AF825946

Crimes of the Powerful

Gregg Barak
Eastern Michigan University, USA

Penny Green
Queen Mary University of London, UK

Tony Ward
Northumbria University, UK

Crimes of the Powerful encompasses the harmful, injurious, and victimizing behaviors perpetrated by privately or publicly operated businesses, corporations, and organizations as well as the state mediated administrative, legalistic, and political responses to these crimes.

The series draws attention to the commonalities of the theories, practices, and controls of the crimes of the powerful. It focuses on the overlapping spheres and interrelated worlds of a wide array of existing and recently developing areas of social, historical, and behavioral inquiry into the wrongdoings of multinational organizations, nation-states, stateless regimes, illegal networks, financialization, globalization, and securitization.

These examinations of the crimes of the powerful straddle a variety of related disciplines and areas of academic interest, including studies in criminology and criminal justice; law and human rights; conflict, peace, and security; economic change, environmental decay, and global sustainability.

Criminology on Trump
Gregg Barak

Indicting the 45th President
Boss Trump, the GOP, and What We Can Do About the Threat to American Democracy
Gregg Barak

Framing Impunity in The Context of State Crime
A Study of Turkish State Criminality Against Kurds (1990–2000)
Sanya Karakas

Citizenship and Genocide Cards
IDs, Statelessness and Rohingya Resistance in Myanmar
Natalie Brinham

For more information about this series, please visit: www.routledge.com/Crimes-of-the-Powerful/book-series/COTP

‘Learning from Rohingya people and experiences, this powerful book connects ID cards and genocide. It reframes citizenship, statehood and ID cards to hold to account, not just the Myanmar government, but the international community.’

Bridget Anderson, *Professor of Migration, Mobilities and Citizenship, University of Bristol, UK*

‘This book examines the links between state registration procedures and mass violence. Foregrounding the voices of Rohingya survivors from Myanmar, it offers human rights advocates and policy makers an important critique and analysis to reflect upon when developing interventions around statelessness and the “legal identity for all” international development agenda.’

Yanghee Lee, *Professor Emeritus, Sungkyunkwan University, & Former UN Special Rapporteur on the situation of human rights in Myanmar (2014 to 2020)*

‘This book offers a brilliant and insightful analysis of how the experiences and understandings of the Rohingya diverge from those of the state and the international actors. This is a timely and extremely valuable contribution to the scholarship on statelessness. It is engaging, exciting and provocative.’

Ratna Kapur, *Professor of International Law, Queen Mary University of London, UK*

‘Myanmar’s misuse of the citizenship law and ID card system is at the heart of the Rohingya suffering and loss. When we tell the stories of our citizenship, our voices are often buried under piles of legalese and paperwork. This book calls for Rohingya knowledge and experience to be put at the forefront of international interventions; a vital read for those working on statelessness and genocide.’

Jaivet Ealom, *CEO of Rohingya Centre of Canada and Author of* Escape from Manus

Citizenship and Genocide Cards

This book draws on Rohingya oral histories and narratives about Myanmar's genocide and ID schemes to critique prevailing international approaches to legal identities and statelessness. By centring the narratives of survivors of state crimes, collected in the aftermath of the 2017 genocidal violence, this book examines the multiple uses of state-issued ID cards and registration documents in producing statelessness and facilitating genocide. In doing so, it challenges some of the international solutions put forward to resolve statelessness.

Rohingya narratives disrupt a simple linear understanding of documenting legal identity that marginalises experiences of these processes. The richly layered accounts of the effects of citizenship laws and registration processes on the lives of Rohingya problematise the ways in which international actors have endorsed state ID schemes and by-passed state-led persecution of the group. This book will be valuable for scholars studying global criminology, state crime, development studies, refugee and migration studies, statelessness and nationality, citizenship studies, and genocide studies.

Natalie Brinham is a researcher and author working on statelessness, ID systems, forced migration, and genocide. She also has many years of experience working in the UK and Southeast Asia in human rights, advocacy, and frontline provision for refugees and migrants. She holds a PhD in Legal Studies from Queen Mary University of London and an MA in Gender, Education and International Development from University College London.

Citizenship and Genocide Cards

IDs, Statelessness and Rohingya Resistance in Myanmar

Natalie Brinham

Routledge
Taylor & Francis Group
LONDON AND NEW YORK

Designed cover image: Mamunur Rashid, Shutterstock

First published 2025
by Routledge
4 Park Square, Milton Park, Abingdon, Oxon OX14 4RN

and by Routledge
605 Third Avenue, New York, NY 10158

Routledge is an imprint of the Taylor & Francis Group, an informa business

© 2025 Natalie Brinham

The right of Natalie Brinham to be identified as author of this work has been asserted in accordance with sections 77 and 78 of the Copyright, Designs and Patents Act 1988.

The Open Access version of this book, available at www.taylorfrancis.com, has been made available under a Creative Commons Attribution (CC-BY) 4.0 license. Funded by Economic and Social Research Council (ESRC)

Any third party material in this book is not included in the OA Creative Commons license, unless indicated otherwise in a credit line to the material. Please direct any permissions enquiries to the original rightsholder.

Trademark notice: Product or corporate names may be trademarks or registered trademarks, and are used only for identification and explanation without intent to infringe.

British Library Cataloguing-in-Publication Data
A catalogue record for this book is available from the British Library

Library of Congress Cataloging-in-Publication Data
Names: Brinham, Natalie, author.
Title: Citizenship and genocide cards : IDs, statelessness, and Rohingya Resistance in Myanmar / Natalie Brinham.
Description: Abingdon, Oxon [UK] ; New York, NY : Routledge, 2024. | Series: Crimes of the powerful | Includes bibliographical references and index.
Identifiers: LCCN 2024031821 (print) | LCCN 2024031822 (ebook) | ISBN 9781032799254 (hardback) | ISBN 9781032799261 (paperback) | ISBN 9781003494539 (ebook)
Subjects: LCSH: Citizenship—Burma. | Identification cards—Law and legislation—Burma. | Statelessness—Burma. | Genocide—Law and legislation—Burma. | Rohingya (Burmese people)—Crimes against. | Rohingya (Burmese people)—Legal status, laws, etc.—Burma.
Classification: LCC KNL2140 .B75 2024 (print) | LCC KNL2140 (ebook) | DDC 342.59108/3—dc23/eng/20240716
LC record available at https://lccn.loc.gov/2024031821
LC ebook record available at https://lccn.loc.gov/2024031822

ISBN: 978-1-032-79925-4 (hbk)
ISBN: 978-1-032-79926-1 (pbk)
ISBN: 978-1-003-49453-9 (ebk)

DOI: 10.4324/9781003494539

Typeset in Sabon
by Apex CoVantage, LLC

For the Rohingya resistance, in all its changing forms.

This work was supported by the Economic and Social Research Council (ESRC), Grant number: ES/Y010345/1. No data was created for this grant.

Contents

Acknowledgements

The research for this book began two weeks before the largest wave of genocidal violence in Myanmar against Rohingya in 2017. I am very grateful to Professor Penny Green and Dr Thomas MacManus, not only for their important intellectual and practical guidance but also for their kindness and support for all through turbulent times.

Thanks to my husband, Zarni, for his encouragement, energy, and support. He showed me that emotion, passion, and a thirst for justice are integral to scholarship. It is this that keeps us moving forwards amid the debilitating pain and suffering of others.

The research for this book would not have been possible without the many Rohingya who helped me with my research or participated in it. My thanks and respect to them reach far beyond the lifetime of the research. They shared with me their time, their knowledge, their pain, their hopes and fears, their friendship, their contacts, and their language skills—all the while providing me with the most incredible hospitality and warmth. I would like to especially thank Sharifah Shakirah, Mohammed S. Anwar, Ali Johar, Neza Mudden, Hussein Johar, Nurul Haque, Khin Maung, Nay San Lwin, Tun Khin, and others who were central to this work but have chosen not to be named.

Abbreviations

AFPFL	Anti-Fascist People's Freedom League
ASEAN	Association of Southeast Asian Nations
BGP	Border Guard Police
BIA	Burma Independence Army
BSPP	Burma Socialist Programme Party
GCM	Global Compact on Migration
GCR	Global Compact on Refugees
GoB	Government of Bangladesh
HRW	Human Rights Watch
INGO	International Non-Governmental Organisation
IOM	International Organisation of Migration
MoU	Memorandum of Understanding
NaSaKa	Hybrid border guard forces deployed in Rakhine State Myanmar.
NGO	Non-Governmental Organisation
NRC (India)	National Register of Citizens
NRS	North Rakhine State
NPR (India)	National Population Register
NV	National Verification
RRRC	Refugee Relief and Repatriation Commission (Bangladesh)
SDGs	Sustainable Development Goals
SLORC	State Law and Order Restoration Council, the military junta in Myanmar from 1988 to 1997
SPDC	State Peace and Development Council, the military junta in Myanmar from 1997. Dissolved in 2011
UDHR	Universal Declaration of Human Rights
UN	United Nations
UNDP	UN Development Programme
UNFPA	UN Population Fund
UNGA	UN General Assembly
UNHCR	UN High Commission for Refugees
UNHRC	UN Human Rights Council
UNICEF	UN International Children's Emergency Fund
UNSR	UN Special Rapporteur
WFP	World Food Programme

Identity documents

	Alternative name	*Description*
Household Registration List	Family list	Records all members of each household. It is mandatory for all residents to be registered on this document.
National Registration Certificates (NRCs)	'Three-fold cards'	Issued from mid-1950s until 1989 (and sometimes after). Although these documents were not officially citizenship cards, in practice they were used as proof of citizenship, as foreigners were registered separately under the Registration of Foreigners Act.
Foreigner Registration Certificates (FRCs)		Issued since independence to foreign nationals.
Union Citizenship Certificates (UCCs)		Union Citizenship Certificates issued under the 1948 Union Citizenship (Election) Act and the 1948 Union Citizenship Election Rules *only* to those who elected for citizenship through residence or naturalisation.
Citizenship Scrutiny Cards (CSCs)	Pink card or Red Card	Issued to 'full citizens' in accordance with the 1982 Citizenship Law. Issued from 1989 until today.
Naturalised Citizenship Scrutiny Cards (NCSCs)	Green card or 'Bengali card'	As above for 'naturalised citizens.'
Temporary Registration Cards (TRCs)	White cards or 'statelessness cards'	These documents were issued if NRCs were lost or if an application for an NRC was pending. They were also issued en masse to Rohingya in North Rakhine State from 1995. In 2015, they were voided.
Form 4		Permissive document needed to travel between townships for white card/NVC holders.

(*Continued*)

(Continued)

	Alternative name	*Description*
TRC slips	Receipt cards	In 2015, voided 'white cards' were collected and replaced with a receipt.
National Verification Cards (NVCs)	'Genocide cards'	Issued from 2015 onwards to former holders of 'white cards' or those who 'needs to apply for citizenship.'
Smart Cards	'UNHCR cards'	Digital identity cards issued to Rohingya refugees in Bangladesh by Government of Bangladesh/UNHCR.

1 Introduction

IDs for Rohingya: 'pathways to citizenship' or 'instruments of genocide'?

Introduction

In August 2017, the Myanmar military launched a 'clearance operation' against the Rohingya in Northern Rakhine.[1] This campaign of terror involved mass killings, mass rape, and the destruction of whole villages (UNHRC Sept 2019). More than three-quarters of a million Rohingya fled across the border into Bangladesh, joining the a quarter of a million registered and unregistered Rohingya refugees who had fled previous waves of violence since the 1990s (Crisp 2018). International media was filled with images of lines of Rohingya stretching into the distance walking into Bangladesh in the monsoon rains, balancing on narrow paths across flooded lands, carrying the injured and the elderly in improvised bamboo slings, smoke from their burning villages billowing behind them. The suffering of the Rohingya, a predominantly Muslim minority, in Buddhist-majority Myanmar captured worldwide attention.

For those of us, Rohingya activists and allies, who had been campaigning since the previous wave of mass violence in 2012 and 2013 to have the crimes against them recognised as genocide, there was an utterly devastating inevitability about events (Zarni and Cowley 2014; Green, McManus et al. 2015). 'Genocide' is defined in international law in Article 2 of the 1948 Convention on the Prevention and Punishment of the Crime of Genocide (hereafter Genocide Convention) as:

> Any of the following acts committed with intent to destroy, in whole or in part, a national, ethnical, racial or religious group, as such: killing of members of the group; causing serious bodily or mental harm to members of the group; deliberately inflicting on the group conditions of life, calculated to bring about its physical destruction in whole or in part; imposing measures intended to prevent births within the group; forcibly transferring children of the group to another group.

After the events of 2017, the abuses against the Rohingya in Myanmar were extensively documented by international human rights bodies. The reports of the Independent International Fact-Finding Mission on Myanmar or IIFFM

DOI: 10.4324/9781003494539-1
This chapter has been made available under a CC-BY 4.0 license.

(UNHRC Sept 2019) and others were framed around this definition of genocide. They provided an evidence base that led to The Gambia filing a case of genocide against Myanmar at the International Court of Justice (ICJ).[2] The field research for this book began two weeks prior to the genocidal violence in August 2017 and finished in December 2019, shortly after I attended the 'provisional measures' public hearing at the ICJ with Rohingya activists (10–12 December 2019). The research and analysis are confined to this period and focus on the immediate aftermath of genocide, in hope that Rohingya knowledge and experience can provide food for thought for researchers, practitioners, and policymakers working on the issues of statelessness and genocide.

In 2024, ICJ proceedings are still pending. Safety and justice for Rohingya have not been secured. More than one million Rohingya in Bangladesh remain confined to camps unable to return home. Conflict in the Rohingya areas of Rakhine State between the Arakan Army, a predominantly Buddhist Rakhine armed group fighting for self-determination, and the Myanmar military have exacerbated the insecurities and injustices for Rohingya in their homelands and increased the risks of further acts of genocide (Human Rights Watch 2024).

Nonetheless, the provisional measures hearing was significant in shifting international and domestic and international perceptions. Not least, the initial judgement provided confirmation that Rohingya are a 'protected group' under international law (International Court of Justice 2020:paragraph 46). This discredited Myanmar's decades-long assertions that Rohingya ethnicity was 'made up' by 'Bengali' migrants to claim land and rights in Myanmar (Khaing Mya Waa 2012).

None of us working on these issues prior to 2017 needed a reminder that genocide is not only a discrete event or a set of events of mass killing, but is instead 'a coordinated plan of different actions aiming at the destruction of essential foundations of the life of national groups' (Lemkin 1944:ix). The processes of intentional destruction of the Rohingya as an ethnic and national group spanned several decades, a process that my coauthor, Zarni, and I characterised in 2014 as a 'slow-burning genocide' (Zarni and Cowley 2014).[3] A key part of this destruction was the production of Rohingya statelessness in Myanmar. This book explores how Myanmar's intentional manufacture and consolidation of Rohingya statelessness did not simply strip Rohingya of their citizenship rights and leave them vulnerable to abuses, but rather was inextricably linked to the broader processes of group destruction. This includes the biological and physical elements of destruction that are contained in the legal definition of genocide, as well as the communal, cultural, religious, intellectual, and economic elements on which all groups anchor their identities, which were key to Lemkin's original conception of genocide in 1944 (Lemkin 1944).

Just as genocide is best understood as a sociological process, rather than a set of discrete events (Feierstein 2014), so too is citizenship stripping or the production of statelessness. It is generally understood that Rohingya were rendered stateless by the 1982 Citizenship Law.[4] The law stripped back the provisions in the 1948 Union Citizenship Act[5] for the acquisition of citizenship through different routes including elected citizenship, marriage, and residence, and made access to 'full' or automatic citizenship almost exclusively dependant on membership of an ethnic group considered 'national' by the Council of State (paragraph 4). The list of ethnic groups was decided entirely at the discretion of the state based on inaccurate and misleading British colonial 'racial' categories prior to the first Anglo/Burma war in 1824 (Zarni and Cowley 2014; Zarni and Brinham 2017). The broad and loosely defined 'racial' categories contained in the 1948 provisions were broken down into a list of 135 national ethnic groups on which the application of the 1982 law and national registration system was based. Rohingya were excluded from this list. This stripped Rohingya of both their rights to nationality and their claim to indigeneity. Whilst it was possible to apply for citizenship based on descent from citizens prior to Myanmar's independence, in practice the evidential requirements and administrative barriers made this process almost impossible for most Rohingya (de Chickera, Arraiza et al. 2021). Whilst the law is deeply significant to the current and future human rights situation in Myanmar, Rohingya oral histories often describe the stripping of their citizenship as a long state-directed campaign that was intertwined with social, economic, and physical destruction. For many, the citizenship law was viewed as simply one weapon used against them in a large arsenal belonging to a hostile militarised state. As one close Rohingya colleague corrected me when I asked about Myanmar's laws, assumptions that security and justice predominantly flow from national law, are reserved for the privileged with experience of living under (semi)functional systems of rule of law.

Rohingya identity, like that of many of Myanmar's ethnic groups, cannot be disentangled from a sense of belonging to the land. The name itself is derived from terms for the Rakhine region which falls within the borders of today's Myanmar (Charney 2007). Rohingya homelands are on the eastern coast of the Bay of Bengal, an area characterised by ethnic and religious diversity, with a long history of international trade, human movement and cultural and intellectual exchange, and shifting centres of power (Amrith 2013). The homelands lie to the east of the Naf River which today marks the boundary between Bangladesh and Myanmar. Rohingya did not come to the region; Imperial powers, states, borders, immigration rules, and identity documents came to the Rohingya.[6] In a world dominated by methodological nationalism in which people and places are assumed to be naturally and timelessly organised into bordered states and bounded nationalities, Rohingya have been displaced in situ in many imaginings, from government officials to the Myanmar public to international policymakers. This has profoundly influenced the different international approaches to resolving the human rights deficits they experience.

A focus on oral histories of IDs and state-issued documents as Chapter 2 explains enables a study of the processes of destruction, state power, and resistance. It facilitates building an understanding of genocide and statelessness in which my own and others' assumptions are interrupted and displaced by the experiences and knowledge of survivors. In Myanmar, Rohingya as a people of place were reconstructed as 'foreigners.' Internationally, they were reconstructed as 'stateless.' This is a story of the violence of that reconstruction, the repercussions, and the struggles to reconstruct belonging.

Rohingya, statelessness, and human rights research

This research was first conceived during the years that I was working on a multi-country project on the human rights of stateless Rohingya from 2010 to 2015. Rohingya were, even then, one of the best-known groups of stateless persons in the world—the term 'stateless' frequently preceded their ethnic identity in the media and other reports. This was one of the reasons our project was designed around Rohingya situations—it built on our organisation's specialisation in statelessness. One afternoon in a flat in Chittagong, statelessness specialists shared food and discussed the human rights situation with a number of Rohingya community leaders. When asked by one of the foreign researchers about Rohingya statelessness, one Rohingya leader replied, 'But Rohingya are not stateless.' An uncomfortable silence followed. The statement undermined the very premise of our project. Later in private, we pondered whether this Rohingya man misunderstood international legal definitions of statelessness, or if this statement meant something more. A similar encounter relating to Rohingya statelessness followed a year later in 2013 in Yangon with a prominent Rohingya politician in Yangon. The query stayed with me. It got me wondering about the tensions that exist between the ways in which Rohingya statelessness has been constructed and approached internationally, and Rohingyas' own experiences and understandings of citizenship and statelessness. In the air-conditioned UN offices in Bangkok, Yangon, and Kuala Lumpur, I thought—and worried—about how the framings of Rohingya statelessness that we drew upon for our research might impact and limit the discussions we were having in advocacy and policy circles, or might mute the dissenting but important voices of Rohingya activists on the topic.

Two years into the project, in 2012, waves of violence against Rohingya in Rakhine State,[7] took the plight of Rohingya from relative obscurity into the international headlines. As human rights researchers working with Rohingya, we tried to mine the testimonies of the survivors for hard facts relating to human rights abuses and the role of the state in the violence. We would filter narratives for evidence; extract the significant events and statements and categorise them in our human rights frameworks, sifting out many of the conflicting or shifting meanings Rohingya themselves had given to the events. On one occasion, I switched off the recording device as my Rohingya interpreter spun off topic and began sobbing in the arms of the stateless Kaman interviewee[8] who, in divulging the destruction of his home and the death of his family members, had expressed remorse at how much he had despised Rohingya in the past. He had a Rohingya grandparent whom he blamed for his own statelessness. Rohingya identities and experiences of citizenship, it seemed, held so much more than their legal status and associated human rights violations. Meanwhile, as human rights researchers, we bemoaned how difficult it was to triangulate information when working with 'hidden communities' and we despaired at the inconsistencies in the narrative details. But when we interviewed Rohingya, they were not only appealing to our human rights frameworks but also drawing on multiple and shifting identities and positions to make meaning from their experiences. In Patel's state crime research, he describes human rights testimony as, 'often presented as ratifying an existing normative discourse about human rights.' A process he describes as undermining, 'original narratives of their own terms of reference in favour of normative international discourses on human rights' (Patel 2012:244). This resonated with my own experiences. This research sets out to consider, then, how Rohingya survivors of state crime disrupt and contribute to international framings of their statelessness.

In doing this, I sought to better understand two paradigms: how statelessness was understood and experienced by Rohingya survivors within the wider processes of state crime and genocide; and how international legal discourses framed the issue of statelessness and approached ending and preventing it. From this base, I was then able to examine where the two framings converged and diverged, and consider how the voices of survivors influenced and informed international approaches. In answering these questions relating to survivors' narratives and experiences, as well as socio-legal perspectives, I developed research approaches that mixed narrative inquiry and oral histories with textual analysis and multi-site ethnographic methods which I describe in Chapter 2.

At the time of the research project's conception, international framings of Rohingya statelessness were largely based on legal and textual analyses of Myanmar's citizenship laws and reflected dominant global notions of statelessness grounded in international law. To a large extent, these analyses were divorced from the political, historical, and social contexts within which Rohingya statelessness had been slowly produced and reproduced. Rohingya statelessness, like statelessness more generally, was almost exclusively viewed in literature as the binary opposite of citizenship (Tonkiss and Bloom 2015). Their legal condition of statelessness was described as resulting from two discrete past events that related to the citizenship law in Myanmar—post-independence bordering in 1948, and the enactment of the 1982 Citizenship Law in Myanmar (Republic of the Union of Myanmar 2013; Tonkin 2018). Thus, Rohingya statelessness was more often understood in human rights literature as a product of gaps and omissions in Myanmar's legal framework relating to citizenship, rather than produced as a set of deliberate and targeted state practices within a broader and ongoing process of genocide. The latter understanding, however, was most often the thread of Rohingya narratives in this research.

Following the 2017 wave of mass violence against the Rohingya in Myanmar (UNHRC Sept 2018), academic and human rights research relating to crimes against humanity, genocide, and statelessness mushroomed. With the majority of Rohingya now residing outside the country in Bangladesh, research participants became more accessible to researchers, journalists, and humanitarian workers. Rohingya voices internationally increased and, in some cases, Rohingya framings of their own experiences were incorporated into academic and human rights research (e.g. Fortify Rights 2019; Olney, Haque et al. 2019). At the same time, the increased use of Rohingya voices in international public fora did not necessarily lead to 'control over representation, interpretation and dissemination' (see also Spivak 1988; Gready 2008:2). With the research for this study, there were two key areas of debate and contestation relating to the international representation of Rohingya voices. First, participants debated how Rohingya voices continued to be interpreted and influenced by the international agencies, governments, INGOs, and their donors. Second, they contested which Rohingya voices and narratives were privileged over others to fit the existing narratives and priorities of international agencies and governments. So, throughout the period of my research, international discourses and approaches to Rohingya statelessness have been in a process of intense flux, negotiation, and contestation. I have been fortunate enough to be a part of some of those discussions and conversations, both observing the changes and continuums and seeking to influence the conversations myself through the type of engaged and activist research that is a feature of state crime scholarship activism (Grewcock 2012:113).

The language of advocacy surrounding Rohingya statelessness shifted in some circles over the course of the research. Technical legal support on reducing statelessness through engagement with the state, such as 'pathways to citizenship' for 'stateless Rohingya,' gave way to the language of international criminal justice including notions such as 'citizenship restoration,' 'accountability,' and 'restitution.' There were also significant pushbacks and counterclaims as different approaches were contested and challenged by various advocacy and policy-making groups vying for influence with competing interests and/or strategic alliances. Such processes are a feature of emerging international discourses (Anderson and Andrijasevic 2008). How and what Rohingya activism took place on international platforms likewise shifted as a result of population movements and the moves to seek accountability through international court procedures. To capture the dynamic nature of both international discourses on statelessness and international Rohingya activism and voice, I needed to develop flexible and evolving research methods and approaches.

In 2024, these framings have evolved and shifted further. The Myanmar-wide violence and conflict following the military coup of 1 February 2021 resulted in a seismic shakeup of international relations with Myanmar. The previous decade, which is explored in this book, was known as the 'transition' period in which the Military leadership was expected to steadily relinquish political power towards more democratic forms of governance. International engagement with Myanmar during this period was characterised by strategic and 'quiet' forms of diplomacy as well as pragmatic humanitarianism often at the expense of human rights approaches (Mahony 2018; Rosenthal 2019). The coup and events that followed saw a resumption of sanctions, disengagement, divestment, and aid delivery through cross-border opposition groups rather than the institutions associated with the Myanmar military (Martin 2023). Further, attitudes towards Rohingya changed, with many of those in the movements resisting military rule offering words of support and acknowledgement to Rohingya refugees (Loong 2023). Israel's ongoing assault on Gaza since October 2023 has also thrust the issue of statelessness and statehood in the context of genocide into the international public consciousness. With connections made between the experiences of Palestinians and Rohingya, international approaches to statehood and citizenship are likely to shift further. Hopefully, this research as a space of reflection on a period following mass state-perpetrated violence can contribute to the increasing exchanges of knowledge between those that work to prevent and understand state criminality, and the statelessness field.

The production of statelessness as state crime

The thread running through this research project is the role of Rohingya survivors in influencing understandings of how statelessness is produced, moving understandings of their statelessness from an issue of state oversight or neglect to one involving the criminal behaviour of the state. International discourses and approaches to Rohingya statelessness over the years have reflected two broader issues. The first issue is how the role of the Myanmar state in the violence perpetrated against Rohingya in Myanmar was framed internationally—whether the situation was understood as one of communal violence and conflict or one of state-led persecution and genocide. The second issue is how citizenship was framed globally as either an area reserved for state discretion or constrained by international law.

How far states can determine and limit their own membership through citizenship laws and practices, and how far international law should be able to limit state power in this regard is a long-standing debate (Siegelberg 2020). In theory, three areas of international law limit state power regarding citizenship: the prohibition against arbitrary deprivation of citizenship, the state duty to provide safeguards against statelessness, and the prohibition against discrimination (Open Society Justice Initiative 2005).[9] Whilst, in practice, many states disregard these limitations, there have been increasing attempts to strengthen human rights norms relating to citizenship (Goldston 2006; Weissbrodt and Collins 2006; Spiro 2011; Foster and Lambert 2016). This conflict or fault line between state sovereignty and human rights law has also been central to the debate in Myanmar regarding Rohingya citizenship. Myanmar citizenship law, according to the United Nations Human Rights Council (UNHRC), is in breach of all three of those areas of international law. The law has arbitrarily deprived Rohingya of citizenship, fails to provide safeguards against statelessness, and discriminates against Rohingya and other minorities on the grounds of race/ethnicity.[10] International pressure to reform Myanmar citizenship law provoked a backlash domestically which invoked the principles of 'self-determination' as a post-colonial nation.[11] Myanmar-resisted foreign interference claiming its national identity should be determined almost exclusively through membership of one of the ethnic groups which the state claimed inhabited Myanmar before colonial rule, known in Burmese as *Taingyintha*.[12] International approaches to addressing the citizenship issue in Myanmar hence took a pragmatic position and largely focused on the second of these three issues—safeguarding against statelessness. Thus, Rohingya citizenship deprivation was approached by international organisations as if it were largely a problem of administrative barriers, a lack of capacity by the state to provide and recognise the correct documentation and gaps and omissions in the legal and administrative framework relating to naturalisation.[13] Whilst the discrimination inherent in Myanmar's citizenship regime is well known and acknowledged by international agencies, pushes for legal reform were approached with caution and placed on the back burner whilst incremental change was sought. Scholars, researchers, and organisations that have been pressing for recognition of crimes against humanity and genocide against Rohingya have increasingly framed the production of Rohingya statelessness by the Myanmar State as criminal behaviour—one of the targeted and arbitrary deprivations of citizenship linked to other crimes (Fortify Rights 2019; UNHRC Sept 2018). Discussion as to whether to approach statelessness in Myanmar as an issue of state crime or of administrative failure continued to dominate policy discussions throughout the data collection period. My research over this period, then, focused on not only how Rohingya framed their statelessness as state crime but also how framings of the production of statelessness as state crime disrupted existing discourses and led to emerging understanding and approaches. Accordingly, I supplemented the qualitative and ethnographic research with analysis of key human rights texts by UN, Government and INGOs and observations of advocacy and policy-related forums and discussions.

Linking statelessness and genocide

The link between statelessness and genocide was first highlighted in literature relating to the European holocaust of the 1930s–1940s (Siegelberg 2020). In particular, the work of Hannah Arendt illustrated how the stripping of Jewish citizenship facilitated and laid the conditions for mass deportations and mass killings—these events became the premise on which she built the oft-quoted notions of citizenship as the 'right to have rights' (Arendt 1958). These ideas were also drawn on in the conceptualisation of statelessness as 'bare life' by which human lives are reduced only to survival (Agamben 1998). As noted earlier, whether the production of statelessness is approached as state crime or not also relates to how the role of the state is understood in relation to broader persecution and violence. Increasingly, after 2017, the term 'genocide' was used to describe the situation for Rohingya in Rakhine State (UNHRC Sept 2018) and attention in turn began to focus on the role of the state ID schemes in the 2016–7 waves of genocidal violence (Fortify Rights 2019; Potter and Kyaw Win 2019). As noted in Chapter 6, genocide is not only a set of discreet events of mass killing and other acts of genocide but also a sociological process. 'Reorganisation genocides' involve the destruction of some identities—such as national and ethnic—and the imposition of new exclusive identities (Lemkin 1944; Feierstein 2014). Genocide scholar, Feierstein (2015:115–127), describes the terror of genocide as a 'technology for transforming, reorganising and destroying identities.' The production of statelessness within genocide can also be understood as a technology for destroying and imposing identities. Approaching statelessness as part of a reorganisation genocide can disrupt the logic behind international approaches to tackling Rohingya statelessness in the ways they seek to engage with the state to reduce statelessness. Genocide featured frequently in Rohingya narratives, as did state intent to destroy their group identity through the production of their statelessness. Thus, a key focus of this research was to examine how Rohingya experienced and described the intersections between identity destruction, statelessness, and genocide.

State crime and resistance

Human rights reports on crimes against humanity and genocide, and international advocacy approaches are in part influenced by Rohingyas' own framings of citizenship deprivation, their activism, and their resistance to state and international actions in regard to citizenship deprivation. This, then, ties into the ways in which state crime scholarship approaches resistance and social audience (Green and Ward 2019). Whilst some scholarship remains focused on criteria-based definitions of what constitutes state crime, such as international law and human rights, other scholarship understands that deviant states and supra-state organisations are unlikely to criminalise their own acts and contends that criminality is social construct (Green and Ward 2004; Lasslett, Green et al. 2015:2). These scholars look to communities of resistance to censure and sanction states where they deviate from these norms (Green and Ward 2012; Lasslett 2012). So a breach of these norms 'does not in itself inscribe state practices with the quality of being criminal, rather it is the *struggles* that emerge in response to these deviant acts which stigmatise state practices and the regimes that author them as being wrong' (Lasslett, Green et al. 2015:5). So the role of resistance is important in naming and understanding the crimes of states (Green and Ward 2012; Lasslett

2012) especially where the criminal nature of a particular set of practices is under dispute, as has been the case with the production of statelessness. The study of resistance in state crime scholarship then, drawing on the concept of 'social audience,' focuses on naming forms of criminal behaviour, making this behaviour publicly visible and putting pressure on the perpetrators to stop and make amends (Green and Ward 2015:214–215).

As such, how Rohingya resist identity destruction and the production of their statelessness was a key area in my research. It was the focus on resistance that led me to look much more closely at narratives relating to identity cards and their absences. Registration and the issuance of identity cards are one of the most frequent encounters between the individual and the state (Hull 2012); hence, ID schemes in Rakhine State and in the refugee camps of Bangladesh have become a key site of resistance for Rohingya (Brinham 2018).

If citizenship is viewed not simply as a status but as a relationship with the state that may be destroyed as part of a process, it is possible to view Rohingya claims to citizenship over several decades as methods to name, make visible, and censure the state for their gradual revocation of that citizenship. The main thrust of Rohingya claim-making processes relating to their citizenship in Myanmar has come not only through acts of resistance such as claiming the name 'Rohingya' against state policy but also through the enactment and performance of citizenship—whether that be through constitution writing, taking part in national cultural events, paying taxes, voting, working in government roles, and other everyday interactions. Such acts potentially place demands on the state and expose the arbitrary revocation of citizenship as part of a criminal process by the state. Thus, in exploring Rohingya narratives, I also looked beyond their stories of identity cards to consider how they enacted and experienced citizenship in Myanmar which, as I discuss in Chapter 5, often disrupted assumptions of their statelessness in ways that highlighted the arbitrary nature of the removal of their status and evidence of citizenship.

Chapter outline

In this chapter, I have provided a background and explained the theoretical underpinnings for this research. In Chapter 2, 'Papers, cards and perilous encounters with the state: Identity documents, oral histories and state crime research,' I focus on IDs and other state-issued documents as central to the research methods developed for this project. Oral histories and narratives about identity documents produced rich data pertaining to state power, social relations, administrative violence, and resistance. They enabled an examination of the intimate relationship between ID systems, identity destruction, and genocide, as well as the interconnections between legal and social identities Chapter 3, 'By-passing State Power and Neutralising State Bureaucracies in International Approaches to Statelessness,' focuses on statelessness.

I explore how archetypal notions of 'the state' and 'the stateless person' have been constructed within global governance agendas and international discourses relating to citizenship and statelessness. I consider statelessness as a discursive concept, exploring how and to what affect 'the stateless person' has been construed as 'invisible' to the state and to international bureaucracies. Drawing on both statelessness scholarship and analysis of key UN texts and campaign material, the chapter explores how archetypal notions of state bureaucracies as neutral or benign, rather than imbued with exclusionary state power, have shaped targets, action plans, and policy approaches. Issues of state crime are largely ignored. This chapter provides context within which to frame Rohingya narratives relating to statelessness and genocide.

Chapter 4 focuses on the history of ID schemes in the Rakhine region, which today falls within the territorial borders of Myanmar. It looks at the period from the British colonial period, up to Burma's independence. It considers the role of colonial categorisation, registration, and ID schemes in consolidating colonial power. It considers how racial and class hierarchies were established and reified, as well as the role of IDs and registration in extracting labour and quelling dissent. It also focuses on the significance of the documenting of 'foreigners' in Myanmar's struggle for independence. It also shows how citizenship and immigration frameworks evolved as Burma gained independence. Chapter 4 provides background as to how authoritarian regimes utilise ID schemes as a form of 'social engineering' (Scott 1998:194). It also provides context to the later chapters which explore how identities and social relations were reorganised under the militarised state.

Chapter 5 considers the citizenship framework and ID scheme that was in place in the early decades of independence, noting how the state 'strategically embraced' minority populations including Rohingya as part of peace pacts (Cowley and Zarni 2017:1). It explores how Rohingya citizenship was experienced and enacted, and considers the meanings attributed by participants to ID cards from this period. It considers how Rohingya in refugee settings collect and collate IDs and registration documents from this era as artefacts that evidence their bonds with the central state, and as evidence of the process of citizenship stripping and state crime that were to follow under the military state.

Chapters 6 and 7 explore genocide and identity destruction in Rohingya ID narratives. Drawing on scholarship relating to genocide as a sociological process and social practice, the chapters focus on the role of Myanmar's ID schemes within the different stages or phases of genocide. Both chapters relate to the period of time from the late 1970s when systematic attempts were made to symbolically and physically destroy Rohingya as a group belonging to Myanmar, up until the genocidal violence of 2016–7. The chapters also explore how Rohingya participants envisaged citizenship as a key element of future safe returns and repatriations from the refugee camps in Bangladesh to their homes in Rakhine. Chapter 6, 'Genocide and Identity Destruction in Rohingya ID Narratives,' explores ID schemes within genocide scholarship, with particular reference to the work of Gregory Stanton (2004, 2017) and Daniel Feierstein (2014, 2015). It also considers how Rohingya narratives often refer to attempts to destroy their identity through state ID schemes as part of a 'masterplan' or state intent relating to genocide. Chapter 7, '"Genocide Cards": IDs, Registration, and the Phases of Rohingya Genocide,' draws predominantly on the scholarship relating to 'reorganising genocides' (Feierstein 2014) to explore Rohingya experiences of Myanmar's registration and ID schemes. It considers how ID schemes were utilised as a technology to reorganise national identities and social relations in such a way as to destroy Rohingya identity and establish a new exclusive national identity without Rohingya.

Chapter 8, 'IDs and International Approaches to Rohingya Statelessness: Towards Social Inclusion or Identity Destruction?,' explores where Rohingya understandings and experiences of the role of state-issued IDs diverge from the approaches of international agencies working to resolve Rohingya statelessness in Myanmar. Referring back to previous chapters, it considers the increasing push within global governance to provide 'legal identities for all' as a method of managing international development projects, international migration, and refugee situations. Whilst the language of legal identities for all is couched within the discourses of human rights and resolving statelessness, Rohingya narratives suggest that approaches that support the provision of Myanmar's IDs and registration served to legitimise an abusive state system and set them on a trajectory away from citizenship recognition, not on a pathway towards citizenship.

The concluding chapter, 'Seeing the State and Criminality in Statelessness,' summarises the findings from the chapters, focusing on how Rohingya narratives from this research have disrupted some of the assumptions about 'the stateless person' and 'the state' that inform international action plans and approaches to reducing and resolving statelessness. In this chapter, I also consider the contributions of this research to scholarship about state crime, legal identities, and statelessness. I outline the value of methodologies that explore the ID narratives of people affected by statelessness. I conclude that better consideration of how people affected by statelessness or citizenship deprivation understand and experience the state and its bureaucracies in statelessness research and policy consideration is vital in assessing and improving the effectiveness of actions to reduce and prevent statelessness. In particular, state crime frameworks and analysis of the potential for ID systems to be utilised by states to do harm are conspicuously absent in the global push for IDs for all.

Notes

1 The name of the country was officially changed from Burma to Myanmar in 1989 under the military junta called State Law and Order Restoration Council (SLORC). The political and ethnic opposition continued to contest the name. It was only after the reforms of 2010 that the term Myanmar became gradually

more accepted. In this book, I refer to Burma and Myanmar interchangeably. Burma is used in historical context and Myanmar in the contemporary context.

2 Application of the Convention on the Prevention and Punishment of the Crime of Genocide (The Gambia vs Myanmar). All documents pertaining to this case are Available at: www.icj-cij.org/case/178 (accessed 05/03/2014).

3 This article was written under my pseudonym, Alice Cowley.

4 Socialist Republic of the Union of Burma (1982). Burma Citizenship Law.

5 Union of Burma, The Union Citizenship Act 1948.

6 In a discussion titled 'The Slow-Burning Genocide of Myanmar's Rohingya' at Harvard Global Equality Initiative Conference, 4 Nov 2014, Amartya Sen said, 'The Rohingya did not come to Burma. Burma first came to the Rohingya.'

7 Rakhine is also referred to as Arakan. Both words come from the same root. The British referred to the region as Arakan. In the 1990s, the name was formally changed to Rakhine. However, many people, particularly those opposed to military rule or the central state, continued to refer to it as Arakan. I use the terms interchangeably throughout. In historical contexts, I refer to the region as Arakan and in contemporary contexts, I use Rakhine.

8 Kaman is an ethno-religious identity. Kaman are Muslim and originate from Rakhine State, Myanmar. Unlike Rohingya, they are included as one of the official 135 'ethnic races of Myanmar' and are, according to the law if not always in practice, entitled to citizenship.

9 (a) The 1948 Universal Declaration of Human Rights Article 15(2) prohibits against the arbitrary deprivation of citizenship, 'No one shall be arbitrarily deprived of his nationality nor denied the right to change his nationality.' The Right to Nationality is considered a fundamental human right. (b) Safeguards against statelessness were first outlined in the 1961 Convention on the Reduction of Statelessness, for example, Article 1, 'A Contracting State shall grant its nationality to a person born in its territory who would otherwise be stateless.' (c) The prohibition of racial discrimination is integral to all human rights instruments. CERD has articulated this principle with regard to citizenship in various recommendations, for example, Committee on the Elimination of Racial Discrimination, 64th Session, 2004, CERD/C/64/Misc.11/rev.3 para 14 'deprivation of citizenship on the basis of race, colour, descent, or national or ethnic origin is a breach of States Parties' obligations to ensure non-discriminatory enjoyment of the right to nationality.'

10 For example, UNHRC (2016: para 26). The Citizenship Law of 1982 is discriminatory and contravenes the prohibition of arbitrary deprivation of nationality. It violates the right of every child to acquire nationality, as it fails to protect the acquisition of citizenship for children born in Myanmar with no 'genuine link' to another State (see CRC/C/MMR/CO/3-4, paras. 41–42). It also gives overly broad power to the Government to revoke citizenship without due protection. It has led and continues to lead to statelessness.

11 Goldston (2006:338) noted that self-determination as a concept in citizenship has maintained its popular appeal in states involved in post-WWII national liberation struggles, such as in Myanmar.

12 In response to UNHRC comments calling for the amendment of the citizenship law, Presidential Spokesperson for Thein Sein, Ye Htut wrote on his Facebook page in 2013, 'Any person ineligible under the law can't be a citizen. This is our sovereign right.' Quoted by Kyaw Hsu Mon (2013). Government Reject UN calls for Rohingya Citizenship. The Irrawaddy.

13 An example of this approach to citizenship reform in Myanmar is Center for Diversity and National Harmony (2019). Myanmar's Citizenship Law: An Analysis.

Bibliography

Agamben, G. (1998). *Homo Sacer: Sovereign Power and Bare Life*. Stanford University Press.

Amrith, S. S. (2013). *Crossing the Bay of Bengal: The Furies of Nature and the Fortunes of Migrants*. Harvard University Press.

Anderson, B. and R. Andrijasevic (2008). *Sex, Slaves and Citizens: The Politics of Anti-Trafficking*. Lawrence & Wishart.

Arendt, H. (1958). *The Origins of Totalitarianism*. Allen and Unwin.

Brinham, N. (2017). Breaking the Cycle of Expulsion, Repatriation and Exploitation for Rohingya. *OpenDemocracy*. www.opendemocracy.net/beyondslavery/natalie-brinham/breaking-cycle-of-expulsion-forced-repatriation-and-exploitation-for-r [Accessed 30/01/2018]

Brinham, N. (2018). 'Genocide Cards': Rohingya Refugees on Why They Risked Their Lives to Refuse ID Cards. *OpenDemocracy*. www.opendemocracy.net/natalie-brinham/genocide-cards-why-rohingya-refugees-are-resisting-id-cards [Accessed 30/01/2019]

Brinham, N. and Y. Cowper-Smith (2019). Rohingya Poets Turn Words into Art of Resistance. *Anadolu Agency*. www.aa.com.tr/en/asia-pacific/rohingya-poets-turn-words-into-art-of-resistance-/1551737 [Accessed 02/10/2019]

Brubaker, R. and F. Cooper (2000). Beyond 'Identity'. *Theory and Society* 29(1): 1–47.

Campbell, R., A. E. Adams, S. M. Wasco, C. E. Ahrens and T. Sefl (2009). Training Interviewers for Research on Sexual Violence: A Qualitative Study of Rape Survivors' Recommendations for Interview Practice. *Violence against Women* 15(5): 595–617.

Center for Diversity and National Harmony (2019). *Myanmar's Citizenship Law: An Analysis*. www.cdnh.org/publication/myanmars-citizenship-law-an-analysis/ [Accessed 08/10/2019]

Charney, M. (2007). Buddhism in Arakan: Theories and Histiographies of the Religious Basis of Ethnonyms. Paper presented at 'Arakan History Conference, Institute of Asian Studies, Chulalongkorn University [Accessed 23/11/2005]

Clandinin, D. J. (2007). *Handbook of Narrative Inquiry: Mapping a Methodology*. Sage.

Cowley, A. and M. Zarni (2017). An Evolution of Rohingya Persecution in Myanmar: From Strategic Embrace to Genocide. *Middle East Institute*. www.mei.edu/publications/evolution-rohingya-persecution-myanmar-strategic-embrace-genocide [Accessed 22/05/2017]

Cowper-Smith, Y. L. (2021). Social Movements That 'Think': Knowledge-Practices of the Rohingya Canadian Social Movement. PhD Thesis. University of Guelph.

Crisp, J. (2018). 'Primitive People': The Untold Story of UNHCR's Historical Engagement with Rohingya Refugees. *Humanitarian Exchange, Humanitarian Practice Network*. 73. https://odihpn.org/magazine/primitive-people-the-untold-story-of-unhcrs-historical-engagement-with-rohingya-refugees/ [Accessed 17/12/2018]

Czarniawska-Joerges, B. (2004). *Narratives in Social Science Research*. Sage.

Czarniawska-Joerges, B., Handelshögskolan, U. Göteborgs, U. Gothenburg, I. Gothenburg Research and E. A. L. School of Business (2010). The Uses of Narratology in Social and Policy Studies. *Critical Policy Studies* 4(1): 58–76.

de Chickera, A., J. Arraiza, Z. Albarazi, G. Field and N. Brinham (2021). Navigating with a Faulty Map: Access to Citizenship Documents and Citizenship in Myanmar. *Institute on Statelessness and Inclusion*. https://files.institutesi.org/Access_to_Citizenship_in_Myanmar_Report.pdf [Accessed 28/12/2021]

Feierstein, D. (2014). *Genocide as Social Practice: Reorganizing Society under the Nazis and Argentina's Military Juntas*. Rutgers University Press.

Feierstein, D. (2015). Debates on the Criminology of Genocide: Genocide as a Technology for Destroying Identities. *State Crime* 4(2): 115–127.

Fortify Rights (2019). *'Tools of Genocide': National Verification Cards and the Denial of Citizenship of Rohingya Muslims in Myanmar*. www.fortifyrights.org/downloads/Tools%20of%20Genocide%20-%20Fortify%20Rights%20-%20September-03-2019-EN.pdf [Accessed 08/10/2019]

Foster, M. and H. Lambert (2016). Statelessness as a Human Rights Issue: A Concept Whose Time Has Come. *International Journal of Refugee Law* 28(4): 564–584.

Goldston, J. A. (2006). Holes in the Rights Framework: Racial Discrimination, Citizenship, and the Rights of Noncitizens. *Ethics and International Affairs* 20(3): 321–347.

Government of the Union of Burma (1948). The Union Citizenship Act.

Gready, P. (2008). The Public Life of Narratives: Ethics, Politics, Methods, in Tamboukou, M., Andrews, M. and Squire, C. (eds), *Doing Narrative Research*. Sage. 137–150.

Green, P., T. McManus and A. de la Cour Venning (2015). Countdown to Annihilation: Genocide in Myanmar. *International State Crime Initiative*. http://statecrime.org/data/2015/10/ISCI-Rohingya-Report-PUBLISHED-VERSION.pdf [Accessed 29/08/2024]

Green, P., T. McManus and A. de la Cour Venning (2018). Genocide Achieved, Genocide Continues: Myanmar's Annihilation of the Rohingya. *International State Crime Initiative*. http://statecrime.org/data/2018/04/ISCI-Rohingya-Report-II-PUBLISHED-VERSION-revised-compressed.pdf [Accessed 29/08/2024]

Green, P. and A. Ward (2012). Civil Society, Resistance and State Crime, in Stanley, E. and McCulloch, J. (eds), *State Crime and Resistance*. Routledge.

Green, P. and T. Ward (2004). *State Crime: Governments, Violence and Corruption*. Pluto Press.

Green, P. and T. Ward (2015). Repression, Resistance and Transition in Burma and Tunisia, in Maloney, C. J. and Chambliss, W. J. (eds), *State Crime: Critical Concepts in Criminology*. Routledge. 210–232.

Green, P. and T. Ward (2019). *State Crime and Civil Activism: On the Dialectics of Repression and Resistance*. Routledge.

Grewcock, M. (2012). Public Criminology, Victim Agency and Researching State Crime. *State Crime* 1(1): 109–125.

Haar, R. J., K. Wang, H. Venters, S. Salonen, R. Patel, T. Nelson, R. Mishori and P. K. Parmar (2019). Documentation of Human Rights Abuses among Rohingya Refugees from Myanmar. *Conflict and Health* 13(1): 1–14.

Habiburahman and S. Ansel (2018). *First, They Erased Our Name: A Rohingya Speaks*. Scribe.

Hull, M. S. (2012). Documents and Bureaucracy. *Annual Review of Anthropology* 41: 251–267.

Human Rights Watch (2024). *Rohingya at Risk in Rakhine Fighting*. www.hrw.org/news/2024/02/09/myanmar-rohingya-risk-rakhine-fighting#:~:text=About%20600%2C000%20Rohingya%20remain%20in,movement%20restrictions%20and%20aid%20blockages [Accessed 01/04/2024]

International Court of Justice (23 Jan 2020). *Order on Provisional Measures: Application of the Convention on the Prevention and Punishment of the Crime of Genocide (Gambia v. Myanmar)*. www.icj-cij.org/public/files/case-related/178/178-20200123-ORD-01-00-EN.pdf [Accessed 06/01/2021]

Khaing Mya Waa (2012). *A Critique of the Expansionist Distorted History of the Bengali with Roots in Chittagong Who Wrap Themselves in the Discourse of Human Rights*. Pan-Wei-Wei Press.

Klempner, M. (2000). Navigating Life Review Interviews with Survivors of Trauma. *The Oral History Review* 27(2): 67–83.

Kyaw Hsu Mon (2013). Government Reject UN Calls for Rohingya Citizenship. *The Irrawaddy*. www.irrawaddy.com/news/burma/govt-rejects-un-calls-rohingya-citizenship.html [Accessed 17/01/2018]

Lasslett, K. (2012). Power, Struggle and State Crime: Researching through Resistance. *State Crime* 1(1): 126–148.

Lasslett, K., P. Green and D. Stanczak (2015). The Barbarism of Indifference: Sabotage, Resistance and State-Corporate Crime. *Theoretical Criminology* 19(4): 514–533.

Lee, R. and J. A. A. González Zarandona (2019). Heritage Destruction in Myanmar's Rakhine State: Legal and Illegal Iconoclasm. *International Journal of Heritage Studies* 26(5): 519–538.

Lemkin, R. (1944). Axis Rule in Occupied Europe: Law of Occupation, Analysis of Government, Proposals for Redress. *Carnegie Endowment for International Peace, Division of International Law*.

Loong, S. (2023). In Myanmar, Generation Z Goes to War. *Current History* 122(843): 137–142.

Mackenzie, C., C. McDowell and E. Pittaway (2007). Beyond 'Do No Harm': The Challenge of Constructing Ethical Relationships in Refugee Research. *Journal of Refugee Studies* 20(2): 299–319.

MacLean, K. (2019). The Rohingya Crisis and the Practices of Erasure. *Journal of Genocide Research* 21(1): 83–95.

Mahony, L. (2018). Time to Break Old Habits: Shifting from Complicity to Protection of Rohingya in Myanmar. *Fieldview Solutions*. www.fieldviewsolutions.org/fv-publications/Time_to_break_old_habits.pdf [Accessed 11/11/2019]

Martin, M. (2023). Rethinking Humanitarian Assistance for Myanmar. *Center for Strategic and International Studies*. www.csis.org/analysis/rethinking-humanitarian-assistance-myanmar [Accessed 01/04/2024]

Metro, R. (2011). History Curricula and the Reconciliation of Ethnic Conflict: A Collaborative Project with Burmese Migrants and Refugees in Thailand. PhD Dissertation, Cornell University.

Newman, E., E. Risch and N. Kassam-Adams (2006). Ethical Issues in Trauma-Related Research: A Review. *Journal of Empirical Research on Human Research Ethics* 1(3): 29–46.

Olney, J., N. Haque and R. Mubarak (2019). We Must Prevent a Lost Generation: Community-Led Education in Rohingya Refugee Camps. *PRIO*. https://reliefweb.int/sites/reliefweb.int/files/resources/Olney%2C%20Haque%2C%20Mubarak%20-%20We%20Must%20Prevent%20a%20Lost%20Generation%20-%20PRIO%20Paper%202019.pdf [Accessed 18/10/2021]

Open Society Justice Initiative (2005). Citizenship and Equality in Practice: Guaranteeing Non-Discriminatory Access to Nationality, Protecting the Right to be Free from Arbitrary Deprivation of Nationality, and Combating Statelessness. *Submission to the United Nations Office of the High Commissioner for Human Rights for Consideration by the UN Commission on Human Rights at Its Sixty-Second Session*. www.justiceinitiative.org/uploads/0d3774dc-821e-4f09-849e-a21e984378a6/citizenship_20051101.pdf [Accessed 17/01/2018]

Patel, I. (2012). The Role of Testimony and Testimonial Analysis in Human Rights Advocacy and Research. *State Crime* 1(2): 235–265.

Perks, R. and A. Thomson (2006). *The Oral History Reader*. Routledge.

Popular Memory Group (2006). Popular Memory: Theory, Politics, Method, in Perks, R. and Thomas, A. (eds), *The Oral History Reader*. Routledge.

Portelli, A. (2006). What Makes Oral History Different?, in Perks, R. and Thomson, A. (eds), *The Oral History Reader*. Second Edition. Routledge.

Potter, R. and Kyaw Win (2019). *National Verification Cards—A Barrier to Rohingya Repatriation, Burma Human Rights Network*. www.bhrn.org.uk/en/report/1090-national-verification-cards-a-barrier-to-rohingya-repatriation-full-report.html [Accessed 08/10/2019]

Republic of the Union of Myanmar (2013). *Final Report of Inquiry Commission on Sectarian Violence in Rakhine State*. https://meriyadh.org/images/pdf/rakhine-commission-report-en-red.pdf [Accessed 05/09/2017]
Riessman, C. K. (2008). *Narrative Methods for the Human Sciences*. Sage.
Riley, A., Y. Akther, M. Noor, R. Ali and C. Welton-Mitchell (2020). Systematic Human Rights Violations, Traumatic Events, Daily Stressors and Mental Health of Rohingya Refugees in Bangladesh. *Conflict and Health* 14(1): 1–14.
Rosenthal, G. (2019). A Brief and Independent Inquiry into the Involvement of the United Nations in Myanmar from 2010 to 2018. *United Nations*. www.un.org/sg/sites/www.un.org.sg/files/atoms/files/Myanmar%20Report%20-%20May%202019.pdf [Accessed 11/11/2019]
Salmon, P. and C. K. Riessman (2008). Looking Back on Narrative Research: An Exchange, in *Doing Narrative Research*. 78–85. Sage.
Scott, J. C. (1998). *Seeing Like a State: How Certain Schemes to Improve the Human Conditions Have Failed*. Yale University Press.
Siegelberg, M. L. (2020). *Statelessness: A Modern History*. Harvard University Press.
Socialist Republic of the Union of Burma (1982). Burma Citizenship Law.
Spiro, P. J. (2011). A New International Law of Citizenship. *American Journal of International Law* 105(4): 694–746.
Spivak, G. C. (1988). 'Can the Subaltern Speak?', in Nelson, C. and Grossberg, L. (eds), *Marxism and the Interpretation of Culture*. Macmillan.
Squire, C., M. Andrews, M. Davis, C. Esin, B. Harrison, L.-C. Hyden and M. Hyden (2014). *What is Narrative Research?* Bloomsbury Publishing.
Stanley, L. (1995). *The Auto/Biographical I: The Theory and Practice of Feminist Auto/Biography*. Manchester University Press.
Stanton, G. H. (2004). Could the Rwandan genocide have been prevented? *Journal of Genocide Research* 6(2): 211–228.
Stanton, G. H. (2017). *The Ten Stages of Genocide, Genocide Watch*. http://genocidewatch.net/genocide-2/8-stages-of-genocide/ [Accessed 20/01/2021]
Tamboukou, M. (2008). A Foucauldian approach to Narratives, in Tamboukou, M., Andrews, M. and Squire, C. (eds), *Doing Narrative Research*. Sage. 102–120.
Tamboukou, M. (2010). *In the Fold between Power and Desire: Women Artists' Narratives*. Cambridge Scholars Publishing.
Tonkin, D. (2018). Exploring the Issue of Citizenship in Rakhine State, in South, A. and Lall, M. (eds), *Citizenship in Myanmar: Ways of Being in and from Burma*. ISEAS. 222–263.
Tonkiss, K. and T. Bloom (2015). Theorising Noncitizenship: Concepts, Debates and Challenges. *Citizenship Studies* 19(8): 837–852.
UNHRC (2016). Situation of Human Rights of Rohingya Muslims and Other Minorities in Myanmar', 32nd session, A/HRC/32/.
UNHRC (Sept 2018). Report of the Independent International Fact-Finding Mission on Myanmar: Report of the 34th Session of the Human Rights Council A/HRC/34/67.
UNHRC (Sept 2019). Detailed Findings of the Independent International Fact-Finding Mission on Myanmar: Report to the 42nd Session of the Human Rights Council, A/HRC/42/CRP.5.
Weissbrodt, D. S. and C. Collins (2006). The Human Rights of Stateless Persons. *Human Rights Quarterly* 28(1): 245–276.
Yuval-Davis, N. (2006). Belonging and the Politics of Belonging. *Patterns of Prejudice* 40(3): 197–214.
Yuval-Davis, N. (2010). Theorizing Identity: Beyond the 'Us' and 'Them' Dichotomy. *Patterns of Prejudice* 44(3): 261–280.

Yuval-Davis, N. (2011). *The Politics of Belonging: Intersectional Contestations*. Sage.
Zarni, M. and N. Brinham (2017). Reworking the Colonial Era Indian Peril: Myanmar's State-Directed Persecution of Rohingyas and Other Muslims. *Brown Journal of World Affairs* 24(1).
Zarni, M. and A. Cowley (2014). The Slow-Burning Genocide of Myanmar's Rohingya. *Pacific Rim Law & Policy Journal* 23(3): 681–754.

2 Papers, cards, and perilous encounters with the state

Identity documents, oral histories, and state crime research

Introduction

In this chapter, I explain how ID narratives provided the most useful way to explore the links between statelessness and genocide. Focusing research on ID cards and registration produced rich data about experiences and understandings of the role of the state in producing statelessness as well as their responses and different forms of resistance. It also enabled the participants to explore the issues of state violence and genocide whilst minimising harms related to interviewing survivors who have experienced trauma.

Health research amongst Rohingya survivors indicates high levels of post-traumatic stress disorder (PTSD), depression, anxiety, and emotional distress (Haar, Wang et al. 2019; Riley, Akther et al. 2020). The process of being interviewed and asked to relate traumatic past events can trigger the symptoms of PTSD (Klempner 2000; Campbell, Adams et al. 2009). Since most of my research took place in the aftermath of the mass killings, mass rape, and mass destruction, one of my concerns was to prioritise well-being and to avoid re-traumatising survivors. The research took place during a period when many human rights organisations and journalists were simultaneously documenting abuses, raising concerns about the impact of 'over-researching' with survivors. During my first visit to the camps in Bangladesh, I was offered what was described by another reflective researcher as a 'menu of human rights violations' by the organisation that was assigned to arrange my visit. They suggested victims of sexual violence on the first morning, gunshot victims in the afternoon and orphaned children the next day. I declined this opportunity to interview at that time, deeply concerned about conducting potentially traumatising interviews when the primary purpose of my research was for my research project rather than broader justice objectives in mind. Instead, I used the time for observations and to familiarise myself with the camp situation. I thought carefully about how to conduct oral history interviews in ways which were not damage-centred—in ways that did not prioritise research findings over well-being and enabled participants to maintain control over what they chose to tell me and what they chose to omit. Identity card narratives provided a way to do this—participants could tell me

DOI: 10.4324/9781003494539-2
This chapter has been made available under a CC-BY 4.0 license.

their own stories, or family and community stories in ways that focused on the meanings they attributed to objects, and from there they could divulge as much or as little about individual or collective violence as they felt comfortable with. I was careful to read the silences, pauses, and contradictions, to respect those awkward moments and not to push beyond them. This was my way of giving greater autonomy and control to participants. As researchers, it is for us to both 'minimise harm' and ensure we aim to 'bring about reciprocal benefits for refugee participants and/or communities'(Mackenzie, McDowell et al. 2007:299). On the basis of this ethical principle, I sought to understand the limitation of my own research before extracting information from survivors of trauma, and tried to ensure that there was a 'favourable ethical cost-benefit ratio' for survivors and research participants (Newman, Risch et al. 2006:29).

As well as encompassing these ethical considerations, ID narratives also provided an excellent entry point for exploring state power, social relations, and identity formation and destruction in ways that captured individual positionality, affect, and emotion, as well as the shifting and evolving structures that framed Rohingya experiences. This chapter explores the role of IDs in the lives of survivors and in state crime and statelessness research.

'This document is like a map of where we belong': IDs and identities

In the early stages of collecting Rohingya oral histories relating to the production of statelessness, it became apparent that many Rohingya narratives about the state's role centred around their identity documents. Many researchers working with diaspora, asylum-seekers, irregular migrants, or stateless persons are familiar with the central role that documents play in lives and narratives of those with precarious or uncertain legal status. As such, scholarship has explored how state power is experienced through state-issued documents (Navaro-Yashin 2007; Sadiq 2009; Hull 2012; Reddy 2015; Williams 2019). Rohingya narratives relating to their documents worked on multiple levels—they were not only evidence of claims to Myanmar citizenship but also state-issued artefacts that could plot policies and practices relating to their diminishing legal status; they were the purveyors of state-ascribed categories that destroyed and imposed (rather than recorded) national, religious, and ethnic identities; they were a series of encounters with the state during which Rohingya resisted identity destruction; and they were objects through which refugees could articulate their hopes, fears, and desires for the future. To illustrate some of the potential for ID narratives to produce rich data, I here draw on the narrative of a Rohingya man called Gulam (not his real name).[1]

As the two young Rohingya interpreters and I were coming to the end of a long day of interviewing in a bamboo shelter in a section of the 'megacamp' still under construction, an older gentleman approached us.[2] He had heard that there was a foreigner in the area who was interested in Rohingya documents, and he had brought one to show me. The tired and hungry faces of the interpreters dropped a little, but out of respect for their elder they resigned themselves to one last interview. As the gentleman, Gulam, carefully unrolled his document, their reluctance gave way to an intense interest. In turn, they gently and silently ran their fingers down the parchment deciphering its old Burmese script, and then erupted into excited chatter that caused other nearby refugees to lean over the bamboo wall in curiosity.

It was a land tenure document belonging to Gulam's ancestors issued by the British colonial administration for the year 1917–8. It detailed the uses of a plot of agricultural land by his Rohingya relatives in northern Maungdaw close to the Indian border. The document was in pristine condition complete with a 1 Anna stamp bearing the head of King George V.[3] Gulam understood that the document had no legal or administrative value—his family, who had remained in the same village until they were expelled in 2017, had passed this land on for other villagers to farm several decades earlier. However, he explained, it was one of his most valued possessions. 'I am a citizen of Burma and I have the right to belong to the land of Arakan. This document shows that. It is like a map of where we (Rohingya) belong,' he told us. My young interpreters cradled the document in their hands and nodded vigorously. It was clear that the document was not only of value to him but also to other Rohingya around him who had an intense thirst for the history of their own people, in particular, for written artefacts and evidence of their past relationships with the states and kingdoms that have governed Rohingya areas. As noted in Chapter 1, a key aspect of Rohingya identity and citizenship that has been denied by Myanmar State institutions is the sense of historical belonging to the land; this document proved Rohingya ties to the land prior to independence. The importance of documents is accentuated by a sense of loss that marks the absence of other documents—whether ones that have been seized, destroyed, or never issued as a result of targeted policies. As Gulam explained, 'the *NaSaKa*[4] took them (Rohingyas' identity documents) away . . . so today they have lost those documents—and it is important to keep these kinds of important historical documents.'

State-issued documents are material objects of law and policy (Hull 2012; Sadiq 2016) and, as Gulam understood, they can be important artefacts of the state (Sadiq 2009). There is a growing body of historically contextualised social science research on statecraft that centres on state-issued documents and paperwork as artefacts that provide insights into how states produce and reproduce nationhood, citizenship, and statelessness through bureaucratic and administrative procedures, and in particular through identity schemes such as identity cards and (biometric) data collection (Caplan and Torpey 2001; Bennet and Lyon 2008; Chhotray and McConnell 2018). Much of this literature draws on Scott's work (1998:65–71) on the categorisation and registration of individuals making populations visible and 'legible' to the state in order to consolidate their power, and on the work of Torpey (2000:4) that understands identity card and passport schemes as central to the building and legitimisation of states by establishing a 'monopoly on the means of movement.' A body of this literature explores how categorisation and identity card schemes shape and influence national, group, and diasporic identities (Brubaker and Cooper 2000; Navaro-Yashin 2007; Hull 2012, 2012; McConnell 2013; Reddy 2015; Williams 2019). Identity card schemes for Rohingya in Myanmar, then, are a useful site through which to explore the state's role in the slow production of Rohingya statelessness.

The central thread in Gulam's unfolding narrative, as with many of the oral histories I collected, was not simply his personal or family history, but the state's attempts to both symbolically and physically destroy Rohingya as a group belonging to Rakhine State. It was a story also of his guile and wit in resisting the attempts of the Myanmar State to erase him from the state records and to erase his group identity. It was a story voiced not only for me but also for the young Rohingya refugees nearby, who hung on his words, searching for messages from history to make sense of and try to take control over their own displacement and survival.

This was not the first time Gulam's document had been in Bangladesh. Gulam had been expelled from Myanmar before, in 1978, along with approximately quarter of a million other Rohingya in what was described by the Myanmar military as an 'immigration operation' but which quickly turned into a campaign of terror (Linquist 1979). Many Rohingya reported having their identity documents confiscated during this time (UNHRC 1996). In 1978–9, Rohingya in Bangladesh were forcibly repatriated to Myanmar (UNHRC 1994; Crisp 2018). Gulam feared that on return, the Myanmar authorities might seize important documents again. He decided that if he had to return to Myanmar 'by the legal route,' which would inevitably involve encounters with state authorities, then the document must stay behind. He hid it with a Bangladeshi family he knew well. He remembered that before he was forced back across the border, an official from an international agency advised all returning Rohingya to keep hold of their ration books. They were told it was an important document as it proved they were returning refugees originally from Myanmar. Sure enough, on Gulam's route between the transit centre and his home village, he was stopped whilst crossing the fields by a member of the armed forces. He showed the ration book, and it was confiscated, never to be returned. Gulam smiled as he told us this. He knew that he had done the right thing leaving his land document behind. After two weeks, Gulam went back across the border 'the sneaky way,' picked up his document, and returned. In the 1990s, following a second round of mass forced repatriations, the National Registration Cards (NRCs) held by his parents and relatives were seized in a household check by the *NaSaKa*. He rolled up the land document, hid it in an iron pipe, and left it in the house where it stayed hidden in the functional and innocuous object until 2017. When Gulam's village was attacked by the Myanmar military in 2017, he managed to flee with just the clothes on his back, drinking water, and the iron pipe containing his document. At the time of the interview, Gulam and many of those around him were worrying about the risk of being forcibly returned to Myanmar again. He told us that he would use the same method again to keep hold of his document—leave it behind and then find a 'sneaky way' to retrieve it. The discussion then moved to the risks of repatriation, their strategies of resistance, and their demands for restoration of their citizenship as a pre-condition of return.

For many Rohingya participants, then, treasured registration documents—such as NRCs and family lists—were also often imbued with an ethnographic significance relating to their group identity, the salience of which outranked their legal and administrative functions of providing access to rights, welfare, and/or forms of citizenship. Rohingya refugees in the camps in Bangladesh had collected together filed copies of outdated or expired identity documents in one community collection with the purpose of showing them to others as a historical record.[5] Through these self-organised archival collections, it was possible, for example, to identify patterns relating to the dates and under which regimes the ethnic, religious, and nationality categorisations changed from Rohingya or Muslim or from citizen to foreigner (see Chapter 5). As Gulam's account demonstrates, whilst such systems organise, categorise, and 'other' people through hegemonic means, such processes are also contested by the documented and the undocumented. Registration and identity documents do not only plot the state's bureaucratic and administrative approaches to citizenship. They are also anthropological objects around which identities are organised, produced, reproduced, destroyed, resisted, contested, mediated, and negotiated (Navaro-Yashin 2007; McConnell 2009; Hull 2012; Reddy 2015; Chhotray and McConnell 2018). For Rohingya, being enumerated, registered, and re-categorised became a hugely important site of resistance, most visibly in the case of the national census in 2014 and the National Verification Cards (NVCs) as explored in Chapter 7. Thus, IDs and registration were points at which Rohingya encountered the violence of the state and so provided useful sites for understanding resistance and contestation.

Narratives relating to IDs, other documents, and their absences, then, can be researched as evidence, as artefacts, and as anthropological objects. All these areas provide ways to explore events, experiences, and affect relating to the production of statelessness and identity destruction and reorganisation.

Narrative research and oral histories

In this section, I explain why narrative research and oral histories provide an effective research approach in critical statelessness and state crime research. Oral history research most often falls within a broader body of narrative research (Portelli 2006:35–36; Czarniawska 2010). Narratives, like oral histories, are accounts or descriptions of a series of connected events. The gaps between state narratives and the narratives of marginalised groups often feature the struggles over constructions of the past. Myanmar's histories in relation to state dominance and its minority populations are also characterised by contestation, conflict, and struggle (Metro 2011). Narrative research moves away from more traditional human rights research that, broadly speaking, seeks to ascertain and triangulate facts relating to violations and to establish degrees of distance between the researcher and the research participants for the purpose of objectivity and validity (Patel 2012). Narrative research focuses rather on subjectivities, multi-layered meaning, and historical experience. The framework provides useful methods for state crime researchers to explore how survivors contest and/or authorise dominant constructions of events and histories in state and international discourses, and how they construct their own individual and group memories, experiences, and identities in narrative forms that produce social action and demand change (see, e.g. Perks and Thomson 2006:1–14; Yuval-Davis 2010; Squire, Andrews et al. 2014). I have identified four ways in which a narrative approach is useful in investigating social histories, identities, and belonging.

First, narratives are understood as 'modes of resistance to existing structures of power' (Squire, Andrews et al. 2014:4). Rohingya have been marginalised in Myanmar society and their histories, heritage, and traditions hidden and erased by the process of genocide and the production of their statelessness (Lee and González Zarandona 2019; MacLean 2019). Narrative frameworks have been integral to approaches that seek to make visible the 'hidden histories' of marginalised or ignored groups. These include black, working-class, or women's histories, often incorporating anti-racist, socialist, and feminist perspectives in order to challenge the assumptions and accepted judgements and demand social action (Stanley 1995; Popular Memory Group 2006; Tamboukou 2010). This approach, then, provides an ideal way to explore how Rohingya narratives are able to influence the larger narratives at international level in ways that demand change and social action, tying in with the notions of resistance and social audience from within state crime scholarship. Written documents are sometimes described as having a 'monopoly' over 'factual credibility' (Portelli 2006:57), which can place communities and groups with oral traditions at a disadvantage in contesting the constructions of the past by dominant group with written (national) histories. Rohingya language has not been widely used as a written language in modern-day Myanmar; oral traditions within the household and community have played a huge part in shaping and maintaining identities and are thus a useful method of inquiry.[6]

Second, narrative research is useful in shifting the focus from the collection of objective facts and instead traces different meanings, understandings, and interpretations of events. Any single narrative also contains imaginings and symbolism (Portelli 2006:37). Narrative research accepts that structures, discourses, and social formations shape personal stories and that individuals may draw from multiple and shifting subject positions. Through these interactions, the impact of structural factors and the significance of social change or upheaval can be traced. Thereby, orality, narrative form, memory, subjectivities, and the relationship between the researcher and research participants all become resources from which meaning and interpretation can be drawn rather than weaknesses relating to credibility (Perks and Thomson 2006:4). This is not to say that facts do not matter; the large body of human rights documentation relating to Rohingya during this period enabled me to check narratives against other bodies of work to ascertain the relationship between facts and meaning. Narrative research often considers the relationship amongst past, present, and future (Popular Memory Group 2006:51; Squire, Andrews et al. 2014). This was a particular feature of Rohingya oral histories within this research, whereby accounts of past mass expulsions, forced repatriations, and identity card schemes were drawn on as resources through which to decipher their futures in Myanmar by weighing up the risks on both sides of the border in Bangladesh and Myanmar, and their current-day situations were reflected backwards (Brinham 2017). Thus, Rohingya group demands and social actions in the present could be traced through the ways in which their narratives interpreted the past.

Third, narrative research is useful in exploring both individual and collective identities. Narrative is understood as providing order to personal and collective identities. Identity in this context is 'a specific kind of narrative in which people tell themselves and others who they are, who they are not and who/how they would like to/should be' (Yuval-Davis 2010:279). All identities are fluid, socially constructed, and are in a process in which they are being (re)constructed, (re)interpreted, and (re)negotiated. They are shaped by both the structures of power and individual subjectivities (Brubaker and Cooper 2000; Yuval-Davis 2006; Riessman 2008). Narratives and oral histories are tied up with the performance and negotiation of social identities and the creation of common platforms for identity (Riessman 2008; Squire, Andrews et al. 2014). They are also constrained by and resist larger and more dominant narrative patterns (Gready 2008; Squire, Andrews et al. 2014). Fluid individual identity narratives and subjectivities are produced within a social and political context that increases in significance as identities come under threat (Yuval-Davis 2010:266). Thus, applying narrative inquiry to identity destruction, formation, and reorganisation can tell us about both the state-led identity destruction projects and the collective resistance and action that are central to this research.

The fourth useful approach from within narrative research relates to the notion of co-constructed narratives. This notion holds that all narratives are produced and shaped by the social context and by the listeners or audience which may or may not be present (Czarniawska 2004; Clandinin 2007; Riessman 2008; Yuval-Davis 2010). This co-construction takes place not only during the interview or focus group but also in the process of interpreting and retelling (Salmon and Riessman 2008). As such, the researcher does not *find* narratives that represent external realities but in the process of interviewing, listening, and interpreting also participates in the production of those narratives. As Phil Salmon notes (quoted in Riessman 2008:31):

> The audience, whether physically present or not, exerts a crucial influence on what can and cannot be said, how things should be expressed, what can be taken for granted, what needs explaining, and so on. We now recognize that the personal account, in research interviews, which has traditionally been seen as the expression of a single subjectivity, is in fact always a co-construction.

This notion offers a way in which to acknowledge the role of the researcher and others in the construction of narratives and use it as a mode of inquiry. It was useful for my research in two ways. First, I was aware that my own positionality often influenced the data I was collecting. I was known to many of the participants as someone who had authored work on Rohingya in the past using the term 'genocide.'[7] Further, I was often known before I entered the room as the wife of a Burmese Buddhist activist who had a prominent voice, including on Rohingya issues, in both Burmese and international circles. Despite my efforts, it was difficult to cast aside these identities in the process of my research. Second, during the data collection period at the urging of Rohingya participants and activists, I retold some of the narratives to a public audience in print form and in advocacy forums to try to influence opinions and highlight neglected issues that were of concern to Rohingya participants relating to citizenship in Myanmar. These articles and presentations were primarily driven by my own ethical need to give something back to the research participants. In the process of retelling to public audiences for particular purposes, I was active in co-constructing the narratives (Salmon and Riessman 2008). In this way, my discussions, conversations, and participation in advocacy forums constituted part of the research. Narratives, as Tamboukou (2008) explains, do not represent external realities but rather are productive. They are not simply determined by the social world but also shaped it.

Research methods

Operation *Nagamin* that reached Rakhine State in 1978 and caused the first major expulsion under the Myanmar military regime of approximately 250,000 Rohingya (Linquist 1979) was most often identified by many Rohingya participants as the start of the production of their statelessness in Myanmar. Furthermore, large-scale expulsions took place in 1991–2, 2012, and 2016–7 (Brinham 2017; Crisp 2018). Additionally, many Rohingya fled systems of persecution in between the major incidents of mass violence. Each of these periods of forced migrations has had differing patterns of onward migration from Myanmar and Bangladesh involving changing routes over land and across the seas (UNHCR 2016, 2017). In order to explore Rohingya experiences across time, I opted to use a multi-site model from which to select participants (see Marcus 1995; Hannerz 2003). The field research took place in Kuala Lumpur in Malaysia; New Delhi in India; Chittagong, the refugee camps near Coxes Bazar and surrounding areas in Bangladesh; and (via signal or in person) with Rohingya in diaspora in Europe and Australia. Diasporic Rohingya communities beyond refugee settlements in Bangladesh have played a vital part in building Rohingya social movements across the years (Cowper-smith 2019).

Since this research was qualitative and focused on meaning and experience rather than broad general findings, in-depth analysis of the narratives of a smaller rather than larger sample group yield better data (Jørgensen and Phillips 2002:120). There were 104 people who participated in the research. I used snowball sampling, which is common in research related to work with refugees or people with precarious legal status, especially where access can be difficult. Snowball sampling involves asking existing participants to recruit further participants for a study (Weiss 1995). This usually involves the help of one or more 'gatekeepers' (Atkinson et al. 2001:29). However, sometimes snowball sampling can slant the data in particular ways, for example, the first participant may reach out to people of a similar social status, age, or political positioning (Weiss 1995). Although it is impossible to eliminate bias in a study such as this, I tried to mitigate such potential slants by using multiple entry points and 'gatekeepers.' For example, in Bangladesh, I drew on the help of four different gatekeepers, one from the 1970s displacements, one from the registered camps from the 1990s expulsions, and two from the 2017 expulsions who had different political allegiances.

I sought a range of participants across different age groups, from different regions of Rakhine State and Myanmar, with a range of political and family-based affiliations. The ages of participants ranged from their late teens to their nineties. Rohingya identities are characterised by regionalisms—first between those within the zone administered as North Rakhine State, who have been subject to segregation and a separate set of persecutory policies, and those residing in other areas of Rakhine State and Myanmar (Amnesty International 2017); second between Maungdaw, Buthidaung, and Rathedaung within North Rakhine State. These regionalisms intersect with different family-based loyalties and political affiliations. I therefore interviewed Rohingya originally from within Rakhine State—Maungdaw, Buthidaung, and Rathedaung; from elsewhere in Rakhine including Sittwe, the state capital, and southern Rakhine; and those who grew up in Yangon and elsewhere in Myanmar.

I made efforts to ensure that both women and men were represented in the research. There were 32 women participants and 72 men. This imbalance reflects several factors: First, gendered norms in Rohingya society include the widespread practice of purdah whereby many women remain in private domestic settings rather than public ones, or often there is a separation of women and men in public spaces (Ripoll 2017; Asia Foundation and Centre for Peace and Justice 2020). In order to ensure a comfortable environment for women participants, I tried where possible to organise women-only focus groups and secure female translators. In the cramped conditions of camps in both Bangladesh and India, there are few private spaces in which to interview or hold meetings, making it much harder to organise spontaneous interviews and discussions with women as I could with men. Women did not self-present requesting to be interviewed as frequently as men did. Fieldwork consisted of narrative interviews, focus groups, observations, and walking histories.

Narrative interviews

Narrative interviewing aims to generate in-depth accounts rather than general or factual statements. It seeks to understand the meaning people attach to experiences and events. It therefore departs from the styles of structured or semi-structured interviews that are common in social science research and shifts to a style that is more conversational and less structured (Riessman 2008:Ch 2). It involves the researcher 'giving up control' of structured questions and allowing participants to speak in their own ways by forging conversational styles. The features of such a style are turn-taking in speaking; associative shifts in topics; 'entrance and exit talk' where narratives transition in and out of accounts of past events to relevant issues; the exploration of associations and meanings that may generate other stories; and discussion of where shifts and turns occur in the conversations (Riessman 2008:24). In the example I provided in Chapter 1, Gulam's account of returning his old land document to Myanmar, narrative shifts frequently occurred that established links between his past experiences and the precariousness of the current situation for Rohingya in Bangladesh. Through a series of associations, his narrative negatively assessed the trustworthiness of the Myanmar government and warned of the threat of future forced repatriations. Since narrative interviews are interactions involving social positioning and co-construction of conversation, the method is sometimes described as being close to ethnographic practice (Mishler 1986; Salmon and Riessman 2008). In Gulam's story, the presence of younger Rohingya impacted the way the story was told—an elder described their collective past in ways that interpreted their current shared situation. The ways in which the younger Rohingya interacted with him and touched the document had as much significance as the language itself. The analysis of narrative interviews involves focusing not only on transcripts of conversations but also on factors such as turns in the conversation, associations, tone, volume, rhythm, pauses, velocity, plots, gestures, emotions, reticence, and points where views conflict (Portelli 2006). Therefore, in addition to the transcripts of the narrative interviews, I also made notes shortly after the events to set the scene and describe gestures, emotions, pauses, and interactions that the transcripts themselves could not fully account for. I provided space for participants to tell stories about their citizenship and their ID cards in their own ways. It allowed me to explore the turns and tangents, the contradictions and elaborations, the silences and the chatter, the interruptions, and the distractions. All of these are both impossible to avoid and a central part of research in crowded refugee camp settings. Narrative interviews ranged in duration between 30 minutes and 3.5 hours.

Focus groups

Focus groups involve the interaction between participants. They can develop ideas collectively and collaboratively to bring forward group priorities and perspectives (Alasuutari, Bickman et al. 2008). The elaboration of stories and themes in focus groups can help researchers 'understand how participants structure and organize their social world' (Hughes and Dumont 1993). One of the key reasons that I chose this method is that the unit of analysis for this research was the group. The method allows for the movement of discussion between personal experiences and collective experiences (Smithson 2000; Alasuutari, Bickman et al. 2008) and so, as Munday (2006) asserts, it can be particularly effective in considering the construction of group identities. Interactions and group dynamics come into focus, as do disagreements and resistances that contribute to the construction of collective narratives (Alasuutari, Bickman et al. 2008). I conducted nine focus groups in Bangladesh, India, and Malaysia. This included eight single-sex groups and one mixed group.

Participant observations

Participant observations and fieldnotes have long formed one of the core components of ethnographic research (Emerson, Fretz et al. 2001). Through observations of the social world, the researcher can explore group and individual interactions and dynamics in ways that supplement interviews and focus groups. In more recent ethnographic work, observations do not just record the social world of the ethnic 'other' but also include reflexivity, positionality, and interactions between social structures and individual subjectivities (Emerson, Fretz et al. 2001). Often observations involve the interactions that take place within certain locations—for example, the refugee camp—or during events with particular cultural significance—for example, memorial days. Observations also provided insights into issues that I would not have been able to gain from interviews alone. For example, the negotiations and contestations and conflicts relating to the strategic concealment of Rohingya identities that occur around the use of irregularly obtained identity documents for accessing education and livelihood opportunities. In all, I recorded 28 sets of observations separate from interviews and focus groups.

'Walking histories' is the term I assigned to a research method I devised in Bangladesh whereby I took two or three Rohingya from different generations of displacement with me on visits to sites in the area with historical or cultural significance in order to generate talk and interpretation of the past.

In this way, we were able to co-construct narratives about Rohingya citizenship, statelessness, and state crime in ways that were more conversational and natural than regular interviews. It was not only the places that generated useful reflections but also the interactions between individual Rohingya with different upbringings, and other local populations. Such visits included:

(a) Shahpuri island at the mouth of the River Naf from which many of the media images of burning villages, arriving refugees, and washed-up bodies were taken in 2017. Our visit, a few weeks before the first anniversary of these assaults, was an act of remembrance in which we visited the places from which the photos had been taken. The island is also a place of cross-border trade, where residents across the years have provided shelter for fleeing refugees and freedom fighters. It is also the area associated with the first Anglo-Burma war in 1824, which enabled Rohingya and Rakhine Buddhist refugees pushed out by the Burman invasion/annexation of Rakhine State to return to their homelands in Rakhine (Phayre 1883; Harvey 1925).

(b) 'No man's land' or 'ground zero' where genocide survivors (not registered by the regular refugee procedures) lived between the Myanmar border fence and Bangladesh territory. At the time, this community had become the frontline in the resistance to repatriations, where they would be approached at the border fence by Burmese and INGO officials to discuss return. The residents' refusal to return at the time made them heroes of endurance and resistance in some of the narratives of some Rohingya participants. The day of the visit came immediately after the worst day of flooding since arrival. Rohingya make-shift homes were waist high in flood water and the community took it in turns standing under umbrellas on the small wooden bridge between Myanmar and Bangladesh and wandering on to the dry lands on the Bangladesh side, watched by armed Bangladeshi border guards from their concrete outpost.

(c) The Buddhist temples in Ramu, a district of Cox's Bazar, to explore shared Buddhist/Muslim histories of the region. We spoke with the Lord Abbot, in his nineties, and who had provided shelter to multi-religious communities during Bangladesh's war of independence and had an interest in multi-religious resistances during the colonial and pre-colonial eras. This and other temples we visited were attacked in religious violence in 2012 and were then under the protection of state security forces. We visited on the anniversary of the 2012 attacks when media and others had come to mark the anniversary.

(d) Some Bangladeshi villages around Ramu Upazila including a small agricultural village that was the relocation site for a Bangladeshi community displaced by climate change. We discussed attitudes of communities to Rohingya, shared borders, identity loss, government and community responses to displacement, etc.

Retelling narratives as politically engaged research

In this research, I did not seek to disengage myself from the political, moral, and ideological issues that motivate it in a quest for 'objectivity.' As such, I took a position similar to that of an action-orientated researcher (Reason and Bradbury 2008:163). I consider myself an active participant in trying to ensure that Rohingya voices are put to the forefront and pushing for greater public spaces for Rohingya activists to be heard on this issue. State crime research is also engaged scholarship (Grewcock 2012). In promoting Rohingya activism, I am not engaging in trying to shift scholarship or indeed international policy to reflect my own informed views but rather to amplify the views of participants through various methods. Such amplification involved assisting participants and key informers with editing journalistic articles for international publication, editing statements by Rohingya organisations, editing speeches for public forums, drafting chapters of Rohingya organisations books based on focus groups with them, and assisting with fundraising and support of genocide memorial efforts. Through playing an active part in these processes, I learnt about the ways in which Rohingya sought to influence public discourses through their activism. I also retold individual narratives from the research in events and conferences involving policymakers, UN officials, and government officials, which aimed to influence international policy relating to Rohingya (in addition and separate from conferences and workshops for developing my research).[8] Rewriting, recontextualising and retelling stories to different audiences whilst maintaining the integrity of the original narratives, is a key aspect of narrative research (Czarniawska 2010:65). It has been possible through these avenues to gage the response to Rohingya narratives that counteract dominant understandings and to use my research in what I consider to be an ethical and publicly engaged way. I also published narrative-centred blogs and articles based on issues that participants have requested are put in the public domain where they feel the issues are being sidelined or silenced, including the role of international organisations in rolling out ID card schemes for refugees and returnees.[9]

The process of ethically conscious and politically engaged research does not come to a neat conclusion at the end of research project. Rather, the relationships and dynamics formed between participants and communities continue to develop and shift. Likewise, the meaning of identity documents, both old and new, in people's lives is in a constant state of flux. The chapters that follow attempt to represent those dynamics projected both into the past and into the future during the limited time period between 2017 and 2019. Chapters 4 to 8 analyse various aspects of the ID narratives in different historical and socio-political contexts. First, however, Chapter 3 provides an important backdrop by exploring the developing international discourses on statelessness.

Notes

1 In53, 27/09/2018, extension 4.
2 'Megacamp' was the unofficial term used to describe all the connected camps for Rohingya in the Coxes Bazar area that comprise the largest refugee camp in the world.
3 The stamp bearing the unit of currency and the King's head indicated it was official documentation issued when Myanmar was administered as part of British India.
4 *NaSaKa* refers to the security forces that operated in Rakhine State at the time.
5 Fg6, 26/07/2018, Kutapalong. See also Greg Constantine's Photographic Work, "Burma's Path to Genocide" https://exhibitions.ushmm.org/burmas-path-to-genocide (accessed 09/06/2021).
6 The significance of oral traditions within Rohingya households is illustrated in Habiburahman and Ansel (2018).
7 See also Green, McManus et al. (2015).
8 These included advocacy and practitioner engagement events at the National Assembly in Paris, Columbia University, the Hague, LSE, UCL, and a think-tank in New Delhi.
9 Articles include Brinham, N. (2017). Breaking the Cycle of Expulsion, Repatriation and Exploitation for Rohingya. Available at: www.opendemocracy.net/beyondslavery/natalie-brinham/breaking-cycle-of-expulsion-forced-repatriation-and-exploitation-for-r (accessed 30/01/2018), Brinham, N. (2018). ""Genocide cards": Rohingya Refugees on Why They Risked Their Lives to Refuse ID Cards." OpenDemocracy, Brinham, N. (2019). "When Identity Documents Produce Exclusion: Lessons from Rohingya experiences in Myanmar", Brinham, N. and Y. Cowper-Smith (2019). "Rohingya Poets Turn Words Into Art of Resistance", Brinham, N., A. D. Tiwari, J. Field, J. Ealom, J. M. Arraiza and A. de Chickera (2020). Locked in and Locked Out: The Impact of Digital Identity Systems on Rohingya Populations, Institute on Statelessness and Inclusion and UN Special Rapporteur on Racism, Zarni, M. and N. Brinham (Jun 2019). New Secretive Deal between UN, Myanmar Smells Foul. Additionally, I assisted activist groups with statements, advocacy, and participated in online conferences/events for practitioners on the preventing refoulement and analysing the production of statelessness in Myanmar.

Bibliography

Alasuutari, P., L. Bickman and J. Brannen (2008). *The Sage Handbook of Social Research Methods*. Sage.

Amnesty International (2017). *Caged without a Roof: Apartheid in Myanmar's Rakhine State*. www.amnesty.org/en/documents/asa16/7484/2017/en/ [Accessed 02/12/2018]

Asia Foundation and Centre for Peace and Justice (2020). *Navigating the Margins: Family, Mobility and Livelihoods amongst Rohingya Refugees in Bangladesh*. https://asiafoundation.org/wp-content/uploads/2020/09/Navigating-the-Margins_Family-Mobility-and-Livelihoods-Amongst-Rohingya-in-Bangladesh.pdf [Accessed 25/03/2021]

Atkinson, P., A. Coffey, S. Delamont, J. Loftland and L. Loftland (2001). *Handbook of Ethnography*. Sage.

Bennet, C. and D. Lyon (2008). *Playing the Identity Card: Surveillance, Security and Identification in Global Perspective*. Routledge.

Brinham, N. (2017). Breaking the Cycle of Expulsion, Repatriation and Exploitation for Rohingya. *OpenDemocracy*. www.opendemocracy.net/beyondslavery/natalie-brinham/breaking-cycle-of-expulsion-forced-repatriation-and-exploitation-for-r [Accessed 30/01/2018]

Brinham, N. (2018). 'Genocide Cards': Rohingya Refugees on Why They Risked Their Lives to Refuse ID Cards. *OpenDemocracy*. www.opendemocracy.net/natalie-brinham/genocide-cards-why-rohingya-refugees-are-resisting-id-cards [Accessed 30/01/2019]

Brinham, N. (2019). When Identity Documents Produce Exclusion: Lessons from Rohingya Experiences in Myanmar. *LSE Blogs*. https://blogs.lse.ac.uk/mec/2019/05/10/when-identity-documents-and-registration-produce-exclusion-lessons-from-rohingya-experiences-in-myanmar/ [Accessed 20/02/2020]

Brinham, N. and Y. Cowper-Smith (2019). Rohingya Poets Turn Words into Art of Resistance. *Anadolu Agency*. www.aa.com.tr/en/asia-pacific/rohingya-poets-turn-words-into-art-of-resistance-/1551737 [Accessed 02/10/2019]

Brinham, N., A. D. Tiwari, J. Field, J. Ealom, J. M. Arraiza and A. de Chickera (2020). *Locked In and Locked Out: The Impact of Digital Identity Systems on Rohingya Populations, Institute on Statelessness and Inclusion and UN Special Rapporteur on Racism*. https://files.institutesi.org/Locked_In_Locked_Out_The_Rohingya_Briefing_Paper.pdf [Accessed 25/05/2021]

Brubaker, R. and F. Cooper (2000). Beyond 'Identity'. *Theory and Society* 29(1): 1–47.

Campbell, R., A. E. Adams, S. M. Wasco, C. E. Ahrens and T. Sefl (2009). Training Interviewers for Research on Sexual Violence: A Qualitative Study of Rape Survivors' Recommendations for Interview Practice.' *Violence against Women* 15(5): 595–617.

Caplan, J. and J. C. Torpey (2001). *Documenting Individual Identity: The Development of State Practices in the Modern World*. Princeton University Press.

Chhotray, V. and F. McConnell (2018). *Certifications of Citizenship: The History, Politics and Materiality of Identity Documents in South Asian States and Diasporas*. Taylor & Francis.

Clandinin, D. J. (2007). *Handbook of Narrative Inquiry: Mapping a Methodology*. Sage.

Cowper-Smith, Y. (2019). The Global Rohingya Diaspora throws Lifelines to Bangladesh and Myanmar. *The Conversation*. http://theconversation.com/the-global-rohingya-diaspora-throws-lifelines-to-bangladesh-and-myanmar-117881 [Accessed 14/10/2019]

Crisp, J. (2018). 'Primitive People': The Untold Story of UNHCR's Historical Engagement with Rohingya Refugees. *Humanitarian Exchange, Humanitarian Practice Network*. 732018. https://odihpn.org/magazine/primitive-people-the-untold-story-of-unhcrs-historical-engagement-with-rohingya-refugees/ [Accessed 17/12/2018]

Czarniawska, B. (2004). *Narratives in Social Science Research*. Sage.

Czarniawska, B. (2010). The Uses of Narratology in Social and Policy Studies. *Critical Policy Studies* 4(1): 58–76.

Emerson, R., R. Fretz and L. Shaw (2001). Participant Observation and Fieldnotes, in Atkinson, P., Coffey, A., Delamont, S., Loftland, J. and Loftland, L. (eds), *Handbook of Ethnography*. Sage.

Gready, P. (2008). The Public Life of Narratives: Ethics, Politics, Methods, in Tamboukou, M., Andrews, M. and Squire, C. (eds), *Doing Narrative Research*. Sage. 137–150.

Green, P., T. McManus and A. de la Cour Venning (2015). Countdown to Annihilation: Genocide in Myanmar. *International State Crime Initiative*. http://statecrime.org/data/2015/10/ISCI-Rohingya-Report-PUBLISHED-VERSION.pdf [Accessed 29/08/2024]

Grewcock, M. (2012). Public Criminology, Victim Agency and Researching State Crime. *State Crime* 1(1): 109–125.

Haar, R. J., K. Wang, H. Venters, S. Salonen, R. Patel, T. Nelson, R. Mishori and P. K. Parmar (2019). Documentation of Human Rights Abuses among Rohingya Refugees from Myanmar. *Conflict and Health* 13(1): 1–14.

Habiburahman and S. Ansel (2018). *First, They Erased Our Name: A Rohingya Speaks*. Scribe.
Hammersley, M. and P. Atkinson (2019). *Ethnography: Principles in Practice*. Routledge.
Hannerz, U. (2003). Being There . . . and There . . . and There! Reflections on Multi-Site Ethnography. *Ethnography* 4(2): 201–216.
Harvey, G. E. (1925). *History of Burma from the Earliest Times to 10 March 1824: The Beginning of the English Conquest*. Longmans, Green and Company.
Hughes, D. and K. Dumont (1993). Focus Groups as Culturally Anchored Methodology. *American Journal of Community Psychology* 21: 775–806.
Hull, M. S. (2012a). Documents and Bureaucracy. *Annual Review of Anthropology* 41: 251–267.
Hull, M. S. (2012b). *Government of Paper: The Materiality of Bureaucracy in Urban Pakistan*. University of California Press.
Jørgensen, M. W. and L. J. Phillips (2002). *Discourse Analysis as Theory and Method*. Sage.
Klempner, M. (2000). Navigating Life Review Interviews with Survivors of Trauma. *The Oral History Review* 27(2): 67–83.
Lee, R. and J. A. A. González Zarandona (2019). Heritage Destruction in Myanmar's Rakhine State: Legal and Illegal Iconoclasm. *International Journal of Heritage Studies* 26(5): 519–538.
Linquist, A. (1979). Report on the 1978–79 Bangladesh Refugee Relief Operation. *UNHCR*.
Mackenzie, C., C. McDowell and E. Pittaway (2007). 'Beyond 'Do No Harm': The Challenge of Constructing Ethical Relationships in Refugee Research. *Journal of Refugee Studies* 20(2): 299–319.
MacLean, K. (2019). The Rohingya Crisis and the Practices of Erasure. *Journal of Genocide Research* 21(1): 83–95.
Marcus, G. E. (1995). Ethnography in/of the World System: The Emergence of Multi-Sited Ethnography. *Annual Review of Anthropology* 24(1): 95–117.
McConnell, F. (2009). Governments-in-Exile: Statehood, Statelessness and the Reconfiguration of Territory and Sovereignty. *Geography Compass* 3(5): 1902–1919.
McConnell, F. (2013). Citizens and Refugees: Constructing and Negotiating Tibetan Identities in Exile. *Annals of the Association of American Geographers* 103(4): 967–983.
Metro, R. (2011). History Curricula and the Reconciliation of Ethnic Conflict: A Collaborative Project with Burmese Migrants and Refugees in Thailand. PhD Dissertation, Cornell University.
Mishler, E. G. (1986). The Analysis of Interview-Narratives, in Sarbin, T. R. (ed), *Narrative Psychology: The Storied Nature of Human Conduct*. Praeger Publishers/Greenwood Publishing Group. 233–255.
Munday, J. (2006). Identity in Focus: The Use of Focus Groups to Study the Construction of Collective Identity. *Sociology* 40(1): 89–105.
Navaro-Yashin, Y. (2007). Make-Believe Papers, Legal Forms and the Counterfeit: Affective Interactions between Documents and People in Britain and Cyprus. *Anthropological Theory* 7(1): 79–98.
Newman, E., E. Risch and N. Kassam-Adams (2006). Ethical Issues in Trauma-Related Research: A Review. *Journal of Empirical Research on Human Research Ethics* 1(3): 29–46.
Patel, I. (2012). The Role of Testimony and Testimonial Analysis in Human Rights Advocacy and Research. *State Crime* 1(2): 235–265.
Perks, R. and A. Thomson (2006). *The Oral History Reader*. Routledge.

Phayre, A. P. (1883). History of Burma: Including Burma Proper, Pegu, Taungu, Tenasserim, and Arakan, from the Earliest Time to the First War with British India. *Susil Gupta.*

Popular Memory Group (2006). Popular Memory: Theory, Politics, Method, in Perks, R. and Thomas, A. (eds), *The Oral History Reader*. Routledge. 43–53.

Portelli, A. (2006). What Makes Oral History Different?, in Perks, R. and Thomson, A. (eds), *The Oral History Reader*. Routledge. 32–42.

Reason, P. and H. Bradbury (2008). *The Sage Handbook of Action Research: Participative Inquiry and Practice*. Sage.

Reddy, M. (2015). Identity Paper/Work/s and the Unmaking of Legal Status in Mae Sot, Thailand. *Asian Journal of Law and Society* 2(2): 251–266.

Riessman, C. K. (2008). *Narrative Methods for the Human Sciences*. Sage.

Riley, A., Y. Akther, M. Noor, R. Ali and C. Welton-Mitchell (2020). Systematic Human Rights Violations, Traumatic Events, Daily Stressors and Mental Health of Rohingya Refugees in Bangladesh. *Conflict and Health* 14(1): 1–14.

Ripoll, S. (2017). Social and Cultural Factors Shaping Health and Nutrition, Wellbeing and Protection of the Rohingya within a Humanitarian Context. *IDS*. https://opendocs.ids.ac.uk/opendocs/ds2/stream/?#/documents/3587036/page/1 [Accessed 14/10/2019]

Sadiq, K. (2009). *Paper Citizens: How Illegal Immigrants Acquire Citizenship in Developing Countries*. Oxford University Press.

Sadiq, K. (2016). Limits of Legal Citizenship: Narratives from South and Southeast Asia, in Lawrance, B. N. and Stevens, J. (eds), *Citizenship in Question: Evidentiary Birthright and Statelessness*. Duke University Press. 165–176.

Salmon, P. and C. K. Riessman, (2008). Looking Back on Narrative Research: An Exchange, in Tamboukou, M., Andrews, M. and Squire, C. (eds), *Doing Narrative Research*. Sage. 78–85.

Scott, J. C. (1998). *Seeing Like a State: How Certain Schemes to Improve the Human Conditions Have Failed*. Yale University Press.

Smithson, J. (2000). Using and Analysing Focus Groups: Limitations and Possibilities. *International Journal of Social Research Methodology* 3(2): 103–119.

Squire, C., M. Andrews, M. D. M. Davis, C. Esin, B. Harrison, L.-C. Hyden and M. Hyden (2014). *What is Narrative Research*? Bloomsbury Academic.

Stanley, L. (1995). *The Auto/Biographical I: The Theory and Practice of Feminist Auto/Biography*. Manchester University Press.

Tamboukou, M. (2008). A Foucauldian Approach to Narratives, in Tamboukou, M., Andrews, M. and Squire, C. (eds), *Doing Narrative Research*. Sage. 102–120.

Tamboukou, M. (2010). *In the Fold between Power and Desire: Women Artists' Narratives*. Cambridge Scholars Publishing.

Torpey, J. (2000). *The Invention of the Passport: Surveillance, Citizenship, and the State*. Cambridge University Press.

UNHCR (2016). *Mixed Maritime Movements*. https://reporting.unhcr.org/sites/default/files/UNHCR%20-%20Mixed%20Movements%20in%20South-East%20Asia%20-%202016%20--%20April%202017_0.pdf [Accessed 09/10/2020]

UNHCR (2017). *Over 168,000 Rohingya Likely Fled Myanmar Since 2012—UNHCR Report*. Retrieved 22 May 2017, from www.unhcr.org/news/latest/2017/5/590990ff4/168000-rohingya-likely-fled-myanmar-since-2012-unhcr-report.html [Accessed 17/05/2020]

UNHRC (1994). Report on the Situation of Human Rights in Myanmar, prepared by Mr. Yozo Yokota, Special Rapporteur, E/CN.4/1994/57.

UNHRC (1996). Report on the Situation of Human Rights in Myanmar, prepared by Mr. Yozo Yokota, Special Rapporteur, E/CN.4/1996/65.

Weiss, R. S. (1995). *Learning from Strangers: The Art and Method of Qualitative Interview Studies*. Simon and Schuster.

Williams, P. (2019). Emigration State Encounters: The Everyday Material Life of a Diaspora Technology. *Political Geography*. 68: 1–11.

Yuval-Davis, N. (2006). Belonging and the Politics of Belonging. *Patterns of Prejudice* 40(3): 197–214.

Yuval-Davis, N. (2010). Theorizing Identity: Beyond the 'Us' and 'Them' Dichotomy. *Patterns of Prejudice* 44(3): 261–280.

Zarni, M. and N. Brinham (Jun 2019). New Secretive Deal between UN, Myanmar Smells Foul. *Anadolu Agency*. www.aa.com.tr/en/analysis-news/new-secretive-deal-between-un-myanmar-smells-foul-/1171661 [Accessed 16/10/2019]

3 By-passing state power and neutralising state bureaucracies in international approaches to statelessness

Introduction

In Chapter 2, I explained how my analysis would focus on both the narratives of Rohingya participants and key human rights texts that outline policy approaches. This dual approach enables me to identify where Rohingya framings of their statelessness as state crime diverged from existing dominant approaches to statelessness. In this chapter, I explore some of those texts, including the mandates and action plans of UN and other international and development agencies working on issues related to the right to nationality, the right to identity, and statelessness.[1] I also supplement the analysis with critiques from within statelessness studies, an emerging critical and interdisciplinary field (Recalde-Vela, Jaghai-Bajulaiye et al. 2019).

The purpose of this chapter is to provide some context on how 'the state' and 'the stateless person' have been constructed within global governance agendas on nationality and statelessness.[2] It considers first how approaches to statelessness evolved in ways that largely by-pass the issues of states' central roles in producing and reproducing statelessness and state crime. It considers how archetypal notions of the 'stateless person' as invisible to states and international bureaucracies have emerged, shaping policies that approach statelessness as a result of state oversight rather than state crime.

In this chapter, I understand statelessness as both a legal/bureaucratic category and an evolving discursive concept within global governance that interacts with policy at the international and national levels. More than a technical legal category, and relating to more than a set of policies, statelessness as a discursive concept relates to a system of knowledge and communication imbued with power which shapes social practices and constructs the way people experience the world. The term 'stateless' also sets the parameters of policy discussions and profoundly influences international policy recommendations and action plans (Fiddian-Qasmiyeh 2016). Discursive concepts such as 'stateless' embody both power relations and subjectivities—as such, they are sites of both domination and resistance (Wetherell 2001; Jørgensen and Phillips 2002). To explain that in more concrete terms, Rohingya narratives throughout this research referred to statelessness not simply as a

DOI: 10.4324/9781003494539-3
This chapter has been made available under a CC-BY 4.0 license.

legal condition but also as a powerful concept that often incorrectly framed their experiences. It often legitimised state narratives that claimed Rohingya had never belonged to Myanmar and approached the lack of recognition of Rohingya citizenship as state oversight rather than a targeted system of persecution (Brinham 2021). Policy approaches framed as addressing their statelessness often promoted the same state registration and documentation processes that Rohingya had experienced as violent and intrinsically linked to genocide (Brinham 2019). Rohingya resistance to state registration and identification, as well as the state discourses that framed and erased their history and identity, was largely ignored by other states and UN agencies as they looked towards solutions at the state and inter-state levels (see Chapter 8). Whilst these issues are explored throughout the thesis, this chapter establishes some key assumptions regarding 'the state' and 'the stateless person' to provide international and historical contexts for state and UN/NGO practices.

Statelessness as a discursive concept that produces archetypal notions of the state and the stateless person is a largely unexplored area within statelessness studies, despite the rich literature within refugee studies. Zetter's work on the formation of 'refugees' and bureaucratic identities (1991:52; Zetter 2007) described how the imposed term of 'refugee' and prescriptive policy-making processes interacted to produce standardised 'refugee' identities. Through these processes, 'needs and aspirations became structured into technocratically manageable programmes with unwanted effects on the lives of the refugees.' Likewise, Malkki (1996), in her seminal essay on the institutionalisation of 'the refugee,' shows how dehistoricised and depoliticised discourses of universal humanitarianism served to silence the voices and sideline the lived experiences of the survivors of Rwanda's 1994 violence and produce an 'archetypal' refugee. A similar, but largely unexplored, process is also true of the 'stateless person.' Sigona (2016:266) argued that, 'the stateless person' is 'an epistemic object and a (global) technology of governance in construction.' Sigona (2016:265) described the discourse relating to statelessness as 'often implicitly assuming homogeneity of experiences,' he noted it 'is more attentive . . . to compliance or not with an ideal-type' than to its dynamic nature. This thesis contributes to addressing this gap in the literature by exploring how statelessness as a discursive category produces certain policy responses based on dehistoricised and depoliticised notions (see also Brinham and Johar 2021). It asserts that notions of the state within statelessness work have been depoliticised and questions of state power, state legitimacy, and state violence have been sidelined (Pillai 2019; Kenny 2020; Van Waas and Brinham 2021).

In this chapter, I first establish how states have become 'the sole legitimate organising unit of global politics' in the international sphere (Siegelberg 2020:6) and why international organisations largely defer to states on matters of citizenship. In considering how state power is by-passed, I also argue that international concerns over statelessness are rooted in human rights on the one hand, and border control on the other. I focus on the convergence of these interests and the implications in terms of promoting oppressive forms of state registration and documentation. Second, I explore the dominant notion of 'invisibility' within campaigns to end statelessness and the way in which these notions shape international action plans to eliminate statelessness. Third, in order to provide context to the Rohingya framings of the production of statelessness as part of a genocidal process that destroys group identity, this chapter also considers how identity has been conceptualised within international approaches to statelessness. I argue that the increasing focus on state recognition of individuals' citizenship status has effectively diverted policy approaches away from experiences of group destruction. The increasing prominence lent to state recognition of individual citizenship status and what constitutes proof or evidence of that recognition has resulted in increasing focus within global governance on the identity document as the purveyor of status, rights, and social goods (Lawrance and Stevens 2017; Bloom and Kingston 2021). The implications of the rise of the ID document in global governance and statelessness work and the impacts on Rohingya are explored further in Chapter 8.

By-passing state power in solutions to statelessness

This section explores how the state has come to be treated as a neutral and depoliticised entity within international approaches to statelessness. This sets the context from which the role of the state in producing statelessness and as a perpetrator of crime is by-passed. The neutralisation of the state and its bureaucracies enables a situation in which state registration and ID systems are construed, not as tools of oppression and persecution but as solutions to the problem of statelessness.

The state as the 'sole legitimate unit of political organisation'[3]

Statelessness, as a discursive concept, is imbued with state power. The meanings related to statelessness have shifted significantly over time with global events and changing configurations of states as a unit of political organisation within the international global order (Sigona 2016; Siegelberg 2020). As Linda Kerber (2007:9) notes:

> Statelessness is a condition that . . . changes over time, dynamically created and re-created by sovereignties in their own interests, defining the vulnerable in ways that affirm the invulnerable, and in the process revealing changing domestic values and changing power relations across international boundaries.

Citizenship and subjecthood during the times of empire, as Chapter 4 explores, were characterised by hierarchies which were differentiated according to race, class, gender, and religion. Different mobilities and rights were assigned to those from the centre of power and those from the peripheries of empire, differentiating between 'white' and 'native (Mamdani 1996; Mamdani 2012; Jayal 2013; Singha 2013; Chhotray and McConnell 2018). Nationality laws were carved out in the interests of states/colonial powers vis-à-vis each other and were not centred on the individual as a rights bearer (Spiro 2011). During the interwar years, where disputes regarding the nationality of individuals or groups arose, nationality was assigned by judges and administrators in the centres of power with little analysis of other states' nationality laws (Siegelberg 2020).

Following the break-up of empires in the interwar years (Romanov, Habsburg, Ottoman) and again during and after WWII, new understandings of citizenship developed and emerged based on the formal equality of states and on notions of individual rights (Kerber 2007; Siegelberg 2020). The formal or 'sovereign equality' of states evolved over centuries but was consolidated as a foundational principle of international organisation after WWII (Kelsen 1944; Ansong 2016). The Charter of the United Nations (Article 2.1) states, 'The Organisation is based on the principle of sovereign equality of all its Members.' Whilst inter-state hierarchies remained, on the formal level, states had equal status in international law, regardless of their political or economic systems, and regardless of their size or level of development (Kelsen 1944; Ansong 2016). This formal equality of states, as Macklin (2015) and Siegelberg (2020) argue, is the foundation on which statist approaches to citizenship were built, whereby states are deferred to in international sphere. Since notions of 'sovereignty' were intrinsically tied to citizenship in the developing international order, states were given broad discretion to determine their own membership. Thus, on an international level, citizenship laws were given a wide berth regardless of a state's political system or human rights record (Spiro 2011; Conklin 2014).

Siegelberg (2020) explored in meticulous detail how statelessness featured in negotiations relating to the Universal Declaration of Human Rights (UDHR) and various human rights treaties during and after WWII. She evidenced how notions of sovereignty dominated discussions relating to citizenship and tempered approaches to statelessness. During the years of the holocaust and WWII, many of Europe's refugees were also stateless (van Waas 2014). It was originally conceived that one international legal framework would cover both refugees and stateless persons. However, it became clear in the negotiations preceding the 1951 Refugee Convention that the issue of limiting state power in the area of citizenship and prevention of statelessness was too contentious and could potentially undermine agreements on refugee protections. As a result, citizenship and statelessness were instead negotiated and covered separately under the two Statelessness Conventions (Siegelberg 2020). Whilst the legal framework relating to the protection of refugees evolved as a relatively robust aspect of international law particularly from the 1960s onwards with the principles of refugee protection incorporated into customary international law, the statelessness framework remained relatively weak (de Chickera 2010; Edwards 2014).

The statelessness framework attempted to place a duty on individual states to both protect those without access to nationality and ensure the right to nationality in cases where the alternative is statelessness. There are two international conventions devoted to addressing statelessness—the 1954 International Convention relating to the Status of Stateless Persons and the 1961 Convention on the Reduction of Statelessness. The 1954 Convention established the definition of a stateless person and set out minimum standards of treatment and protection of stateless persons. The 1961 Convention focused on the reduction of statelessness. It requires states to confer nationality where a person would otherwise be stateless (focused primarily on conferring at birth), and not withdraw nationality where it would otherwise render someone stateless. Statelessness scholarship points to weaknesses relating to the Statelessness Conventions in five key areas: low ratification,[4] the lack of an oversight mechanism,[5] reservations,[6] (excessive) reverence to state concerns over sovereignty and border control,[7] and that the Conventions have developed on a separate trajectory to broader human rights frameworks.[8] State power to deny citizenship to populations with links to the state, then, was left largely unchecked within the foundational framework.

Siegelberg (2020:6) argues that the state as the 'sole legitimate organising unit of global politics' to which the international sphere deferred was also consolidated in the decades that followed WWII as decolonisation occurred. As the European empires dissolved (e.g. British, Dutch, French) and independence movements grew, self-determination as a concept rose in prominence within the international order (Siegelberg 2020). Self-determination is the right of 'all peoples' to 'determine their political status and freely pursue their economic social and cultural development.'[9] The principle is enshrined in the Charter of the United Nations and in customary international law.[10] Self-determination was the subject of intense debate within international law, in particular, its focus on collective rather than individual rights. In matters of sovereignty and citizenship, it had a heightened significance (Siegelberg 2020). A key aspect of self-determination was the right of newly independent states that had seceded from colonial powers to freely choose their own political membership. This consolidated the notion that recognised states should be deferred to in matters of citizenship and that all states should be treated as formal equals within the international state system. The consolidation of state power at the international level meant that in practice international organisations largely deferred to states (Spiro 2011; Conklin 2014).

Within this international context, Burma gained independence from Britain shortly after WWII, after intense conflict in the region between colonial Britain and imperialist Japan. As Chapter 4 explores, independent Burma's citizenship law sought to establish the boundaries of both territory and membership with India and Pakistan. To a large extent, the citizenship law was a product of negotiations with these post-colonial states, as well as Britain, and was also influenced by socialism.[11] It largely balanced notions of indigeneity, with other links to the country, as well as loyalty and elective citizenship. It was after the advent of military rule in 1962, where debates relating to self-determination were playing out internationally, that the military state in Burma began to reorganise inter-ethnic relations and notions of citizenship around more exclusive and exclusionary forms of national identity (Zarni and Brinham 2017; Charney 2018). By the time these exclusions were encoded in the 1982 Citizenship Law, the Burmese state had sweeping powers to establish the rules in ways that breached non-discrimination norms and effectively withdrew nationality from Rohingya and other minorities (de Chickera, Arraiza et al. 2021). The British acting Head of Mission to Myanmar in private correspondence captured the tension between self-determination of colonised peoples and discrimination in the then-newly enacted 1982 Burma Citizenship Law:

> The new law is blatantly discriminatory on racial grounds. If the new procedures that are being prepared turn out to be as rigorous as we suspect they will be, then the Law may in practice be even more discriminatory than its text pretends. On the other hand, it would be possible to argue that the new Law is a generous and far-sighted instrument to resolve over a period of time an awkward legacy of the colonial era.[12]

Despite the fact that the 1982 law, then, was blatantly discriminatory and denied many the right to nationality, no were few avenues through which international pressure could be placed on Burma to comply with international non-discrimination norms in citizenship rules.

The alignment of statist and human rights interests in matters of statelessness

This section considers how reducing statelessness and assigning a nationality to every person relates to both statist and human rights concerns. It highlights the implications of the alignment of these interests in terms of lending state registration and identification projects' legitimacy and resources.

Statelessness as a statist concern

As noted, citizenship is linked to national sovereignty, with states retaining broad discretion to determine their own membership (see also Goldston 2006; Spiro 2011).[13] Nationality law, thus remains within 'the reserved domain' of states (Conklin 2014) and has been described as 'the last bastion in the citadel of sovereignty' (Spiro 2011: 746). However, this discretion is not absolute and is limited, at least in theory, by human rights obligations.

The Convention on Certain Questions Relating to the Conflict of Nationality Laws (The Hague 1930) states:

> It is for each State to determine under its own law who are its nationals. This law shall be recognised by other States in so far as it is consistent with international conventions, international custom, and the principles of law generally recognised with regard to nationality.
>
> (Article 1)[14]

During the interwar years, concern over statelessness and nationality did not start out in international law as a human rights issue but rather an issue of 'order management' between states (Spiro 2011) or a conflict between states as to the nationality of individuals or groups.[15] Stateless people were regarded as those who fell through the gaps between different states' nationality rules to be resolved through arbitration (Siegelberg 2020). This notion persisted until after the 'end' of the Cold War when international technical legal assistance to better coordinate different countries' nationality laws dominated international approaches to preventing statelessness (Foster and Lambert 2016). Statelessness was viewed as an 'anomaly' within this inter-state system (Weis 1979; de Chickera 2010).

The stateless person in the first half of the 20th century was often depicted in popular fiction as a pirate or a cross-border criminal that represented a threat to both the national security and the international state systems (Siegelberg 2020). These ideas of the stateless person being a point of conflict between states and a security threat are also prevalent today.[16] It has become more salient as countries in both the global north and south have attempted to harden the boundaries of both their territory and membership drawing on national security concerns to do so (Kingston 2013; D'Costa 2016). Often notions of race and national security intersect with the growth in surveillance technology to produce hard borders (Jones 2016; UNHRC Nov 2020). These bordering processes function through not only physical/territorial borders but also the rules of membership such as citizenship laws and immigration rules (UNHRC Nov 2020). Recent attention has been drawn to situations in which these bordering processes have involved citizenship stripping, for example, in Assam, India where the National Registration of Citizens (NRC) has disproportionately excluded people with Bengali heritage (Arraiza, Aye et al. 2020), and in the Dominican Republic where people of Haitian descent have increasingly been excluded from Dominican citizenship (Hayes de Kalaf 2020).

From the perspective of border control when a person is stateless, they are 'unremovable' from a country where they are considered to be staying unlawfully.[17] This may result in conflict between the states where that person has lived, or may become an 'inconvenient aberration' for state officials (Macklin 2015:231). Citizenship and associated documentation procedures are sometimes described as operating as a global filing system, which allocates each person to at least one state, thereby providing a return address for other states. This optimises a receiving state's power to deport noncitizens (Macklin 2015:231). The notion of Rohingya as 'unremovable' due to their statelessness drives many of the concerns for states hosting Rohingya refugee and migrant worker populations, and shapes international relations. Following the mass expulsions of Rohingya to Bangladesh in 2017, for example, Bangladesh simultaneously condemned Myanmar's human rights record in relation to Rohingya and attempted to force Myanmar's hand to repatriate them whilst the violence was ongoing (Brinham 2017; Crisp 2018). Likewise, in Malaysia and Thailand, concerns over the refugee flows and 'maritime movements' of Rohingya since 2006 relate to their un-removability which has led to many being trapped in indefinite detention (Equal Rights Trust 2010). Statist concerns about Rohingya's statelessness as un-removability have often overridden concerns about individuals' access to human rights, resulting in a lack of durable solutions for Rohingya refugees and situations of protracted displacement and inter-generational statelessness outside Myanmar (Maung Thein Shwe, Field et al. 2021).

Statelessness as a human rights issue

Statelessness as a human rights concern rose in prominence in the post-war years. As Spiro (2011: 698) explained:

> Only with the dawn of the human rights revolution in the mid-twentieth century did international law come tentatively to pose an alternate conception of nationality, one that took rights into account- but even then, only in ways that minimally affected the identity function of national rules.

Negotiations around the right to nationality in the 1948 Universal Declaration of Human Rights (UDHR) were centred around notions of legal personhood and concerns over the universality of human rights (Siegelberg 2020). Whilst in theory rights should apply to everyone by virtue of being human, in reality the right to nationality provided access to most other rights, hence the inclusion of Article 15 (1) in the UDHR. Human rights literature points out that the human rights framework has developed significantly since the post-war years and that the framework relating to noncitizens and individual human rights has strengthened considerably (Lawrance and Stevens 2017:7). Despite this, there is still an almost universal understanding that a lack of citizenship continues to have a severe impact on the enjoyment of broader human rights (Belton 2015:36). As such, the right to a nationality or citizenship is considered a fundamental human right and provisions relating to nationality and the prevention and reduction of statelessness are contained in a series of other human rights instruments.[18]

Myanmar has acceded to three of the relevant human rights treaties—Convention on the Rights of the Child (CRC), Convention on the Elimination of all forms of Discrimination Against Women (CEDAW), and the Convention on the Rights of Persons with Disabilities (CRPD), although compliance has been weak. There has been a series of submissions, recommendations, and concluding observations relating to nationality and the lack of safeguards against statelessness in Myanmar issued by CRC and CEDAW.[19] Nonetheless, statelessness in Myanmar has spiralled since the 1990s, particularly in North Rakhine State (NRS) where the majority of Rohingya live (European Network on Statelessness and Institute on Statelessness and Inclusion 2019). Despite its inclusion elsewhere in human rights law, the right to nationality has, in Myanmar and throughout the globe remained unenforceable and is described as 'a right without a remedy' since in many cases, it is not clear which states have an actionable duty to grant citizenship (Goldston 2006:58).

There is a growing movement that attempts to clarify, articulate, and strengthen human rights norms relating to the right to nationality (Weissbrodt and Collins 2006; Spiro 2011; Foster and Lambert 2016). Goldston (2006:341) argued in 2006 that the prohibition of racial discrimination could in the future provide important constraints on state practices in relation to citizenship deprivation. The right of every individual not to be arbitrarily deprived of nationality is guaranteed under international law. Of note in the case of Myanmar is that nationality cannot be denied on the basis of race, nationality, ethnicity, or religion (Human Rights Council 14/12/2009: para 80). In practice, however, states continue to arbitrarily deprive people of their nationality with impunity (Kenny 2020). Kenny (2020) considers statelessness as a result of arbitrary deprivation of nationality under international criminal law. He argues that the legal framework of crimes against humanity of apartheid, persecution, 'other inhumane acts,' deportation or forced transfer, as well as the crime of genocide, may provide a means to redress arbitrary deprivation of nationality. Many of these efforts to move citizenship deprivation under the purview of international criminal law draw on the example of Rohingya in Myanmar and underline the international impunity that Myanmar has enjoyed in this regard (Pillai 2019; Kenny 2020).

Despite this growing movement to re-centre statelessness in rights and justice (Spiro 2011; Foster and Lambert 2016), the notion of statelessness as cause of discrimination that can be remedied through the state recognition of each individual's legal status, rather than a consequence of state persecution, remains dominant.

The alignment

In terms of ensuring each human being has a formal citizenship and the ability to prove that citizenship through state documents, both statist and human rights approaches to statelessness have the same objectives. Macklin

(2015:231–232), in considering citizenship as a filing system recording migrants' return addresses, argued:

> If statelessness represents a human rights deficit, one view is that citizenship-any citizenship-fills the void. This view aligns with the statist approach to nationality, which trades on the formal equality of states. This alignment between statist and human rights orientation is compelling to a point, but it only satisfies the goal of perfecting the filing system.

The alignment, then, between human rights and statist interests relating to border control may drive momentum to address the problem of statelessness. However, it can also mean that state interests and objectives that are not centred on human rights can be legitimised through the promotion of registration systems and technologies that are assumed to promote access to rights and services for marginalised populations (Brinham 2019). For example, state registration and ID systems as well as citizenship verification drives can be promoted as ways to reduce statelessness (Brinham, Tiwari et al. 2020; Manby 2020, 2021). Meanwhile, these identification and registration procedures can be used for the purposes of surveillance, oppression, and exclusion (Torpey 2000; Lyon 2001; Bennet and Lyon 2008; Breckenridge 2008). They can be used as bordering technologies to establish and maintain the hard borders of membership, as well as hard territorial boundaries (UNHRC Nov 2020). This tension between state ID systems as effective and efficient methods of governance on the one hand, and oppressive tools of surveillance on the other, is explored in a rich and developing academic literature (Caplan and Torpey 2001; Bennet and Lyon 2008). As I consider in Chapter 8, statist and human rights interests have further aligned with the global drive for universal state registration and identification documents. International development, human rights, and corporate interests have converged in the 'legal identity for all' agenda (Gelb and Manby 2016; Manby 2020). The growth in national and refugee digital ID systems has been driven by the SDGs, the World Bank ID4D projects, and growth of the private digital ID technology sector (ibid).

The stateless person and invisibility

The online marketing material for the UNHCR Campaign to end statelessness 2021 featured the translucent outline of a smiling man through which the reader can see a bustling city full of busy people. The caption reads, 'I BELONG, no longer invisible, no longer stateless. Everyone has the right to a nationality. Act now to end statelessness.' In this section, I consider how notions of the stateless person as invisible both to the state and to international agencies have gradually evolved to dominate mainstream international campaigns to end statelessness. I consider how invisibility constructs the problem of statelessness as being produced by state oversight or state neglect. As such, the role of the state in deliberately producing statelessness is largely by-passed. This can result in inappropriate or harmful policy approaches to tackling statelessness. In particular, notions of the stateless person as invisible or unseen by the state contribute to dominant policy responses that advocate for increased state registration and documentation, which Rohingya narratives challenge as enabling systems of persecution, apartheid, and genocide (see Chapters 7 and 8).

State bureaucracies and visibility

Since the end of WWI, as new and old states attempted to mark out the boundaries or their membership and establish themselves as 'modern' and 'efficient,' states have increasingly governed through bureaucracies and state categorisation, registration, and documentation processes (Scott 1998; Scott, Tehranian et al. 2002; Weber 2006; Thompson 2008). It was during this period, for example, that the passport emerged as a mandatory document for international travel (Torpey 2001). Since WWI, states have increasingly documented individuals within their physical borders as a method of constructing themselves as efficient and modern. Registration and documentation of individuals and related categorisation processes make populations visible or 'legible' (Scott 1998). By making populations visible and legible, states control movement and access to resources and rights. Categorisation of citizens enables states to 'embrace' populations through the provision of rights, welfare, and movement (Scott 1998; Torpey 2000). Efficient governance is often understood as being based on the visibility and legibility of populations. Within this paradigm, the stateless person is understood to exist outside of the state bureaucracy and is therefore administratively and legally 'invisible' to state and according to supra-national organisations who rely on states for national-level data. Hence, stateless people are also conceived of as being 'illegible' for national and international development programming, for human rights advocacy and campaigns, and for the purposes of migration management.[20] Problematically, within international statelessness work, state bureaucracies and processes of counting, identifying, and documenting populations—or lifting people out of a state of invisibility—are most often constructed as neutral or benign (Van Waas and Brinham 2021; Zalc 2021). Rather, as Scott (1998) and Torpey's (2000) work shows, the processes of identification, categorisation, and documentation are key technologies of state power through which states build, consolidate, and legitimise their power (Lyon and Bennett 2008). They enable states to draw the boundaries of their 'imagined communities' through the provision of citizenship to some populations whilst at the same time excluding others. Registration and documentation do not simply record a set of neutral facts about individuals but are also integral to the functions of state surveillance and securitisation. They sort, structure, and order populations in ways that construct the state, as well as frame and shape an individual's lived experiences (Sharma and Gupta 2006). State categories, as Scott (1998:83) explains, do not simply chart the demographic landscape but also shape everyday experience and become 'the authoritative tune to which most of the population must dance.' As I explain in Chapter 8, they are also a state technology through which national identities can be destroyed and reorganised as part of the social practice of genocide. Dominant notions of invisibility, then, and the resultant policy recommendation that calls for more registration, more categorisation, and more citizenship verification in some cases can not only by-pass state power but actually assist in consolidating and legitimising it at the international level. So, the notions of 'invisibility' that dominate international campaigns and approaches to statelessness only factor in some of the functions of state registration and documentation processes—the functions that 'embrace' and not the functions that 'exclude' (Scott 1998; Torpey 2000; Scott 2009).

The developing mandate of UNHCR and the rise of invisibility

In this section, I consider how UN mandates, action plans, and campaigns have evolved over time to focus so predominantly on notions of 'invisibility,' and the need for proof or evidence of state recognition of citizenship status. I argue that just as states have been by-passed as the main producers of statelessness, so too has the violence of their bureaucracies.

Studies of bureaucracies in Nazi Germany and Nazi-occupied Europe reveal how the counting, categorising, and documenting of Jewish and other minority populations were integral to genocide (Caplan 2013; Zalc 2021). These populations became hypervisible to the Nazi regime thus facilitating their ghettoisation, denationalisation, and deportation (ibid.). Although the statelessness framework was developed largely in response to the events of WWII, notions of invisibility rather than hypervisibility have gained increasing prominence in statelessness work (Poladoghly 2021).

UNHCR's mandate on statelessness developed over time with increasing resources and focus placed on the issue since the 1990s. State accession to the 1954 and 1961 UN Statelessness Conventions was initially low in comparison to other conventions with only 35 state parties as signatories up until the 1990s.[21] UNHCR was designated as the body which would examine individual claims and protect stateless individuals,[22] but the organisation did not have a broader mandate relating to statelessness until the early 1990s (de Chickera 2010; Kingston 2013; van Waas 2014; Seet 2016).

State secession at the end of the Cold War

Following the break-up of the soviet bloc and Yugoslavia from 1991 onwards, statelessness as a concept became increasingly prominent again. States seceded from the soviet bloc and socialist forms of national identity were replaced by more ethnically and culturally defined notions, resulting in a potentially precarious legal status for those who fell between the gaps of different nationality laws. In response to the large-scale state secession during this period, UNHCR's mandate on statelessness was reasserted and became a renewed focus within the organisation (Seet 2016). In 1995, the UN General Assembly formally entrusted the UNHCR with a global mandate to 'identify, prevent and reduce statelessness and protect stateless persons.'[23] Specifically, the UN General Assembly (UNGA) requested UNHCR to 'provide relevant technical and advisory services pertaining to the preparation and implementation of nationality legislation.'[24] As such, UNHCR had a mandate to protect stateless persons, but the focus of that mandate was to provide technical legal assistance to states in order to prevent statelessness.

This technical assistance was conceived of as 'non-political' (UNHCR 2013) and hence should not undermine the sovereignty or self-determination of new states. Statelessness approaches accordingly focused on the coordination between nationality laws, attempting a careful balance of advising states how to tweak their nationality laws to reduce statelessness. Stateless people were perceived to fall between the gaps between nationality laws (Kingston 2013; Seet 2016). Meanwhile, the role of states in producing 'bureaucratic ethnic cleansing' through their citizenship frameworks was approached with caution (Hayden 1996). The focus of this technical legal expertise was on state recognition of new citizens and the provision of formal legal status, and thus approaches were predominantly focused on making sure nobody fell outside the international filing system of nationality and ensuring that all populations were visible and legible for effective governance in the new states and internationally. Statelessness scholars have described this period as one in which statelessness was largely approached as a 'technical problem' requiring technical legal solutions, rather than as a fundamental human rights issue (Spiro 2011; Foster and Lambert 2016). This approach also characterised UNHCR's initial approach to Rohingya citizenship in Myanmar in the 1990s which remained reverential to Myanmar's sovereignty (see, e.g., Zaw Min Htut 2003). Rohingya statelessness was approached not as an issue of citizenship stripping but rather as one in which they needed more state registration to lift them out of a state of invisibility to the state in order to be set on a trajectory from statelessness towards citizenship, as explored in Chapter 8 (ibid.). Many Rohingya contrastingly argued that state registration and documentation from the 1990s onwards had set them on a trajectory from citizenship towards statelessness, as explored in detail in Chapter 7.

The rediscovery of statelessness

The 2010s also saw the further revival of statelessness as an issue internationally. In 2011, UNHCR prioritised statelessness as a 'budgetary pillar' (Kingston 2013:74). State commitments to international legal frameworks relating to statelessness increased, marked by a UNHCR Ministerial Meeting on statelessness in 2011 (UNHCR 2014). Statelessness also became an increasing focus for international NGOs, with several organisations established that were dedicated to the issue of statelessness (Kingston 2013). This growth in interest in the topic during this period has been described as the 'rediscovery' of statelessness (Blitz and Lynch 2011; Edwards and Waas 2014). The re-emergence of the issue was generally understood to have been driven by key personalities within UNHCR who advocated for the issue to be prioritised.[25] Between 2011 and 2015, there were 49 accessions to the two Statelessness Conventions (UNHCR). In 2014, UNHCR launched the 'I Belong campaign' which aimed to bring different agencies and civil society organisation together to eradicate statelessness by 2024.[26] The prominence of statelessness as an international issue, then, had increased internationally, driven predominantly by priorities set within UNHCR. The rediscovery of statelessness has led to both increasingly amorphous meanings attributed to statelessness and an increasingly coordinated and formalised global approach to its occurrence.[27] The issue of statelessness was reasserted internationally as a fundamental human rights issue—expanding beyond the 1990s focus on state succession and legal technical solutions addressing gaps between nationality laws (Spiro 2011; Foster and Lambert 2016). This time the scope of the problem was defined more broadly, re-establishing the significance of discrimination in nationality laws and their application (UNHCR 2014:Actions 3&4). The resultant international approach was more comprehensive.

UNHCR's 10-point Global Action Plan (2014–24) that accompanied the I Belong campaign recommended 'one or two' of a large scope of measures, depending on the country context (UNHCR). These measures ranged from directly tackling discrimination in citizenship laws and civil registration procedures (Action 3&4), to a softer focus on the administrative procedures relating to birth registration (Action 7), provision of documents to those entitled to citizenship (Action 8), and expanding access to naturalisation procedures to enable stateless persons to regularise their legal status over time (Action 6) (UNHCR 2014). Meanwhile, the global campaign frequently drew on the language that equated statelessness with invisibility. The public-facing campaigns attempted to address discrimination by making the issue more visible to the general public and thus shifting domestic and international opinions. Whilst the action plan recommended tackling discrimination in registration processes and laws, the problem of statelessness was simultaneously reinforced in public campaigns as a problem of invisibility to state bureaucracies and thus a matter of state oversight. Despite the relatively broad scope of the action plan's approaches, UNHCR's and other UN agencies' pragmatic need to continue to engage with states on statelessness and their broader mandates, and the relative power of states vis-à-vis international organisations, established a tendency to veer towards the softer approaches on which international agencies could engage with states. Other international agencies followed the same trajectory.[28]

Rohingya statelessness was largely approached from within the same paradigms. In selecting the 'one or two' measures under the Global Action Plan, the softer approaches were pragmatically chosen by UN agencies in order to engage with Myanmar. This was broadly in line with other approaches to the Rohingya situation in Myanmar, whereby the UN Resident Coordinators Office in Myanmar and associated UN agencies prioritised engagement with the military and military/civilian government over directly challenging state abuses (Mahony 2018; Rosenthal 2019). International approaches included attempts to identify stateless Rohingya; ensure Rohingya were documented with a view to reducing statelessness over the long-term and inter-generationally; and expand access to the 'naturalisation' provisions in the citizenship law by relaxing administrative barriers (Brinham 2019).[29] Over the years, UNHCR was pragmatically reticent in calling for changes in the 1982 Citizenship Law itself.[30] Furthermore, the issue of Rohingya claims to citizenship through their group identity was consciously sidelined in favour of not disputing the state narrative. Such claims were perceived as 'political' and thus off limits.[31] This is despite the fact that Rohingya were arbitrarily stripped of their citizenship en masse.[32] Likewise, other international agencies such as UNICEF avoided using the term 'Rohingya' and continued to use the term 'communal violence' to refer to the state-led abuses of 2012–3 (UNICEF 2013). It was largely convenient and strategic when engaging with the Myanmar State, to imply that Rohingya statelessness was not a direct result of state persecution but rather a result of state oversight that could be resolved through more efficient and better documentation processes.[33]

The focus on expanding state registration processes and the provision of IDs grew in global contexts, as well as the Rohingya context, after 2015. This was driven by the global international development agenda developed through the Sustainable Development Goals (SDGs), as well as new approaches to 'migration management' through the Global Compacts (de Chickera 2018; Guild and Basaran 2018; United Nations 2018). Consultations on the development of the SDGs of 2015 were viewed within the statelessness field as a significant opportunity to ensure that the issue of statelessness was addressed within the global development agenda (UNHCR 2017; Bloom, Manby et al. 2019). The guiding principle of the SDGs was 'leave no one behind' (United Nations System 2017). Linked to this was the increasing prominence of the notion that stateless people were 'invisible' to states and in the international sphere; that being left out of national data and statistics resulted in being excluded from national development initiatives (UN Sustainable Development Group 2019). Sustainable Development Goal 16 was to 'promote peaceful and inclusive societies for sustainable development, provide access to justice for all and build effective, accountable and inclusive institutions at all levels.' Included within the targets for this goal was SDG 16.9, 'By 2030, to provide legal identity for all, including birth registration.' Legal identities as a form of state recognition have been closely associated with approaches to reducing and preventing statelessness, as explained in this chapter. The addition of this target, then, was significant for those seeking to raise the international profile of the issue. Within the statelessness movement, this SDG was viewed as an opportunity to build more momentum to address the global problem of statelessness and its impacts (UNHCR 2017; Bloom, Manby et al. 2019; UN Sustainable Development Group 2019).

Amongst all the talk of invisibility, Rohingya narratives throughout this research described not their invisibility in Myanmar but their hypervisibility to state surveillance systems (Brinham 2019, 2019). The notions of an archetypal stateless person that is 'invisible' to state and to international agencies have over decades been consolidated leading to policy approaches that engage with rather than challenge the state and accordingly by-pass peoples' experiences of targeted state campaigns of exclusion and persecution. Stateless experiences are thus homogenised as invisibility.[34] 'The stateless person' as an object of national and global governances then produces recommendations of more state registration and more identification documents, with little assessment of the harm this may produce, as I will explore throughout the rest of this thesis (Brinham 2019; Manby 2021).

By-passing crimes against the group

This section provides context to Rohingya framings of the production of statelessness as part of a genocidal process that destroys group identity, as explored in Chapters 7 and 8. In doing so, it considers the links between citizenship and identity in statelessness literature. In Lemkin's original conception of genocide, a term which he coined before its incorporation into international law (Frieze and Lemkin 2013; Siegelberg 2013), he referred to 'the destruction of the national pattern of the oppressed' as a central component of genocide and group destruction' (Lemkin 1944). By this, he meant the systematic erasure of ethnic, religious, or other 'national groups' from the broader citizenship body by dominant groups controlling the state. Lemkin's long struggle to have genocide recognised as an international crime in part resulted from his approach of focusing on crimes perpetrated against the group rather than the individual. The individual within international law had gained prominence over groups in the WWII and post-WWII years (Frieze and Lemkin 2013; Siegelberg 2013; Sands 2016). He argued that a crime against the group is fundamentally different from a crime against the individual (Lemkin 1944). This significance of group destruction over individual victimhood was similarly asserted in Rohingya narratives of genocide and identity destruction as I will explore in Chapter 8. In this section, I argue that the increasing prominence given to individual citizenship status has diverted policy approaches away from experiences of group destruction.

Citizenship: from identity to state identification

In the past notions of group, membership and identity were understood to be integral to citizenship and accordingly approaches to resolving statelessness focused on minority groups. In the post-WWII human rights framework, these gave way to more individualistic notions of citizenship and approaches focused on state recognition of individuals and reducing the number of stateless individuals within national territories rather than group rights (Siegelberg 2020). As imperialist systems crumbled (Czarist Russia, Ottoman, Astro-Hungarian) and new states formed during and after WWI, concerns arose regarding the potential statelessness of minority groups, and the instability that this could cause for the developing state system and international organisations, in particular, for the League of Nations (ibid.). These concerns were largely dealt with under the minority treaties that required majority groups in states to provide protections, rights, and citizenship to minority groups within their territories. Under this system, the group—not just the individual—was an important unit of political organisation and able to make appeals to the League of Nations (ibid.).

The 1930s saw the rejection of the minority treaties in Poland, Germany, and elsewhere in Europe, as well as the rise of fascism which led to mass denaturalisations and denationalisations (Sands 2016; Siegelberg 2020; Zalc 2021). In the majority of cases, denaturalisation was linked either directly or indirectly to membership of a minority group with Jewish people constituting the largest group impacted (Zalc 2021). The human rights framework that emerged in post-WWII, partly in response to the failure of the minority treaties, increasingly focused on the individual as the bearer of rights with groups losing political traction (Siegelberg 2013; Sands 2016; Siegelberg 2020). The Nazi genocide had exposed the dangers of citizenship based solely on racial criteria and international discussions moved on to ensuring balance in the criteria through which individuals acquired citizenship. In the post-WWII years, individual citizenship status was understood to be acquired through one or more of three main avenues: through the citizenship of parents and/or grandparents or *jus sanguinis*; through birth on the territory or *jus soli*; and through naturalisation provisions, for example, through marriage, long-term residence, or other significant links to a state (Weil 2001). As the British and other European empires broke up in the post-WWII years, post-colonial citizenships were often based on notions of indigeneity but balanced with these three ways that individuals acquire nationality (Manby 2016; de Chickera, Arraiza et al. 2021).

Myanmar's citizenship framework after independence, as explored in Chapter 4, largely achieved a balance that enabled both indigenous groups and those that had other significant links with the country to acquire nationality and equal citizenship rights including through residency and birth on the territory (de Chickera, Arraiza et al. 2021). Contrastingly under the 1982 Citizenship law, full citizenship is acquired almost exclusively through membership of a state-ascribed list of 'national ethnic groups,' and there are no provisions that allow for citizenship acquisition through birth on the territory, marriage to a citizen, long-term residence, or other objective criteria.[35] As notions of citizenship and belonging in Myanmar were increasingly consolidated around notions of belonging to an ethnic group, citizenship in the international sphere was increasingly founded on notions that decoupled individual rights from group identities (Howard-Hassmann 2015).

Divorcing citizenship status from group identity

Citizenship since the emergence of the post-WWII human rights framework has often been described as being constituted of three interrelated and overlapping aspects: legal, political, and identity based (Cohen 1999; Joppke 2007; Tonkiss and Bloom 2015).[36] This I refer to in this book as the trinity of citizenship. The legal aspect describes citizenship as status, or as the formal membership of a state and the rules of access associated with it. Citizenship status is understood to provide admittance to a bundle of civil, political, and social rights, which vary from state to state (Marshall 1950). Citizenship status in line with the formal equality of states does not distinguish between different types of political governance—the status is recognised internationally, whether citizenship is granted under a liberal democracy or, for example, a totalitarian state.

The political aspect of citizenship is generally associated with democratic principles and denotes active participation in national affairs or governance of the state. The concept draws on classical Greek definitions of democratic citizenship as opposed to the subjecthoods of monarchies, colonial rule, or authoritarian rule (see Dagger 1997). The legal and political aspects of citizenship are sometimes differentiated from one another by the characteristics of 'thin' and 'thick' citizenship (Tilly 1995:8; Sadiq 2009:21–22)—the first relating to the status plus bundle of rights provided by the state and the second relating to how individuals actively participate in society. Descriptions of 'thick' citizenship have been further qualified by notions such as 'active' and 'activist' citizenship which describe how individuals interact with the state (Isin and Nielson 2008:38; Isin 2009).

The third aspect, citizenship as identity, refers to how individuals conceive of themselves and act in relation to their membership of a group. This aspect has been studied from within sociology and political science and draws on notions such as loyalty and belonging (Yuval-Davis 2006; Isin and Nielson 2008; Anderson, Gibney et al. 2011; Yuval-Davis 2011; Belton 2015). Typically, identity in citizenship studies refers to a person's sense of identity as it relates to the state and national belonging. Joppke (2007:38), for example, describes 'citizenship as identity' as addressing 'the unity and integration of society . . . closely connected with the semantics of nation and nationalism.' Identity in citizenship studies may also relate to membership of groups that are associated with the nation-state, such as indigenous or ethnic groups, and may refer to an individual's interactions with other (non-ethnic) state-ascribed or state-associated categories (Tilly 1995; Isin and Wood 1999). Citizenship studies have sometimes conceptually broadened to delink citizenship from its relationship with the state, incorporating concepts such as sexual, multicultural, or ecological citizenship (Isin and Turner 2002;

Joppke 2007). However, since this study is concerned with *de jure* statelessness, I draw on Joppke's notion of identity as an 'intrinsically state-related concept' (2007:38).

Theorisations of the third aspect of citizenship, identity, have been strongly influenced since the 1990s by the entrenchment of the human rights regime (Spiro 2011). Contemporary theories of citizenship, such as universalist and post-national approaches, have framed citizenship around individual rights rather than collective identities—people are understood to claim and enjoy citizenship in different countries that do not always reflect their ethnic or cultural identity (Benhabib 1999; Sassen 2003; Benhabib 2004; Soysal 2004). These theories have gained increasing prominence, particularly in understanding the dynamic nature of citizenship in the global north. Within these theories, there has been a 'decoupling of rights and identity' (Soysal 2004; Howard-Hassmann 2015). As an issue of justice in an age of mass mobility, claims to citizenship based on long-term residence and the individual human right to citizenship are often viewed as trumping claims based solely on membership of an ethnic, cultural, or 'national' group (Carens 2013). A person may enjoy and enact rights as a citizen of a particular state, and yet that citizenship may only be loosely associated with the multiple and shifting collective identities of that person. Contrastingly, in Myanmar, ethnic identity, which is framed by the ethno-centric citizenship law, has been at the heart of claims to citizenship and cannot be decoupled from rights. Ethnic identity remains salient in the ongoing formation of a post-colonial national identity (Ganesan and Hlaing 2007; South 2008; Zarni and Brinham 2017). Rohingya claims to Myanmar citizenship are often not simply claims to citizenship status and its attached bundle of rights but are also more fundamentally identity-based claims. Through membership of a distinct ethnic community—Rohingya– individuals claim their affiliation and historical belonging to Myanmar (Jilani 1999; Nural Islam 2018). International agencies, in Myanmar as elsewhere, engage in approaches that view citizenship as status but largely circumvent 'citizenship as identity' which is viewed as inherently 'political.'[37] For example, these approaches have included naturalisation and the provision of state-issued documents. Yet, at the heart of the pursuit for justice within Rohingya collectives, as this thesis explores is the pursuit of identity citizenship and associated safety and protections.[38]

Meanwhile, in international approaches to statelessness, whilst the language of belonging has been incorporated into the public face of the UNHCR-led I Belong campaign, the focus of the 10-point action plan remains firmly rooted in securing state recognition of formal citizenship status for more individuals. This emphasis on formal status in statelessness work has been further reflected and consolidated by the clarification of definitions relating to statelessness. A stateless person in international law is anyone 'not considered a national by any state under the operation of its law' (Article 1, 1954 Convention relating to the Status of Stateless Persons). The

1954 Statelessness Convention was negotiated and established in the wake of the holocaust and the Second World War (WWII), when the vast majority of stateless persons were also refugees. As such, the definition contained in the 1954 Stateless Convention was largely conceived of as filling the gaps that were not covered by the 1951 Refugee Convention (van Waas 2014; Siegelberg 2020). At the time it was incorrectly understood that all *de facto* stateless persons would be outside their countries of origin and fall under the protections of the Refugee Convention (Goldston 2006:60; Weissbrodt and Collins 2006:262; Weissbrodt and Divine 2015).

Debate continued within the statelessness field regarding the scope of the term *de facto* statelessness.[39] There was no single definition of *de facto* statelessness and the term was 'mobilised inconsistently' (Lawrance and Stevens 2017:22). It was sometimes used to describe a situation in which people may be entitled to citizenship status but were unable to prove that entitlement. In other situations, it described a situation in which a person had no 'effective nationality,' and so was unable to access rights as a citizen or be protected by their government (Massey 2010; Belton 2015). The boundaries between *de jure* and *de facto* statelessness in the 1954 Convention lacked clarity. For example, it remained unclear whether people who had the right under the law to citizenship status, but were, in fact, denied citizenship documents in administrative processes, should be regarded as *de jure* stateless or not. In 2014, UNHCR published further guidance on the wording 'under the operation of its law.' According to this guidance, whether a person is considered *not* to be a national was described as a 'mixed question of fact and law' (UNHCR 2014:Article 23). So, any person who is 'in fact' not recognised by any state as a national is considered stateless, regardless of whether they may be entitled to citizenship under national laws. This angle on the definition of statelessness has further consolidated the focus on citizenship status as state recognition and the lack of provision of ID cards as a factor in determining statelessness.

Concurrently, many Rohingya participants in this research claimed that they were citizens of Myanmar who had been denied proof of their citizenship by a criminal regime. For example, 'We are not stateless! We are already a state! We have built our nation. We also have all our documents. Why are they calling us stateless?'[40] Rohingya objections to the term stateless were sometimes rendered irrelevant by international policymakers and largely dismissed as Rohingya not understanding their own legal condition.[41] This was because statelessness as an evolving discursive concept had reduced citizenship to state-issued evidence of a formal status—in material terms, citizenship had been reduced to particular documents issued by a state—in this case, a criminal state.[42] Rohingya objections to the term stateless were based on understandings that this discursive concept could undermine belonging and simultaneously have a profoundly negative impact on policy approaches.[43] Even as the genocide unfolded, international bodies promoted more state-issued documents and registration as pathways to a lower tier of citizenship that termed them 'Bengali' and 'made them into foreigners.'[44] These approaches were perceived as part of the genocidal destruction of their identity as a people of Myanmar.

Conclusion

This chapter has explained how homogenised and archetypal notions of 'the stateless person' as a technocratically manageable object of global governance have emerged. Within this paradigm, 'the stateless person' is largely conceived of as 'invisible' to the state and to international development actors, predominantly as a result of state oversight or neglect. Accordingly, international action plans and campaigns to end statelessness have largely prescribed the same remedies for 'the stateless person' regardless of whether they became stateless as result of being overlooked by the state, or as a direct result of state crime. Crucially, action plans and international policies also approach the state through the same framework regardless of organisational behaviours or the abuses they have committed. This is linked to the post-war consolidation of an international legal order based on the 'formal equality of states'(Kerber 2007; Siegelberg 2020).

In showing how international conceptions of citizenship have increasingly moved towards individualism and away from notions of group identity and the group as a unit of political organisation, this chapter has set a context through which to understand the significance of citizenship and citizenship stripping to Rohingya participants of this research. It provides background as to how Myanmar's physical and symbolic destruction of Rohingya group identity has been by-passed and avoided in international approaches to statelessness in favour of 'reducing' the overall number of stateless persons and promoting the expansion 'naturalisation' provisions. Citizenship has largely been reduced in international spheres to the provision of IDs. Additionally, it has explained how the international political order which largely defers to states has meant that the role of the state in bureaucratic violence and citizenship stripping is also frequently ignored. The chapter that follows considers the historical significance of identity documents in Rakhine State.

Notes

1 This includes UNHCR (statelessness mandate as well as identity management for refugees, IDPs and humanitarian assistance), IOM (Global Compact on migration and migration management), UNICEF (child's right to nationality and identity), World Bank Group (ID4D projects), and global tech companies (National level civil registrations and ID infrastructures).

2 Global governance is 'the formal and informal bundle of rules, roles and relationships that define and regulate the social practices of states and non-state actors in international affairs' (Slaughter, Tulumello et al. 1998). The United Nations (UN) is a key institution of global governance as are markets, financial institutions, and NGOs. Barnett and Duvall (2005) identify four forms of power related to global governance: compulsory, institutional, structural, and productive. Productive

power is particularly relevant to the concept of 'statelessness' since it operates through knowledge and discourse that shape social life.

3 This quote is from Siegelberg (2020:6).

4 Ratification was particularly low during the first 50 years of the convention compared to treaties of the same era (Bloom 2013). There were 49 ascensions between 2011 and 1215 following a push by UNHCR. However, as of January 2018, there were still only 89 State Parties to the 1954 Convention and 70 State Parties to the 1961 Convention (see UNHCR, "Statelessness Conventions" www.unhcr.org/uk/un-conventions-on-statelessness.html (accessed 24/01/2018)).

5 UNHCR has had an evolving mandate to oversee the Convention since 1961. However, this is an advisory rather than supervisory role. This has had an impact on implementation. For this reason, the Conventions have been described as 'orphan Conventions' (see van Waas (2014). The UN Statelessness Conventions. Nationality and Statelessness under International Law. A. Edwards and L. van Waas, Cambridge, p.74).

6 See Bloom (2013:14).

7 E.g. 'The text displays the unfortunate hallmarks of an international compromise shaped by. . . tension between states' sovereign interests in the field of nationality and the shared interest of avoiding statelessness—it stops short of prescribing obligations that will decisively eliminate statelessness in all circumstances' van Waas (2014:75).

8 E.g. see de Chickera (2010).

9 International Covenant on Civil and Political Rights (ICCPR) 1966 Article 1 (1).

10 For more information on self-determination, see Minority Rights Group, "Self-Determination" Available at: https://minorityrights.org/law/self-determination/ (accessed 10/11/2021).

11 The negotiations are outlined in correspondence from British archival records collected in Tinker, H., A. Griffin and S. R. Ashton (1984). Constitutional Relations between Britain and Burma: Burma—The Struggle for Independence 1944–48, Her Majesty's Stationary Office. The socialist character of the constitution is evident in the 1947 Constitution of the Union of Burma.

12 Quoted in Tonkin (2018:234).

13 International Covenant on Economic, Social and Cultural Rights, Article 1 states, 'All peoples have the right of self-determination. By virtue of that right they freely determine their political status and freely pursue their economic, social and cultural development.'

14 This is echoed in the 1961 Statelessness Convention.

15 'International law had something to say about nationality, but only as a matter of order management. The early law of nationality was bounded by the interests of states vis-a-vis each other, not the interests of individuals' (Spiro 2011: 698).

16 In certain situation, states deprive individuals of citizenship on the basis of them being a threat to national security, for example, Shamima Begum due to her Islamic State connection. This has caused conflicts between states and arguments that individuals without nationality are a greater threat to national security. See Institute on Statelessness and Inclusion (2019). Principles on the Deprivation of Nationality as a National Security Measure.

17 See, for example, Kett (2017).

18 This includes the International Covenant on Civil and Political Rights 1966 (ICCPR), Article 24 (3) 'every child has the right to acquire a nationality'; UN Convention of the Rights of the Child 1989 (CRC), Article 7 (1) 'The child shall be registered immediately after birth and shall have the right. . . to acquire a nationality'; UN Convention on the Elimination of All Forms of Discrimination against Women 1979 (CEDAW), Article 9 (1) 'States Parties shall grant women equal rights with men to acquire, change or retain their nationality' and (2) 'States

Parties shall grant women equal rights with men with respect to the nationality of their children'; International Convention on the Elimination of All forms of Racial Discrimination, 1965 (ICERD), Article 5 'States Parties undertake to prohibit and to eliminate racial discrimination in all its forms and to guarantee the right of everyone, without distinction as to race, colour, or national or ethnic origin, to equality before the law, notably in the enjoyment of. . . (diii) the right to nationality.' Provisions are also contained within the Convention on the Nationality of Married Women, the Convention on the Rights of Persons with Disabilities (CRPD), and the International Convention on the Protection of the Rights of All Migrant Workers and Members of Their Families. For a further list of extracts from treaty provisions relating to statelessness and nationality, see UNHCR, 2009 Extracts relating to nationality and statelessness from selected universal and regional human rights instruments www.unhcr.org/4517da8e2.html (accessed 20/01/2018).

19 E.g. Committee on the Rights of the Child, 2014, 59th session, Concluding remarks: Myanmar, articles 41–44. CRC/MMR/3–4 Committee on the Right of the Child, 2004, 36th session, Concluding remarks: Myanmar, articles 64&65, CEDAW, 2016, Concluding Observations: Myanmar Articles 32&33 CEDAW/C/MMR/CO/4–5, CEDAW, 2008, Concluding Observations: Myanmar Articles 30–33 CEDAW/C/MMR/CO/3. The term 'stateless' increasingly occurs in these treaty body documents on Myanmar from 2004 onwards. This coincides with UNHCR's increasing focus on their statelessness mandate and engagement with international Civil Society Organisations (CSOs) on statelessness. See also Kingston (2013); Seet (2016).

20 See, for example, UNICEF and UNHCR Being Invisible: Children Living in Statelessness.

21 United Nations Treaty Collection Available at: https://treaties.un.org/pages/ViewDetailsII.aspx?src=TREATY&mtdsg_no=V-3&chapter=5&Temp=mtdsg2&clang=_en (accessed 24/04/2021).

22 General Assembly Resolutions 3274 (XXIX) of 10 Dec 1974 and 31/36 of 30 Nov 1976

23 General Assembly Resolution 50/152 of 21 Dec 1995

24 *Ibid*

25 Discussion during 2017 New York academic meeting on Statelessness, Citizenship & Inclusion, 5–9 Jun 2017, New York University, Open Society Foundation, and the Institute on Statelessness and Inclusion.

26 Further Information on the I Belong Campaign Available at: www.unhcr.org/ibelong/ (accessed 11/11/2021).

27 Manley, M. and S. Persaud (2009) note, 'Behind the Label "Statelessness" We Find a Broad Range of Issues, Many of Them Quite Complex, Including Birth Registration, Nationality Legislation, State Succession, Migration and International Law.' The authors then go on to describe the broad international approach under the headings 'protection' and 'prevention and reduction.'

28 E.g. UNICEF's approaches involve engaging at the national level on the softer issues of birth registration.

29 Similar approaches have been critiqued in the situation of Kurdish citizenship deprivation in Syria. See Bahram (2021).

30 There are few public documents available on UNHCR's approach to Rohingya statelessness or human rights abuses because they strategically approached these issues through closed-door meetings and back-door diplomacy. These findings are based on the conversations and meetings that I had with various international staff working in Myanmar for UN and NGOs as part of my work between 2010 and 2020 (organisations' names kept confidential) as well as interviews for this research with Rohingya who had worked for UNHCR and partner organisations.

31 See UNHCR (Feb 2012). UNHCR Style Companion. P25 'The term Rohingya should be avoided. The term "refugee from northern Rakhine State" could be used in the context of a regional update or in a report on activities in Bangladesh; alternatively the word "Muslim population" or "Muslim residents" could be used for a report on activities in Myanmar.'
32 In Chapter 5, I lay out the evidence that Rohingya were previously understood to be citizens of Myanmar, despite common misconceptions. Notable in UNHCR's Analytical Framework for Prevention, Reduction, and Protection is that although arbitrary deprivation of nationality is mentioned 13 times in the annexed human rights treaties, in the body of the framework the term is not mentioned once. Irwin and Manley (2008).
33 See footnote 30.
34 See also Thomas Reuters Foundation News Stateless: The World's most invisible people, UNHCR What is Statelessness, UNICEF and UNHCR Being Invisible: Children Living in Statelessness.
35 Socialist Republic of the Union of Burma, 1982. Burma Citizenship Law.
36 Joppke, C. (2007) describes these as citizenship as status, citizenship as rights and citizenship as identity.
37 I use Joppke's terms to describe the different aspects of citizenship in this instance—citizenship as status, citizenship as rights, and citizenship as identity.
38 An example of this is the joint statement in Jan 2018 of 21 Rohingya community groups on concerns over the repatriation of refugees from Bangladesh. Conditions 6 and 7 of this statement articulate the necessary pre-conditions for return relating to citizenship. Condition 6 relates to citizenship rights and condition 7 to identity citizenship. '6 The Myanmar government must restore their full Myanmar citizenship ensuring all rights and freedoms—security of life, property, honour, dignity, freedom of religion, movement, education, marriage, employment etc.—without any infringement, restriction, and discrimination in all affairs of their national activities. 7. The Myanmar government shall recognize the "Rohingya ethnicity" allowing them to peacefully co-exist in Arakan/Rakhine State as equals with their "collective rights" on par with other ethnic nationalities of the country.'
39 The final article of the 1954 Statelessness Convention addresses the issue of de facto stateless persons with a non-binding recommendation: 'that each Contracting State, when it recognizes as valid the reasons for which a person has renounced the protection of the State of which he is a national, consider sympathetically the possibility of according to that person the treatment which the Convention accords to stateless persons.'
40 Fg6, 26/07/2018, Kutapalong. This resistance is also explored in Brinham, N. (2021). 'We Are Not Stateless! You Can Call Us What You Like, but We Are Citizens of Myanmar!'Rohingya Resistance and the Stateless Label.
41 Personal correspondence and email exchanges, 20–26/06/2019.
42 Fg6&7, 26/07/2018, Kutapalong.
43 Fg2&3 22–23/04/2018, Kuala Lumpur.
44 Fg6, 26/07/2018, Kutapalong.

Bibliography

Anderson, B., M. J. Gibney and E. Paoletti (2011). Citizenship, Deportation and the Boundaries of Belonging. *Citizenship Studies* 15(5): 547–563.

Ansong, A. (2016). The Concept of Sovereign Equality of States in International Law. *GIMPA Law Review* 2(1): 14–34.

Arraiza, J., Phyu Zin Aye and M. Shakirova (2020). Fighting Imagined Invasions with Administrative Violence: Racism, Xenophobia and Nativism as a Cause of

Statelessness in Myanmar, the Dominican Republic and Assam (India). *Statelessness & Citizenship Review* 2(2): 195–221.

Bahram, H. (2021). Too Little Too Late? Naturalisation of Stateless Kurds and Transitional Justice in Syria, in Bloom, T. and Kingston, L. (eds), *Statelessness, Governance, and the Problem of Citizenship*. Manchester University Press. 264–275.

Barnett, M. and R. Duvall (2005). Power in International Politics. *International Organization* 59(1): 39–75.

Belton, K. (2015a). Rooted Displacement: The Paradox of Belonging among Stateless People. *Citizenship Studies* 19(8): 907–921.

Belton, K. (2015b). Statelessness: A Matter of Human Rights, in Howard-Hassmann, R. E. and Walton-Roberts, M. (eds), *The Human Right to Citizenship: A Slippery Concept*. University of Pennsylvania Press. 31–43.

Benhabib, S. (1999). Citizens, Residents, and Aliens in a Changing World: Political Membership in the Global Era. *Social Research* 66(3): 709.

Benhabib, S. (2004). *The Rights of Others: Aliens, Residents and Citizens*. Cambridge University Press.

Bennet, C. and D. Lyon (2008). *Playing the Identity Card: Surveillance, Security and Identification in Global Perspective*. Routledge.

Bhabha, J. and M. Matache (2015). Are Children's Rights to Citizenship Slippery or Slimy?, in Howard-Hassmann, R. E. and Walton-Roberts, M. (eds), *The Human Right to Citizenship: A Slippery Concept*. University of Pennsylvania Press. 131–144.

Blitz, B. K. and M. Lynch (2011). *Statelessness and Citizenship: A Comparative Study on the Benefits of Nationality*. Edward Elgar.

Bloom, T. (2013). *Problematising the Statelessness Conventions, UNU-GCM Policy Report*. https://i.unu.edu/media/gcm.unu.edu/publication/684/unu-gcm-policy-report-02-01-problematizing-the-conventions-on-statelessness.pdf [Accessed 21/03/2017]

Bloom, T. and L. N. Kingston (2021). Introduction: Opening a Conversation about Statelessness, Governance, and the Problem of Citizenship, in *Statelessness, Governance, and the Problem of Citizenship*. Manchester University Press. 1–16.

Bloom, T., B. Manby and B. Khadija (2019). Why Citizenship is Relevant to Sustainable Development: Considerations for the 2019 High Level Political Forum. *European Network on Statelessness*. www.statelessness.eu/sites/default/files/2020-09/ENS-Citizenship-SDGs-High_Level_Political_Forum_2019-briefing.pdf [Accessed 12/05/2021]

Breckenridge, K. (2008). The Elusive Panopticon: The HANIS Project and the Politics of Standards in South Africa, in Bennett, C. J. and Lyon, D. (eds), *Playing the Identity Card: Surveillance and Identity in Global Perspective*. Routledge. 39–56.

Brinham, N. (2017). Breaking the Cycle of Expulsion, Repatriation and Exploitation for Rohingya. *OpenDemocracy*. www.opendemocracy.net/beyondslavery/natalie-brinham/breaking-cycle-of-expulsion-forced-repatriation-and-exploitation-for-r [Accessed 30/01/2018]

Brinham, N. (2018). 'Genocide Cards': Rohingya Refugees on Why They Risked Their Lives to Refuse ID Cards. *OpenDemocracy*. www.opendemocracy.net/natalie-brinham/genocide-cards-why-rohingya-refugees-are-resisting-id-cards [Accessed 30/01/2019]

Brinham, N. (2019). When Identity Documents Produce Exclusion: Lessons from Rohingya Experiences in Myanmar. *LSE Blogs*. https://blogs.lse.ac.uk/mec/2019/05/10/when-identity-documents-and-registration-produce-exclusion-lessons-from-rohingya-experiences-in-myanmar/ [Accessed 20/02/2020]

Brinham, N. (2021). 'We Are Not Stateless! You Can Call Us What You Like, but We are Citizens of Myanmar!' Rohingya Resistance and the Stateless Label, in Bloom,

T. and Kingston, L. (eds), *Statelessness, Governance, and the Problem of Citizenship*. Manchester University Press. 342–355.

Brinham, N. and A. Johar (2021). *Lending Legitimacy to a Murderous Military: What's in the 'Stateless' Label for Rohingyas?, Critical Statelessness Studies, University of Melbourne.* https://law.unimelb.edu.au/centres/statelessness/resources/critical-statelessness-studies-blog/lending-legitimacy-to-a-murderous-military-what-is-in-the-stateless-label-for-rohingyas [Accessed 08/10/2021]

Brinham, N., A. D. Tiwari, J. Field, J. Ealom, J. M. Arraiza and A. de Chickera (2020). *Locked In and Locked Out: The Impact of Digital Identity Systems on Rohingya Populations, Institute on Statelessness and Inclusion and UN Special Rapporteur on Racism.* https://files.institutesi.org/Locked_In_Locked_Out_The_Rohingya_Briefing_Paper.pdf [Accessed 25/05/2021]

Caplan, J. (2013). 'Ausweis Bitte!' Identity and Identification in Nazi Germany, in About, I., Brown, J. and Lonergan, G. (eds), *Identification and Registration Practices in Transnational Perspective: Papers, People and Practices*. Palgrave. 224–242.

Caplan, J. and J. C. Torpey (2001). *Documenting Individual Identity: The Development of State Practices in the Modern World*. Princeton University Press.

Carens, J. (2013). *The Ethics of Immigration*. OUP USA.

Charney, M. (26 Feb 2018). A State Myth of 'National Race' and the Tatmadaw's War on the Rohingya and other Myanmar Ethnic Groups. Paper presented at Berlin Conference on Genocide.

Cheesman, N. (2017). How in Myanmar 'National Races' Came to Surpass Citizenship and Exclude Rohingya. *Journal of Contemporary Asia* 47(3): 461–483.

Chhotray, V. and F. McConnell (2018). *Certifications of Citizenship: The History, Politics and Materiality of Identity Documents in South Asian States and Diasporas*. Taylor & Francis.

Cohen, J. L. (1999). Changing Paradigms of Citizenship and the Exclusiveness of the Demos. *International Sociology* 14(3): 245–268.

Conklin, W. E. (2014). *Statelessness: The Enigma of the International Community*. Hart Publishing.

Crisp, J. (2018). 'Primitive People': The Untold Story of UNHCR's Historical Engagement with Rohingya Refugees. *Humanitarian Exchange, Humanitarian Practice Network*. 732018. https://odihpn.org/magazine/primitive-people-the-untold-story-of-unhcrs-historical-engagement-with-rohingya-refugees/ [Accessed 17/12/2018]

Dagger, R. (1997). *Civic Virtues: Rights, Citizenship and Republican Liberalism*. Oxford University Press.

D'Costa, B. (2016). *Borders, Boundaries and Statelessness*. Routledge.

de Chickera, A. (2010). *Unravelling Anomaly: Detention, Discrimination and the Protection Needs of Stateless Persons*. Equal Rights Trust.

de Chickera, A. (2018). *GCM Commentary: Objective 4: Ensure That All Migrants Have Proof of Identity and Adequate Documentation*. https://rli.blogs.sas.ac.uk/2018/11/08/gcm-commentary-objective-4/ [Accessed 14/05/2021]

de Chickera, A., J. Arraiza, Z. Albarazi, G. Field and N. Brinham (2021). Navigating with a Faulty Map: Access to Citizenship Documents and Citizenship in Myanmar. *Institute on Statelessness and Inclusion*. https://files.institutesi.org/Access_to_Citizenship_in_Myanmar_Report.pdf [Accessed 28/12/2021]

Edwards, A. (2014). The Meaning of Nationality in International Law in an Era of Human Rights: Procedural and Substantive Aspects, in Edwards, A. and van Waas, L. (eds), *Nationality and Statelessness under International Law*. Cambridge University Press.

Edwards, A. and L. V. Waas (2014). *Nationality and Statelessness under International Law*. Cambridge University Press.

Equal Rights Trust (2010). *Trapped in a Cycle of Flight: Stateless Rohingya in Malaysia*. www.equalrightstrust.org/sites/default/files/Trapped%20in%20a%20cycle%20of%20flight%20Stateless%20Rohingya%20in%20Malaysia.pdf [Accessed 21/10/2017]

European Network on Statelessness and Institute on Statelessness and Inclusion (2019). *Statelessness in Myanmar: Country Position Paper*. https://statelessjourneys.org/wp-content/uploads/StatelessJourneys-Myanmar-final.pdf [Accessed 11/11/2019]

Fiddian-Qasmiyeh, E. (2016). On the Threshold of Statelessness: Palestinian Narratives of Loss and Erasure. *Ethnic and Racial Studies* 39(2): 301–321.

Foster, M. and H. Lambert (2016). Statelessness as a Human Rights Issue: A Concept Whose Time Has Come. *International Journal of Refugee Law* 28(4): 564–584.

Frieze, D. and R. Lemkin (2013). *Totally Unofficial: The Autobiography of Raphael Lemkin*. Yale University Press.

Ganesan, N. and Kyaw Yin Hlaing (2007). *Myanmar: State, Society and Ethnicity*. Institute of Southeast Asian Studies.

Gelb, A. and B. Manby (2016). *Has Development Converged with Human Rights? Implications for the Legal Identity SDG*. www.cgdev.org/blog/has-development-converged-human-rights-implications-legal-identity-sdg [Accessed 17/12/2018]

Goldston, J. A. (2006). Holes in the Rights Framework: Racial Discrimination, Citizenship, and the Rights of Noncitizens. *Ethics and International Affairs* 20(3): 321–347.

Guild, E. and T. Basaran (2018). *The UN's Global Compact for Safe, Orderly and Regular Migration: Analysis of the Final Draft and Monitoring Implementation, Refugee Law Initiative*. https://rli.blogs.sas.ac.uk/themed-content/global-compact-for-migration/ [Accessed 14/05/2021]

Hayden, R. M. (1996). Imagined Communities and Real Victims: Self-Determination and Ethnic Cleansing in Yugoslavia. *American Ethnologist* 23(4): 783–801.

Hayes de Kalaf, E. (2020). Making Foreign: Legal Identity, Social Policy and the Contours of Belonging in the Contemporary Dominican Republic, in Cruz-Martinez, G. (ed), *Welfare and Social Protection in Contemporary Latin America*. Routledge. 101–117.

Howard-Hassmann, R. E. (2015). Introduction: The Human Right to Citizenship, in Howard-Hassman, R. E. and Walton-Roberts, M. (eds), *The Human Right to Citizenship: A Slippery Concept*. University of Pennsylvania Press. 1–18.

Institute on Statelessness and Inclusion (2019). *Principles on the Deprivation of Nationality as a National Security Measure*. www.institutesi.org/year-of-action-resources/principles-on-deprivation-of-nationality [Accessed 02/11/2021]

Irwin, E. and M. Manley (2008). Statelessness: An Analytical Framework for Prevention, Reduction and Protection. *UNHCR*.

Isin, E. (2009). Citizenship in Flux: The Figure of the Activist Citizen. *Subjectivity* 29(1): 367–388.

Isin, E. and G. Nielson (2008). *Acts of Citizenship*. Zed Books.

Isin, E. and B. S. Turner (2002). *Handbook of Citizenship Studies*. Sage.

Isin, E. and P. K. Wood (1999). *Citizenship and Identity*. Sage.

Jayal, N. G. (2013). *Citizenship and Its Discontents: An Indian History*. Harvard University Press.

Jilani, A. (1999). *The Rohingya of Arakan: Their Quest for Justice*. Privately Published.

Jones, R. (2016). *Violent Borders: Refugees and the Right to Move*. Verso Books.

Joppke, C. (2007). Transformation of Citizenship: Status, Rights, Identity. *Citizenship Studies* 11(1): 37–48.

Jørgensen, M. W. and L. J. Phillips (2002). *Discourse Analysis as Theory and Method*. Sage.

Kelsen, H. (1944). The Principle of Sovereign Equality of States as a Basis for International Organization. *The Yale Law Journal* 53(2): 207–220.
Kenny, C. (2020). Legislated Out of Existence: Mass Arbitrary Deprivation of Nationality Resulting in Statelessness as an International Crime. *International Criminal Law Review* 20(6): 1026–1067.
Kerber, L. K. (2007). The Stateless as the Citizen's Other: A View from the United States. *The American Historical Review* 112(1): 1–34.
Kett, L. (2017). Locked in Limbo: The Continued Detention of Stateless Persons in the UK. *European Network on Statelessness.* www.statelessness.eu/blog/lockedinlimbo-continued-detention-stateless-persons-uk [Accessed 30/01/2018]
Kingston, L. N. (2013). A Forgotten Human Rights Crisis: Statelessness and Issue (Non)Emergence. *Human Rights Review* 14: 73–87.
Lawrance, B. N. and J. Stevens (2017). *Citizenship in Question: Evidentiary Birthright and Statelessness.* Duke University Press.
Lemkin, R. (1944). Axis Rule in Occupied Europe: Law of Occupation, Analysis of Government, Proposals for Redress. *Carnegie Endowment for International Peace, Division of International Law.*
Lyon, D. (2001). *Surveillance Society: Monitoring Everyday Life.* McGraw-Hill Education (UK).
Lyon, D. and C. J. Bennett (2008). Playing the Identity Card: Understanding the Significance of Identity Card Systems, in Bennet, C. J. and Lyon, D. (eds), *Playing the Identity Card: Surveillance and Identification in Global Perspective.* Routledge. 3–20.
Macklin, A. (2015). Sticky Citizenship, in Howard-Hassmann, R. E. and Walton-Roberts, M. (eds), *The Human Right to Citizenship: A Slippery Concept.* University of Pennsylvania Press. 223–239.
Mahony, L. (2018). Time to Break Old Habits: Shifting from Complicity to Protection of Rohingya in Myanmar. *Fieldview Solutions.* www.fieldviewsolutions.org/fv-publications/Time_to_break_old_habits.pdf [Accessed 11/11/2019]
Malkki, L. H. (1996). Speechless Emissaries: Refugees, Humanitarianism, and Dehistoricization. *Cultural Anthropology* 11(3): 377–404.
Mamdani, M. (1996). *Citizen and Subject: Contemporary Africa and the Legacy of Late Colonialism.* Princeton.
Mamdani, M. (2012). *Define and Rule: Native as Political Identity.* Harvard University Press.
Manby, B. (2016). *Citizenship in Africa: A Comparative Study.* African Minds.
Manby, B. (2020). Legal Identity for All and Statelessness: Opportunity and Threat at the Junction of Public and Private International Law. *Statelessness and Citizenship Review* 2(2): 248–271.
Manby, B. (2021). The Sustainable Development Goals and 'Legal Identity for All': 'First, Do No Harm'. *World Development* 139: 105343.
Manley, M. and S. Persaud (2009). UNHCR and Responses to Statelessness. *Forced Migration Review* 32.
Marshall, T. H. (1950). *Citizenship, Social Class and Other Essays.* Cambridge University Press.
Massey, H. (2010). Legal and Protection Policy Series, UNHCR and de facto Statelessness, UNHCR. www.unhcr.org/en-us/4bc2ddeb9.pdf [Accessed 11/12/2020]
Maung Thein Shwe, J. Field and N. Brinham (2021). Failure to Protect: The denial of Status, Detention and Refoulement of Rohingya in India. *Institute on Statelessness and Inclusion.* https://files.institutesi.org/Rohingya_Refugees_in_India_Brieifing_Paper.pdf [Accessed 11/12/2021]
Nural Islam (2018). Rohingya and Nationality Status in Myanmar, in South, A. and Lall, M. (eds), *Citizenship in Myanmar: Ways of Being in and from Burma.* ISEAS. 264–278.

Pillai, P. (2019). Taking Statelessness Seriously: Linkages to Mass Atrocities? *Opinio Jurist*. http://opiniojuris.org/2019/01/28/taking-statelessness-seriously-linkages-to-mass-atrocities/ [Accessed 05/10/2021]

Poladoghly, J. (2021). On Statelessness and Hypervisibility. *Critical Statelessness Studies Blog*. University of Melbourne. https://law.unimelb.edu.au/centres/statelessness/resources/critical-statelessness-studies-blog/on-statelessness-and-hypervisibility [Accessed 12/12/2021]

Recalde-Vela, M. J., S. Jaghai-Bajulaiye and C. Vlieks (2019). The State of Statelessness Research: 5 Years Later. *Tilburg Law Review* 24(2): 139–141.

Rosenthal, G. (2019). A Brief and Independent Inquiry into the Involvement of the United Nations in Myanmar from 2010 to 2018. *United Nations*. www.un.org/sg/sites/www.un.org.sg/files/atoms/files/Myanmar%20Report%20-%20May%202019.pdf [Accessed 11/11/2019]

Sadiq, K. (2009). *Paper Citizens: How Illegal Immigrants Acquire Citizenship in Developing Countries*. Oxford University Press.

Sands, P. (2016). *East West Street: On the Origins of Genocide and Crimes Against Humanity*. Weidenfeld and Nicolson.

Sassen, S. (2003). Towards Post-National and Denationalised Citizenship, in Isin, E. F. and Turner, B. S. (eds), *Handbook of Citizenship Studies*. Sage.

Scott, J. C. (1998). *Seeing Like a State: How Certain Schemes to Improve the Human Conditions Have Failed*. Yale University Press.

Scott, J. C. (2009). *The Art of Not being Governed: An Anarchist History of Upland Southeast Asia*. Yale University Press.

Scott, J. C., J. Tehranian and J. Mathias (2002). The Production of Legal Identities Proper to States: The Case of the Permanent Family Surname. *Comparative Studies in Society and History* 44(1): 4–44.

Seet, M. (2016). The Origins of UNHCR's Global Mandate on Statelessness. *International Journal of Refugee Law* 28(1): 7–24.

Sharma, A. and A. Gupta (2006). *The Anthropology of the State: A Reader*. Blackwell.

Siegelberg, M. L. (2013). Unofficial Men, Efficient Civil Servants: Raphael Lemkin in the History of International Law. *Journal of Genocide Research* 15(3): 297–316.

Siegelberg, M. L. (2020). *Statelessness: A Modern History*. Harvard University Press.

Sigona, N. (2016). Everyday Statelessness in Italy: Status, Rights, and Camps. *Ethnic and Racial Studies* 39(2): 262–279.

Singha, R. (2013). The Great War and a 'Proper' Passport for the Colony: Border-Crossing in British India, c.1882–1922. *The Indian Economic and Social History Review* 50(3): 289–315.

Slaughter, A.-M., A. S. Tulumello and S. Wood (1998). International Law and International Relations Theory: A New Generation of Interdisciplinary Scholarship. *American Journal of International Law* 92(3): 367–397.

Socialist Republic of the Union of Burma (1982). Burma Citizenship Law.

South, A. (2008). *Ethnic Politics in Burma: States of Conflict*. Taylor & Francis.

Soysal, Y. N. (2004). Postnational Citizenship: Reconfiguring the Familiar Terrain, in Nash, K. and Scott, A. (eds), *The Blackwell Companion to Political Sociology*. Blackwell. Ch 31, pp. 333–334.

Spiro, P. J. (2011). A New International Law of Citizenship. *American Journal of International Law* 105(4): 694–746.Thomas Reuters Foundation News, Stateless: The World's Most Invisible People. (webpage) https://news.trust.org/packages/stateless-the-worlds-most-invisible-people1/ [Accessed 17/11/2021]

Thompson, S. (2008). Separating the Sheep from the Goats: The United Kingdom's National Registration Programme and Social Sorting in the Pre-Electronic Era, in Bennett, C. J. and Lyon, D. (eds), *Playing the Identity Card: Surveillance, Security and Identification in Global Perspective*. Routledge. 145–162.

Tilly, C. (1995). Citizenship, Identity and Social History. *International Review of Social History* 40(S3): 1–17.
Tinker, H., A. Griffin and S. R. Ashton (1984). Constitutional Relations between Britain and Burma: Burma—The Struggle for Independence 1944–48. *Her Majesty's Stationary Office.*
Tonkin, D. (2018). Exploring the Issue of Citizenship in Rakhine State, in South, A. and Lall, M. (eds), *Citizenship in Myanmar: Ways of Being in and from Burma.* ISEAS. 222–263.
Tonkiss, K. and T. Bloom (2015). Theorising Noncitizenship: Concepts, Debates and Challenges. *Citizenship Studies* 19(8): 837–852.
Torpey, J. (2000). *The Invention of the Passport: Surveillance, Citizenship, and the State.* Cambridge University Press.
Torpey, J. (2001). The Great War and the Birth of the Modern Passport System, in Caplan, J. and Torpey, J. (eds), *Documenting Individual Identity: The Development of State Practices in the Modern World.* Princeton University Press. 269–270.
UN Conventions
Convention on Certain Questions Relating to the Conflict of Nationality Laws (The Hague 1930)
The Charter of the United Nations, 1945
Convention on the Punishment and Prevention of Genocide, 1948.
Convention relating to the Status of Refugees, 1951
Convention relating to the Status of Stateless Persons, 1954
Convention on the Reduction of Statelessness, 1961
International Covenant on Civil and Political Rights, 1966 (ICCPR)
Convention on the Elimination of all forms of Discrimination against Women, 1979 (CEDAW)
Convention on the Rights of the Child, 1989 (CRC)
Convention on the Rights of Persons with Disabilities, 2006 (CRPD)
Global Compact on Refugees, 2018.
Global Compact on Safe, Orderly and Regular Migration, 2018.
UNHCR (Feb 2012). *UNHCR Style Companion.* www.refworld.org/docid/4fe30f9a2.html [Accessed 21/05/2017]
UNHCR (2013). The Mandate of the High Commissioner for Refugees and His Office. Webpage. www.unhcr.org/5a1b53607.pdf [Accessed 15/05/2021]
UNHCR (2014). Handbook on Protection of Stateless Persons under the 1954 Convention Relating to the Status of Stateless Persons. www.unhcr.org/uk/protection/statelessness/53b698ab9/handbook-protection-stateless-persons.html [Accessed 11/11/2019]
UNHCR (2017). The Sustainable Development Goals and Addressing Statelessness. www.refworld.org/pdfid/58b6e3364.pdf [Accessed 12/05/2021]
UNHCR I Belong: Global Action Plan 2014–2024. www.unhcr.org/54621bf49.html [Accessed 17/05/2021]
UNHCR UN Conventions on Statelessness. Webpage. www.unhcr.org/uk/un-conventions-on-statelessness.html [Accessed 01/05/2021]
UNHCR What is Statelessness? Webpage. www.unhcr.org/ibelong/wp-content/uploads/UNHCR-Statelessness-2pager-ENG.pdf [Accessed 17/11/2021]
UNHRC (Dec 14 2009). Human Rights and Arbitrary Deprivation of Nationality, 13th Session, A/HRC/13/34.
UNHRC (Nov 2020). Report of the Special Rapporteur on Contemporary Forms of Racism, Racial Discrimination, Xenophobia and Related Intolerance, A/75/590.
UNICEF (2013). *UNICEF Says Inter-Communal Violence in Rakhine State Must End for the Sake of Myanmar's Children.* https://reliefweb.int/report/myanmar/unicef-says-inter-communal-violence-rakhine-state-must-end-sake-myanmar%E2%80%99s-children [Accessed 02/11/2021]

UNICEF and UNHCR Being Invisible: Children Living in Statelessness. www.unhcr.org/centralasia/wp-content/uploads/sites/75/2019/09/03_BEING-INVISIBLE-CHILDREN-LIVING-IN-STATELESSNESS.pdf [Accessed 17/11/2021]
United Nations (2018). Report of the UNHCR: Part II Global Compacts, A/73/12.
United Nations System (2017). Leaving No One Behind: Equality and Non-Discrimination at the Heart of Sustainable Development. https://unsceb.org/sites/default/files/imported_files/CEB%20equality%20framework-A4-web-rev3.pdf [Accessed 12/05/2021]
UN Sustainable Development Group (2019). Leaving No One behind: An UNSDG Operational Guide for UN Country Teams.
van Waas, L. (2014). The UN Statelessness Conventions, in Edwards, A. and van Waas, L. (eds), *Nationality and Statelessness under International Law*. Cambridge. 64–87.
van Waas, L. and N. Brinham (2021). The Statelessness Pandemic. *Project Syndicate*. www.project-syndicate.org/onpoint/statelessness-denaturalization-past-and-present-by-laura-van-waas-and-natalie-brinham-2021-10 [Accessed 26/10/2021]
van Waas, L. and M. J. R. Vela (2017). *Nationality and Statelessness*. Oxford Bibliographies.
Weber, M. (2006). Bureaucracy, in Sharma, A. and Gupta, A. (eds), *The Anthropology of the State: A Reader*. Blackwell.
Weil, P. (2001). Access to Citizenship: A Comparison of Twenty-Five Nationality Laws. *Citizenship Today: Global Perspectives and Practices* 17: 17–35.
Weis, P. (1979). *Nationality and Statelessness in International Law*. Brill.
Weissbrodt, D. S. and C. Collins (2006). The Human Rights of Stateless Persons. *Human Rights Quarterly* 28(1): 245–276.
Weissbrodt, D. S. and M. Divine (2015). Unequal Access to Human Rights: The Categories of Noncitizenship. *Citizenship Studies* 19(8): 870–891.
Wetherell, M. (2001). *Discourse Theory and Practice: A Reader*. Sage.
Yuval-Davis, N. (2006). Belonging and the Politics of Belonging. *Patterns of Prejudice* 40(3): 197–214.
Yuval-Davis, N. (2011). *The Politics of Belonging: Intersectional Contestations*. Sage.
Zalc, C. (2021). *Denaturalized: How Thousands Lost Their Citizenship and Lives in Vichy France*. Harvard University Press.
Zarni, M. and N. Brinham (2017). Reworking the Colonial Era Indian Peril: Myanmar's State-Directed Persecution of Rohingyas and Other Muslims. *Brown Journal of World Affairs* 24(1): 53–76.
Zaw Min Htut (2003). Human Rights Abuses and Discrimination on Rohingyas. *Burmese Rohingya Association Japan*.
Zetter, R. (1991). Labelling Refugees: Forming and Transforming a Bureaucratic Identity. *Journal of Refugee Studies* 4(1): 39–62.
Zetter, R. (2007). More Labels, Fewer refugees: Remaking the Refugee Label in an Era of Globalization. *Journal of Refugee Studies* 20(2): 172–192.

4 State power and identification schemes in Rakhine

From the British colonial period to Burma's independence

Introduction

In the previous chapter, I explored how international policy frameworks relating to statelessness have largely approached state bureaucracies and ID systems as being inherently neutral or benign. Meanwhile, Rohingya participants for this research overwhelmingly experienced Myanmar's ID schemes as oppressive and violent. This chapter builds on notions from the work of Torpey (2000; Torpey 2001) and Scott (1998) that state categorisation, registration, and IDs are key to consolidating and legitimising the power of states. It considers key developments in the history of registration and IDs in Rakhine from the British colonial period to the early independence period after 1948. Registration and ID systems provide a useful window through which to consider state power, resistance, and the changing social structures of citizenship (Hull 2012; McConnell 2013). The chapter considers the role of IDs during the British colonial period in establishing and reifying race and class hierarchies as well as extracting labour and quelling dissent and the significance of documenting foreigners in Myanmar's struggle for independence. In this chapter, I draw parallels between the tiered ID systems of the British colonial period and associated ethnic and class hierarchies and Myanmar's contemporary ID system. This chapter also establishes how citizenship and national identities were organised in the lead-up to independence and in post-independence Myanmar. This provides context to the ways in which the militarised state was to later reorganise identities and social relations through the citizenship framework. This reorganisation involved the destruction and erasure of the Rohingya as a group belonging to Rakhine, Myanmar (covered in Chapters 7 and 8).

In this chapter, I draw on four main categories of sources. First, I draw on Indian and Burmese scholarship on IDs and citizenship in the region. Second, I draw on official sources such as accounts of British colonial administrators including reports of the Anglo-Burma wars, narratives from census documents, and 'riot inquiries' which reported on pro-independence rebellions; official British correspondence, meeting notes, and other documents relating to constitutional relations between Britain and Burma in the

DOI: 10.4324/9781003494539-4
This chapter has been made available under a CC-BY 4.0 license.

lead-up to independence (1944–8);[1] legal documents relating to independence, citizenship, and immigration including the constitution, treaties/agreements, and laws.[2] Third, I draw on unpublished personal correspondence between Burma's independence leaders M.A. Raschid (hereafter Raschid), Aung San, described as the 'Father of the Nation,'[3] U Nu, first Prime Minister of independent Burma,[4] and other significant figures.[5] Raschid was a close colleague and friend of Aung San. He was Burmese-Indian and served on the constitution drafting committee and in various ministerial positions in independent Burma. He was arrested and imprisoned following Ne Win's military coup of 1962 and latterly fled to Pakistan. The relevance of his correspondence to this research is that he helped negotiate with the independence leaders from Pakistan and India, resolved disputes on the incorporation of Rohingya areas (Maungdaw and Buthidaung) within Myanmar's borders, and was significant in negotiations relating post-colonial citizenship and India/Pakistan/Burma relations. Fourth, I draw on findings from the oral histories collected as part of this research. These include findings from 'walking histories,' in which I travelled with Rohingya in Bangladesh from different generations of displacement to sites on or next to the border, and to areas in Bangladesh with shared Buddhist/Muslim heritage and populations to generate oral histories (see Chapter 2); and interviews and focus groups conducted with Rohingya participants relating to identity documents and independence.[6]

The first section of this chapter focuses on Rohingya as a borderland people with their homelands in today's Myanmar. It considers how Rohingya oral histories described being caught between various clashing colonial and authoritarian regimes as these powers fought over the boundaries around their territory and their membership. The second section considers the colonial legacies of ID systems. The third section focuses on IDs, registration, and the independence struggle.

Clashing imperialisms, forced displacement, and the 'myth of 1824'

> We are five times refugees, so we need international commitment to return – recognition as Rohingya—and citizenship. In the second world war, Japan and Britain told us we were in Myanmar. If we were not told that, we would not need to return. Let them face me now, with the current presidents. Let me meet them and I will tell them how it is (Rohingya refugee in Bangladesh).[7]

In this section, I consider notions of state power from the Rohingya narratives to provide a backdrop to perceptions of today's state-building, bordering, and ID schemes in Myanmar. Within narratives relating to the pre-independence period, Rohingyas' deep and long-standing relationship with the land in Arakan/Rakhine was thrust to the forefront. Descriptions of this relationship often intersected with references to loss and longing. Narratives also focused on the group's powerlessness as their lands and their communities that once straddled today's borders were sliced up by clashing colonial and authoritarian states. The purpose of this section is not to provide a detailed history of the region but to highlight how state power and belonging were perceived in a historical context, based on the understanding that oral histories are fundamentally a meaning-making rather than fact-generating process (Perks and Thomson 2006; Portelli 2006). As noted, in oral histories, today's meanings are often reflected backwards (Popular Memory Group 2006).

Myanmar's 1982 Citizenship Law (Section 3) states:

> Nationals such as the Kachin, Kayah, Karen, Chin, Burman, Mon, Rakhine or Shan and ethnic groups as have settled in any of the territories included within the State as their permanent home from a period anterior to 1185 B.E., 1823 A.D. are Burma Citizens.[8]

1823 was the year before the first Anglo-Burma war (1824–26). Thus, the law attempted to privilege Myanmar's pre-colonial populations in acquisition of citizenship to rectify the demographic shifts that resulted from economic migration during the British colonial period. However, the borders and populations of the region prior to, and during, the British period were not stable or fixed (Amrith 2013; Charney 2016, 2018). The citizenship law and broader historical constructions drawn on by the military state suggested that Arakan/Rakhine region was part of a bounded pre-colonial Burmese state with a largely stable population that was invaded and colonised by the British (Charney 2018). A large body of historical work challenges these notions. Instead, it describes shifting and overlapping centres of power or *mandalas* with waxing and waning control over peripheral areas (Winichakul 1997). The power bases consisted of multi-ethnic courts, dependent for labour on prisoners of war, slave labour, and populations imported from the peripheries (Than Tun 1959; Lieberman 1978; Scott 2009; Charney 2016). Scholarship describes unstable identities and porous boundaries amongst clan-based, linguistic, and territorial identities with ethnic identity drawn on intermittently as strategic interactions with groups in power (Lehman 1967; Leach 1973; Lieberman 1978; Scott 2009).

Rakhine State, naturally separated from the rest of Myanmar by the *Yoma* mountain range but connected to Bengal and beyond by the major trade routes of the river and sea, was far more closely connected culturally, economically. and administratively in the past to the Bengal region than to central Burma. Populations were mobile across what is now the border between Bangladesh and Myanmar and a large proportion of the Rakhine populations identified as Muslim as well as Buddhist and Hindu long before the British period (Charney 2016, 2018). Regional, ethnic, linguistic, and religious identities in this region shifted, developed, or were subsumed over time with the structures of governance, resistance identities, and subjectivities (Lehman

1967; Leach 1973; Lieberman 1978). Amrith (2013:1) described the areas which incorporate Rohingya homelands, as being the centre of trade and communications, later severed in the post-WWII era by physical and conceptual boundaries between Myanmar, Bangladesh, and India, and also between South and Southeast Asia.

> The Bay of Bengal was once a region at the heart of global history. It was forgotten in the second half of the twentieth century, carved up by the boundaries of nation-states, its shared past divided into the separate compartments of national histories. The regions that gave shape to the postwar organization of academic knowledge— the 'areas' of area studies— drew a sharp distinction between 'South Asia,' on one hand, and 'Southeast Asia,' on the other: the line between them ran right through the middle of the Bay.

Section 3 of the 1982 Citizenship Law, then, was part of a broader anti-colonial revisionist history that re-imagined Myanmar as a bounded state with a stable population and fixed ethnic identities that pre-dated the British colonial period. This is what Charney (2016) refers to as 'the myth of 1824.' Participants for this research also challenged this myth, highlighting the interconnected and dynamic nature of this region and impact of expansionist states. For example:

> In the past, Arakan extended beyond the Naf river. Chittagong was a part of Arakan. In fact, today's Rohingya derive from the same populations as the Hindus in Rakhine today. The Burman's came late to the region. Then later they began the Burmanisation of Arakan or Rohang. It's an imperialist project that continues today.[9]

In 2018 fieldwork, I travelled with two Rohingya men to Shahpuri island, now part of Bangladesh, at the mouth of the River Naf where Myanmar and Bangladesh meet.[10] Shahpuri, the two Rohingya men explained, was the place in which the first Anglo-Burma war began in 1824. The East India Company, which dominated Bengal at the time claimed the almost deserted island of Shahpuri in 1823.[11] In an act of aggression aimed at the British with whom there had been many border disputes, the island was then attacked and occupied by troops of the Burmese *Konbaung* dynasty. This led to the British declaration of war in March 1824 (Phayre 1883; Harvey 1925). The two Rohingya men described the nearby Coxes Bazar area as 'a place built by the British' prior to this time, that was 'full of refugees—both Rohingya and Buddhist Rakhine.' They explained that the multi-religious population was pushed out of what is today's Rakhine State by the *Konbaung* kingdom from central Burma that had annexed parts of Arakan and tyrannised the populations there (see also Phayre 1883; Harvey 1925). The British entry into Burma, in these narratives, enabled Arakan's Buddhist, Muslim, and other populations to repatriate to their homes in Arakan/Rakhine (see also Hall 1945).

Oral histories of this period reflected how local populations were caught up in the conflict between the British and Burmese. In explaining the need for solidarity and compassion for today's Rohingya refugees, a Bangladeshi Buddhist Lord Abbott in *Ramu* and a Bangladeshi artist together reflected on local shared histories.[12] They told stories to Rohingya of the Buddhist refugee Arakan King, *Chinbyan,*[13] *who in the early 1800s sheltered in the local caves and raised a multi-religious following that rebelled against the Konbaung* and, at the same time, evaded the British East India Company troops in the area. In his earlier years, the Lord Abbot rediscovered these caves whilst meditating and later introduced the artist to them.[14] The stories of the caves were also a part of their own historically grounded notions of Bangladesh's sovereignty and independence, in which Rohingya and Buddhist Rakhine alike played a part.

Conflicts between warring state powers and resulting forced displacement of this period were themes repeated throughout Rohingya oral histories. The most frequent reference in the narratives relating to the collision of imperialisms across shared lands was the Second World War (WWII). Rakhine State was the site of some of the fiercest fighting of WWII as imperial Britain clashed with imperial Japan resulting in aerial bombings and scorched-earth tactics. Troops allied with the British fought to defend British India against Japanese assaults. British troops were predominantly non-white colonial forces (African and Asian). Meanwhile, the Burma Independence Army was formed with the support of the Japanese. This pitted local populations against one another in Arakan and elsewhere in Myanmar (Irwin 1945). As one research participant explained:

> It was during World War II that the relationship really soured (between local populations in Rakhine)—that was because the British predominantly used the Muslims and the Japanese predominantly used the Buddhists.[15]

During the Japanese occupation, refugees and evacuees fled to British-controlled areas in India in 1942. These populations were Indians and Burmese-Indians from other parts of Burma, as well as the multi-religious and multi-ethnic populations of Arakan. 1942 was a time of communal violence that led to mass and indiscriminate killings of both Muslim and Buddhist populations (Aman Ullah 2024). These populations, including Indians, were granted the right of return between 1945 and 1948 when the British resumed administrative control of Burma after the war (Mohan 1955).

The trip to Shahpuri island, mentioned earlier, took place a few weeks before the first anniversary of the launch of the military campaigns of genocidal violence against Rohingya (25 August 2017).[16] It was an act of remembrance and reflection. We visited the sites from which the well-known media photographs were taken a year earlier during the campaign of terror in Myanmar and the resultant exodus: the narrow path beside the flooded river where a continuous line of refugees trudged towards safety; the sandy beach where the washed-up bodies had been lined up; the border guard post from which the images of burning villages across the water were taken. As we travelled by boat, watching 'Rohingya' cattle from Rakhine State grazing on the flooded island pastures between the two countries, the two men reflected together on the changing nature of the borders and the refugees who had walked the very same route over centuries. One of the men had arrived in Bangladesh as part of the forced migration from General Ne Win's Burma in the 1970s, and the other forced from Aung San Suu Kyi's Myanmar in 2017. One educated in Bengali, the other in Burmese—though they shared friends, leaders, kinships, and histories. As we walked, they made plans to teach one another their languages. A house we visited was run as a halfway house for the Rohingya quietly passing backwards and forwards across the borders until the 1990s. The owner suggested that around 80% of the families that inhabited the island, though now Bangladeshi, had roots on the Myanmar side of today's borders. He explained that his home became subject to raids since the mass expulsions of approximately 200,000 Rohingya from Myanmar in the early 1990s, which gave rise to increased securitisation of the border areas in Bangladesh.

It was not only Rohingya that passed these borderlands but people also fled to Rohingya areas from Bangladesh (then East Pakistan), fleeing persecution by the Pakistani armed forces. Older Rohingya I interviewed recalled sheltering women and children from the Bangladesh side of the border in their homes in Maungdaw, protecting them from the sexual violence that was a feature of the genocide in Bangladesh prior to independence in 1971.[17] A local Bangladeshi man explained that his late father, the first MP for his area in independent Bangladesh, had fled to Maungdaw during this time along with 30,000 others, where he was sheltered in Rohingya homes for three months before returning. Seven years later, he explained, when Rohingya fled across into Bangladesh his father had tried his best to persuade the central government in Dhaka to help the refugees more, but according to his telling of the history, the central government had not understood the strength of the local affiliations and shared histories.[18]

Narratives of the past, then, were related as a core aspect of today's Rohingya identities. They often reflected current-day interpretations of events and Rohingya identities, whereby state-building projects cut through the middle of Rohingyas' geographic and social worlds, overwhelming their communities and resulting in forced migrations. This stands in stark contrast to the Myanmar State narratives of Bengalis migrating to a Buddhist region of Arakan during and after the British colonial period; and to the myth of a pre-existing bounded predominantly Buddhist nation under threat from the Muslim migrant 'other' at its 'western gate' (Zarni and Brinham 2017).

Rohingya participants, then, challenged these revisionist histories and 'the myth of 1824.' They critiqued the notions of Myanmar as a national community separate and distinct from South Asian influences. Their own histories were described as being erased or subsumed within the 'lies' and 'false' histories of Buddhist nationalism.[19]

Colonial categories and their legacies

In this section, I consider how British colonial categorisation and identification schemes differentiated between ethnic, religious, and class groups, establishing hierarchies that enabled the regime to govern, extract labour, and protect their economic and political interests. It draws parallels with today's citizenship hierarchies and authoritarian control in Myanmar. It focuses on how categorisation and identification systems in India and Burma during the British colonial periods were born primarily out economic expedience. As economies became export focused and labour intensive, the colonial regime sought to ensure mobility of the populations of British India as a supply of labour throughout the British Empire. Following the abolition of slavery, both indentured and 'free' labour were supplied through schemes which required a mixture of licensing and open borders (Amrith 2013).[20] ID systems were deeply racialised and hierarchical, seeking to maintain British superiority and privilege (Mongia 1999). Roy (2016) asserts that there was a resultant shift of consciousness from social identities to more individualised legal and bureaucratised identities as colonial categories assumed an economic and social use that could be drawn on or resisted. During and after WWI and as resistance to colonial rule grew, ID systems were implemented as a form of surveillance and control through which to suppress internal opposition and external threats as the British sought to maintain dominance and exclusivity over the economies and territories within the empire (Mongia 1999; Singha 2013; Sriraman 2018).

Prior to WWI in 'the British Raj,' a plethora of documents were issued according to different bureaucratic processes that were regionally and socially stratified. ID schemes were shaped not only by the imperatives of colonial governance but also by the practices of district officials and by resistance, negotiation, and strategic compliance from various Indian interest groups including the educated and elite groups seeking to break the 'colour bar' that differentiated between 'white' and 'native' subjects and prevented them from entering other parts of the empire (Singha 2013). Scholarship shows how bureaucratic identification schemes in British India did not simply reflect but also shape identities (Mongia 1999; Singha 2000; Sadiq 2009; Sriraman 2011; Roy 2016). Bureaucratic processes and categories in post-independence India and Pakistan also built on colonial administrative foundations, framed identities, and forged notions of citizenship (Sadiq 2009; Hull 2012, 2012; Sadiq 2016; Chhotray and McConnell 2018). Similarly, in contemporary Myanmar, the legal framework and the post-1989 colour-coded ID schemes have shaped and reified ethnic identities and aided the establishment of a citizenship hierarchy (Nyi Nyi Kyaw 2015; Cheesman 2017). This perspective provides contrast to the dominant notions within development and human rights discourse described in Chapter 3 that construe legal identities as simply representing pre-existing facts about individuals that will help individuals access their rights (also see Brinham 2019).

Identification, enumeration, and categorisation

A body of literature on British identification systems in India has focused on how both fingerprinting and photography employed *eugenic* scientific approaches in an attempt to correlate racial types with criminal characteristics (Sengoopta 2003; Cole 2009). This scholarship also points to the broader racial stereotypes that framed identification processes in the British Raj. Sections of the Indian population lobbied for the photograph to be used on their documents, since they were used on European passports and IDs. Fingerprinting, on the other hand, was associated with the British identification of 'criminals' and 'criminal tribes' (Singha 2000; Roy 2016). Similar notions of essentialist and fixed-racial and class typography informed the registration and census/enumeration processes in British India including Burma in 1911, 1921, and 1931 (Bennison 1933; Crosthwaite 1912; Smart 1917).

Racial and ethnic classifications and categorisations in the British colonies are often described as forming the foundations for divide-and-rule policies (Mamdani 1996; Singha 2000; Mamdani 2012). Essentialist ethnic and racial stereotypes were also a feature of colonial capitalism and often pitted 'lazy natives' against 'industrious' migrants (Alatas 2013).[21] Racial tropes associated Bamar (the dominant Burmese ethnicity) with criminality and 'dacoity' or banditry (Crosthwaite 1912), the Arakanese Buddhists as 'indolent,' and Chittagonians as 'industrious' (Smart 1917). In fact, ethnic categories in colonial Burma were not always accurate and did not always reflect the realities on the ground but nonetheless became socially significant themselves when deployed as part of a broader project of British economic and political dominance (see also Lehman 1967; Leach 1973; Lieberman 1978; Scott 2009). As Amrith (2013:184) explained in the context of Burma:

> The ethnic division of labor that pitted Indian landlords against Burmese tenants and immigrant plantation workers against local cultivators was partly a matter of design— the classic imperial strategy of 'divide and rule'— and partly unplanned, in the sense that, once established by intent or by accident, these patterns tended to replicate themselves.

These British categories in contemporary Myanmar continue to inform the ethnic classifications on which the 1982 Citizenship Law's *taingyintha* criteria rest and provide the basis on which to deny citizenship to Rohingya, individuals of mixed parentage, and others (Cheesman 2017; Nyi Nyi Kyaw 2017; European

Network on Statelessness and Institute on Statelessness and Inclusion 2019; Kyaw 2019). The colonial categorisation process is assumed in some scholarship and policy analyses relating to the 1982 Citizenship Law to be neutral, objective, and rigorous, rather than part of a flawed economic and governance project (reflected in work such as Leider 2018; Tonkin 2018). Ethnic groups within such accounts are assumed to exist largely unchanged until today. The accuracy and validity of these categories, as well as the essentialist premise on which they have been based, are challenged in Rohingya narratives. For example:

> If it is true that the Rohingya do not exist, then it is also true that the Rakhine do not exist. If we go by the British records as they do, we will see the British referred to Mohammedans, Arakanese and Moghs—a term which is rejected. The Moghs and the Arakanese became Rakhine, and the Mohammedans became Rohingya.[22]

This comment reflects the fact that British categorisation processes, established as part of an approach to make colonised populations in Burma 'legible' and thus 'governable,' were imperfect. Linguistic, ethnic, religious, national, and residence categories were inaccurately and inconsistently recorded over time even by administrators own admissions (Bennison 1933). The conceptual confusion and inaccuracies between categories caused considerable resentment by those who were wrongly recorded. Thus, the 1931 census, towards the end of British rule when the separation of Burma from India was being considered, attempted to enumerate which side of the India/Burma border individuals were domiciled. Collecting census data at different times during the rice season produced different results, which failed to capture the nature of circular and seasonal migration. Earlier censuses categorised people differently from the 1931 census and produced wide margins of error (Bennison 1933). 'Arakan Mohammedans,' the category within which many Rohingya fell was moved from the inaccurate category of 'Indian races' to 'Indo-Burman races' between the 1921 and 1931 censuses in an attempt to rectify past inaccuracies that conflated language and ethnicity with territorial belonging (Bennison 1933). These categories later provided inaccurate proxies for national belonging that failed to capture the long-standing demographic realities of the borderlands. Census data provided shaky ground on which to retrospectively establish one's ethnic existence in modern Myanmar under the 1982 Citizenship Law.

Campaigning on the part of Burmese Muslims more generally to be recategorised occurred particularly in the lead-up to independence. The categories conflated ethnic/linguistic/religious identities with national/residence categories and assumed them to belong to India, Chittagong, or Bengal. As Yegar (1972:63) noted,

> The Burmese Muslims resented the fact that the government (British India) considered them part of the Indian community and lumped them together in one category in census and other statistical reports.

For example, Myanmar and Rakhine Muslims battled long and hard against the terms ascribed to them such as 'Zerbadi,'[23] which referred to people of mixed heritage, 'Mohammedan' and 'Indo-Burman Races,' campaigning particularly in the lead-up to separation from India in 1937 to be known as 'Burmese Muslims' and to be given minority status. It was not until 1941 that the colonial government agreed to remove the term 'Zerbadi.'[24] In the lead-up and years surrounding independence, notions of belonging in Burma cemented around ethnicity, and minority status was not granted on a religious basis to groups such Muslim or Christian (Yegar 1972).

This process of state powers ascribing inaccurate and unwanted categories to Rohingya and conflating the ethnolinguistic terms with citizenship categories remains at the heart of Rohingya grievances. As this book explores, they have consistently resisted being registered under the terms 'Bengali' and 'foreigner' including in the national census (2014) and in Myanmar's ID schemes, particularly since new ID cards were introduced in 2015.

International travel documents

By the mid-19th century, passports and travel documents in India were in widespread use to regulate both international and internal travel. Passports and travel documents—first issued by the East India Company and later by the Crown—were an introduction provided for those considered respectable and loyal. They offered safe passage and consular protection for British subjects travelling to and from India (Singha 2000; Roy 2016). Certificates of identity and other travel documents were also issued at different times in British India to restricted groups of 'natives' such as the elite, scholars, pilgrims, *lascars* (seamen), and military personnel/*sepoys* (un-commissioned military personnel) (Singha 2000, 2013; Roy 2016).

Over time, through ID schemes, the British 'expropriated the legitimate means of movement' (phrase used by Torpey 2000:4) and monopolised the authority to determine who could move within and cross the borders of British India. These documents established a racial hierarchy with different mobilities assigned to different groups based on race and class characteristics. They provided 'white' British people with extensive mobilities to travel into and through the British-controlled territories. Meanwhile, some 'native' people were granted limited rights to travel for specific purposes (Sharma 2020). They were initially largely barred from entering other parts of the empire. By the early 20th century, some groups of Indians trying to reach the wealthier parts of the British Empire such as Canada and Australia lobbied against the 'colour bar' in international migration (Mongia 1999). These groups pushed for passports that enabled them mobilities that were more equal to those issued to 'white' British people. This resulted in the 'Australian passport' and from 1912 the 'British India passport' that was issued only to some Indians of 'certain means and respectability' (Singha 2013:313 see also Mongia 1999; Roy 2016).

By 1917 when attempts were made to standardise the passport, there were eight different kinds of official passport (four red and four black) issued in India in addition to a plethora of other bureaucratic documents in use (Mongia 1999; Singha 2013; Roy 2016). The much-criticised tiered and colour-coded ID system of citizenship ID cards in Myanmar today that was introduced in 1989 has similarities with the ID card schemes in British India and in wartime Britain, where ID cards were also colour-coded according to racial or national origin in order to identify security threats (Agar 2001; Thompson 2008).

The pilgrim passport and later pilgrim pass were issued in 1882 to Muslims for the purpose of *Hajj* (pilgrimage). It offered them a mobility that was not always accorded to other populations. This pass enabled Muslims on pilgrim travel documents to trade and forge international links (Singha 2013). However, the movement of Muslims to the Middle East drew suspicion and concern relating to pan-Islamic, anti-imperialist movements. As Britain entered WWI such mobility placed Muslims travelling to areas under Ottoman influence under greater suspicion and surveillance. Security concerns during and after WWI resulted in the Passport Act of 1920 which made the passports for international travel mandatory.[25] Travel was restricted out of British India by limiting the issuance of passports and visas (Jayal 2013; Singha 2013; Roy 2016; Sriraman 2018). Singha (2013) argues that Muslim pilgrims were exempted from restrictions as their travel documents provided a technology through which the Government of India could put them under surveillance to gather information about enemies. Also, on the basis of the 1920 Passport Act, attempts were made to prevent the re-entry into India of some Indians, including Muslims. This included those believed to be connected with the Irish republican Sinn Fein movement, Bolshevik groups, and certain Islamic groups believed to be involved in anti-imperialism or 'sedition' (Singha 2013).

The transnational mobility of Muslim populations was similarly cast as a threat to the nation of Burma by Ne Win, as he spelled out in his speech prior to the enactment of the 1982 Citizenship Law.[26] Rohingya narratives also underlined the importance after independence of travel documents and passports issued for the purpose of *Hajj*. A treasured Burmese passport dated 1954 was brought out during an interview in India issued to a Rohingya man from Maungdaw for travel to Saudi Arabia.[27] Passports and visas issued for pilgrimages continued to enable international mobility for Burmese Muslims and Rohingya in independent Burma. This provided commercial opportunities and international business connections as well.[28] One high-status interviewee explained how the ID systems for *Hajj* changed over time, as suspicions of Muslim mobilities grew and Rohingya statelessness was slowly produced in Myanmar. He explained that he had been on *Hajj* and travelled throughout the Middle East on multiple occasions in his lifetime. The initial travel documents and visas were issued from Yangon. Towards the end of 1980s, the internal journey between Maungdaw and Yangon became increasingly expensive and difficult, so his travel documents and *Hajj* visa were later obtained from Bangladesh instead.[29] These mobilities and links with Saudi Arabia, Malaysia, and Pakistan were framed as a security threat in contemporary Myanmar, just as they were in 20th-century British India embodying concerns relating to a potential pan-Islamic, anti-nationalist movement. This framing underpinned the everyday experiences for the Rohingya in north Rakhine. Female participants in particular explained how extortion rates, accusations, and harassment during household checks increased if security forces believed there were family members who had travelled to Saudi Arabia.[30]

Controlling internal movement

For travel to the interior of British India, Europeans, and other foreigners required passports during the period of the East India Company. These rules were implemented in order to maintain the Company's monopoly control over trade and access to resources. A variety of internal travel documents were issued by district officers to Indians. These documents functioned to provide safe passage to prominent persons (Singha 2013). By 1864, when the Foreigners Act was introduced, attempts had been made to consolidate the administrative processes under British Crown and thus attempt to monopolise control over movement within British India. In order to do this, a ban was enforced on the issuance of non-standardised internal passports (Singha 2013). The 1864 Foreigners Act was the first law to govern migration into British India including lower Burma. It was meant to prevent unauthorised movement of non-British subjects into, within, and through British India, and was not initially meant to stem the flow of 'native' populations between the regions of the British Empire within the Bay of Bengal (Amrith 2013). Burma was run as a province of India by the British from the time it was annexed (in three stages as a result of three wars from 1824 to 1885) until its separation from India in 1937. During this time, there was a free flow of largely undocumented populations between these areas of the British Empire. At end of the 19th century increased, as agricultural production and industry intensified, these population movements increased (Mohan 1955; The Riot Inquiry Committee 1939). However, Amrith (2013) characterises movements of this period as largely 'circular' in the people tended to move back and forth rather than settle in other parts of the British Empire within the Bay of Bengal.

With the advent and aftermath of WWI, the internal borders between India, the provinces (including Burma) and the 'princely states'[31] became more significant. Rising British concerns relating to the threat of pan-Islamic and anti-imperial movements across the Empire and, later, over the spread of Bolshevism hardened internal borders. Although the 1864 Foreigners Act was introduced to ward against outside economic and security threats, as resistance to colonial rule grew the law was increasingly deployed against Indians/Burmese who were viewed to be 'troublesome.' By 1917, the rules that enforced registration and restricted movement for 'foreigners' were also being applied to those considered to be working against the interests of the crown. Such individuals could be sent back or deported to the region of their origin (Singha 2013). The same 1864 Foreigners Act, amended in 1948, was also used from the 1990s onwards as a basis upon which to deny Rohingya the right to travel internally between districts without a 'license,' even though they were not documented as foreigners (NUI Galway 2010).[32]

Colonial economies and labour extraction

During the British colonial era, there were clear class differentiations relating to the issuance and non-issuance of travel documents. Documents were issued for indentured labourers or 'coolies' to travel to specific areas of the British Empire such as Mauritius, the West Indies, and Fiji to work in labour-intensive agriculture such as sugar production. Indentured labour was organised through the East India Company and latterly the Crown. It was a form of bonded labour which was ostensibly 'voluntary' but, as the literature makes clear, it was instead a new form of slavery following abolition. The certificates for indentured labour were in essence a way in which labour could be identified and maintained as property and tracked should they abscond (Amrith 2013; Jayal 2013; Roy 2016). Meanwhile, labour and economic migration from other areas of British India into Ceylon, Malaya, Burma, and the Straits flowed freely across both land and sea without checks. It was this type of undocumented, largely circular movement of people that formed the largest share by far of labour migration within the British Empire (Amrith 2013; Singha 2013). Labour was organised through debt and brokered by labour gangs. It was, however, described as 'free' labour since it was not officially regulated by the state. With the lack of documentation, it was outside the official purview of the state authorities. Nonetheless, financial incentives and subsidies were offered by the British administration to encourage such migration to Burma due to the particularly rapid intensification of agriculture and industry for export after the opening of the Suez Canal in 1869 (The Riot Inquiry Committee 1939). Singha (2013) argued that the non-issuance of ID documents to 'free' labour was a deliberate strategy, so as to meet the labour supply needs in agriculture, mines, and ports in Ceylon, Malaya, Burma, and the Straits.

It was not only the working classes that were mobile across the India/Burma frontiers but also other classes of Indians. Indians worked in the colonial security services and administration as well as in the commercial sector, and it was their high visibility and dominance in these sectors that was perceived by many Burmese as a source of grievance. The privileging of Indian workers over Burmese by the British was often seen as a deliberate policy of divide and rule by the British (The Riot Inquiry Committee 1939). There was resentment against the Indian commercial and money-lending classes at the time. The money-lending sector was dominated by the *chettias* from Tamil

Nadu. In some rural areas of Burma, the *chettias* had amassed as much as 25% of the land from debt recovery in the 1930s, as Burma struggled with the impact of the 1929 Great Depression and the collapse of global rice prices (The Riot Inquiry Committee 1939). As such Indian economic migration into Burma was often construed as the 'Indian Peril' within the early independence movement (Zarni and Brinham 2017).

After the coup of 1962, as the myths of Burma as a bounded and stable state that pre-existed British colonialism was mobilised, notions of 'the Indian Peril' as a threat to Burma's sovereignty were reworked within state discourses. Rohingya, as a long-standing community in the border areas of Rakhine, were wrongly subsumed with these perceptions of the threat of colonial-era migrations on Burmese sovereignty (ibid.).

This section has considered the identification and categorisation system as Britain attempted to assert authority and administrative and economic control over India and Burma. It has established some of the legacies of the categories and the tiered and hierarchical ID systems implemented in the colonial era. The following section builds on this and explores the significance of registration and IDs in Burma's attempts to forge an independent and sovereign state from the ruins of colonial rule and WWII.

Burma's struggle for independence and the registration of foreigners

In the 1920s and 1930s, an independence movement in Burma emerged out of the Buddhist Sangha and the student movements in Rangoon. This nationalist movement grew in momentum, with increasing rebellions amongst both the urban and rural working classes, such as the Hsaya San rebellion and the port and prison rebellions in Rangoon (Government of Burma 1931; The Riot Inquiry Committee 1939; Than Tun 2012). The rising consciousness around both labour organising and nationalism sometimes pitted migrant Indian and Burmese groups against one another, leading to demands regarding the curbing of migration from elsewhere in British India and the registration of Indian labour (Mohan 1955). For example, the port uprising on 1930 was triggered by Burmese labourers crossing the Indian picket lines (The Riot Inquiry Committee 1939). It was estimated that net Indian immigration to Burma was only approximately 10,000 per year between 1918 and 1938. Despite this decrease in immigration levels to Burma post-WWI, anti-Indian sentiments grew based on increased land ownership by Indians and their dominance of key sectors of the economy, coupled with the economic hardships resulting from the Great Depression (The Riot Inquiry Committee 1939). By the 1930s, the press in Burma and some sections of the *Thakin*[33] independence movement were harnessing popular suspicions of undocumented Indian populations to mobilise the urban and rural working classes towards the purpose of building the independence movement. Along with the call for internal borders came demands to better register and document labourers and other classes of Indians (The Riot Inquiry Committee 1939; Mohan 1955). The independence movement in Burma, then, was intrinsically linked to struggles relating to class, race, and ethnicity vis-à-vis both the white British colonisers and their Indian neighbours. The movement, however, also sometimes transcended notions of race—some of the key student strike organisers included Burmese-Indians and Muslims who worked alongside other independence leaders after independence (Maung Maung 1956).[34] The role of key Muslims in the independence movement and in early nation-building was frequently referred to in Rohingya narratives as one which has been downplayed by today's Burmese nationalists.[35]

Burma's separation from India

In 1937, Burma was separated from the rest of British India and was to be administered separately under the 1935 Government of Burma Act. Quelling rebellions through the containment and surveillance was one of the factors in the British move to separate Burma from the rest of British India. Nonetheless, following separation the Burmese nationalists continued to be dominated by British polices and were still unable to assert control over the borders or limit immigration from India. This resulted in further rebellions in 1938 (The Riot Inquiry Committee 1939).[36] Following Burma's separation from India in 1937, immigration into Burma was planned to be regulated under the 1935 Government of Burma Act (section 138). Under the new arrangements, Burma was not able to restrict the entry for British subjects domiciled in the UK, but it was to be able to govern the migration of British subjects domiciled in India (section 44). In areas other than immigration, the 1935 Burma Act protected all British subjects including those domiciled in India from discrimination. Nonetheless, a British Order that covered the first years after separation, ensured that immigration from India was subject to the same arrangements that were in place prior to separation—in other words, no restriction of movement.[37] This was put in place due to commercial concerns that immigration controls would impact trade and tariff arrangements between Burma and India. The Order was not to be terminated until April 1942 (Mohan 1955).

The Commission of Inquiry on Indian Immigration in 1939 outlined immigration measures to be taken to quell the rising anti-Indian violence. It recommended passports and visas be made mandatory for entry of all Indians into Burma, that Indians already in Burma should be registered, and that all unskilled labour in the ports should be registered (Baxter, Tut et al. 1941). As such, in 1941, an immigration agreement was negotiated between Burma and India that would have seen significant restrictions on entry into Burma of British subjects domiciled in India, dividing them into different visa categories depending on their existing links to Burma. Indians already in Burma were to be documented into three categories: Indians who were born in Burma and chose to make it their permanent home were entitled to remain domiciled in Burma and retain their rights; those who had been in Burma for more than seven out of the last nine years were considered 'privileged immigrants' and allowed to continue living in Burma with limits; those who did not meet either of the criteria would be subject to the same immigration controls as new immigrants (Mohan 1955). The 1941 immigration agreement between Burma and India, however, was neither signed off by the King nor implemented. War broke out between Britain and Japan and the agreement was interrupted (ibid.).

There was organised resistance in India to the migration arrangements with Burma, in particular, against two clauses—one which required literacy in order to enter Burma and a second that attempted to prevent unions/marriages between Burmese and Indians, legislating for deportation in such cases (Mohan 1955). The riot inquiry report described how Burmese nationalism at the time highlighted Indian-Burmese marriages as a perceived threat to the nation and to Buddhism (The Riot Inquiry Committee 1939). The different categories of Indians within the Burma/India immigration agreement according to place of birth, length of residence, and loyalty, were to remain significant as the citizenship criteria was negotiated in the lead-up to independence in the 1948.[38] At this time, there was considerable unease amongst those who considered themselves Burmese and were Muslim or had cultural and social links in India. A flurry of negotiations and resistance ensued in an attempt to shape these bureaucratic categories (Yegar 1972).

Issues relating to the categorisation and documentation of people with mixed Buddhist-Muslim or mixed-ethnic parentage under the 1982 Citizenship rules persist today (Kyaw 2019). For example, one interviewee described how, since his parentage was mixed Rakhine Buddhist and Kaman (one of the Muslim categories of *taiyintha*), he was recategorised by the state authorities in 2011 as 'Bengali,' refused citizenship documentation, and made subject to internal movement controls.[39] The issue of inter-marriage and the status of the children of such unions has continued to be an issue of deep contestation relating to citizenship and belonging. Such concerns were also echoed in the nationalist discourses relating to the 'protection of race and religion' bills that were adopted in 2015, which, inter alia, effectively prevented Buddhist women from marrying non-Buddhist men.[40]

This section has considered how the demands for borders and documentation of foreigners in the independence movement were largely thwarted following Burma's administrative separation from India. War in Burma ushered in new conflicts as well as new physical and conceptual boundaries between Burma and India. It caused large-scale forced migrations and new negotiations over who to document as evacuees and returnees. Meanwhile, globally WWII brought the disintegration of the British Empire, and the birth of new independent nations that were to be constructed from negotiated borders and ID schemes. The following section focuses specifically on registration, documentation, and the relevance of border demarcation in Rakhine to citizenship and its 'others' in Burma.

WWII and its aftermath: interruption of the registration of foreigners

In 1942, Japan, having assisted the *Thakins* in the formation of the Burma Independence Army (BIA), occupied large parts of Burma. The British retreated to defend India. There was fierce fighting in the Rohingya areas of Rakhine as Britain defended against Japanese entry into India. This predominantly Rohingya region was to pass backwards and forwards between the warring empires more than any other area in Burma. Britain re-captured Maungdaw and Buthidaung three times between 1942 and 1945 (Tinker, Griffin et al. 1984). In 1942, as a result of the occupation of Burma, there was an exodus/evacuation of approximately 500,000 Indians and Burmese-Indians out of Burma. This was almost half the total population. Many died on route (Tinker 1959; Naorem 2020). Other Burmese also fled including many of the populations of Rakhine—both Rohingya and Buddhist Rakhine. In 1943, with the support of the Japanese, Burma declared independence from Britain, but it was to be short-lived (Tinker, Griffin et al. 1984). In 1945, the British re-entered and reclaimed Burma. Following the surrender of Japan, the region was placed under temporary direct rule with a view to full independence. In the three years before Burma gained independence from Britain, the Burma/India immigration agreement negotiated in 1941 was not in force. Instead, the British focus was on ensuring a labour and skills supply for post-war reconstruction. In June 1945, it was agreed between Burma and India that evacuees in India from the period of Japanese occupation would be issued with evacuee documents to facilitate their return to Burma. Even those unskilled labourers who would have been treated as new immigrants under the 1941 immigration arrangements were issued with evacuee documents and able to return. This was resented by some Burmese (Mohan 1955) and was to be the first of many international disagreements and negotiations over repatriation documents for Myanmar's displaced populations, which still continue today.[41]

Burmese-Indians in Burma continued to fear for their safety after the war. On 27 December 1945, Nehru, who was to be the first Prime Minister of India, wrote a letter to prominent Burmese-Indian, Raschid, urging him to return to Burma and tell Burmese-Indians in the country that, for their 'personal safety,' they should 'throw their lot in with the Burmese' and not expect any 'special treatment' from India.[42] In the lead-up to independence, many assurances were to be made by the Burmese leadership to those Burmese-Indians whose loyalties lay with Burma. In a radio address, two weeks before independence Tin Tut, key negotiator of the Nu-Atlee or the independence agreement and first Minister of Foreign Affairs,[43] said:

> Discount the evil rumours of impending catastrophe for Burma in general and for Burma Indians in particular and believe that the great body of the Burmese people are not thinking of ill-treatment or expulsion.[44]

Migrant labour into Burma was encouraged between 1945 and 1948 due to the imperative to rebuild the economy in Burma—particularly in rice-growing Rakhine. Between 1943 and 1944, famine had killed 2–3 million people in the Bengal province of India. It also impacted local populations of Assam and other regions as well as the refugees and evacuees who had fled Burma since 1942 (Naorem 2020). One of the trigger factors of the Bengal famine was the interruption of harvests and the subsequent distribution of rice produced in Rakhine as a result of Japanese offensives.[45] Thus, there was a sense of urgency in bringing a migrant labour force into Rakhine and Burma to rebuild agriculture and other parts of the Burmese economy. Despite the pragmatism, the situation did not go unchallenged. By 1947, when Raschid departed for talks regarding the border demarcation between Maungdaw and Bengal with the Chief Minister of Bengal, the press in Burma misreported his visit as relating to immigration concerns in Maungdaw and Buthidaung.[46] Nonetheless, the Burmese leadership also understood the need for migrant labour from India/Bangladesh. Their nationalist logic was not to stop migration but to manage and regulate it through ID schemes in ways that had not been permitted under the British. On the eve of independence, the Council of Ministers agreed that the movement of 8,000 labourers and 2,000 mill labourers across the Arakan-Chittagong border should be permitted, but that 'some form of permit or identity-card be devised for checking whether seasonal labourers go back before the year.'[47]

In the lead-up to independence, there was much discussion between Burmese, British, Indian, and Pakistani representatives on borders, immigration, and who should be documented as a 'Burmese national.' In January 1947, Aung San by then leader of the pre-independence government, set off for talks with Nehru in Delhi, Jinnah in Karachi,[48] and Atlee in London[49] to negotiate independence arrangements. Prior to his departure, rumours began circulating that the Muslim League, founders of Pakistan, wanted Maungdaw and Buthidaung to be included within Pakistan after partition, on the basis that the districts were predominantly Muslim. The rumour began from statements exchanged between Suhrawardy, Chief Minister of Bengal, and U Saw, former Prime Minister of British Burma, who was to join the London talks with Aung San and who was later to assassinate him and his cabinet.[50] The border issue was discussed between Aung San and Jinnah, President of the Muslim League. Jinnah reassured Aung San—and the Burmese people in a press statement—that the Muslim League had no intention of annexing Maungdaw/Buthidaung, nor ever had, suggesting the press had circulated unsubstantiated rumours.[51] Meanwhile, Aung San's close Burmese-Indian colleague, Raschid, was tasked by U Nu—the future prime minister of independent Burma, with meeting and discussing the matter with Suhrawardy in north Bengal. Original correspondence between Raschid and U Nu also shows that the suggestion of Maungdaw/Buthidaung becoming part of

Pakistan had been put to rest by Suhrawardy and the Muslim League. Raschid also wrote to U Nu that whilst some British military officers may have made promises to Muslims in Maungdaw/Buthidaung, the suggestion was not initiated or sanctioned by the British government.

Raschid also noted that Suhrawardy's comments had arisen from his assumption that the vast majority of people living in northern Rakhine 'retained cultural contacts with Chittagong.' Raschid responded that 'while this may be correct, the bulk of people were domiciled in that part of the country.'[52] This statement clarifies that Rohingya were not migrants to the areas but were rather caught up in the religious, cultural, and linguistic notions of nationality that framed independence negotiations relating to citizenship in Pakistan, India, and Burma. A draft of the public statement to be made following these meetings read, 'The AFPFL's[53] attitude towards minorities in the country are well-known. The AFPFL will do all it can to redress the genuine difficulties that people of the Maungdaw and Buthidaung area may have.'[54] According to Rohingya narratives and articles, this redress included citizenship. Aung San and the AFPFL's approach to citizenship on the eve of independence was to try to pragmatically and strategically embrace minorities under 'one citizenship' based on the principles of equality and non-discrimination (The Union Citizenship Act 1948:Articles 10–15). In 1946, Aung San had visited Maungdaw.[55] This visit featured in several of the fieldwork narratives relating to citizenship. During this visit, he spoke to Muslim populations in a strategic effort to assure them of their belonging and secure their loyalty towards building a united independent Burma.[56]

Amongst other issues discussed between the Burmese delegation and the British Government in January 1947 in London was the question of the term 'Burmese national.' It was defined for the purposes of the elections regarding who could stand for office and who should be registered to vote.[57] During these talks, it was noted that there was difficulty differentiating between those Indians who were migrant and those who were permanently settled—particularly since much of the population tended to move backwards and forwards between India and Burma on a regular basis.[58] The term Indian used during these discussions was predominantly used as a racial term rather than one referring to a place of origin. These discussions were relevant to Rohingya since by this time they were recorded as an 'Indo-Burman race.' It was agreed in London that 'Burmese national' would mean any person born in Burma *and* living in Burma for at least eight out of ten years.[59] Two letters from Raschid to Aung San immediately after his return from London urged him to reconsider this definition, noting that under this definition he and two other close colleagues of Aung San's in the Burma independence movement would not pass as nationals. He himself was born in India during his mother's temporary visit to the country, despite Burma being his home since birth. He suggested using born *or* domiciled instead of born *and* domiciled.[60] In a press statement on return, Aung San noted that the definition of 'Burmese National' vis-à-vis Burmese-Indians needed to be considered more fully.[61]

The way forward was found whereby elective citizenship based on a mixture of settled status and loyalty was introduced into definitions. Thus, by the time the constitution was drafted in July 1947, the definition of citizen included those who were born in any part of the British 'dominions', had lived in eight out of ten years in Burma (either from the date of independence or from 1942 to allow for wartime evacuation), and who intended to make Burma their permanent home (Union Citizenship Act 1948, Article 11). The significance of the elective nature of citizenship can be underlined by the different choices made by Raschid and his brother Raul. The first, born in India and raised in Burma, elected for Burmese citizenship and was a cabinet minister for 15 years until he was imprisoned following Ne Win's military coup in 1962. The second was born and raised in Rangoon, Burma but elected Indian citizenship. He was a close colleague of Nehru and, serving under his government in India, became Indian ambassador to Burma.[62]

Further concerns were raised regarding Burmese nationality by British administrators with regard to the treaty to be signed for the purpose of independence. After the assassinations of Aung San and his cabinet, there was a rise in anti-British sentiment as popular opinion viewed the British as implicated in the assassinations. It soon became clear that Burma would not join the Commonwealth.[63] Without a commonwealth citizenship as a backup, concerns were raised regarding potential statelessness and the protection of those who may be dual nationals. The populations of concern were primarily Anglo-Burmese who could be eligible for either Burmese or British citizenship, but as dual nationals may not be protected by British consular services. Also of concern were the Burmese-Indians who could be entitled to either citizenship or none depending on gaps between future citizenship laws.[64] In the end, Burma was to bar dual nationality for Burmese citizens (The Union Citizenship (election) Rules 1948) and the treaty between UK and Burma was, after much discussion, only to contain provision for a declaration of alienage from Burma for those individuals who elect for British citizenship but did not address the possibility of statelessness.[65] Such rules against dual nationality can contribute over time to statelessness since those who lose rights to one nationality may also not be able to establish links to another (European Network on Statelessness and Institute on Statelessness and Inclusion 2019).

This section has considered how discussions and negotiations relating to borders and definitions of 'Burmese nationals' were to impact documentation processes in the lead-up to independence. The next section turns to the ID schemes after independence in Burma.

Early independence ID schemes: the construction of foreignness and the multi-ethnic embrace

On 4 January 1948, Burma became independent from the UK. The updated 1864 Foreigners Act, the 1947 Emergency Immigration Act, and the 1940

Registration of Foreigners Act came into force (Mohan 1955). After two decades, the demands of Burma's nationalist movement to register and document Indians, Pakistanis, and Chinese were finally realised. The business of reconstructing a multi-ethnic nation from a social landscape devastated by the impact of divide-and-rule policies and war began. ID schemes were a key technology through which Burma could materialise its new sovereign borders and embrace populations through the provision of rights and welfare. The first priority, then, was not documenting Burma's populations as citizens, but the registration and regulation of its 'foreign' populations.

The Registration of Foreigners Act required foreigners to register with government authorities on arrival, when travelling to different areas of the country, and prior to exit (to obtain an exit permit). It also required the managers/owners of houses with foreign guests staying to report to the local authorities. Under this act, all foreigners were provided with Foreigner Registration Cards (FRCs). From 1950, passports and visas were required for Indians/Pakistanis wishing to enter Burma (Mohan 1955). In a departure from the 1935 Government of Burma Act, the 1947 Constitution made clear differentiations between the rights of citizens and of foreigners. Significantly it prevented foreigners from owning and utilising agricultural land, addressing the grievances of the past (Article 220).

Citizens, on the other hand, did not need to register or obtain IDs in the early years of independence. The vast majority of people throughout the country operated under the assumption that they were automatic citizens and thus did not need to be documented. There were frequent references in Rohingya narratives to the absence of FRCs in their community, whereby the absence of these documents was the proof of belonging. For example, 'We are not FRC people. Not foreigners.'[66] Only those who needed to travel for work, pilgrimage, or other reasons needed to obtain documents. The constitution of 1947, and in particular definitions of citizenship contained within it, in the early years of independence was deeply influenced by international socialism. The constitution stipulated the relationship of the state to peasants and workers (Chapter 3); limited the private ownership of land (section 30), provided protection for workers (section 31); and put in place the foundations for nationalisation of industry and business (section 23, 2018–9). It also underlined that 'there is one citizenship throughout the union; that is to say there shall be no citizenship of the unit as distinct from the citizenship of the Union [sic]' (section 10). In other words, it did not differentiate between those who were citizens on the basis of the ethnic indigeneity and those who naturalised or elected for citizenship. This citizenship thus formed the basis for equal rights for all citizens (Chapter II).

Rohingya narratives relating to independence were very clear that they felt a part of the new the multi-ethnic nation and were on an equal footing with all other citizens of Burma. One elderly gentleman, for example, reminisced about independence day as follows:

> I studied at the Deoband University in India. When I heard that independence was coming, I hurried back to Maungdaw from university. I remember that day very clearly—I felt so happy and overjoyed when I attended the independence celebrations. So happy. I remember very clearly that the Rohingya became citizens of Burma at that time.[67]

Muslim independence leaders were frequently referred to as providing further evidence of equal citizenship. Abdul Razak[68] and Raschid[69] were most frequently mentioned. In such narratives, participants positioned themselves in relation to their broader religious rather than ethnic affiliations, within which Rohingya were part of a broader marginalised group. For example, 'So, Abdul Razak asked Aung San, "where is our (Muslim) state?" Aung San replied, "Burma and Muslim are the same. We are one. There is no need to separate it."'[70]

Participants often noted that Aung San and Abdul Razak, a Muslim member of his pre-independence cabinet, were killed in the same incident along with other members of the cabinet almost six months before independence. As such, inferences were often drawn between the joint fate of Aung San and Abdul Razak, and the later fate of Rohingya citizenship and ethnic recognition under Ne Win's military rule. Narratives on Aung San/U Razak's assassinations sometimes turned abruptly towards the later cleansing of Muslims and non-Buddhists from the armed forces and the country's leadership.[71]

It was not until 1955 that ID documents were made mandatory and rolled out across the country, although the penetration of this scheme remained incomplete. These ID cards were called 'National Registration Certificates' (NRCs). They provided everyone with the same access to rights and in that respect gave a material form to the equalising aspects of citizenship that were described as a feature of post-WWII citizenships (see Marshall 1950). Issuing the same card to all was a calculated departure from the British system of classed and raced categorisation schemes. Many Rohingya were issued these NRCs from the 1950s onwards. It was the most frequently referred to proof of state recognition of their citizenship in fieldwork narratives. Although the cards were not officially proof of citizenship, they were *de facto* citizenship cards since anyone who was not a citizen was not entitled to it—instead noncitizens had to register and were issued FRCs. They were the only individual identity documents used within the country to access citizenship rights (European Network on Statelessness and Institute on Statelessness and Inclusion 2019). As I will examine in the following chapter, it was this non-differentiated ID scheme that Rohingya research participants spoke about with nostalgia, loss, and longing—as a promise of peace that was broken, and as evidence of how a citizenship they once possessed was stolen from them by the post-1962 military regime.

Conclusion

In this chapter, I have explored some of the parallels between colonial identification schemes prior to Burma's independence and today's ID schemes in Myanmar. I have also shown how in the lead-up to, and in the early years of independence, north Rakhine State was incorporated within Myanmar and citizenship and equal rights were provided to Rohingya. The ID schemes of newly independent Burma were a marked and intentional departure from the hierarchical identification schemes developed by the British. They were intended as an equalising technology and a strategic embrace of minorities in a multi-ethnic post-conflict situation. The following chapter considers how Rohingya oral histories describe the periods prior to military rule in Myanmar through ID card narratives.

Notes

1 These are compiled in two large volumes by Tinker, Griffin et al. (1984).
2 For the purpose of this study, these documents were approached as historic artefacts rather than legal documents per se. For historical approaches to constitutions, etc., in citizenship studies, see Hayden (1996).
3 Aung San was the founder of the Burma armed forces and was instrumental in the fight for independence. He was assassinated six months before Burma gained independence. He is also father of Aung San Suu Kyi, Myanmar's *de facto* leader prior to the military coup of 1 Feb 2021.
4 Nu was also a close comrade of Raschid in the pro-independence student movement. He was Prime Minister for three parliamentary periods between 1948 and 1962, before Ne Win took over in a military coup. His government included Rohingya, Muslims, and Burmese-Indians.
5 Permission was obtained from the son of the late Raschid to draw on the personal correspondence for research purposes. There are 37 documents in all—12 letters, 13 original newspaper cuttings, and 2 photos.
6 I identified significant historic moments from the oral histories and narratives. These included the British entry into Rakhine; war and exodus in Japanese-occupied Rakhine from 1942; Aung San's visit to Maungdaw in 1946; the demarcation of borders between Burma and East Pakistan (now Bangladesh) in 1947; the assassination of Aung San in 1947; the advent of independence in 1948; the establishment of the Mayyu district in 1961.
7 Rohingya man in his seventies. In44, Thayingkhali camp, 25/09/2018.
8 The Union Citizenship Act of 1948 3(1) had a similar definition of 'indigenous race' but included a more expansive definition of 'citizen.'
9 In34, Chittagong, 02/08/2018. Rohang is an old name for Rakhine from which the word 'Rohingya' is thought to derive. See Charney, M. (2007). The Naf river forms part of today's border between Myanmar and Bangladesh.
10 Ob11, Shahpuri, 30/07/2018.
11 The East India Company preceded the British Crown in controlling vast areas of the Indian sub-continent, and commanded twice as many troops as the British national armed forces Dalrymple (2020).
12 In39, Ramu Central Buddhist Temple, 31/07/2018.

13 Known by the British as King Bering. Also see Harvey (1925). Hall (1945).
14 Ob20, Ramu, Coxes Bazar, 31/07/20218.
15 In35, 02/08/2018, Chittagong.
16 Ob11, 30/07/2018, Shahpuri.
17 In44, 25/09/2018, Thayingkhali.
18 Ob22, 28/09/2018, Ramu.
19 Lies and trickery on the part of Myanmar in relation to citizenship and history were a common theme, referred to in all focus groups and in 29 individual interviews.
20 Legislation passed in 1807 banned British subjects and British ships from trading in enslaved people. Slavery in plantations in British colonies continued for a further 30 years.
21 There are numerous studies of how colonial ethnic categories—or the taxonomy of race—in other contexts such as Africa were used to form the basis of divide-and-rule strategies, Apartheid, and later the social significance of the categories formed the basis of mass violence, for example, between Hutus and Tutsis in Rwanda. See, for example, Mamdani, M. (1996). Citizen and Subject: Contemporary Africa and the Legacy of Late Colonialism. And Longman, T. (2001). Identity Cards, Ethnic Self-Perception, and Genocide in Rwanda. Documenting Individual Identity.
22 In35, Chittagong, 02/08/2018.
23 Zerbadi was a term originally used to denote the children of mixed Muslim or Indian and Burmese parentage but became a category into which many Burmese Muslims were conflated. Burmese Muslims considered it derogatory in that it emphasised their foreignness and 'strangeness' over their Burmese identity (Yegar 1972). The British census report of 1933 records this dispute as follows: 'Objection has often been raised against the use of the word Zerbadi, but no satisfactory substitute has been suggested. . . A leaflet was actually issued by this society instructing all Muslims permanently resident in Burma to return themselves at the census as Burma Muslims. This was stopped at once and a Press Communique was also issued explaining that the instructions for the census did not provide for any entry such as "Burma Muslims"' (p231).
24 'On August 18, 1941, U Ba Oh, inserted an announcement in the press which contained the Governments' notification (of the discontinuation of the term Zerbadi) and summarised the ten-year struggle that had proceeded it. This was the last activity of the Burma Muslim Society, for it was shortly thereafter that the Japanese invaded the country,' Yegar, M. 1972 pp. 16, 21–22 Quoting Silver Jubilee 'Burman Muslims: Their status in Burma,' Government of Burma's communiqué, published by the Burma Moslem Society, Rangoon 9 Aug 1941.
25 Indian Passport Act (Act XXXIV of 1920)
26 'Some of them -kalas to be frank- did not go back to their kala-pyi, but went to Singapore, Hong-Kong or America. . . They are not trustworthy. . . they are engaged in bad business.' General Ne Win (8 Feb 1982). Speech on the 1982 Citizenship Law: Meeting Held in Central Meeting House, President House, Ahlone Rd, Translated by Working People's Daily. 'Kala' is a derogatory term for Muslims and people of South Asian descent. 'Kala-pyi' means 'country of kalas.'
27 In56, 03/10/2018, New Delhi.
28 In33, 30/07/2018 Tekaf; In44, 25/09/2018 Thayingkhali.
29 In44, 25/09/2018 Thayingkhali, Bangladesh.
30 In19, 27/04/2018 Kuala Lumpur; In1, 12/08/2017, New Delhi; In35, 02/08/2018, Chittagong.
31 'Princely' states were semi-sovereign, governed by local rulers but subject to indirect rule by the British Crown. There were hundreds of princely states throughout the region.

32 The documents that served the same role as 'licenses' are referred to in Rohingya narratives as Form 4s.
33 *Thakin* was a term of address for the British that was adopted as a term of respect by members of the Burmese independence movement. Its meaning is close to 'comrade.'
34 Dr Maung Maung, who was editor of *The Guardian* in Burma and author of this article, which lays out the important role this Burmese-Indian played in the independence movement, was later one of the key drafters for the 1982 Citizenship Law which drafted with the purpose of excluding Burmese-Indians. Raschid, who was featured in this article, was arrested and detained after the 1962 coup. He was later exiled to Pakistan.
35 Fg6, 26/07/2018, Kutapalong.
36 Through the Government of Burma Act 1935.
37 See British parliamentary discussion of Government of Burma (immigration) Order. Available at: https://api.parliament.uk/historic-hansard/lords/1937/mar/04/government-of-burma-immigration-order (accessed 26/01/2020).
38 In the 1947 Constitution of Burma, Union Citizenship Act 1948.
39 In63, 25/04/2018, Kuala Lumpur. Also see Burma Human Rights Network (2018). European Network on Statelessness and Institute on Statelessness and Inclusion (2019).
40 See UNHRC, 27/05/2015, Myanmar: UN Rights Experts Express Alarm at Adoption of First of Four 'Protection of Race and Religion' Bills Available at: www.ohchr.org/EN/NewsEvents/Pages/DisplayNews.aspx?NewsID=16015&LangID=E (accessed 27/01/2020).
41 For example, ongoing discussions between Bangladesh, Myanmar, and UNHCR over returnee documents for Rohingya and between Thailand and Myanmar for returnees from Thailand.
42 Raschid's personal correspondence, on file.
43 Tin Tut was assassinated by a car bomb in Sept 1848.
44 Document 573 Broadcast by U Tin Tut from the Burma Broadcasting Service IOR: M/4/2748 in Tinker, Griffin et al. (1984).
45 One of the main causal factors of the famine is understood to be the feeding and distribution policies of the British, which diverted limited supplies away from local populations to support war efforts elsewhere. See Sen (1977).
46 There are four original press clippings from 22 February 1947 on file—two referring to the visit being related to border demarcation and two reporting the visit as relating to an 'influx of Indians.' From original correspondence from Raschid, U Nu, and the Chief Minister of Bengal relating to this visit, it is clear that the only purpose of the visit was to clarify border demarcation.
47 Document 563 Council of the Ministers, 19th meeting, Minute 12 (5,6,7,8) IOR: M/4/2555 in Tinker et al. (1984).
48 Jinnah was first Governor General of Pakistan.
49 Attlee was British Prime Minister of the time.
50 U Saw had been identified in the riot inquiry report of 1939 as an instigator of the anti-Indian movement in the 1930s. He did not sign on to the Atlee-Aung San agreement or 'white paper' that resulted from the London talks in 1947. Seven months later, he was involved in planning the assassination of Aung San and his cabinet and was later hanged.
51 Original press clipping—'Jinnah repudiates Maungdaw claim: Aung San in expresses complete satisfaction' 8/01/1947 Reuters, Karachi.
52 Letter from Raschid to U Nu dated 18/02/1947. Additionally, there are three letters between U Nu, Suhrawardy, and Raschid that introduce him as key negotiator and confirming the dates of the meeting.

53 Anti-Fascist People's Freedom League, key leaders of the period included Aung San and U Nu.
54 Public statement drafted by Raschid for U Nu contained in the correspondence dated 18/02/1947.
55 Letter from Aung San to Raschid dated 29/03/1946 confirms this visit stating that he has 'very recently returned from Arakan.'
56 Also see Siddique, The Rohingya Problem—Why? Speech delivered on 15 Aug 2012 at Thammasat University, Bangkok Available at: www.eurasiareview.com/29082012-the-rohingya-problem-why-speech/ (accessed 28/01/2020).
57 Copies of the original records from the 'Burma Conversations' of Jan 1947 and the 'white paper' pertaining to this are collected and reproduced in Tinker, Griffin et al. (1984). This reference refers to paper 193, 3rd meeting, Record II CAB133/3.
58 *Ibid* and doc. 218, 5th meeting, Further Statement by the Burma Delegation, L/PO/9/17.
59 *Ibid* document 258, Conclusions reached in the Conversations between His Majesty's Government and the Delegation from the Executive Council of the Governor of Burma, Jan 1947. Cmd. 7029.
60 Two letters from M.A. Raschid to Aung San dated 2 Feb 1947 and 6 Feb 1947.
61 Document 267, Bogyoke Aung San speaks to Press Conference M/4/2590, Tinker, Griffin et al. (1984).
62 Letter dated 19/11/1946 from Raschid to Aung San noting his resignation from Government of India to work with Aung San. Article/obituary of M.A. Rauf, original cutting, 'Prominent Rangoonite Dies in Toronto.' Working People's Daily, 8/6/67.
63 Recorded in the letters, telegrams, and correspondence of Sir Hubert Rance, the last Governor of British Burma, prior to and after the death of Aung San on 19 Jul 1947, collected in Tinker, Griffin et al. (1984).
64 Document 468, Cabinet: India and Burma Committee, I.B (47) 43rd Meeting & Document 533, Cabinet Commonwealth Affairs Committee Paper C.A. (47) in *Ibid.*
65 Treaty between the Government of the United Kingdom and the Provisional Government of Burma, 1948, Article 3.
66 In47, 26/09/2018, Camp 14 & In40, 24/08/2018, Balukhali.
67 In32, 28/07/2018, Balukhali.
68 Minister of Education prior to independence and Head of Mandalay division of the AFPLF.
69 Close colleague of Aung San and U Nu. Served as Minister in four different departments post-Independence.
70 In44, 25/09/2018, Teknaf. NB. There is no evidence that this conversation actually took place. Imagined dialogues were a common narrative device in the research.
71 Referred to in three focus groups and four interviews.

Bibliography

Agar, J. (2001). Modern Horrors: British Identity and Identity Cards, in Caplan, J. and Torpey, J. (eds), *Documenting Individual Identity: The Development of State Practices in the Modern World*. Princeton University Press. 101–120.

Alatas, S. H. (2013). *The Myth of the Lazy Native: A Study of the Image of the Malays, Filipinos and Javanese from the 16th to the 20th Century and Its Function in the Ideology of Colonial Capitalism*. Routledge.

Aman Ullah (2024). *The History of Rohingya until 1948*. Naing Win Htut (Publisher).

Amrith, S. S. (2013). *Crossing the Bay of Bengal: The Furies of Nature and the Fortunes of Migrants*. Harvard University Press.

Baxter, J., T. Tut and R. Desai (1941). Commission of Inquiry Report on Indian Immigration. Department of Commerce and Industry, Government of Burma.
Bennison, J. J. (1933). Census of India 1931, Volume XI, Burma Part I—Report. Rangoon, Office of the Supdt., Government Printing and Stationery, Burma.
Brinham, N. (2019). Looking Beyond Invisibility: Rohingyas' Dangerous Encounters with Papers and Cards. *Tilburg Law Review* 24(2): 156–169.
Burma Human Rights Network (2018). *Corruption and Discrimination Plague Burmese Passport System.* www.bhrn.org.uk/en/report/1051-bhrn-releases-report-on-discrimination-against-muslim-passport-applicants.html [Accessed 03/04/2019]
Charney, M. (2007). Buddhism in Arakan: Theories and Histiographies of the Religious Basis of Ethnonyms. Paper presented at 'Arakan History Conference, Institute of Asian Studies, Chulalongkorn University [Accessed 23/11/2005]
Charney, M. (2016). State and Society in Arakan from the Fourteenth Century: From Inclusion to Polarisation and Exclusion: Myanmar's Democratic Transition and the Rohingya Persecution. Paper presented at Research Conference on Myanmar's.
Charney, M. (26 Feb 2018). A State Myth of 'National Race' and the Tatmadaw's War on the Rohingya and other Myanmar Ethnic Groups. Berlin Conference on Genocide.
Cheesman, N. (2017). How in Myanmar 'National Races' Came to Surpass Citizenship and Exclude Rohingya. *Journal of Contemporary Asia* 47(3): 461–483.
Chhotray, V. and F. McConnell (2018). *Certifications of Citizenship: The History, Politics and Materiality of Identity Documents in South Asian States and Diasporas.* Taylor & Francis.
Cole, S. A. (2009). *Suspect Identities: A History of Fingerprinting and Criminal Identification.* Harvard University Press.
Crosthwaite, C. (1912). *The Pacification of Burma: London.* Edward Arnold.
Dalrymple, W. (2020). *The Anarchy: The Relentless Rise of the East India Company.* Bloomsbury.
European Network on Statelessness and Institute on Statelessness and Inclusion (2019). Statelessness in Myanmar: Country Position Paper. *Stateless Journeys.* https://statelessjourneys.org/wp-content/uploads/StatelessJourneys-Myanmar-final.pdf [Accessed 11/11/2019]
General Ne Win (8 Feb 1982). Speech on the 1982 Citizenship Law: Meeting held in Central Meeting House, President House, Ahlone Rd, Translated by Working People's Daily.
Government of Burma (1931). Report on the Rebellion in Burma up to 3rd May, 1931 and Communique issued by the Government of Burma 19th May 1931.
Hall, D. G. E. (1945/1886). *Europe and Burma: A Study of European Relations with Burma to the Annexation of Thibaw's Kingdom.* ed. H. Milford. Oxford University Press.
Harvey, G. E. (1925). *History of Burma from the Earliest Times to 10 March 1824: The Beginning of the English Conquest.* Longmans, Green and Company.
Hayden, R. M. (1996). Imagined Communities and Real Victims: Self-Determination and Ethnic Cleansing in Yugoslavia. *American Ethnologist* 23(4): 783–801.
Hull, M. S. (2012a). Documents and Bureaucracy. *Annual Review of Anthropology* 41: 251–267.
Hull, M. S. (2012b). *Government of Paper: The Materiality of Bureaucracy in Urban Pakistan.* University of California Press.
Irwin, A. (1945). *Burmese Outpost..* Collins.
Jayal, N. G. (2013). *Citizenship and Its Discontents: An Indian History.* Harvard University Press.
Leach, E. (1973). *Political Systems of Highland Burma.* Berg.

Lehman, F. K. (1967). Ethnic Categories in Burma and the Theory of Social Systems, in Kunstadter, P. (ed), *Southeast Asian Tribes, Minorities, and Nations*. Princeton University Press.

Leider, J. P. (2018). Conflict and Mass Violence in Arakan (Rakhine State): The 1942 Events and Political Identity Formation, in South, A. and Lall, M. (eds), *Citizenship in Myanmar: Ways of Being in and from Burma*. ISEAS. 193–221.

Lieberman, V. B. (1978). Ethnic Politics in Eighteenth-Century Burma. *Modern Asian Studies* 12(3): 455–482.

Longman, T. (2001). Identity Cards, Ethnic Self-Perception, and Genocide in Rwanda, in Caplan, J. and Torpey, J. (eds), *Documenting Individual Identity: The Development of State Practices in the Modern World*. Princeton University Press.

Mamdani, M. (1996). *Citizen and Subject: Contemporary Africa and the Legacy of Late Colonialism*. Princeton.

Mamdani, M. (2012). *Define and Rule: Native as Political Identity*. Harvard University Press.

Marshall, T. H. (1950). *Citizenship, Social Class and Other Essays*. Cambridge University Press.

Maung Maung (1956). Profile: M.A. Raschid. The Guardian III(14).

Maung, M. I. K. (1986). The population of Burma: An analysis of the 1973 Census, East-West Center.

McConnell, F. (2013). Citizens and Refugees: Constructing and Negotiating Tibetan Identities in Exile. *Annals of the Association of American Geographers* 103(4): 967–983.

Mohan, R. (1955). Immigration Policy of Burma in Relation to India: A Brief Survey. *The Indian Journal of Political Science* 16(2): 165–170.

Mongia, R. V. (1999). Race, Nationality, Mobility: A History of the Passport. *Public Culture* 11(3): 527–555.

Naorem, D. (2020). Japanese Invasion, War Preparation, Relief, Rehabilitation, Compensation and 'State-Making' in an Imperial Frontier (1939–1955). *Asian Ethnicity* 21(1): 96–121.

NUI Galway (2010). *Crimes against Humanity in Western Burma: The situation of the Rohingyas*. www.nuigalway.ie/media/intranet/Crimes-Against-Humanit-in-Western-Burma.pdf [Accessed 03/05/2017]

Nyi Nyi Kyaw (2015). Alienation, Discrimination, and Securitization: Legal Personhood and Cultural Personhood of Muslims in Myanmar. *The Review of Faith & International Affairs* 13(4): 50–59.

Nyi Nyi Kyaw (2017). Unpacking the Presumed Statelessness of Rohingyas. *Journal of Immigrant and Refugee Studies* 15(3): 269–286.

Nyi Nyi Kyaw (2019). Adulteration of Pure Native Blood by Aliens? Mixed Race Kapya in Colonial and Post-Colonial Myanmar. *Social Identities* 25(3): 345–359.

Perks, R. and A. Thomson (2006). *The Oral History Reader*. Routledge.

Phayre, A. P. (1883). *History of Burma: Including Burma Proper, Pegu, Taungu, Tenasserim, and Arakan, from the Earliest Time to the First War with British India*. Susil Gupta.

Popular Memory Group (2006). Popular Memory: Theory, Politics, Method, in Perks, R. and Thomas, A. (eds), *The Oral History Reader*. Routledge. 43–53.

Portelli, A. (2006). What Makes Oral History Different?, in Perks, R. and Thomson, A. (eds), *The Oral History Reader*, Second Edition. Routledge. 32–42.

The Riot Inquiry Committee (1939). Interim Report of the Riot Inquiry Committee. Rangoon: Govt. Printing and Stationary. Government of Burma.

Roy, H. (2016). Paper Rights: The Emergence of Documentary Identities in Post-Colonial India, 1950–67. *Journal of South Asian Studies* 39(2): 329–349.

Sadiq, K. (2009). *Paper Citizens: How Illegal Immigrants Acquire Citizenship in Developing Countries*. Oxford University Press.

Sadiq, K. (2016). Limits of Legal Citizenship: Narratives from South and Southeast Asia, in Lawrance, B. N. and Stevens, J. (eds), *Citizenship in Question: Evidentiary Birthright and Statelessness*. Duke University Press. 165–176.

Scott, J. C. (1998). *Seeing Like a State: How Certain Schemes to Improve the Human Conditions Have Failed*. Yale University Press.

Scott, J. C. (2009). *The Art of Not Being Governed: An Anarchist History of Upland Southeast Asia*. Yale University Press.

Sen, A. (1977). Starvation and Exchange Entitlements: A General Approach and Its Application to the Great Bengal Famine. *Cambridge Journal of Economics* 1(1): 33–59.

Sengoopta, C. (2003). *Imprint of the Raj: How Fingerprinting Was Born in Colonial India*. Macmillan.

Sharma, N. (2020). *Home Rule: National Sovereignty and the Separation of Natives and Migrants*. Oxford University Press.

Siddique (2012). The Rohingya Problem—Why? Keynote Speech Delivered at the International Conference on 'Contemplating Burma's Rohingya People's Future in Reconciliation and (Democratic) Reform,' Held on August 15, 2012 at the Thammasat University, Bangkok. www.eurasiareview.com/29082012-the-rohingya-problem-why-speech/ [Accessed 13/02/2020]

Singha, R. (2000). Settle, Mobilize, Verify: Identification Practices in Colonial India. *Studies in History* 16(2): 151–198.

Singha, R. (2013). The Great War and a 'Proper' Passport for the Colony: Border-Crossing in British India, c.1882–1922. *The Indian Economic and Social History Review* 50(3): 289–315.

Smart, R. B. (1917). Burma Gazetteer: Akyab District, Volume (A). Rangoon: Superintendent, Government Printing and Stationery, Union of Burma.

Sriraman, T. (2011). Revisiting Welfare: Ration Card Narratives in India. *Economic and Political Weekly* 46(38): 52–59.

Sriraman, T. (2018). *In Pursuit of Proof: A History of Identification Documents in India*. Oxford University Press.

Than Tun (1959). History of Burma: AD 1300–1400. *Journal of the Burma Research Society* 42(2): 119–134.

Than Tun (2012). Review of Maitrii Aung Thwin, the Return of the Galon King: History, Law, and Rebellion in Colonial Burma: Ohio University Research in International Studies. *Journal of the Economic and Social History of the Orient* 55(1): 183–186.

Thompson, S. (2008). Separating the Sheep from the Goats: The United Kingdom's National Registration Programme and Social Sorting in the Pre-Electronic Era, in Bennett, C. J. and Lyon, D. (eds), *Playing the Identity Card: Surveillance, Security and Identification in Global Perspective*. Routledge.

Tinker, H. (1959). *The Union of Burma: A Study of the First Years of Independence*. Oxford University Press.

Tinker, H., A. Griffin and S. R. Ashton (1984). Constitutional Relations between Britain and Burma: Burma—The Struggle for Independence 1944–48. *Her Majesty's Stationary Office*.

Tonkin, D. (2018). Exploring the Issue of Citizenship in Rakhine State, in South, A. and Lall, M. (eds), *Citizenship in Myanmar: Ways of Being in and from Burma*. ISEAS. 222–263.

Torpey, J. (2000). *The Invention of the Passport: Surveillance, Citizenship, and the State*. Cambridge University Press.

Torpey, J. (2001). The Great War and the Birth of the Modern Passport System, in Caplan, J. and Torpey, J. (eds), *Documenting Individual Identity: The Development of State Practices in the Modern World*. Princeton University Press.
Union of Burma (1864). *Foreigners Act, India Act III.*
Union of Burma (1920). *The Passport Act, India Act XXXIV.*
Union of Burma (1935). *Government of Burma Act.*
Union of Burma (1940). *Registration of Foreigners Act.*
Union of Burma (1947). *Constitution of the Union of Burma.*
Union of Burma (1947). *Emergency Immigration Act.*
Union of Burma (1948). *Foreigners (Amendment) Act.*
Union of Burma (1948). *The Union Citizenship Act.*
Union of Burma (1948). *The Union Citizenship (Election) Act.count.*
Union of Burma (1949). *Residents of Burma Registration Act.*
Union of Burma (1951). *Residents of Burma Registration Rules.*
Winichakul, T. (1997). *Siam Mapped: A History of the Geo-Body of a Nation*. University of Hawaii Press.
Yegar, M. (1972). *The Muslims of Burma*. O. Harrassowitz.
Zarni, M. and N. Brinham (2017). Reworking the Colonial Era Indian Peril: Myanmar's State-Directed Persecution of Rohingyas and Other Muslims. *Brown Journal of World Affairs* 24(1): 53–76.

5 IDs as evidence of state crime and artefacts from the early decades of independence

Introduction

IDs issued by the Burmese state during the first decades of independence prior to the military coup of 1962 were a central feature of Rohingya narratives regarding their citizenship. Fieldwork narratives relating to this period described strong bonds between the central state and Rohingya, as the state strategically embraced Rohingya populations through citizenship and cultural recognition of their belonging to the multi-ethnic national community. This chapter considers the significance of IDs from these decades in evidencing the later military practices of citizenship stripping and identity destruction.

This chapter first considers how Rohingya citizenship in Burma was experienced and enacted during the period before the military coup of 1962. Second, it considers how IDs and state documents issued to Rohingya under the 1947/8 citizenship framework were used as evidence of state 'theft' or citizenship stripping. The chapter frames these experiences of citizenship within a 'trinity of citizenship'—status, rights, and identity—outlined in Chapter 3 (see also Joppke 2007). In considering the identity aspect of citizenship, the chapter also explores how state-issued identity and registration documents were preserved by Rohingya survivors as artefacts of Rohingya identity to highlight and resist the processes of identity destruction during the years of military rule.

The IDs explored in this chapter were issued between 1948 and 1989. Most were issued in the early years of independence which was largely a period of parliamentary democracy (1948–62).[1] The chapter also considers the changes during the period of military rule under Ne Win from 1962.[2] Ne Win oversaw the military operation, *Nagamin,* in 1978 that resulted in the forced expulsion of approximately 200,000 to 250,000 Rohingya into Bangladesh.[3] This was followed by the forced repatriation of most of these Rohingya refugees in 1978–9 (Linquist 1979; Abrar 1995; Pittaway 2016; Crisp 2018); and the subsequent drafting and enactment of the 1982 Citizenship law, which excluded Rohingya as a part of the ongoing production of their statelessness (Arraiza and Vonk 2017; Nyi Nyi Kyaw 2017). The

DOI: 10.4324/9781003494539-5
This chapter has been made available under a CC-BY 4.0 license.

period covered by the chapter ends with the roll-out of a new colour-coded ID scheme in 1989. This ID scheme came shortly after the 1988 nationwide uprising, when the State Law and Order Restoration Council (SLORC), a military junta, assumed control over the state (Smith 1999).[4] The ID scheme enabled SLORC to exert tighter control over the border areas as they cracked down on opposition to military rule and multiple ethnic insurgencies. It further allowed them to establish a bureaucratic system that segregated Rohingya communities in North Rakhine State and systematised the process of stripping Rohingya of citizenship recognition (Fortify Rights 2014; Amnesty International 2017).

Chapter 3 revealed how IDs in statelessness studies were most frequently referred to as evidence or proof of whether a state recognises individuals as citizens or not (Sadiq 2016; Kingston 2017; Stevens 2017). State categorisation and ID systems were crucial tools available for states to build and maintain power, by establishing a monopoly control over freedom of movement and access to rights and benefits (Scott 1998; Torpey 2000; Lyon and Bennett 2008). This chapter also considers identity documents as artefacts of the state, and the material objects of law and policy (Hull 2012; Sadiq 2016). ID narratives and documents provide a lens through which to explore both notions of state power and individual subjectivities (Hull 2012; Chhotray and McConnell 2018; Reddy 2015; Navaro-Yashin 2007). In this regard, IDs can also be mediators between individual subjects and the social world (Latour 1999; Hull 2012). Torpey (2001:5) describes identity documents as having both 'emancipatory and repressive aspects' in that they enable states to 'embrace' some people and 'exclude' others in ways that produce non-citizens. Rohingya narratives reflecting on the early decades of independence often highlighted the emancipatory aspects of IDs issued in the decades after independence. These notions were often juxtaposed with the repressive and destructive aspects that characterised the IDs they held from the 1990s onwards.

Citizenship as a strategic embrace and a peace pact

This section considers how Rohingya citizenship in the early decades of independence was spoken about in the field research. It focuses first on how the recognition of Rohingya citizenship and national belonging was part of a strategic embrace on the part of the post-independence state (Cowley and Zarni 2017; Zarni and Brinham 2017). Second, it considers the ways in which citizenship was experienced and enacted by Rohingya in terms of rights and duties.

The citizenship bond between the state and the Rohingya was often described by research participants as an embrace on the part of the state, whereby Rohingya citizenship was recognised, bestowed, and reasserted by the state/military as part of a peace agreement and a guarantee against future conflict. This pragmatic approach to citizenship is featured in narratives relating to the time when borders were settled in the lead-up to independence. For example:

> In the past, we Rohingya wrote a letter to the British requesting that we become part of Pakistan, but they just ignored it. So, Aung San said 'I will take care of them.' After he went to London, he came to visit Akyab and he basically told us, 'I will give you a blank cheque.' This agreement was decided by Aung San and Jinnah.[5]

Nonetheless, border and minority issues across Burma were far from settled in the post-independence years. Against the backdrop of multiple ethnic insurgencies across the country, groups of both Rakhine Buddhists and Rohingya took up arms in the 1950s both demanding greater autonomy (Smith 1999). Some of the Rohingya 'mujahedeen' continued to demand to be incorporated into Pakistan. Recognition of Rohingya as citizens and as a group belonging to the region was reasserted on surrender, as recounted by participants.[6] This recognition also came with the establishment of Mayyu district—today's North Rakhine State—as a homeland for Rohingya to be administered separately from the rest of Rakhine by the central state.[7] Participants in the research referred to the speech of Brigadier Aung Gyi that recognised the Rohingya belonging in Burma (15 Nov 1961).[8] Citizenship, recognition, and land as part of a pact of peace between Rohingya and the central state were described by one participant in this way:

> the government told them that if you surrender, if you drop your weapons, we will recognise you and give you your rights. So, believing the government words, the Rohingya rebels—they dropped their weapons before the Myanmar government. But the government has now forgotten all the promises that they gave to the rebels. This is another example of the Burmese (government) making things up.[9]

The various ways in which the state later denied Rohingya citizenship were repeatedly referred to in narratives as dishonesty and broken promises on the part of the state—a reneged pact and a broken peace. For example, 'We are citizens and natives. The government until now wants to delete us from the ethnic groups, so they lie. They lie to the world. They lie to the world that there is no Rohingya.'[10]

The recognition of Rohingya as an ethnic group, and as a group belonging to Burma was also a strong theme throughout the Rohingya narratives relating to this period. Its significance was that cultural and ethnic recognitions were denied by the state during the military period as a slow process culminating in the denial of individual citizenship status in the 1980s. For example:

> Rohingya culturally participated in Union Day in February[11]—Rohingya always participated. So, Ne Win first he took away this. Then he stepped up this '74 operation and '78 king dragon operation[12]—they wiped away 250,000. And then he did the citizenship law.[13]

One of the ways in which the state was understood to embrace Rohingya prior to the Ne Win period was the state recognition of their language, culture, and history in the Rakhine region. Rohingya narratives often drew attention to where they participated in state-organised cultural celebrations and events, where the term Rohingya was used by associations registered by the state, and where it appears in state-authorised publications and speeches by members of the military and government.[14] For example, participants noted the term Rohingya was used in high school geography textbooks, an official state encyclopaedia, state-run newspapers, military journals, speeches by U Nu and Brigadier Aung Gyi, State announcements, and radio broadcasts.[15] They also noted that Rohingya student organisations at Yangon University were registered along with other ethnic organisations.[16] Furthermore, Arakan Muslims—a category incorporating ethnic Rohingya—were also referred to as indigenous, including in the speech of first president of Burma, Sao Shwe Thaike.[17]

One of the most common examples of state cultural recognition within the narratives was the regular broadcasts of Rohingya language programmes on the national radio between 1961 and 1965. Some older Rohingya participants remembered listening to the programme and described feeling a deep sense of belonging and connection when they heard Rohingya voices and language broadcast across the nation.[18] Younger Rohingya continued to refer to the programme, nostalgically as the era when the state embraced Rohingya as their own.[19] In the camps in Bangladesh, I spoke with one of Rohingya radio presenters.[20] He believed himself to be over 100 years old and was carried to the camp from his home by his grandsons in 2017. From 1961 to 1965, he recited a prayer from the Quran before the Rohingya language news on the national radio that was broadcast from Yangon. He explained that the radio broadcasts were an important part of building a multi-ethnic nation:

> The government in 1961 wanted to recognise all the ethnic nationalities in the same way. All the other ethnic nationalities of Burma were given an opportunity to broadcast their languages on state radio. The Rohingya were amongst them. Nobody said that we Rohingya did not belong to Burma during this period; We were equal with others.

He explained how, in 1965, with the country then under the military rule of Ne Win, the radio broadcasts were shut down. When the programmes were later reopened, Rohingya language was 'cancelled.' He recalled feeling at that time a sense of very deep foreboding for the future of the Rohingya as a group in Myanmar; he, and many others, thought this cancellation was deeply symbolic of the denationalisation and erasure processes that were to come.

Enacting citizenship

For their part, Rohingya participated in national affairs and building independent Burma. Fieldwork narratives emphasised these 'thick' aspects of citizenship (Tilly 1995:8; Sadiq 2009:21–22) as part of their bond with the state (see Chapter 3). The examples provided included political participation in national and local elections such as voting and standing for public office until 2015; the payment and records of formal and informal taxes; working in other public sector jobs ordinarily reserved for citizens of Myanmar including public administration, the judiciary, and state education and health sectors; serving in the state security forces including the police force and army; and drawing state pensions.

Political participation

Rohingya and Muslims from Rakhine who contributed to constitution writing or nation-building were often referred to including Sultan Mahmood[21] and Abdul Gaffar.[22] Narratives also emphasised Rohingya that were elected as Members of Parliament in the past. This included not only those who stood for office in the elections that took place prior to the military coup of 1962 but also those elections that took place during military rule, the unrecognised elections of 1990, and the elections of 2010. Rohingya were elected to public office in 1936, in preparation for the separation for the administrative separation of Burma from India in 1937. The significance is that, unlike after independence, there was a quota system in place whereby 'Burmese nationals' occupied a separate category from 'Chinese' or 'Indian.' The two Rohingya elected under this system were classed under the category 'Burmese national' (Ahmad 2009; Nay San Lwin 2012). Four participants had relatives who had been elected MPs in independent Burma. Additionally, there were many different references to particular local MPs. Those most frequently mentioned were Shwe Maung who served as an MP from 2010 to 2015[23] and Kyaw Min, who was elected in 1990 and was a member alongside Aung San Suu Kyi of the Committee Representing the People's Parliament (CRPP). The presence of Rohingya MPs was held up as proof of the state recognition and Rohingya's active participation in the processes that continued to shape the modern nation.

Rohingya also voted in national elections prior to the separation of Burma from India in 1936, up until their voting rights were removed before the 2015 elections. This included elections during the Ne Win era; the elections of 1990s in which the NLD won a landslide victory, but the results were not recognised; the constitutional referendum of 2008 and the general election of 2010 which brought in a military/civilian leadership lead by ex-General Thein Sein. Participants spoke fondly of the experience of voting. For example:

> I enjoyed voting very much because our relatives for a long, long time had been voting. They voted in every election. So, we also enjoyed it . . . we thought that in a very short time we will get citizenship cards. We expected that.[24]

Voting was frequently referenced as state recognition of their historic citizenship, a duty, and a bond with the state.

Serving in the national security forces

Modern citizenship regimes are understood to arise in part from the historic need to build states by raising armies of loyal citizens. Thus, citizenship is intrinsically linked to both national service and recruitment into the national security forces (Torpey 2000; Torpey 2001; Tilly 2003; Scott 2009). The strategic alliance and national incorporation of ethnic groupings, territories, and forces including Rohingya—and the exclusion of Indians and other foreigners in the forces—were important aspects of state-building and the citizenship regime in 1947–8.[25] This was a key part of the strategic embrace. It was therefore pertinent that narratives relating to how individual Rohingya were recognised as citizens often referred to those who had served in the state security forces after independence. This included the police, the army, and the navy.[26] Prior to independence, Rohingya commonly held positions in the security sector under the British. Many of those already recruited remained in position after independence.[27] Other family members spoken about were recruited into the forces during the independence period.[28] Under military rule, Muslims and Christians were slowly purged from the military in the upper ranks and then lower. Rohingya presence in the security sector was important in the narratives not simply because it proved the state recognition of Rohingyas' loyalty to the state but also because having mixed-ethnic and religious security forces was seen as a vital component in ensuring Rohingyas' safety, security, and state protection. One Rohingya man who fled Burma/Myanmar in 1978, 1992, and 2017, explained how this impacted Rohingya in the 1990s:

> Before, there were so many Rohingya officers in the security forces. Muslim people were some of the most important people. Many of the Rank 3 officers were Muslim. So many officers. After, step by step, the Muslim officers were removed. They dropped all the Muslim officers that were already there—and did not recruit Rohingya anymore . . . . After that we were not safe. They tortured us.[29]

The lack of ethnic and religious diversity in the upper ranks of the military was thus viewed as an obstacle to return for refugees, which often informed their demands for international protection before they return.[30]

Government sector jobs

Whilst government sector jobs are not necessarily used as an indication of citizenship recognition in other national contexts, in Burma/Myanmar they held a particular significance. Employment in government roles including civil administration, the education and health sectors, were reserved for citizens. Further, entrance to university education for particular professions such as doctors, lawyers, and engineers was also barred (Arraiza and Vonk 2017; de Chickera, Arraiza et al. 2021; Ealom 2021:ch1&2). Thus, narratives of citizenship recognition often focused on either their own work or relatives' work in these sectors. Participants explained that, much like the security sector, the recruitment of Rohingya into these sectors slowed down in the 1980s and Rohingya were slowly removed from positions.[31] One participant worked as a staff member in the Home Ministry for 33 years and was given a pension and an honorary certificate for his long service. He explained, 'When I applied to be officer of Burma, at that time my form clearly mentioned that I was a Burmese citizen. If not, we are not allowed to become an official.'[32]

He explained that he was forced into retirement in 2006. He was told that in order to keep his job, he would have to shave his beard off which, as a Muslim, he refused. In 2016, he was told that he needed to go through the national verification process and accept a National Verification Card (NVC) that identified him as a noncitizen. He refused. Thereafter, he was unable to travel from his home in the north to Maungdaw town in order to draw his pension.

The most frequent references to work in the government sector as citizenship recognition related to teaching in government schools. Although Rohingya were not recruited and were 'pushed out' of the formal education sector from the 1990s onwards, there were several references to relatives, who at the time of the research remained in post. One participant noted that his father was a teacher for 35 years. His elder sister was also a head teacher and remained in post in 2017. She applied in 1989. He noted that he could not become a teacher because he applied after 1990.[33]

This section has explained how recognition of both Rohingya group status and their individual citizenship status within post-independence Burma was drawn on in fieldwork narratives to contrast with their diminished status today. These narratives described a systematic state-led process that deliberately erased their histories as citizens of independent Burma and produced their statelessness over time. The following sections focus specifically on ID narratives.

State power, resistance, and ID narratives

IDs are often imbued with memories and emotions relating to resistance and oppression (Navaro-Yashin 2007; Hull 2012; Reddy 2015; Chhotray and McConnell 2018). Thus, the meanings attributed to IDs and their significance to social relations and relationships between the individual and the state shift and transmute over time (Latour 2005; Hull 2012). Many participants spoke about and treated IDs from the early decades of independence as some of their most treasured possessions. The documents themselves over time became endowed with memories and nostalgia of a bygone era—a time of equality and recognition. Some Rohingya had gone to extraordinary lengths to keep hold of their documents and their narratives contained elements of sacrifice and heroism. Participant ID narratives were endowed with affect and emotion, which provided stark contrast to the neutrality often attributed to paperwork and state bureaucracies by state and international agencies (Hoag 2011). In order to analyse the ID narratives, I therefore drew on themes that emerged from the research relating to affect/emotion. These themes included belonging, hope, fear, loss, grief, honour, stigma, and shame. I considered the ways Rohingya spoke about their documents from this period. Additionally I explored the ways in which they preserved them, touched them, presented them and, the ways in which other Rohingya interacted with the documents.

ID and registration documents most often discussed in fieldwork narratives relating to this period were National Registration Cards (NRCs).[34] They were issued to Myanmar citizens across the country, including Rohingya, from the 1950s until 1989.[35] Blue cards were issued to men and pink to women. Unlike today's identity cards, NRCs did not record ethnicity or religion. They were not colour-coded according to a hierarchy of citizenship as later ID cards were (pink/red for full citizenship; blue for 'associate' citizenship; green for 'naturalised' citizenship; white for those whose applications were being processed). Burmese passports and occasionally high school certificates and student registration cards from this period were also spoken about. Additionally, the changes in the way ethnicity, nationality, and religion were recorded on the family lists or household registration cards also featured as explanations of the ways in which Rohingya statelessness had been slowly produced by the state. Family lists were also key documents required for citizenship applications (de Chickera, Arraiza et al. 2021). Other documents talked about and preserved to prove Rohingya ethnic identity included the application forms for citizenship cards from 1989 onwards which detailed genealogy, and repatriation documents from 1978 to 1979 which recorded their ethnicity as Rohingya. Frequently these documents, which were associated with citizenship recognition and equality, were juxtaposed in narratives with stories of ID documents issued after 1989.[36]

IDs as evidence of state crime: looted and stolen citizenships

The most dominant thread of Rohingya narratives concerning IDs from this period was to counteract the state discourses which suggested that Rohingya had never belonged to Myanmar or were not fully Burmese. For example:

> My father and mother both had the NRC card. So, therefore my nationality is Burmese. I am a citizen of Burma because my father and my mother belong to Arakan. How can my nationality not be Burmese?[37]

In this way, the participants were drawing on the notion of IDs as pieces of evidence to prove a crime—citizenship stripping. Rohingya participants in discussing their NRCs were highlighting that citizenship was once rightfully theirs, and had been 'stolen' from them by the state.[38]

> Our citizenship has been stolen from us. Rohingya statelessness is not an accident of history, it was deliberately produced by the Myanmar military as a part on the ongoing genocide.[39]

In explaining this, narratives also appealed to notions that the removal or withdrawal of the right to citizenship was a breach of international norms.[40] Within statelessness scholarship and advocacy, it is often noted that although the right to nationality is inscribed in international law, state responsibility to provide nationality to stateless individuals is harder to establish. The arbitrary deprivation of citizenship, however, is a clear breach of international law, as discussed in Chapter 3 (Goldston 2006; Weissbrodt and Collins 2006; Spiro 2011). Rohingya narratives were constructed to prove that they are not simply people who fell through the gaps between Burmese and Bangladesh citizenship laws, but rather that the state had systematically attempted to strip them of their once well-established citizenship.[41] They called on international agencies and bodies to stop supporting the state's attempts to register and document Rohingya under ID schemes that did not recognise their citizenship or ethnicity. For example, one focus group vocally and energetically agreed with the participant who said:

> A thief will never admit that he stole things. And the Burmese government will never admit that they stole our citizenship. We are worrying about UNHCR—that they may work against the interests of survivors of genocide.[42]

In discussing the issues of international justice, reparations, and restitution, another participant explained that citizenship was a core component:

> The military generals should be punished for what they have done to us . . . We need to be provided again with citizenship—citizenship with full dignity and security. We need everything that has been looted from us—everything should be returned.[43]

From 2012 onwards, two contrasting international approaches to tackling statelessness in Myanmar emerged. On the one hand, approaches recommended tackling statelessness within the existing legal domestic framework or making technical tweaks to the existing laws, rules, and administrative processes (Center for Diversity and National Harmony 2019). Essentially these approaches have sought to engage with the state and remain deferential in matters relating to citizenship and documentation. These approaches were predominantly promoted by international and domestic organisations that engaged closely with the state, including UN organisations (Mahony 2018). The other approach contrastingly challenged the notion within international law that states reserve the sovereign right to determine their members through their citizenship laws. Instead, such approaches attempted to place the production of statelessness firmly within the purview of human rights violations and establish limits regarding the discretion states reserve in their citizenship laws and practices (Pillai 2019; Kenny 2020). These approaches emphasised the issues of citizenship stripping and racial discrimination (Goldston 2006;

Weissbrodt and Collins 2006; Spiro 2011). They called for the 'immediate' reform of the 1982 Citizenship Law and related practices based on the principles of non-discrimination; the reform of the judicial system and constitution in Myanmar; and most importantly the restitution or restoration of full citizenship rights (as opposed to citizenship verification or 'pathways to citizenship') for Rohingya (Fortify Rights 2019; International Commission of Jurists 2019). This approach was advocated largely by human rights organisations operating predominantly outside the country such as International Commission of Jurists, Burma Campaign UK, and Fortify Rights. Rohingya research participants consistently called for the latter approach, emphasising state culpability and the need for citizenship restoration. The public speeches of Rohingya activists during the period of this research project also drew on this perspective, looking to shift international discourses and approaches into alignment with their own perspectives which located the solution to their citizenship stripping within the broader approaches of genocide prevention and international justice.[44]

The following section looks in more depth at how Rohingya ID narratives draw upon the early decades of Myanmar's independence to establish their citizenship in Myanmar and is framed by key concepts within citizenship studies.

IDs and the trinity of citizenship: status, rights, and identity

Rohingya ID narratives relating to the early decades of independence reflected the notions that citizenship is constituted by three interrelated component parts: status, rights, and identity. They emphasised how IDs during this period provided recognition of their legal status as citizens and access to equal rights. Most emphatically, they reflected on how IDs supported a framework of social relations within which individual Rohingya belonged as part of a national Burmese community.

IDs and citizenship status

ID documents that proved Rohingya citizenship status dominated conversations in the early decades of independence. However, the absence of other documents that were issued to foreigners or naturalised citizens was also referenced as proof of automatic citizenship. The absence of FRCs, which were issued to foreigners in Myanmar, amongst Rohingya communities was referred to as evidence of their citizenship.[45] Similarly, Union Citizenship Certificates in Myanmar were issued under the 1948 Union Citizenship (Election) Act and the 1948 Union Citizenship Election Rules *only* to those who elected for citizenship through residence or naturalisation. They were not issued to those who qualified for automatic citizenship through membership of a national/indigenous group. Rohingya claims to citizenship within the narrative research were based emphatically on automatic citizenship. As such, mention of Union Citizenship Certificates only arose in one interview.

This participant showed a picture of a letter from the Citizenship Election Officer dated 1949 issued to his grandfather which stated he need not apply for citizenship as he belonged to an indigenous group of Burma according to an affidavit submitted to the authorities.[46] The absence, not the existence, of Union Citizenship Certificates was thus described as proof of automatic citizenship.

NRCs were the most frequently cited form of ID used to describe an era of citizenship recognition and equality. These references mostly related to participants' own or family members' citizenship status. Many kept pictures of their family member's NRCs on their mobile phones. Others kept and presented the original documents during interview in order to tell their family histories. They often requested me to either take photos of NRCs or record the names, issue numbers, and other details from the documents. This was part of a broader recording and validation process relating to the co-construction of narratives referred to in the methodology. Some of these IDs were 50–60 years old and were frayed, faded, or torn. They were handled tenderly and passed around other Rohingya carefully; they were often photocopied several times and the copies preserved as well, reflecting how treasured these objects were both by their 'keepers' and by the broader community. Almost all the narratives emphasised that Rohingya held the same cards as all other citizens of Myanmar and were thus evidence of family citizenship status and their own right to citizenship status today. For the most part, 'the keepers' and their families understood that they held limited legal value under the existing citizenship framework and conditions in Myanmar, although it was often hoped that they could be used to prove citizenship in the future.[47]

The removal of NRCs as proof of citizenship

State authorities including immigration, local authorities, and the border guard forces removed Rohingya NRCs from the 1970s onwards through a mixture of practices which featured frequently in Rohingya ID narratives. Since the removal of documents was a historic practice and human rights, documentation in Rohingya areas of Rakhine State was limited, especially prior to the mid-1990s, published information on historic removal practices are limited and retrospective. At the time this research project was conceived, there was a common misconception that most Rohingya had never been recognised as citizens or issued IDs in independent Burma. Since then, research has challenged these notions, showing that Rohingya were recognised as citizens and highlighting how documents were confiscated or destroyed (Cheesman 2017; Nyi Nyi Kyaw 2017; Fortify Rights 2019; UNHRC Sept 2019). Nonetheless, these accounts have not explored historical state practices of document removal due to the lack of evidence from the time.

The ways in which IDs were removed were significant in the fieldwork narratives, since the methods evidenced practices that were systematic and state directed. Many of the incidents of ID removal were spoken about within the context of military 'campaigns' and 'operations' and included the 'seizure,' 'confiscation,' or 'snatching' of their own or family members' documents.[48] Some practices of removing documents fell within the 1982 Citizenship law and associated administrative rules, for example, the requirement to surrender the NRCs of deceased relatives.[49] Some practices did not, such as the ripping up or burning of IDs during military operations, which was often referred to as being so widespread as to indicate orders for higher ranks (see also Fortify Rights 2019). Rohingya narratives rarely differentiated between these practices. When asked, participants explained that they did not lack knowledge of the citizenship rules, but rather understood that the law and rules functioned to persecute them and to consolidate and legitimate the state's power. As such, they understood that the state authorities operated outside of a framework of rule of law.[50]

> Even if Rohingya got citizenship under changes to the law, we would still face problems because there is no rule of law . . . The international community, they don't understand the real situation . . . it is very hard for them to imagine. It's like a poultry farm—we are the chickens. They (the State authorities) are the poultry farmers coming and catching a person—a random person.[51]

The first state attempt to remove Rohingya NRCs as proof of their citizenship was, according to the narratives, during Operation *Zabae* (jasmine) in 1974. This was described as a 'hidden operation' in which new security checkpoints were set up between townships in northern Rakhine. When Rohingyas' IDs were checked at these security posts, they were taken and not returned.[52] A second narrative noted that some IDs were also confiscated at the local government offices as part of this operation.[53] The significance of this operation as a narrative thread was that it preceded the better known 1978 immigration and security operation known as *Nagamin,* which turned into a campaign of terror in which at least 200,000 Rohingya fled to Bangladesh (Linquist 1979; Zarni and Cowley 2014). Operation *zabae* was therefore used to evidence a systematic and sustained plan by the state to remove Rohingya legal status and physical presence in the country.

The second chronological mention of NRCs being confiscated was during and after Operation *Nagamin*. This operation began in Buthidaung in 1978. One participant came from the first town in which the operation started. He explained that Rohingya were asked to produce their IDs and when they did so, the documents were seized. Rohingya were then arrested on immigration charges and violence was used against them.[54] News of both the seizure of IDs and the arrests and violence spread to other Rohingya areas including Maungdaw causing many to flee in fear.[55] Of four participants who were interviewed about fleeing to Bangladesh in 1978 and their experiences of repatriation, all identified the confiscation of IDs as widespread in 1978–9.

One stated that his family's NRCs had been confiscated during the operation itself.

> In 1978, I fled to Bangladesh with my family. I was 15 years old . . . At that time, my mum and dad had documents from U Nu—the NRCs. These all were taken away when we were driven out of the country.[56]

Another explained that protecting IDs and other documents was the main reason his family fled:

> In 1978, there was a flash inquiry by government—Nagamin. So, in the night-time the government was taking documents from the Rohingya. At that time in Buthidaung, Rathedaung, all documents were collected. But we were near to the Bangladesh border, so the news had already spread. The people who were alerted—we could hide all our documents. My father and mother protected those documents. They thought if we stay here any longer, they will take away every document. It will be better if we can save our documents. With this idea, my father and mother fled to Bangladesh in 1978 only to protect those documents. They left them hidden in Rakhine state and then collected them when they went back.[57]

The third explained that his family's documents were confiscated along with others at the repatriation centre a few days after his return.

> After the hand over from Bangladesh to Burma, we were kept in a transit camp or centre for maybe no more than one week on the Burma side. During that time, it was only for the Burmese authorities to check the documents. At that time, they took all the documents to check them. They did not give them back. Then they let us out from the transit centre and told us to go with no documents. After the documents were taken, our lives became more difficult.[58]

A fourth participant recounted that his refugee documents, which he was told to keep as proof of his Burmese origins, being confiscated by an armed officer on his journey between the repatriation centre to his home village.[59] There were other reports of the confiscation of documents at checkpoints in the 1980s and 1990s—both personal accounts and stories of close family members.[60]

After the 1982 Citizenship Law was enacted, there were also various ways in which NRCs were removed under the citizenship rules. The two most frequently cited means of formal removal, related to applications for new citizenship cards in 1989 and house-to-house collection of 'cancelled' or 'void' cards. Following the period of nationwide unrest in 1988 and the change in military leadership, militarisation and securitisation of the border areas increased. This included the rolling out of a new ID Scheme from 1989 onwards, which colour-coded citizenship cards according to the 1982 citizenship Law (Arraiza and Vonk 2017; European Network on Statelessness and Institute on Statelessness and Inclusion 2019; International Commission of Jurists 2019). According to the narrative research, many Rohingya applied under this application process often referred to as 'form-2 applications.' They submitted their NRCs for this process, expecting to receive new citizenship cards in return. Instead, the authorities kept the NRCs and did not issue new citizenship cards.

> In 1989 the Myanmar government declared that we must return this card (NRC). We filled the form and applied. Unfortunately, the Myanmar government provided the other ethnic nationalities with their citizenship cards, but they didn't return our citizenship cards. In 1994 and 1995, then they provided these cards instead (white cards).[61]

Others had their NRCs removed during house-to-house visits by immigration or local authorities or in attempting to pass through checkpoints. Local government offices kept lists of who still held the NRCs and asked people to submit them to the office. All participants noted that they did not want to relinquish the IDs. Some did so because they felt they had no choice as otherwise they risked arrest. After the death of a relative, remaining family members would be told to submit their NRCs or risk arrest. These moments featured frequently in the narratives. 'I did not trust them, but at that time the NaSaKa had so much power. They could do anything. So, I gave the NRC.'[62]

The final way in which NRCs were removed was through attacks on homes by military or civilians during different periods. Some who fled were forced to leave documents behind and others had their homes burned or otherwise destroyed with their documents inside. These accounts predominantly related to events of 2012–3 and 2016–7.

Hidden and treasured IDs

As mistrust of the state's registration and documentation procedures grew, some of the participants went to extraordinary lengths in order to keep hold of their own and family NRCs as proof of their citizenship. One participant when asked why she had hidden her parent's documents from the state authorities at considerable risk to herself, said:

> When the military and authorities heard that my father died, they came to take back his NRC, but our relatives had suggested to us not to show and not to give it—to tell them that it was lost already and to keep it for the future. And now my brother's wife is the keeper. My elder Uncle said that one day Burmese authorities might ask who has had citizenship cards. Maybe they will be able to get land or maybe they will be able to get citizenship. He said, 'your children may get facilities you should keep it.'[63]

Another participant related how he had spent seven months in 2006 in Buthidaung prison rather than relinquish his late father's NRC card. His sentence was reduced from three years on the payment of a fine. He was sentenced to hard labour and described the prison conditions as 'horrifying.' He explained that the state authorities maintained a list of all people in his village who had not yet relinquished their NRCs. After his father's death, they asked him to return it, and when he said it was lost, the *NaSaKa* came to his house and arrested him. He explained:

> My father had told me there was a meeting to take back the NRCs in his time. But my father did not agree to give it. Before my father died, he told me, 'Please take this card. It is legal proof of your nationality. It is very important for you. And for our future generations.' That is why I kept this card—for our honour.[64]

Many participants spoke about their documents being one of the few items they fled with when leaving Myanmar. One participant explained how he kept his family's NRC, family lists, and all the land documents that were issued yearly wrapped and locked in a box that he kept buried on the land outside his house. He sometimes moved the position of the box to keep the documents safe in case of household searches. It was buried and hidden for decades until he fled in 2017.[65]

The ways in which participants described securing, treasuring, and hiding their family members' NRCs and other documents reflected understandings of the importance of IDs as evidence of Myanmar's recognition of their individual citizenship status, and also the citizenship status of the Rohingya as a group.

State trickery and lies

The removal of documents from Rohingya was understood by most to be in order to deliberately remove evidence of the existence of Rohingya people in Myanmar. Participants repeatedly stated that they would not show their family member's original NRCs to Myanmar State authorities, even if they were told that this may provide them with a pathway to citizenship in Myanmar. The most frequent reason provided was that the Myanmar State could not be trusted to recognise or return these documents, reflecting the dominant theme in oral histories of the ways in which the state authorities had 'lied,' 'tricked,' or 'forced' Rohingya to relinquish them in ways that were officially sanctioned through ID and registration practices. Often the trickery involved promises of providing other IDs.

> The Burmese government have many tricks. Even if they write Burmese citizen, they will give us a card. But after a few years, they will mention something—they will write some symbol or something. Then after 5 years, 10 years, they will come and say 'No. Your card is separate. Your card is different. Give us it back.'[66]

Many noted historical patterns and described this as a deliberate state-directed attempt to remove proof of Rohingyas' past citizenship status.

> During Burma independence, Rohingya and other fought together for independence. We had equal rights until 1962. 1962 was the start of the 'master plan' for the Rohingya community.'[67]

Many narratives also emphasised that the state authorities had consistently maintained records of who had been issued with NRCs, despite denying their right to citizenship. Often old family lists were referred to, on which the NRC reference numbers were recorded in order to show how records were systematically maintained.

> The authorities have a record of everyone who had one, so they visit houses to take them back. The authorities knew from their records who had been issued with NRCs in the past- and records of who had died or was no longer on the household list. So, they would go to the houses and tell people to return them. Then there was no proof anymore.[68]

Under the 1982 Citizenship Law, those who were citizens prior to the date when the law came into force remain citizens (section 6). However, the NRCs were not accepted as evidence of Rohingya citizenship despite the fact that they functioned as such. Further, under the current citizenship rules, the burden of proof of citizenship is placed on the individual applicant, not the state authorities. Relaxing evidentiary requirements in the administrative practices relating to citizenship applications in Myanmar, particularly with regard to the recognition of NRCs issued prior to 1982, has been a mainstay of international recommendations relating to the reduction of statelessness in Myanmar (Center for Diversity and National Harmony 2019; Advisory Commission on Rakhine State Aug 2017). Despite this, reluctance and resistance of Rohingya to produce family IDs in front of authorities remained. This was expressed as a continued lack of trust and the lack of any tangible guarantees regarding their safety or citizenship in Myanmar.

> People had to hide their NRCs. So, although many people now in Arakan have NRCs, they cannot produce them before the authorities—they will be confiscated . . . when the Myanmar Minister went to refugee camps, one of the people tried to show his NRC to the Minister. He said, 'No, no, no! This one was issued in Ne Win's era. So, this is not valid anymore.' So, for him the law that was formed in 1982 under Ne Win's era is valid but the citizenship cards issued during his era are not valid.[69]

The personal investments and risks taken in order to hide and secure NRCs and other documents from this period were revealed in the ways in which

Rohingya in the camps in Bangladesh and elsewhere in exile collected, presented, and copied their documents, and asked them to be photographed and recorded by outsiders. During this research, I had conversations with three different professional photographers who had photographed and exhibited on the theme of Rohingya and their documents. Another Rohingya had approached me regarding a museum exhibition on Rohingya identity in which NRCs were a part of the exhibit. During research in New Delhi, towards the end of the interview one Rohingya man asked his mother to bring out a package of old documents including her father's Myanmar passport dated 1954. He told me that he had been afraid to show the documents to anyone before—even to UNHCR on applying for a refugee card.[70] My Rohingya guide afterwards expressed surprise that he had never shown these to people before. The process of feeling able to present and show these documents to others revealed much about both fear of authorities and the significance of IDs as evidence of citizenship status.

IDs and citizenship rights

NRC cards provided access to the same set of rights and benefits available to all other citizens of Burma including free movement throughout the country, access to work in the government sector, entry into the armed forces, political participation, and access to university and professional training. As such they were described in Rohingya narratives as evidence of their citizenship status and as documents from which 'rights flow' (Van Waas 2015), similar to the way IDs predominantly feature in statelessness literature (Oppenheim and Powell 2015; Van Waas 2015; Gelb and Manby 2016; Institute of Statelessness and Inclusion 2018).

> From 1955 in Myanmar, they provided us with this card (showing the NRC card). With this card, we Rohingya received benefits like all other people. This card was given to ALL the citizens the same—they all got one card. We got the same rights, equal rights with other ethnic groups together.[71]

The equal rights and the welfare that were accessible to Rohingya during the era of the NRCs included access to healthcare, education, professional jobs, and government sector jobs including the security sector. Political rights, such as voting and standing for office, were attached to both NRCs and the 'white cards' that were issued in the mid-1990s to Rohingya populations.

The most frequent connection made between ID cards and equal rights with other citizens of Myanmar related to the right to travel freely and to live anywhere within Myanmar until the early 1990s.

> Before the 1990s, there was no difference and no discrimination. I never saw it . . . We could move freely and even my brother brought me to

> Yangon for schooling with a plane on his Burmese ID. I had only my school certificate . . . At the time, there was no racism. There was Rohingya, there was Christian, there was Muslim, all together.[72]

The new ID scheme that began in 1989, in effect, nullified the NRC cards held by Rohingya in Rakhine State. This was followed by an increased number of checkpoints, particularly in northern Rakhine State and other border areas of Myanmar. It was also followed by the mass expulsions of Rohingya to Bangladesh in the early 1990s and then repatriations, as well as the subsequent establishment of the new hybrid border guard forces in northern Rakhine, known as the *NaSaKa*. These forces became notorious for their implementation of restrictions of movement, for developing surveillance and informer systems, and the widespread practices of extortion and human rights abuses (Human Rights Watch 1996; NUI Galway 2010; Fortify Rights 2014).

Despite the new ID scheme, NRCs could still sometimes be utilised to move around and function elsewhere in Myanmar, especially in and around Yangon, but not under the NaSaKa in northern Rakhine.[73]

> I used to have an NRC. I had this registration number here (showed the number). An immigration officer asked to check our ID when I was travelling to Buthidaung. Then he took it away. This was after NaSaKa came to our place. It was very different after they took the NRCs. Every checkpoint they ask for money. When we had the NRCs, we could travel easily. But then we were facing discrimination. After, it was very difficult to travel one section to another.[74]

For many of the participants, freedom of movement within Burma was not within their living memory and many had not travelled far beyond their homes before leaving the country. Their own experiences were framed by the increasing restrictions that came into place from the early 1990s onwards. Those restrictions were described through other documents including white cards and form 4s, which were required to travel to the next town and often restricted their right to education, healthcare, and employment.

> All of these rights have been taken away along with the citizenship cards. The right to freedom of worship and then right to medical access and healthcare. The Myanmar government has taken our rights step by step starting from 1962 until now. When we are sick and we have to get medical treatment, we are not allowed to get there. We cannot get to schools and universities and also if we want to travel to Maungdaw, Buthidaung or Sittwe or Yangon, we are not allowed.[75]

Thus, for younger generations, the NRCs of older relatives were endowed with freedoms and rights. Contrastingly, white cards held from the 1990s onwards held in a system of apartheid (Amnesty International 2017), in which

Rohingya were segregated from other Burmese populations and prevented from living, travelling, and connecting to areas outside of North Rakhine State (Fortify Rights 2014). They were made subject to a separate set of local policies based on tight restrictions and controls, including requiring permission to get married and limiting families to two children (NUI Galway 2010).

IDs without rights

NRCs were almost always spoken about, then, nostalgically as IDs which enabled Rohingya in the past to access equal rights. Citizenship status, as recognised in state-issued IDs in the past, came with a bundle of rights attached. Narratives often turned sharply to provide contrast with citizenship and IDs cards issued under the more recent IDs—white cards (from 1995 until 2015) and NVCs (from 2015 onwards). These IDs were characterised as being devoid of rights but rather held in systems of surveillance and restrictions. 'Green cards,' which were provided to a limited few who had successfully applied for 'naturalised' citizenship were also spoken about in the Rakhine context as cards without rights.[76] At the time of research, NVCs were issued to Rohingya and showed that the holder needed to apply for citizenship.[77] NVCs supposedly enabled Rohingya to access limited rights including freedom of movement between townships in Rakhine. In practice, at best they provided the same very limited rights that had been attached to 'white cards' before they were voided in 2015. This limited set of rights included being allowed to apply for travel permission within Rakhine (form 4s) and enabled them to obtain licenses for work including fishing and trading, and enabled them to travel to markets. One participant explained:

> People from the other side—other countries—they are saying that the NVC card is not meaning rights. The cards do not contain any rights. So why would you take it? Don't take it. NVC and white card are same meaning. Until now, they are not containing rights, so no reason to take it.[78]

However, the NVCs were enforced, as discussed further in Chapter 7, not so much by attaching rights to these cards but by implementing such severe restrictions of basic rights on those who did not hold the cards, that their livelihoods, health, and food security were severely affected.

> As with the white cards, they were saying similar things like, 'this card is compulsory otherwise you cannot go to Maungdaw, you can't go to Buthidaung, you can't go from village to village. In order for you to be able to travel, you must hold this card.' My family said, 'Okay. Even if you don't allow us to travel anywhere, we will die. But we won't accept this card.'[79]

In a very small minority of cases, Rohingya obtained 'green cards' officially called Naturalised Citizenship Scrutiny Cards (NCSCs).[80] Green cards provided them with access to the second tier of citizenship rights, such as freedom of movement and access to education and healthcare, but not all. Working in government jobs, involvement in politics, and land rights, for example, are limited (1982 Law, section 53c). Naturalised citizenship is provided, amongst other criteria, on the basis of ancestral residence prior to Myanmar's independence (1982 Law: section 42) and not on the basis of membership of a group indigenous to Myanmar. For Rohingya, the card carries the stigmatising term 'Bengali.' Further, in practice green cards for Rohingya and Muslims in Rakhine State did not provide access to freedom of movement or other rights.

> That citizenship card is for foreigners. There is Bengali written on it. With other cards, citizens can move freely everywhere, and they can enjoy the government facilities. They can enjoy the government jobs. But these Rohingya cannot enjoy these things.[81]

Officially, citizenship cards enabled movement. Nonetheless, restrictions of movement remained in place for Muslim populations in Rakhine, including for those from *taingyintha,* such as Kaman from the area affected by the 2012–3 violence.[82] Restrictions resulted both from curfews, martial law and local policies relating to the containment of displaced populations and those within the townships of North Rakhine State. They also resulted from the broader security and safety concerns of the bearers relating to the campaigns and hostility of local non-Muslim populations to the issue of citizenship for Muslims. These factors combined to mean that in practical terms, rights did not flow from citizenship cards or citizenship status. In narratives, this was often contrasted with the NRCs from which rights flowed. For example, 'If you pass the national verification, you take the citizenship card, but still your situation is the same like other people who are not citizens.'[83]

> Even the local Rakhine people protest against those citizenship cards for the Rohingya. Those with cards live in the same conditions. Even he got the citizenship card, there is no change to his conditions. He is just the same like others. It is just to show the foreigner and show the Rohingya that they are providing the citizenship card. But now we can realise that still they have a dirty mind.[84]

NRCs and other IDs during the early decades of independence, then, were understood in similar ways to classic notions of ID cards from within citizenship and statelessness studies to be the material objects of law that provide citizenship status plus access to a bundle of rights. Within the research, one of the narrative purposes of NRCs was to contrast with later ID cards such as white cards, NVCs, and green cards which were understood as ID cards from which rights did not flow.[85] The negative impacts of the new cards including stigmatisation, 'locking-in' statelessness (Manby 2018), and identity destruction, then, were understood to vastly outweigh their benefits. This contrasted with the ways in which NRCs and IDs of the past were understood to be endowed with rights. Rohingya narratives drew on these respective differences between the NRCs and NVCs.

IDs and citizenship identity

State-issued IDs are often linked in statelessness literature to the third component of the trinity of citizenship—belonging or identity. IDs are understood to lend an individual along with status and access to rights, a sense of belonging to a national community. In turn, the possession of a state-issued ID enables an individual to be accepted as a member of the broader national community (Yuval-Davis 2006). Rohingya participants also spoke about their past IDs in the context of their national and group identities—of belonging and social acceptance into the national fold.

The main intersecting group identities spoken about in the narratives were Burmese/Myanmar, referring to a multi-ethnic, multi-religious national identity; Arakan/Rakhine Muslim, referring to an identity that denoted both religion and belonging to the lands of Arakan/Rakhine; and Rohingya, referring to an identity that is ethnolinguistic, and denotes a belonging to lands of the historic region known as Rohang/Rakhine/Arakan. Both Arakan/Rakhine Muslim and Rohingya as group identities were in themselves inextricable from claims to Burmese identity and citizenship, since they were rooted in notions of belonging to the lands/region of Rakhine now incorporated within the boundaries of Myanmar. These ethnic and religious identities were, for the most part, spoken about not in opposition to Burmese national identities but rather as claims to a broader Burmese national identity. Where acts of resistance to ID schemes occurred, they were described as resistance to the military and ruling elite projects—not based in opposition to national belonging.[86]

For the majority of participants, individual Rohingya who held citizenship IDs in the past held a significance that reached beyond the status claims of that individual and their descendants. These IDs were of historic significance to Rohingya as a group belonging to Myanmar.

> The reason that I am keeping this document especially, is because the *NaSaKa* took Rohingya documents away. It is important for us to keep these kinds of important historical documents.[87]

This was reflected in the acts of collecting IDs both in digital form and in files in the Bangladesh refugee camps. They were collected by Rohingya organisations[88] as records of Rohingya group belonging to show to other Rohingya in the camp, so that they could learn about their own history. They were also used to show or exhibit to visitors to the camps, as artefacts of Rohingya national identity in Burma.[89] In one office in the camp, I was presented with ancestral documents from five individual participants, as well as five ring binders full of photo copies of various different ID documents, all of which told a collective story of Rohingya group identity in Burma and the slow production of statelessness. These collections were discussed and emphatically referred to as a group record of belonging.

> *Participant 1:* 'These documents are collected together for records . . . All are Rohingya -collected from people in the camp.'
> *Participant 2:* 'They show everything. Rohingya, Religion. Everything. We are collecting everything so we can show our citizenship.'90

As such, the copies of ID documents and registration documents from the past became the artefacts of a shared group history and identity. These different IDs, registration documents and forms that had been collected by Rohingya groups in the camps to exhibit to both Rohingya and foreigners connected different religious, ethnic, and national aspects of Rohingya identities. Based on these collections, some types of documents were of particular note, as outlined later.

As noted throughout this chapter, copies of NRCs that had been collected and filed were talked about as evidence that community members were part of a collective Burmese national identity. For example:

> My father and mother also had them. 90% of Rohingya had their NRC cards in the past. We are not foreigners. We are Burmese.[91]

Since NRCs from the period did not contain ethnic or religious markers, they were used to evidence a direct link between members of the camp and refugee communities and their national identity as Burmese.

Family lists or household registration cards from prior to the 1990s were collected and spoken about in three ways. First, the reference numbers of NRCs were recorded on the family cards and were used to plot when Rohingya were stripped of their Burmese identity. These records showed inter-generationally when the targeted non-issuance of national ID cards began. Since older household members had their ID numbers recorded and younger ones did not, they showed that the issuance of national IDs slowed down from the 1970s and had stopped by the 1980s.

Second, family lists issued or altered by state authorities after the *NaSaKa* forces were deployed in North Rakhine State in the mid-1990s were compared with family lists from before this period. Reference to the *NaSaKa* was important because these hybrid forces were established and deployed specifically to control Rohingya populations of North Rakhine State and implemented a specific set of local restrictions and policies that targeted Rohingya populations (NUI Galway 2010; Amnesty International 2017). Comparison of family lists was used to plot the time period when the term 'Bengali' was imposed on Rohingya populations. Family cards from before the *NaSaKa* period recorded the biodata of individuals in the 'ethnic nationality' column as 'Muslim' or sometimes 'Rohingya.' A separate column for religion carried the term 'Islam.'[92] Later family lists, issued from the mid-1990s onwards, categorised the same household members under the ethnic category of 'Bengali' and the religious category of 'Islam.' Narratives that described these documents explained the recategorization.

> They removed Rakhine Muslim and replaced it with Bengali. After the repatriations, they started changing it . . . . It was for all the families. From NaSaKa time. That time they started taking the group photo. Due to group photo, they asked us to bring all the documents of the family. Then the government said that there were some documents with Rohingya or nationality Muslim on. So that time they took it off. The old documents were banned. Then, newly, they provided the documents where they used the term Bengali. Systematically they took away all our documents. Fortunately, we managed to save our documents. Otherwise, most families have returned them.[93]

As such, taken as a collection the family lists showed how the term 'Bengali' was imposed through the *NaSaKa*. Whilst the replacement of the terms 'Rohingya' and 'Muslim' with the term 'Bengali' was not official policy, the acts of reclassification and recategorisation were attributable within the narratives to the state rather than to the discretion of individual officers.

> Muslim was changed to Bengali on our documents by the inquiry team. They were from different departments—military, security forces, immigration, civilian. They told us that this is the order from the top.[94]

The third way in which the family cards were discussed also related to the changes that occurred under the *NaSaKa*. The *NaSaKa* was understood to have been established as a response to the mass repatriations from Bangladesh to North Rakhine State during 1993–4. New systems of surveillance and extortion were brought in during this period. More regular house-to-house checks were carried out, as well as surprise checks, using the family list to check for absences and additions to the household. The *NaSaKa* began photographing each family outside house. In the narratives, these photographs marked the move from the family cards as a useful proof of identity and residence to a state technology of surveillance and intrusion.[95] The family cards and associated photographs in narratives became the basis for extortion and arbitrary arrest.[96] Officers could strike people off the family list if they were not present at the time of household inspection. Since the family lists were primary proof of residency in Burma/Myanmar, such acts effectively cancelled residency. This meant that people who were crossed off had no right to remain or right to return to Burma/Myanmar. Crossings out and deletions were marked in pen by the civilian/security inspection team on the family lists. They also carried related remarks made by the officer. As such, participants were able to describe the moment at which family members were 'struck off' the family list during household inspections or effectively had the right to reside in Myanmar removed. For example, one participant explained how his brother was struck off the list whilst in hospital for an operation in Bangladesh. He never returned to Myanmar.[97] The photographs of the house and family were also often referred to in relation to concerns about Myanmar's attempts to collect biometric data or obtain biometric data from Bangladesh/UNHCR records of refugees.[98]

Other documents kept as part of the group collections which were used to evidence Rohingya identity were 'Form 2s,' which were the application forms filled in for citizenship cards that were to replace the NRCs. Applications began in 1989. Some copies of these application forms filled out by Rohingya were kept as part of group collections of documents.[99] These forms were submitted using the term 'Rohingya' and recorded family trees going back generations. As such, they were used as evidence of Rohingya identity as part of the broader Burmese national identity. Rohingya participants also kept records of the registration 'receipt' documents issued to Rohingya refugees returning from Bangladesh in 1978–9. Some of the documents recorded individuals as 'Rohingya.'[100] These documents were issued by Bangladesh and became the basis on which individuals were accepted back to Myanmar. They were, accordingly, used to show how Rohingya identity was accepted and recognised by both states (Bangladesh and Myanmar) in the past.

> When people were repatriated from Bangladesh, they issued this repatriation form at the reception centre—there also a lot of people were identified as a Rohingya.[101]
>
> In 1978, we couldn't take any documents. My father was the secretary of village, under the chairman during the repatriations to our village. So, on the repatriation papers, they mentioned 'Rohingya.' We were listed as Rohingya.[102]

These repatriation documents were also used to contrast the ways in which they were, at the time of research, categorised on their refugee documents issued by the Bangladesh government/UNHCR. They were categorised as 'Forcibly Displaced Myanmar Nationals (FDMN)' without any mention of Rohingya ethnicity.[103] This was a source of concern and anxiety since the refugee cards were viewed not simply as providing access to protections and services in the camps but also as an identity document that may be used in relation to future returns, future identity recognition, and citizenship (see also Brinham 2018).[104]

Whilst white cards, as noted in this chapter, were most often associated with repression, they were also sometimes used to evidence the increasing imposition of the term Bengali as part of a slow process driven by unofficial and 'hidden' policies (Fortify Rights 2014; Fortify Rights 2019). In the first few years of issuance in 1994–5, many Rohingya were issued white cards which designated them as 'Muslim.' In the years that followed, this was changed to 'Bengali.'

> On the white cards, in the column of the race, they put Bengali by force even if we do not agree to it. All the cards issued later in the 1990s—everyone used Bengali but not in the early stages of issuing white cards.[105]

The practice of recording people as Bengali despite the ways in which they self-identified began in NRS and spread to other areas of Rakhine including Sittwe/Akyab and in the southern areas of Rakhine (Kyaw Phyu and Kyaw Taw).[106] The term 'Bengali' was also imposed on some people of Muslim or mixed-ethnic heritage across Myanmar. The manner in which this has been imposed elsewhere is arbitrary and depends on the township office and the discretion of the individual officers (de Chickera, Arraiza et al. 2021).

After the changes in the ID scheme in 1989, ethnic identifiers were recorded on all citizenship and ID cards, further cementing the significance of ethnicity in national identity and social relations (Nyi Nyi Kyaw 2015; Cheesman 2017; Nyi Nyi Kyaw 2017). As Tilly pointed out, identity is always constructed in relation to dominant groups and often in resistance to domination (Tilly 1995). 'Rohingya' as a more salient ethnic identity than the broader religious identity of 'Muslim' was explained in focus groups as a response to the state's reclassification of the community as 'Bengali.' This they related back to the white cards.

> Rohingya people used to refer to themselves as Muslim because they are not much concerned with what is Muslim and what is Rohingya. So sometimes they used Rohingya and sometimes not. So, if you ask them, 'who are you?' They will answer, 'we are Muslim Arakanese.'[107]
>
> In the beginning of the white card, they used Muslim –nationality Muslim. For two years, they mentioned Muslim on that card. After 1996–7, they started using the term Bengali. Then people started to refuse it. Then they started a new thing—in the villages, if there is no white card in their hand, no one is allowed to get married. If there

> is no white card, they will not be allowed to move or travel in Buthidaung, Maungdaw. If there is no white card, he will not be able to apply to for the job anywhere.[108]

Rohingya understandings of the use of white cards to socially sort people according to an ethnic and citizenship hierarchy reflect some of the critical work from within statelessness studies that not only view ID cards as the harbingers of individual rights but rather associate them with processes of social and racial sorting and the reification of group identities (Balaton-Chrimes 2014; Reddy 2015).

The collecting and sharing of histories about state-issued IDs and registration documents, then, revealed how documents of the past represented shared ethnic, religious, and national identities. Within ID narratives, it was the identity aspect of the trinity of citizenship that featured most prominently. The acts of collating IDs were a form of resistance to identity erasure. The value of state-issued documents from the past in terms of identity revival renewal outweighed their significance as legal documents. Such IDs were often contrasted with the IDs issued since the 1990s. As Chapter 6 explores, white cards issued from 1995 to 2015, and NVCs issued from 2015 onwards, were not simply IDs devoid of national identity. They were IDs that erased and destroyed Rohingya as a group belonging to Rakhine, Myanmar.

Conclusion

This chapter has explored how Rohingya narratives underlined the state's embrace of the first decades of independence. They highlighted how both individual citizenship and state recognition of Rohingya as a group belonging to Myanmar were experienced and enacted. Rohingya participants understood that from the citizenship status provided by IDs during this period, rights and welfare flowed, as well as belonging and national identity. In this way, state-issued IDs from prior to military rule functioned as the harbingers of inclusive citizenship, reflecting the notions inherent in the literature and international policy documents explored in Chapter 3.[109]

IDs associated with citizenship status were treasured and preserved, sometimes in the hope they could be used in the future to prove individual citizenship status. IDs belonging to Rohingya were also collated, recorded, and exhibited to demonstrate Rohingya identity as a group belonging to post-independence Myanmar and to resist identity destruction and erasure. Identity maintenance, renewal, and revival are important acts of resistance and survival in communities that have been colonised or 'damaged' by state entities (Vizenor 1994, 2008). Such acts of resistance and survival have been central to Rohingya activism since the events of 2017 (Brinham and Cowper-Smith 2019; Cowper-smith 2019).

Rohingya narratives from this research also focused on IDs of the early independence era to draw attention to, and provide evidence of, later crimes perpetrated by the state including citizenship stripping and persecution targeting the Rohingya as a group. The equalising and emancipatory functions of state-issued IDs issued prior to 1989 were often juxtaposed with the repressive and destructive properties of IDs issued after this time. ID and registration schemes brought in after 1989 were understood to be void of status, rights, and identity. Rather they were understood to lock in restrictions and deny rights and identities. As the following chapter will explore, they were also understood to destroy Rohingya identity as a group belonging to Rakhine and re-categorise them as an ethnic and national 'other.' These repressive and destructive properties of IDs highlighted in Rohingya narratives sat in contrast with the function of state IDs and registration as pathways towards citizenship assumed within the approaches to reducing statelessness that by-passed state power and associated statelessness with invisibility (see Chapter 3). Rather Rohingya ID narratives described Myanmar's IDs as setting them on a trajectory away from citizenship towards statelessness. The repressive and destructive aspects of state registration and IDs contained in Rohingya narratives were closer to those explored in academic literature on state-building that describe how states legitimise and maintain power through their bureaucracies and ID schemes (Scott 1998; Torpey 2000; Caplan and Torpey 2001; Scott, Tehranian et al. 2002).

The dangers associated with ID schemes also informed the way that Rohingya understood their futures. Amongst their consistent demands regarding return to Myanmar from Bangladesh were citizenship and recognition of their ethnic identity.[110] As such, IDs without full citizenship status, rights, and identity were overwhelmingly rejected and, as the next chapter explains, formed one of the main focal points for group resistance to the central state.

Notes

1 The parliamentary period was for the most part under the leadership of Nu, with a nine-month interim under Ba Swe (Jun 1956–Mar 1957). Furthermore, there was a 'caretaker period' in Oct 1958–Apr 1960 in which the military took control to 'restore order' under Ne Win. In Mar 1962, Ne Win and the Burma Socialist Programme Party (BSPP) took over in a military coup.

2 Ne Win was chairman of the BSPP and served as *de facto* leader under various official titles until 1988.

3 Numbers were disputed between Myanmar and Bangladesh. For UNHCR figures, see Crisp (2018).

4 SLORC (State Law and Order Restoration Council) was reorganised in 1997 and rebranded the State Peace and Development Council (SPDC).

5 In35, 02/08/2018, Chittagong. The 'blank cheque' refers to citizenship and rights (ascertained in further conversation). On the 'blank cheque' speech, see Siddique (2012). This strategic approach is also backed up by the Raschid correspondence referred to in Chapter 4.

6 One participant was present at the surrender ceremony. In33, 30/07/2018, Teknaf.
7 Kyaw Win, Mya Han and Thein Hlaing (1991).
8 On 15 Nov 1961, Brigadier Aung Gyi, Deputy Chief of Staff for the Army, delivered an address at the ceremony of the Mujahadin Surrender explaining that many of the ethnic groups of Myanmar lived on both sides of the national borders, such as the Karen and the Shan, and the Rohingya were one such group. He urged that within Myanmar they be treated as 'close relatives.' This was recorded in the official publications of the Ministry of Defence as 'The future of Mayyu' and 'The second Mujahidin surrender ceremony.'
9 Fg5, 28/04/2018. Additionally, correspondence on file.
10 Fg3, 23/04/2018, Kuala Lumpur.
11 Marks the day on which the Panglong agreement was signed on 12 Feb 1947, which unified multiple ethnic nationalities and territories, which became Burma.
12 Referring to Operation Jasmine of 1974, when Rohingya NRCs were removed and Operation *Nagamin,* which was the citizenship scrutiny operation generally referred to as the first mass expulsion.
13 In65, 26/06/2019, The Hague.
14 For more information and sources for similar references, see Nay San Lwin (2012)
15 Fg2–6 (2018, KL and Bangladesh), In64&65, 26/06/2018, The Hague; In34&35, 02/08/2018, Chittagong.
16 In64 & In65, 26/06/2019 The Hague.
17 Fg2, 22/04/2018, Kuala Lumpur; Fg5, 28/04,2018, Kuala Lumpur.
18 E.g. Fg5, 28/04/2018, Kuala Lumpur.
19 In65, 26/06/2019, The Hague.
20 In32, 28/07/2018, Balukhali.
21 Served as Minister for Health and Education under Nu.
22 Served as a parliamentary secretary under Nu. In65, 26/06/2019, The Hague.
23 For a complete list of Rohingya MPs as well as the ways in which Rohingya were recognised by the state, see Nay San Lwin (2012).
24 In40, 24/09/2018. Balukhali. This extract relates to the 2008 vote on the constitution. At this time, Rohingya had Temporary Registration Cards (TRCs) or 'white cards,' which many hoped would be replaced with full citizenship cards after military rule.
25 See notes from the Jan 1947 negotiations between the British and Burmese delegations. Original notes contained in Tinker, Griffin et al. (1984).
26 Narratives mentioned eight relatives who had served in the police and nine relatives who had served in the army or the navy. Some Rohingya families specialised inter-generationally in the security sector, thus some interviewees referred to multiple family members serving in the forces. Two Rohingya participants said they had themselves served in the army. Another two had spent time with different family members who were in the security forces in Yangon and Kachin State during the 1980s before their own movement as Rohingya was restricted within the country. There were mentions of at least two Rohingya still serving in the police. Fg1, 13/08/2017, New Delhi & Fg4, 27/04/2018, Kuala Lumpur.
27 In56 & In57, 03/10/2018, Delhi. In64, 26/06/2019, The Hague.
28 The recruitment of Rohingya slowed down during the Ne Win period but continued—albeit in small numbers—into the 1980s Fg4, 17/04/2018, Kuala Lumpur. In40, 24/09/2018, Balukhali. In64, 26/06/2019, The Hague.
29 In42, 28/09/2018, Balukhali.
30 Fg6 &fg7 26/08/2018, Kutapalong.
31 Four participants emphasised that they either worked or had relatives who worked in the civil service or township administration; ten in government schools;

two in government hospitals; one as a lawyer and three working in the export trade which required government licensing. Often extended families specialised in particular jobs or economic roles across generations. Teaching in particular applied intergenerationally to certain families.

32 Fg6, 26/08/2018, Kutapalong.

33 Fg1, 13/08/2017, New Delhi. NB. This was a few weeks prior to the violence of 2017 when his sister was still in post.

34 These were sometimes also referred to as 'threefold' cards, or by the first letters of the issue numbers, e.g. 'AK card.' In53, 27/09/2018, extension 4 camp.

35 They were issued under the 1949 Residents of Burma Registration Act and the 1951 Residents Burma Registration Rules. Although no longer issued, NRCs elsewhere in Burma/Myanmar outside of north Rakhine continued to be used as a form of ID providing access to rights and services for those who had been unable to obtain citizenship cards under the colour-coded scheme until today. See de Chickera, Arraiza et al. (2021).

36 These were predominantly first the Temporary Registration Cards (TRCs) or 'white cards' that were largely issued between 1995 and 2015, associated with restrictions of movement, state surveillance, apartheid, and oppression; and National Verification Cards (NVCs), associated with identity destruction and genocide (see Chapter 7).

37 Fg6, 26/07/2018, Kutapalong.

38 Fg6, 26/07/2018, Kutapalong.

39 In61, 23/10/2018, Kuala Lumpur.

40 The 1948 Universal Declaration of Human Rights Article 15(2) prohibits against the arbitrary deprivation of citizenship, 'No one shall be arbitrarily deprived of his nationality nor denied the right to change his nationality.' The Right to Nationality is considered a fundamental human right.

41 Most Rohingya have also been unable to secure Bangladesh citizenship. Although the citizenship laws in Bangladesh have *jus soli* and naturalisation provisions, in practice, Rohingya born in Bangladesh or married to Bangladeshis have been excluded from citizenship through civil documentation procedures (Hoque 2016). However, it is important to note that the overwhelming thrust of the narratives in this research was of Rohingya claiming their right to citizenship in Myanmar, not the countries into which they were displaced.

42 Fg6, 26/07/2018, Kutapalong. The last sentence was in the context of activism and resistance relating to the 'secret' negotiations of an MOU between Myanmar, Bangladesh, UNHCR and UNDP relating to repatriations and the issuance of UNHCR/GoB 'smart cards' to replace the cards issued by the GoB/IOM. See Zarni and Brinham (Jun 2019).

43 In47, 26/09/2019, camp 14.

44 For example, the speeches of Rohingya activists during the World Conference on Statelessness, the Hague, 26 Jun 2018.

45 In40 24/09/2018, Balukhali; In49, 26/09/2018, camp 14.

46 Copy of letter on file. In64, 26/06/2019, The Hague.

47 In a limited number of cases, it had been possible for Rohingya to obtain 'naturalised citizenship,' sometimes known as 'Bengali' citizenship since it required them to register under Bengali ethnicity. This application process required excessive documentary evidence including the original NRCs of all grandparents and parents. Many Rohingya feared disclosing the existence of these IDs to Myanmar State authorities based on past experiences lest they be confiscated or destroyed.

48 These practices were the subject of discussion in five focus groups and 31 interviews.

49 Section 20 of the 1982 Citizenship Law stipulates that cancelled IDs must be surrendered to the Ministry of Home Affairs and failure to return cancelled IDs

including for deceased persons shall be liable to imprisonment for a term of ten years and to a fine. This was included supposedly to deal with the potential for IDs to be fraudulently transferred to other persons but amongst Rohingya effectively criminalised the saving of evidence required for citizenship applications (which require evidence of parents' and grandparents' citizenship).

50 Rule of Law was discussed in this focus group within the eight principles outlined by Bingham. These relate to the core principle of the rule of law, 'that all persons and authorities within the state, whether public or private, should be bound by and entitled to the benefit of laws publicly and prospectively promulgated and publicly administered in the courts.' Bingham, T. (2011). The Rule of Law.
51 Fg1, 13/08/2017, New Delhi.
52 In65, 26/06/2019, The Hague.
53 In64, 26/06/2019, The Hague.
54 Fg5, 28/04/2018, Kuala Lumpur.
55 One of the collections of photocopied documents provided to me by Rohingya sources for research purposes was a collation of international and Bangladeshi newspaper articles from the aftermath of Operation *Nagamin* in 1978. They included investigative reports using the terms such as 'terror,' 'mass rape,' and 'apartheid.'
56 In42, 24/09/2018, Balukhali.
57 In43, 25/09/2018, Jolatoli.
58 In41, 24/09/2018, Balukhali.
59 In53, 27/09/2018, extension 4.
60 e.g. In24, 26/07/2018, Teknaf; In56, 03/10/2018, Kharjurikhaas; New Delhi; In45, 26/09/2018, Hakimpara.
61 In40, 24/09/2018, Balukhali.
62 In53, 27/09/2018, extension 4.
63 In18, 27/04/2018, Kuala Lumpur.
64 In50, 27/09/2018, extention 4 camp.
65 In40, 24/09/2018, Balukhali.
66 Fg4, 27/04/2018, Kuala Lumpur.
67 Fg6, 26/07/2018, Kutapalong.
68 In21, 29/06/2018, WhatsApp from Melbourne.
69 Fg3, 23/04/2018, Kuala Lumpur.
70 In57, 03/10/2018, Kharjurikhaas, New Delhi.
71 Fg6, 26/07/2018, Kutapalong.
72 In40, 24/09/2018, Balukhali
73 Fg4, 27/04/2018, Kuala Lumpur.
74 In45, 26/09/2018, Hakimpari.
75 F5, 28/04/2018, Kuala Lumpur.
76 Naturalised citizenship required applicants to have a long list of documentary evidence. The requirements were different depending on the office and the officer in charge but always included NRCs of all parents and grandparents. They also required excessive 'unofficial fees' or bribery, which was prohibitive to most. On arbitrary decision-making, for abuse of discretion and bribery, see de Chickera, Arraiza et al. (2021).
77 NVCs originally carried the term 'Bengali.' This term from 2016 was omitted. Nonetheless, many Rohingya referred to concerns about the term Bengali being 'written behind the card' (Fg7, 26/07/2018, Kutapalong).
78 In14, 25/04/2018, Kuala Lumpur.
79 Fg5, 28/04/2018, Kuala Lumpur.
80 No Rohingya with green cards were interviewed for this research. Testimonies from those who had green cards are available in de Chickera, Arraiza et al. (2021).
81 In40, 24/09/2018, Balukhali.

82 In62 & In63, 25/04/2018, Kuala Lumpur.
83 In45, 26/09/2018, Hakimpara.
84 In40, 24/09/2018, Balukhali.
85 Some statelessness literature has highlighted how discrimination can remain even after citizenship status is provided to stateless persons. See Blitz and Lynch (2011).
86 For example, on the first anniversary of the Aug 2017 atrocities, Rohingya in the refugee camps in Bangladesh demonstrated en masse, showing their connections to Myanmar and their desire to return given the right conditions. Rohingya youth gathered in the open spaces in the camps, dressed in Myanmar school uniform, and waved small Myanmar flags.
87 In53, 27/09/2018, extension 4.
88 Including but not limited to: Arakan Society for Peace and Human Rights (ASPHR).
89 These collections were not only shown to me but also shown to other researchers.
90 Fg7, 26/08/2018, Kutapalong.
91 Fg6, 26/08/2018, Kutapalong.
92 This also showed how religious and ethnic identities were conflated in state categorisations in independent Burma, just as they had been in the colonial era when Rohingya were categorised as ethnically 'Mussalman' or Muslim (see Chapter 4).
93 In40, 24/09/2018, Balukhali.
94 In43, 25/09/2018, Jamtoli.
95 In40, 24/09/2018, Balukhali, In30 &31, 28/07/2018, Balukhali.
96 There were 48 references to separate incidences of extortion associated with IDs and registration documents in the fieldwork data. Further, references to oppressive state surveillance and securitisation occurred throughout.
97 In30, 28/07/2018, Balukhali.
98 Fg6,7,8&9, Jul–Oct 2018, Kutapalong, Hakimpara & New Delhi.
99 Provided to me during Fg7, 26/07/2018. Copies on file.
100 As with many documents from the period, the way in which people were recorded was not always consistent and varied with the time period, individual self-identification, and the individual issuing officers involved.
101 In65, 26/06/2019, The Hague.
102 In43, 25/09/2018, Jolatoli.
103 Some of the earliest refugee registration cards issued in the first few months after the Aug 2017 exodus stated 'FDNM (Rohingya).' Copies of cards on file. Rohingya was later removed. This was assumed in Rohingya narratives to be an act of appeasement by the Bangladesh government to the Myanmar government in hope of early repatriation agreements.
104 It should be noted as a principle of non-discrimination, good practice in international agencies to omit ethnic markers on ID cards. Often noted in this regard is the Rwandan genocide in which ethnic markers on ID cards identified victims to the perpetrators. See Longman, T. (2001).
105 Fg5, 28/04/2018, Kuala Lumpur.
106 In21, 29/06/2018, skype from Melbourne.
107 Fg5, 28/04/2018, Kuala Lumpur.
108 In43, 25/09/2018, 25/09/2018, Jolatoli.
109 See also Oppenheim and Powell (2015), van Waas (2015), Gelb and Manby (2016), Manby (2018).
110 Fg6&7, 26/07/2018, Kutapalong. Banners covering the walls of the office used for these focus groups included repatriation demands. They included safety and security, return direct to their lands, and citizenship and ethnic recognition. These three focuses were repeated consistently across all the focus groups and interviews.

Bibliography

Abrar, C. R. (1995). Repatriation of Rohingya Refugees. *UNHCR's Regional Consultation on Refugee and Migratory Movements, Colombo.*

Advisory Commission on Rakhine State (Aug 2017). *Towards a Peaceful, Fair and Prosperous Future for the People of Rakhine: Final Report.* www.rakhinecommission.org/app/uploads/2017/08/FinalReport_Eng.pdf [Accessed 05/06/2018]

Ahmad, S. U. (2009). Rohingya Members of Parliament in Burma. *Arakan Monthly.*

Amnesty International (2017). *Caged without a Roof: Apartheid in Myanmar's Rakhine State.* www.amnesty.org/en/documents/asa16/7484/2017/en/ [Accessed 02/12/2018]

Arraiza, J. M. and O. Vonk (2017). Report on Citizenship Law: Myanmar. *GlobalCit 14, European University Institute.* https://cadmus.eui.eu/bitstream/handle/1814/48284/RSCAS_GLOBALCIT_CR_2017_14.pdf?sequence=1&isAllowed=y [Accessed 05/06/2019]

Aung Gyi (Brigadier) (15 Nov 1961). The Future of May Yu: Address at the Ceremony of the Mujahadin Surrender Ceremony. Ministry of Defence: The Burmese Language Transcript is Available in, Special Issue on May Yu, Current Affairs (or Khit Yay), Ministry of Defence, the Union of Burma, 12(6).

Balaton-Chrimes, S. (2014). Statelessness, Identity Cards and Citizenship as Status in the Case of the Nubians of Kenya. *Citizenship Studies* 18(1): 15–28.

Bingham, T. (2011). *The Rule of Law.* Penguin UK.

Blitz, B. K. and M. Lynch (2011). *Statelessness and Citizenship: A Comparative Study on the Benefits of Nationality.* Edward Elgar.

Brinham, N. (2018). 'Genocide Cards': Rohingya Refugees on Why They Risked Their Lives to Refuse ID Cards. *OpenDemocracy.* www.opendemocracy.net/natalie-brinham/genocide-cards-why-rohingya-refugees-are-resisting-id-cards [Accessed 30/01/2019]

Brinham, N. and Y. Cowper-Smith (2019). Rohingya Poets Turn Words into Art of Resistance. *Anadolu Agency.* www.aa.com.tr/en/asia-pacific/rohingya-poets-turn-words-into-art-of-resistance-/1551737 [Accessed 02/10/2019]

Caplan, J. and J. C. Torpey (2001). *Documenting Individual Identity: The Development of State Practices in the Modern World.* Princeton University Press.

Center for Diversity and National Harmony (2019). *Myanmar's Citizenship Law: An Analysis.* www.cdnh.org/publication/myanmars-citizenship-law-an-analysis/ [Accessed 08/10/2019]

Cheesman, N. (2017). How in Myanmar 'National Races' Came to Surpass Citizenship and Exclude Rohingya. *Journal of Contemporary Asia* 47(3): 461–483.

Chhotray, V. and F. McConnell (2018). *Certifications of Citizenship: The History, Politics and Materiality of Identity Documents in South Asian States and Diasporas.* Taylor & Francis.

Cowley, A. and M. Zarni (2017). An Evolution of Rohingya Persecution in Myanmar: From Strategic Embrace to Genocide. *Middle East Institute.* www.mei.edu/publications/evolution-rohingya-persecution-myanmar-strategic-embrace-genocide [Accessed 22/05/2017]

Cowper-smith, Y. (2019). The Global Rohingya Diaspora Throws Lifelines to Bangladesh and Myanmar. *The Conversation.* http://theconversation.com/the-global-rohingya-diaspora-throws-lifelines-to-bangladesh-and-myanmar-117881 [Accessed 14/10/2019]

Crisp, J. (2018). 'Primitive People': The Untold Story of UNHCR's Historical Engagement with Rohingya Refugees. *Humanitarian Exchange, Humanitarian Practice Network.* 732018. https://odihpn.org/magazine/primitive-people-the-untold-story-of-unhcrs-historical-engagement-with-rohingya-refugees/ [Accessed 17/12/2018] de Chickera, A., J. Arraiza, Z. Albarazi, G. Field and N. Brinham (2021). *Navigating with a Faulty Map: Access to Citizenship Documents and Citizenship in Myanmar, Institute on Statelessness and Inclusion*. https://files.institutesi.org/Access_to_Citizenship_in_Myanmar_Report.pdf [Accessed 28/12/2021]

Ealom, J. (2021). *Escape from Manus: The Untold True Story*. Penguin Viking.

European Network on Statelessness & Institute on Statelessness and Inclusion (2019). *Statelessness in Myanmar: Country Position Paper*. https://statelessjourneys.org/wp-content/uploads/StatelessJourneys-Myanmar-final.pdf [Accessed 11/11/2019]

Fortify Rights (2014). *Policies of Persecution: Ending Abusive State Policies Against Rohingya Muslims in Myanmar*. https://fortifyrights.org/downloads/Policies_of_Persecution_Feb_25_Fortify_Rights.pdf [Accessed 03/05/2017]

Fortify Rights (2019). *'Tools of Genocide': National Verification Cards and the Denial of Citizenship of Rohingya Muslims in Myanmar*. www.fortifyrights.org/downloads/Tools%20of%20Genocide%20-%20Fortify%20Rights%20-%20September-03-2019-EN.pdf [Accessed 08/10/2019]

Gelb, A. and B. Manby (2016). Has Development Converged with Human Rights? Implications for the Legal Identity SDG. *Center for Global Development*. www.cgdev.org/blog/has-development-converged-human-rights-implications-legal-identity-sdg [Accessed 17/12/2018]

Goldston, J. A. (2006). Holes in the Rights Framework: Racial Discrimination, Citizenship, and the Rights of Noncitizens. *Ethics and International Affairs* 20(3): 321–347.

Hoag, C. (2011). Assembling Partial Perspectives: Thoughts on the Anthropology of Bureaucracy. *PoLAR: Political and Legal Anthropology Review* 34(1): 81–94.

Hoque, R. (2016). Report on Citizenship Law: Bangladesh, Globalcit 14 European University Institute. https://cadmus.eui.eu/bitstream/handle/1814/44545/EudoCit_2016_14Bangladesh.pdf [Accessed 29/08/2024]

Hull, M. S. (2012). Documents and Bureaucracy. *Annual Review of Anthropology* 41: 251–267.

Human Rights Watch (1996). *The Rohingya Muslims: Ending a Cycle of Exodus?* www.hrw.org/reports/pdfs/b/burma/burma969.pdf [Accessed 21/10/2018]

Institute of Statelessness and Inclusion (2018). *Paperless People Podcast 2: The Legal Identity Dilemma*. www.institutesi.org/forum/podcasts.php [Accessed 10/05/2020]

International Commission of Jurists (2019). *Citizenship and Human Rights in Myanmar: Why Law Reform is Urgent and Possible*. www.icj.org/wp-content/uploads/2019/06/Myanmar-Citizenship-law-reform-Advocacy-Analysis-Brief-2019-ENG.pdf [Accessed 03/04/2020]

Joppke, C. (2007). Transformation of Citizenship: Status, Rights, Identity. *Citizenship Studies* 11(1): 37–48.

Kenny, C. (2020). Legislated Out of Existence: Mass Arbitrary Deprivation of Nationality Resulting in Statelessness as an International Crime. *International Criminal Law Review* 20(6): 1026–1067.

Kingston, L. N. (2017). Worthy of Rights: Statelessness as a Cause and Symptom of Marginalisation, in Bloom, T., Tonkiss, K. and Cole, P. (eds), *Understanding Statelessness*. Routledge. 17–34.

Kyaw Win, Mya Han and Thein Hlaing (1991). *Myanmar Naing Ngan Yay (Burma's Politics)*. Volume 3 (years 1958–1962), republished in Universities Press.

Latour, B. (1999). On Recalling ANT. *The Sociological Review* 47(1): 15–25.

Latour, B. (2005). *Reassembling the Social: An Introduction to Actor-Network-Theory*. Oxford University Press.

Linquist, A. (1979). Report on the 1978–79 Bangladesh Refugee Relief Operation. *UNHCR*. www.burmalibrary.org/en/docs/LINDQUIST_REPORT.htm [Accessed 28/12/2018]

Longman, T. (2001). Identity Cards, Ethnic Self-Perception, and Genocide in Rwanda, in Caplan, J. and Torpey, J. (eds), *Documenting Individual Identity: The Development of State Practices in the Modern World*. Princeton University Press.

Lyon, D. and Bennett, C. J. (2008). Playing the Identity Card: Understanding the Significance of Identity Card Systems, in Bennet, C. J. and Lyon, D. (eds), *Playing the Identity Card: Surveillance and Identification in Global Perspective*. Routledge.

Mahony, L. (2018). Time to Break Old Habits: Shifting from Complicity to Protection of Rohingya in Myanmar. *Fieldview Solutions*. www.fieldviewsolutions.org/fv-publications/Time_to_break_old_habits.pdf [Accessed 11/11/2019]

Manby, B. (2018). 'Legal Identity' and Biometric Registration in Africa. *Newsletter of the American Political Science Association's Organized Section on Migration and Citizenship* 6(2).

Navaro-Yashin, Y. (2007). Make-Believe Papers, Legal forms and the Counterfeit: Affective Interactions between Documents and People in Britain and Cyprus. *Anthropological Theory* 7(1): 79–98.

Nay San Lwin (2012). Making Rohingya Stateless. *New Madala*. www.newmandala.org/making-rohingya-statelessness/ [Accessed 07/02/2020]

NUI Galway (2010). *Crimes against Humanity in Western Burma: The Situation of the Rohingyas*. www.nuigalway.ie/media/intranet/Crimes-Against-Humanit-in-Western-Burma.pdf [Accessed 03/05/2017]

Nyi Nyi Kyaw (2015). Alienation, Discrimination, and Securitization: Legal Personhood and Cultural Personhood of Muslims in Myanmar. *The Review of Faith & International Affairs* 13(4): 50–59.

Nyi Nyi Kyaw (2017). Unpacking the Presumed Statelessness of Rohingyas. *Journal of Immigrant and Refugee Studies* 15(3): 269–286.

Oppenheim, B. and B. M. Powell (2015). Legal Identity in the 2030 Agenda for Sustainable Development: Lessons from Kibera, Kenya. *Open Society Foundation*. https://www.justiceinitiative.org/uploads/0a6472de-a975-4a3b-b3ad-2b979891d645/legal-identity-2030-agenda-lessons-kibera-kenya-2051216.pdf [Accessed 29/08/2024]

Pillai, P. (2019). Taking Statelessness Seriously: Linkages to Mass Atrocities? *Opinio-Jurist*. http://opiniojuris.org/2019/01/28/taking-statelessness-seriously-linkages-to-mass-atrocities/ [Accessed 05/10/2021]

Pittaway, E. (2016). Rohingya Refugees in Bangladesh: A Failure of the International Protection Regime, in Adelman, H. (ed), *The Protracted Displacement in Asia: No Place to Call Home*. Routledge.

Reddy, M. (2015). Identity Paper/Work/s and the Unmaking of Legal Status in Mae Sot, Thailand. *Asian Journal of Law and Society* 2(2): 251–266.

Sadiq, K. (2009). *Paper Citizens: How Illegal Immigrants Acquire Citizenship in Developing Countries*. Oxford University Press.

Sadiq, K. (2016). Limits of Legal Citizenship: Narratives from South and Southeast Asia, in Lawrance, B. N. and Stevens, J. (eds), *Citizenship in Question: Evidentiary Birthright and Statelessness*. Duke University Press. 165–176.

Scott, J. C. (1998). *Seeing Like a State: How Certain Schemes to Improve the Human Conditions Have failed*. Yale University Press.

Scott, J. C. (2009). *The Art of Not being Governed: An Anarchist History of Upland Southeast Asia*. Yale University Press.

Scott, J. C., J. Tehranian and J. Mathias (2002). The Production of Legal Identities Proper to States: The Case of the Permanent Family Surname. *Comparative Studies in Society and History* 44(1): 4–44.

Siddique (2012). The Rohingya Problem—Why? Keynote Speech Delivered at the International Conference on 'Contemplating Burma's Rohingya People's Future in Reconciliation and (Democratic) Reform,' Held on August 15, 2012 at the

Thammasat University, Bangkok. www.eurasiareview.com/29082012-the-rohingya-problem-why-speech/ [Accessed 13/02/2020]
Smith, M. (1999). *Burma: Insurgency and the Politics of Ethnicity*. Zed Books.
Spiro, P. J. (2011). A New International Law of Citizenship. *American Journal of International Law* 105(4): 694–746.
Stevens, J. (2017). Introduction, in Lawrance, B. N. (ed), *Citizenship in Question: Evidentiary Birthright and Statelessness*. Duke University Press.
Tilly, C. (1995). Citizenship, Identity and Social History. *International Review of Social History* 40(S3): 1–17.
Tilly, C. (2003). *The Politics of Collective Violence*. Cambridge University Press.
Tinker, H., A. Griffin and S. R. Ashton (1984). Constitutional Relations between Britain and Burma: Burma—The Struggle for Independence 1944–48. *Her Majesty's Stationary Office*.
Torpey, J. (2000). *The Invention of the Passport: Surveillance, Citizenship, and the State*. Cambridge University Press.
Torpey, J. (2001). The Great War and the Birth of the Modern Passport System, in Caplan, J. and Torpey, J. (eds), *Documenting Individual Identity: The Development of State Practices in the Modern World*. Princeton University Press. 269–270.
UNHRC (Sept 2019). Detailed Findings of the Independent International Fact-Finding Mission on Myanmar: Report to the 42nd Session of the Human Rights Council, A/HRC/42/CRP.5.
van Waas, L. (2015). The Right to Legal Identity or the Right to Legal ID? *European Network on Statelessness*. www.statelessness.eu/blog/right-legal-identity-or-right-legal-id [Accessed 17/12/2018]
Vizenor, G. R. (2008). *Survivance: Narratives of Native Presence*. University of Nebraska Press.
Vizenor, G. R. (1994). *Manifest Manners: Postindian Warriors of Survivance*. Wesleyan University Press.
Weissbrodt, D. S. and C. Collins (2006). The Human Rights of Stateless Persons. *Human Rights Quarterly* 28(1): 245–276.
Yuval-Davis, N. (2006). Belonging and the Politics of Belonging. *Patterns of Prejudice* 40(3): 197–214.
Zarni, M. and N. Brinham (2017). Reworking the Colonial Era Indian Peril: Myanmar's State-Directed Persecution of Rohingyas and Other Muslims. *Brown Journal of World Affairs* 24(1): 53–76.
Zarni, M. and N. Brinham (2019). New Secretive Deal between UN, Myanmar Smells Foul. *Anadolu Agency*. www.aa.com.tr/en/analysis-news/new-secretive-deal-between-un-myanmar-smells-foul-/1171661 [Accessed 16/10/2019]
Zarni, M. and A. Cowley (2014). The Slow-Burning Genocide of Myanmar's Rohingya. *Pacific Rim Law & Policy Journal* 23(3): 681–754.

6 Genocide and identity destruction in Rohingya ID narratives

Introduction

The following two chapters explore, through ID card narratives, how statelessness was understood and experienced by Rohingya survivors within the wider processes of genocide. Both genocide and identity destruction were central strands in these narratives. Associations were also often made between registration practices and the physical destruction of the group, communities, and lands.[1] It became evident as I conducted the research that, in narrating the stories of their identity cards, participants were often relating not just their individual experiences of administrative violence but also the story of a genocide against their people. Accounts of the state's use and abuse of identity card schemes were used to show a historic trail of intent to destroy the Rohingya as a national group belonging to Rakhine State, Myanmar. State terror, mass violence, killings, and the destruction of lands and properties were frequently associated with state registration schemes. Identity cards singled Rohingya out for persecution and enabled systems of segregation and institutionalised discrimination that were a part of a genocidal process (Green, McManus et al. 2018; Brinham 2019; Fortify Rights 2019). The state's policies and practices relating to identity cards and registration were understood to deliberately reorganise national identities in ways that erased Rohingya from the national consciousness and made them 'unimaginable' as part of a national community.[2] This chapter explores these aspects of genocide and identity destruction that featured within the narratives. In doing so, it draws on previous chapters that described how identities are socially constructed, fluid, and relational (Leach 1973; Lieberman 1978; Tilly 1995:75; Scott 2009), and that state registration and identity card practices do not neutrally record facts about populations but are key tools through which states shape and reify identities and construct, destruct, and reconstruct social relations (Scott 1998; Torpey 2000).

For the purposes of the following two chapters, I draw on sociological understandings of genocide as a process. These notions were first outlined in Lemkin's original work in which he coined the term 'genocide' and were later built on by key genocide scholars working on 'stages of genocide,' including

DOI: 10.4324/9781003494539-6
This chapter has been made available under a CC-BY 4.0 license.

Feierstein (2014; Feierstein 2015) and Stanton (1998). In the first section of this chapter, I focus on the role of ID cards and registration schemes within sociological understandings of genocide. In the second section, I provide an overview of Myanmar's national verification process and its National Verification Cards (NVCs), with a focus on identity destruction and resistance.

IDs, intent, and the 'masterplan'

Throughout the research, ID schemes were referred to as an intrinsic part of a genocidal plan that aimed to destroy the Rohingya as a group belonging to the Rakhine region of Myanmar. Changes over time in ID schemes described by Rohingya participants were drawn on to narrate the genocidal intent of successive regimes. Rohingya oral histories undertaken for this research, without exception, did not describe their citizenship as being stripped from them by the 1982 Citizenship law alone but rather described a state-led process beginning prior to the campaign of terror and the mass expulsions of 1978 and continuing until today. They described four or more cycles of expulsion and repatriation across four decades (1978, 1991–2, 2012, and 2016–7). They told of how the state's efforts to denationalise them through legal and administrative practices intensified before and after each of these expulsions and in response to the repatriations. These practices included the nullification, confiscation, destruction, and targeted non-issuance of IDs. Accounts often made associations or skipped between the bureaucratic practices of past regimes and today's military and civilian leadership as though they were part of a continuous process driven by the same objective.[3] For example, 'The architect of the genocide plan was Ne Win—then it was handed to Khin Nyunt and Than Shwe—Now even Suu Kyi is involved.'[4]

Within the legal context, intent in genocides has proved to be notoriously hard to ascertain since perpetrators rarely leave explicit evidence of intent and/or often erase and destroy evidence of their crimes as part of the 'denial' stage of genocide (Totten and Bartrop 2009; Sands 2016). Further, as both Stanton and Feierstein elaborate, both human and state intentionalities are complex and crimes of any kind almost always involve more than one single intent.[5] Nonetheless, genocide differs from other atrocity crimes in that it necessarily involves a deliberate plan or a concerted and coordinated attempt to destroy a group of people. This is central to all legal and sociological definitions of genocide.[6] As such, in the absence of explicit statements or documents of intention, genocide scholarship often explores genocidal intent by examining policies, practices, and ideologies (Cox 2017) or the 'systematic widespread pattern of actions that have the foreseeable consequence of destroying a group.'[7] Identification policies and practices that change over decades, and reflect ideologies relating to citizenship can therefore shed light on intent. Rohingya oral histories of their ID cards for this research, frequently inferred this intent, often referring to a 'masterplan' or a long-term military strategy with the overarching objectives of erasing and destroying the Rohingya as a group belonging to Rakhine State, Myanmar.[8] For example:

> After the repatriations, the Burmese government used new policies to drive us out. The 1982 Citizenship law . . . the white card method in the 1990s . . . the 2017 genocide crisis and the NVC cards, they are all to drive us out. This is the masterplan of the Burmese government.[9]

The above statement reflects many other occurrences in the research, in which Rohingya participants evidenced the existence of a coordinated plan to erase and destroy them as a group, through the sustained use and abuse of registration policies, identity card practices, citizenship laws, and an underlying Islamophobic, racist (anti-South Asian), and Buddhist nationalist state ideology. In Chapter 5, I examined how the shift in ideologies as a result of the period of military rule beginning in 1962 was actualised through citizenship laws and registration rules and policies that attacked the foundations of Rohingya identity and the social fabric of their communities in northern Rakhine. I explained how in the early decades after Myanmar's independence, national identity was largely based on a multi-ethnic, multi-religious national identity in which belonging was established through a mixture of ethnic belonging and loyalty to the state. In this chapter, I further explore genocide through Rohingya accounts of identification and registration policies and practices.

State identification and registration practices in genocides

Genocide as a sociological and legal term

In this first section, I outline how genocide is understood and utilised within this chapter. The term genocide was first coined by Raphael Lemkin in Axis Rule in Occupied Europe (1944) and was used to describe the deliberate and systematic destruction of ethnic or 'national' groups.[10] He described genocide as 'a coordinated plan of different actions aiming at the destruction of essential foundations of the life of national groups, with the aim of annihilating groups themselves' (1944:ix). Importantly, his original conception described broad sociological and political notions of the destruction of group identities that went beyond the biological or physical destruction of the group. He outlined how the objectives of genocide were the 'disintegration of the political and social institutions of culture, language, national feelings, religion and economic existence of national groups, and the destruction of the personal security, liberty, health, dignity and even the lives of the individuals belonging to such groups' (1944:ix).

Lemkin, a lawyer himself, campaigned relentlessly to have the crime of genocide incorporated into international law. His work was largely driven by the conviction that crimes that targeted people based on their membership of a distinct group were fundamentally different from those that targeted individuals (Frieze and Lemkin 2013; Siegelberg 2013). He argued that this warranted a separate approach in international criminal law. This went against the grain of broader international legal discussions at the time, which had shifted away from the thinking behind the minority protection treaties of the interwar years that focused on collectives and groups of people as the unit of international law, towards more individualistic notions of legal personality that formed the basis for the post-war human rights treaties (Siegelberg 2020). In this regard, he was often at odds with his contemporary, Hersch Lauterpacht, who was instrumental in developing the Crimes against Humanity framework and establishing the foundations of international law in post-war years (Frieze and Lemkin 2013; Siegelberg 2013; Sands 2016). When genocide was enshrined in international law in 1948 in the Convention on the Prevention and Punishment of the Crime of Genocide (hereafter Genocide Convention), the definition moved away from the broader sociological concepts contained in Lemkin's original work, to focus on the specific acts that constituted the crime genocide. As such it was defined as:

> Any of the following acts committed with intent to destroy, in whole or in part, a national, ethnical, racial or religious group, as such: killing of members of the group; causing serious bodily or mental harm to members of the group; deliberately inflicting on the group conditions of life, calculated to bring about its physical destruction in whole or in part; imposing measures intended to prevent births within the group; forcibly transferring children of the group to another group.
>
> (Article 2)

This legal definition, then, limited genocide to the intentional physical and biological destruction of groups, having omitted such crucial dimensions as the destruction of cultural, religious, communal, intellectual, and economic foundational institutions on which all groups anchor their identities.

Human rights documentation on the Rohingya genocide has tended to focus on these acts of genocide in order to contribute to building a case for genocide determination in international legal processes (UNHRC 16th Sept 2019; International Court of Justice 23 Jan 2020; UNHRC Sept 2018).[11] Since 2017, such research has established a loose correlation between state ID schemes and the acts of genocide defined in the Genocide Convention. The International Independent Fact-Finding Mission or IIFFM (UNHRC Sept 2018:68), for example, stated:

> The Government has denied the Rohingya access to essential life-saving and life supporting goods and services as punishment for refusing to accept the NVCs. Rohingya believe their refusal to accept NVCs in 2017 has led to the genocidal 'clearance operations.'

Further, a human rights report focused on Myanmar's NVCs raised questions 'as to whether and how the NVC process and the 1982 Citizenship Law relate to two prohibited acts of genocide: (1) causing serious mental harm to Rohingya, and (2) deliberately inflicting on Rohingya conditions of life calculated to bring about its physical destruction in whole or in part' (Fortify Rights 2019).

Despite the dominance of the Genocide Convention's definition of the crime, scholarship in genocide has continued to explore sociological, cultural, political, and economic factors relating to group destruction that were at the heart of Lemkin's original conception of genocide. These broader frameworks in exploring the meanings and experiences survivors attached to state ID schemes.

The 'group' and identification practices in genocide scholarship

Notions of what constitutes a 'group' have evolved as anthropological and sociological thought has increasingly moved away from the colonial and pre-WWII concepts of fixed and biologically defined racial and national groups, towards an understanding of groups and associated identities as shaped or influenced by the processes of social construction (Arnold 2002; Hinton 2002). In situations of genocide, these group identities are thus understood as being, in part, constituted through power relations between victim and perpetrator groups. As described in previous chapters, national and ethnic identities are better understood as relational, cultural, historical, and contingent (Tilly 1995:5–6). As such, they are shaped not only by the structures of the state and the international order but also by subjectivities.

Since its conception, genocide scholarship has interrogated various aspects of the Genocide Convention's definition. One relevant discussion relates to the limitations of defining the victim group as 'national, ethnical, racial or religious.' This limitation precluded situations of genocide that involve the destruction of social and political groups (Harff and Gurr 1988), as well as groups in which membership is constituted through the multiple overlapping characteristics that are most often a feature of intersecting group identities (Feierstein 2014).[12]

In 2019, the findings of the International Court of Justice (ICJ) (23 Jan 2020:52) that Rohingya are a 'protected group' and thus fall within the genocide definition was significant for Rohingya participants in this research. This was not simply because it was a legal lynchpin that enabled the *Gambia vs Myanmar* genocide case to proceed but also because it provided Rohingya with official international recognition of their identity that had been denied by the Myanmar government, and which they described as being persistently erased as part of a genocidal process.[13]

Whilst the ethnic group Rohingya falls within the international legal definition of genocide, this research draws on the more expansive sociological understandings of the characteristics of groups impacted by genocide. Definitions that refer to 'any human group' or a 'collective' provide space for group identities to be multiple, intersectional, and overlapping (Harff and Gurr 1988; Charney 2009; Fein 2009). As noted in earlier chapters, all group identities are subject to the processes of social construction. Further, the construction, destruction, and reconstruction of ethnic, racial, religious, and national groups are in part determined by state categorisation and identification processes including citizenship laws, constitutions, and state ID policies and practices (Scott 1998; Torpey 2000). In the case of the Rohingya in Myanmar, where even the term Rohingya has been contested, victims' and perpetrators' constructions of national and ethnic groups collide with one another (International Court of Justice 23 Jan 2020:14). The parameters of fluid group identities can shift according to strategic and pragmatic responses to administrative violence and state policies. As such, this chapter predominantly explores the destruction of Rohingya identity but additionally considers the intersecting religious, linguistic, and cultural identities that arose in field research with Rohingya. These intersecting identities were understood as being under threat from the Myanmar State. Simultaneously, participants also drew on these identities as a survival strategy when identifying as Rohingya was too dangerous.[14] The other intersecting group identities that most often arose in the narrative research were Arakan/Rakhine Muslim and Burmese/Myanmar Muslim.[15]

Understanding groups in this way as fluid, malleable, and subject to state constructions and categorisation provides an underpinning for analysis of genocide as a social process which reshapes social relations in ways which 'construct, destroy and reorganize the social fabric' (Feierstein 2014:104). State identification and registration practices within this framework are key state technologies through which the objectives of a genocide are achieved, whereby state categorisation procedures do not simply neutrally record biographic facts about human beings, but bring identities into being and destroy them (Scott 1998; Torpey 2000). As such, state registration and identification practices can be understood as key weapons of genocide in a state's arsenal.[16]

ID cards and early warning systems

Genocide is often described within scholarship, not as a set of discrete events of mass killing or other acts of genocide but as a sociological process and a social practice (Stanton 1998; Stanton 2004; Feierstein 2014; Feierstein 2015; Green, McManus et al. 2015). This provides researchers with a framework to examine how the conditions of genocide develop within particular contexts and to recognise the vulnerabilities of specific groups before, during, and after the culmination of mass violence. Several research frameworks based on 'stages of genocide' have developed, which inform scholarship and provide the basis for early warning systems for civil society organisations that monitor xenophobia and impending genocide.

The work of Stanton (2017), on the ten stages of genocide, has been particularly influential within these civil society organisations.[17] These stages are classification; symbolisation, discrimination, dehumanisation, organisation, polarisation, preparation, persecution, extermination, and denial. Within this framework, the first two stages are particularly relevant to state ID card and registration schemes. The classification stage distinguishes racial, ethnic, religious, and national characteristics limiting the possibilities of mixed, heterogeneous, or fluid identities and creating the conditions for polarisation. Symbolisation lends the categorisation process a set of names or symbols that, when 'combined with hatred' (2017:para 2), actualise the conditions and social relations that polarise society and produce persecution and genocidal violence. The most powerful and complete way in which states categorise, classify, and symbolise peoples, as well as monopolise their control over human movement, is through their national registration and ID systems (Scott 1998; Torpey 2000).[18] Stanton notes that in the Rohingya situation, symbolisation first occurred when their national ID cards were removed by state authorities.[19] A legal brief by the Simon Skjodt Centre for the Prevention of Genocide (2020) also draws on these notions of symbolisation in the Rohingya genocide. The brief concludes that the revocation of citizenship enabled the systematic denial of rights and was closely linked with the processes of 'othering.' Further, it concludes that the systematic denial of the right to participate in public affairs, which was linked to the removal of Rohingyas' white cards in 2015, forged an environment conducive to the perpetuation of continuing serious human rights abuses.

Stanton notes that his ten 'stages' are perhaps better understood as ten 'processes' which are 'not always linear' and can 'occur simultaneously.'[20] This is significant in the Rohingya situation, since classification and symbolisation through the use of ID cards did not simply precede genocidal violence but rather evolved over decades alongside the broader processes of genocide and mass violence. Rohingya participants in this study most often pinpointed not one but three past state practices that were viewed as significant markers in the reification of ethnic identities in Myanmar, the 'othering' of their communities, and the deterioration of social relations in Rakhine State. First, when Myanmar's colour-coded national identity cards were rolled out throughout the country from 1989 onwards, a process under which many Rohingya were left without citizenship cards. Second, when 'white cards' or temporary residence cards were issued to Rohingya from the mid-1990s, it marked them out as a group whose citizenship and national belonging were precarious, temporary, and uncertain. Third, when the state attempted to issue Rohingya with National Verification Cards (NVCs) that were understood to permanently cement a status of unbelonging and exclusion. It was these processes of classification and symbolisation that were understood to underlie and actualise the persecution and genocidal violence.[21]

Mass violence both preceded and followed the implementation of these ID schemes. The structures of segregation, isolation, and apartheid also developed in different areas of Rakhine State both before and after the unleashing of mass violence. This included, but was not limited to, the containment of Rohingya in apartheid conditions in North Rakhine State under the *NaSaKa* from the early 1990s onwards, and the use of camps to detain Rohingya, Kaman, and other groups displaced by the 2012 state-sponsored violence (see also Fortify Rights 2014; Amnesty International 2017). For example, one participant explained his experiences following repatriation from Bangladesh in 1993:

> The Myanmar government dreamed of deleting us for a long time—this was their plan. So, *NaSaKa* and the white cards were sent to our area. The movement for our people was stopped. If you want to go to another place, you have to take the permission from the authority of the village. So, if you want to stay in another village, you have to report at night. If you do not report and the police or NaSaKa find you, they will sentence you. Six months.[22]

These segregations were also associated in Rohingya narratives with state refusal to replace destroyed identity documents and the forced issuance of white cards (pre-2015) and latterly NVCs (2016 onwards).

Reorganising genocides and ID schemes

Feierstein (2014) also developed a framework of six stages of genocide. Feierstein's work focuses on 'reorganising genocides,' in which the ultimate aim of a genocide is to reorganise identities and social relations in such a way as to deny the existence of the victim group. He drew on Lemkin's original conception of genocide as a dual process that is both destructive and creative in that it aims to not only 'destroy the national pattern of the oppressed group' but also 'impose the national pattern of the oppressors' (2002:27–28). Reiterated in more contemporary social science language, Feierstein (2014:126) describes the central aim of a reorganising genocide, as being to 'transform the society in which genocide takes place by destroying a way of life embodied by a particular group, and thus reorganizing social relations with the rest of society.' Myanmar's destruction of Rohingya identity as part of the process of reconstructing a more exclusive national identity devoid of its historical linkages with South Asia and its demographic realities is a 'reorganising genocide.' As such, Feierstein's framework lends itself to exploring the construction, destruction, and reconstruction of identities in Myanmar as this applies to identity cards and registration.

Feierstein's six stages of genocide are stigmatisation or the construction of a negative 'other'; harassment, in which there is a shift from symbolic to physical violence; isolation, in which separate social, geographic, economic, and political spaces are carved out in ways that sever social ties with the rest of society; policies of systematic weakening, involving the physical and psychological destruction of the group through conditions of life such as overcrowding, underfeeding, lack of healthcare, and physical violence; and extermination, including the killing and physical disappearance of members of the group who 'once embodied certain types of social relations.' The sixth and final stage of Feierstein's model, symbolic enactment, captures the continuing and ongoing destruction and after mass annihilation. This stage shifts the focus onto the new types of society and social relations that are reconstituted in the process. This stage is significant for work on ID cards and genocide and will be explored in greater detail in this chapter.

Feierstein, like Stanton, asserts that the stages he has developed are not always enacted as a linear sequence of events[23] but rather the stages can overlap and recur. He explains that the six stages form a cycle. The final stage is an attempt to close the cycle and if the disappearance of a group through discursive and other symbolic means is not achieved, 'the cycle might begin again' (2014:126). Likewise, Rohingya oral histories plotted a cycle of violence, recategorisation, and redocumentation that occurred and recurred over decades.

The implementation of the NVC scheme from 2015 onwards was largely viewed as an attempt to permanently erase the Rohingya from Myanmar's national identity. Previous attempts to re-categorise Rohingya in ways that erased evidence of their existence through the census, the citizenship law, household, and individual documentation schemes, were largely understood as only partially achieving this aim. Myanmar's campaigns of terror in 1978 and 1992–3 failed in their attempts to permanently remove Rohingya from Myanmar, in part due to the mass repatriations from Bangladesh that followed. This failure caused the cycle to begin again. For example:

> White cards were sent in the name of NaSaKa. The operation resulted in refugees going to Bangladesh and the white cards were a direct response to their return. (They were) saying that everyone who had been outside the country was not Burmese. Repatriations and white cards were directly linked.[24]

Likewise, state ID schemes only partially achieved the symbolic erasure of Rohingya as a group. Resistance to the processes of erasure and persecution rather resulted in the unintended consequence of strengthening Rohingya resistance, identity, and consciousness.[25] For example:

> All our educated people are being arrested and targeted for the reason that they do not accept the NVCs. The educated people are targeted because they know their history so the government target them—because part of knowing your history is knowing why the Rohingya people should reject NVCs.[26]

Resistance and lack of closure of the cycle raised the stakes, as the state increasingly resorted to coercion and force from 2016 onwards, whereby the implementation of Myanmar's ID scheme became inextricably linked in Rohingyas' accounts and narratives to the genocidal violence of 2016–7 (UNHRC Sept 2018:68).

Feierstein's six-stage framework was utilised and adapted by the International State Crime Initiative (ISCI) in two reports on Rohingya genocide (Green, McManus et al. 2015; Green, McManus et al. 2018). The first report, written after the 2012–3 violence, documented the first four of these stages of genocide and concluded that the situation was at the stage four—systematic weakening. The second report, written after the 2017 violence focused on the fifth stage of the genocide—extermination—and aspects of the sixth stage—symbolic enactment—which had occurred in the months following the 2017 violence and exodus. The state use of citizenship denial and IDs were included in the report. For example, the authors point out that the denial of Rohingyas' citizenship in Myanmar through the 1982 Citizenship Law was 'central to Myanmar's dehumanisation campaign' (2015:56). They explain that NVCs represented 'a crude attempt to involve Rohingya in their own identity denial' (2018:41) and that they were used to 'identify the Rohingya as outsiders before unleashing the final stages of the genocide' (2018:18). The following section builds on this analysis by focusing on the use of IDs within the process of reorganising genocides. In doing so, it considers the role of state IDs within recurring and overlapping stages of a genocidal process. ID and registration schemes and practices, that both precede and follow mass violence, can simultaneously function within the stigmatisation, symbolic enactment, and other stages of genocide.

NVCs and Rohingya resistance to identity destruction

This section provides an overview of attempts to implement the nationality verification and associated NVCs. It draws predominantly on fieldwork data, cross-checked, and supplemented by findings and recommendations from published reports. The verification of Rohingyas' citizenship began in Myanmar in the aftermath of the 2012–3 violence, and NVCs were issued from 2015 onwards (Fortify Rights 2019; Human Rights Watch 2020). NVCs were described by participants in interviews and focus groups as 'genocide cards' or 'tools of genocide' (see also Brinham 2018; Fortify Rights 2019). This section explores why they were described as such. Group resistance through non-compliance and civil disobedience related to the NVCs was a recurring theme throughout the fieldwork. It provides a background to genocide analysis in the rest of the chapter on ID cards and the stages of genocide.

In interviews and focus groups, NVCs were rarely spoken about in isolation from Myanmar's historic genocidal and identity destruction processes, or separately from hopes for safe futures for Rohingya in Myanmar. ID card narratives were imbued with strong emotions relating to the group struggle against a common oppressor—the militarised state (see also Brinham 2019). Refusal to participate in the registration scheme formed one of the most significant strategies of Rohingyas' collective resistance to the state's destruction of their group. As such, the NVC scheme resulted both in the strengthening of Rohingya as a resistance identity[27] and was understood to have triggered state violence and physical destruction as the state authorities became increasingly frustrated by this form of resistance.[28] NVC narratives were imbued with notions of heroism, sacrifice, betrayal, and collaboration.[29] The determination and strength of relatives and friends who remained in the Rohingya homelands of Rakhine State and continued to resist NVCs were spoken about in terms of sacrifice for the Rohingya people.

> My mother and my brother are still there. They are very strong. They say, 'This is our Rohingya land—we would rather die here than take NVC.' Even if it is hard to eat and survive without NVC, they still stay there.[30]

Resistance to the issuance of cards resulting in beatings, arrest and abuses by security forces, was described as heroism.[31] The failure of a few Rohingya diasporic leaders to condemn Myanmar's use of NVCs was spoken about as a betrayal of the Rohingya cause. For example, shortly before one field visit, a US-based Rohingya leader (name withheld for confidentiality) had made a public statement to the effect that 'resettlement' in Rakhine and 'peace' was more important than the pursuit of international justice. Many of the participants wanted to voice their opposition to his statement, such as

> (Irritation and tutting) 'Why he say that? Why resettle!? There is a huge difference between resettle and repatriate. Resettle means just NVC card. If you don't get justice, then abuse will not stop.'[32]

INGOs and UN agencies who told their Rohingya staff to accept NVCs in order to continue their work in Northern Rakhine were described as collaborators.[33]

> For the white card, UNHCR provided help. It was a tool of genocide. So is the NVC. To get salary for UNHCR, you would have to go to the bank. You have to use your NVC card to get there. They are not paying salary without the NVC. If this is not forcing them, then how do you think?. . . They are linking with Myanmar government and following the genocide law.[34]

Rohingya who had been coerced into accepting NVCs described their shame as they hid their cards from others.

> Until now, I did not tell the people in the village that I accepted the NVC because I was very ashamed and worried. If the people know that I accepted the NVC, it won't be good for me . . . I knew well that this card is not good for us, but I was the 'responsible person.'[35] If I did not accept the NVC, I would have been fired from my position. And I was not able to move. I was inside the BGP headquarters with the guns pointed at me.[36]

Overall, many of the participants had become invested in resisting NVCs and the national verification process as part of their struggle against genocide, and accordingly articulated their hopes for justice, restitution, and Rohingya futures in Myanmar as being without NVCs or similar ID schemes.

The National Verification process for Rohingya populations was first attempted under President Thein Sein in 2014 in the aftermath of violence and displacement, to determine whether Rohingya and other Muslims in the IDP camps[37] were eligible for citizenship under the 1982 Citizenship Law (Fortify Rights 2019). At the time, NVC cards were not issued as part of the verification process. The registration categories for this verification denied Rohingya the right to self-identify, instead labelling them 'Bengali.' For this reason, the scheme was met with widespread resistance from displaced populations detained in camps. As a result, it was put on hold (Advisory Commission on Rakhine State Aug 2017).

In 2015, across the country, the white cards that Rohingya had held since the mid-1990s were nullified and collected in, in a move to block Rohingya from voting in the general election. This move followed a failed lobby in parliament to have voting rights removed for white card holders (BROUK 2015). A receipt, popularly known as 'receipt card,' was provided in return for the white cards. The receipt cards did not contain biographic data and could not be used to apply for travel permissions, marriage permissions, licenses for work, or other administrative permissions.[38] They were described as 'useless,' and several participants in the Bangladesh refugee camps explained that they had discarded the receipt cards.[39] With most Rohingya now without individual identity documents, Thein Sein's government attempted to issue new identity cards known as Identity Cards for Nationality Verification (ICNVs). They were ostensibly issued as part of the broader national verification process for Rohingya populations but rarely resulted in citizenship applications (Advisory Commission on Rakhine State Aug 2017). When they were piloted, Rohingya were recorded on the cards as 'Bengali.' These cards were largely resisted by Rohingya populations who understood that the card scheme attempted to erase their ethnic identity and lock in a noncitizenship or foreigner status.[40]

In 2016, under Aung San Suu Kyi's NLD government, the ICNV cards were relaunched and rebranded as National Verification Cards (NVCs), this time without the term 'Bengali' displayed on the card. The colour of the card was also changed to blue.[41] Nonetheless, there was continued resistance and fear of the process amongst Rohingya groups. The data collection questions included asking 'applicants' when and by what method they arrived in Myanmar, and other questions that underlined for Rohingya that the cards were issued to foreigners who needed to apply to be citizens, not those who had a valid claim to ancestral belonging.[42] As such they undermined Rohingyas' claim to citizenship by right, as opposed to by application and naturalisation. This highlighted that the problems inherent in Myanmar's personal identification system are not only the ethnic and religious data displayed on national identity cards but also the personal data retained by the state. In Rohingya narratives, these data were frequently referred to with suspicion as to what was 'written behind the cards.'[43]

The Myanmar government claimed that NV and NVCs would provide 'a pathway to citizenship'[44] in that it would establish individuals' legal identity and enable them to apply for citizenship, which some Rohingya would be entitled to if they could provide evidence of two previous generations of permanent residency to apply for citizenship (European Network on Statelessness and Institute on Statelessness and Inclusion 2019). However, the right to apply for citizenship went directly against the Rohingyas' collective stance that they were citizens by birth, and should not have to file citizenship applications and thus expose themselves to discriminatory and arbitrary determination processes.[45] This national verification approach was viewed as compliant with the recommendations of Myanmar's Rakhine Inquiry Commission report of 2013 (Republic of the Union of Myanmar 2013:vi) and some other key domestic actors.[46] Such approaches noted the 'sensitivities' and practical barriers to reforming the citizenship law. Instead, they proposed an approach to tackling the Rohingya citizenship issue which would expand access to citizenship for some Rohingya under the existing provisions of the 1982 Citizenship Law by reducing the administrative hurdles and the evidentiary burdens (de Chickera, Arraiza et al. 2021). Even by August 2017 immediately prior to the genocidal violence, the 'Kofi Annan Commission' recommended expanding the NVC scheme as an initial measure towards tackling the citizenship issue. The second stage they recommended, which was not acted on, was tweaking the 1982 citizenship law to bring it into compliance with international law (Advisory Commission on Rakhine State Aug 2017).[47] As such, the NVC scheme was supported by some international agencies.[48] Across the course of this research, the credibility of the national verification as a 'pathway to citizenship' was undermined. There were indefinite delays (UNHRC 16th Sept 2019), with only a small number of people being issued citizenship cards three years after the scheme began.[49] Additionally, the few who applied within Rakhine State and did receive citizenship IDs (both NCSCs and CSCs) found that the cards were not endowed with any more rights than the white cards. Most significantly, they were still subject to the restrictions of movement within and outside Rakhine State.[50]

For many Rohingya, the problems were far more fundamental than these barriers to implementation. The scheme attacked the foundations of their group identity as one belonging to Rakhine State Myanmar. Rohingya had good reason to doubt the intentions of the Myanmar leadership. The white cards of the past were officially issued as 'temporary' cards whilst citizenship cards were processed. They functioned for such purposes elsewhere in Myanmar, but for Rohingya they indefinitely suspended their legal status in limbo (European Network on Statelessness and Institute on Statelessness and Inclusion 2019) and as such were sometimes described as 'stateless cards.'[51] NVCs were also not viewed by participants as a step towards a more stable legal status but rather permanently cemented their unbelonging, with the cards explicitly stating that the holders were required to have their citizenship verified.[52] For example:

> The government organised the village meeting about the NVCs through the village chairman. They told us, 'If you do not take this card, you cannot live in this country.' But we are not foreigners, and we are not illegals. The place where we live—it is our 500 years ancestral land. We settled it. Before it was just jungle.[53]

Additionally, whist in theory national verification would enable more Rohingya to apply for citizenship, in practice, for most the evidentiary obstacles remained insurmountable. Citizenship applications required them to submit NRCs and other documents from parents and grandparents, with the evidentiary burden placed on the applicants. Decades of systematic destruction, confiscation, and targeted non-issuance of citizenship and identity documents for Rohingya meant that very few were able to prove their right to citizenship under these provisions, even if they wished to apply (de Chickera, Arraiza et al. 2021). Whilst the burden fell on the applicant to produce evidence, the state authorities were understood to have that evidence in their possession. The fact that Rohingya applicants were required to still have these documents that had been systematically removed and evidence of them denied, in order to apply for citizenship, was relayed with bitterness in interviews. Some participants had invested too much emotionally in saving old documents to risk handing them over to state authorities. The documents of their relatives had been carefully hidden from the state authorities. They had risked abuse and arrest for doing so. Many expressed fear in revealing these IDs to state authorities for an application process lest they be confiscated.[54] The application process, based on historical experience, was thus often described as a 'trick' to further remove evidence of their historic belonging.[55] In practice, there were only a small number of cases in which citizenship applications were pursued beyond the issuance of the NVCs themselves (Brinham, Tiwari et al. 2020).[56]

The most dominant opinion expressed in field research was that allowing oneself to be documented under this ID scheme and under these provisions of the citizenship rules was a betrayal of their group identity. As such, it was also a betrayal of the united Rohingya resistance to the state processes of identity destruction.

> They are demanding that the Rohingya are from Bangladesh . . . . How is it possible that they are demanding once again that we are Bengali people? That we must again apply for citizenship—and stay there by their permission . . . . It is better to die than to take this NVC. For one year before I left, they had been pressurising us. Even some of the people are still in the jail. They were put in the jail because they refuse or deny the NVC . . . . Everyone has been denying it.[57]

Although NVCs did not carry an ethnic designation, the 'green cards' or naturalised citizenship cards (NCSCs) issued to a few successful Rohingya applicants carried the term 'Bengali' and, as such, were endowed with a deep sense of shame and stigma. Additionally, many participants were clear that until ethnic and religious identity was removed from *all* ID cards in Myanmar, the stigma would remain. This was because the absence of an ethnic or religious designation on cards, in itself, inferred a 'foreign' or 'Bengali' status.[58] The citizenship application process, then, was often viewed as divisive within the community, with applicants in northern Rakhine sometimes considered to be 'selling out' the group cause for individual gain.

> People are criticising them. They are saying if one or two persons take it, then all of us will need to take it . . . . People are getting information from outside, 'Don't take NVC card.' But some people are thinking, if we need to survive here, we need to take it. We cannot follow other people from outside.[59]

As such, the promotion of citizenship application processes without providing Rohingya with an automatic right to citizenship was sometimes understood as a tactic by which the state could 'divide-and-rule' Rohingya communities.[60] Citizenship by application undermined the attempts to organise and present a unified group resistance by offering citizenship to a minority that were more educated and more financially sufficient (albeit a second-class one) whilst consigning the majority of Rohingya to a precarious noncitizenship status.[61]

Conclusion

In summary, refusal to register for NVC cards was a key group strategy to resist identity destruction. NVCs were resisted, in part, because they did not provide or lead to the trinity of citizenship:—legal status, citizenship rights, or national belonging (see Chapter 3). They were also understood as a form of identity destruction in and of themselves that cemented a noncitizen or foreigner status. This status stigmatised them and marked them out for persecution. Feelings expressed in interviews towards the Rohingya holders of NVCs were not uniform, and in some cases changed during the course of the fieldwork. Initially, a greater degree of anger and frustration was directed towards NVC holders. In the period 2017–8, NVCs were endowed with a deep sense of injustice and shame. Rohingya participants described how they felt towards those who underwent the registration process. Holders were often spoken about with derision. For example:

> Some people accepted the NVC, who are very close with the government—like the officials and the village chairman or the business men . . . I hate all those who accept the NVCs. We are citizens of Burma so we do not need to accept the foreigner cards . . . NVC is not for us.[62]

Some participants defended individuals who had accepted the NVCs, providing justifications as to how these individuals were tricked, forced, or outmanoeuvred by the state authorities. As such holding one was also sometimes explained as a sign of weakness.[63] Participants who admitted taking NVCs themselves described how they hid this fact from the community, and some confessed their shame to the interpreters and myself.[64]

Other opinions, particularly as time went on, accepted the pragmatic survival choices made by those who held NVCs. Resistance to genocide and identity destruction was also understood as maintaining 'feet on the ground' in the homelands in Rakhine. Within this paradigm, accepting an NVC card in order to remain in the homelands was accepted as a strategy choice.[65] Nevertheless, the NVC card remained in all Rohingya narratives, a powerful symbol of the state's attempts to destroy Rohingyas' belonging and identity, and an indication of Rohingyas' capacity to unite as a group to resist such attempts. Having provided an overview of the national verification process and NVCs in Myanmar, the following chapter examines the NVCs within Feierstein's six stages of genocide.

Notes

1 These associations are most evident in the narrative turns or jumps made between identity cards and physical violence.

2 The notion of national identities as 'imagined communities' was coined in Anderson (1991). In reorganisation genocides, the victims of genocide and expulsion become 'othered' in such a way as to make them 'unimaginable' as part of the national identity. See Feierstein, D. (2014).

3 For more information on these cycles, see 'bureaucratic cleansing' in Brinham (2019)
4 In34, 02/08/2018, Chittagong.
5 The Question of 'Intent' in Genocide: A Public Dialogue, Free Rohingya Coalition livecast with Gregory Stanton and Daniel Feierstein, 25/01/2021
6 For example, 'Genocide. . . is intended rather to signify a coordinated plan of different actions aiming at the destruction of essential foundations of the life of national groups, with the aim of annihilating the groups themselves' Lemkin (1944); and 'acts committed with intent to destroy, in whole or in part a national, ethnical, racial or religious group' CCCPG Article 2; and 'Genocide is sustained purposeful action by a perpetrator to physically destroy a collectivity directly or indirectly' Fein (1993).
7 Stanton speaking at: The Question of 'Intent' in Genocide: A Public Dialogue, Free Rohingya Coalition livecast with Gregory Stanton and Daniel Feierstein, 25/01/2021.
8 The term 'masterplan' was used in six interviews and two focus groups.
9 Fg8, 26/09/2018, Hakimpara.
10 He uses the term 'national group' in his work to refer to shared cultural heritage, not the term 'nationality' that is now used in international law to denote the legal aspects of 'citizenship.' For explanation of the evolution of this term, see Siegelberg (2020).
11 The notable exception is the International State Crime Initiative's reports which focuses on the process rather than the acts of genocide. Green, McManus et al. (2015, 2018).
12 This includes the atrocities, which was inflicted on the multi-religious and ethnically diverse populations of East Pakistan, today's Bangladesh, during their struggle for liberation from Pakistan in 1971, which has not been internationally recognised as genocide. The issue of non-recognition recurred throughout the fieldwork research in Bangladesh including during a field trip to the Liberation War Museum in Dhaka, Bangladesh on 17/11/2017, Dhaka.
13 Observations, 12/12/2019, attending the International Court of Justice hearing, The Hague.
14 For example, playing down ethnic 'Rohingya' identities and playing up 'Myanmar Muslim' religious identities when living in parts of Myanmar beyond northern Rakhine, or concealing Rohingya identities and drawing on the Bangladesh upbringings to avoid harassment by authorities or locals in Bangladesh.
15 Also, dual identities were spoken about in the context of identity destruction such as Rohingya/Bangladeshi and Rohingya/Malaysian. Exploration of these is beyond the scope of this research.
16 Whilst this chapter is focused on Rohingya experiences of Myanmar's ID and registration systems, there are other situations in which state classification and identification systems combined with exclusionary citizenship laws have been applied to heterogeneous and mixed populations resulting in the polarisation of national, ethnic, and religious identities and thus increasing the risks of genocide. These include identity cards that differentiated between Tutsis and Hutus in Rwanda (Longman 2001); categorisation of former Yugoslavians as for example 'Serb' and 'Bosnia' (Hayden 1996); and the denationalisation, identification, and classification of German Jews in Nazi Germany (Caplan 2013).
17 E.g. Genocide Watch, The Sentinel Project, The Holocaust Memorial Trust, etc.
18 The examples provided in Stanton's work include ID cards that distinguished between Hutus and Tutsis in Rwanda and the use of the star to symbolise Jews in Nazi-occupied Europe to polarise previously mixed and heterogeneous populations along ethnic and racial lines.

19 The Question of 'Intent' in Genocide: A Public Dialogue, Free Rohingya Coalition livecast with Gregory Stanton and Daniel Feierstein, 25/01/2021.
20 The Question of 'Intent' in Genocide: A Public Dialogue, Free Rohingya Coalition livecast with Gregory Stanton and Daniel Feierstein, 25/01/2021.
21 There are similar accounts in Fortify Rights (2019).
22 In13, 23/04/2018, Kuala Lumpur.
23 See discussion in The Question of 'Intent' in Genocide: A Public Dialogue, Free Rohingya Coalition livecast with Gregory Stanton and Daniel Feierstein, 25/01/2021.
24 Fg6, 26/07/2018, Kutapalong.
25 Fg3, 23/04/2018, Kuala Lumpur. Tilly notes that national and ethnic identities can be formed in resistance as strategic interactions (Tilly, 1995).
26 In32, 28/07/2018, Balukhali.
27 Fg2, 22/04/2018, Kuala Lumpur; FG6, 26/07/2018, Kutapalong; Fg8, 28/09/2018, Hakimpara.
28 In47, 26/09/2018, Camp 14; In48, 26/09/2018, Camp 14; In50, 27/09/2018, Extension 4.
29 Fieldwork data were coded according to affect/emotion relating to ID cards. These were some of the recurring affects.
30 In14, 26/04/2018, Kuala Lumpur; Fg4, 27/04/2018, Kuala Lumpur.
31 In46, 26/07/2018, Camp 14.
32 In40, 24/09/2018, Balukhali. In contrast, Rohingya IDPs in Rakhine state—many children—staging public protests, apparently at the urging of the elders, against the NVC push during a well-publicized visit by UN officials to the IDP camps were celebrated by the communities as an act of defiance and resistance.
33 These opinions were consistent with findings in Fortify Rights (2019).
34 Fg6, 26/07/2018, Kutapalong; also Fg8, 26/09/2018, Hakimpara.
35 Meaning the person with administrative responsibilities for 100 houses.
36 In51, 27/09/2018, Extension 4.
37 125,000 Rohingya and other Muslims who were forcibly displaced by state-led violence in 2012–3 remained contained in camps at the end of 2020. The IDP camps are also referred to as detention camps (Human Rights Watch, Fortify Rights) due to the policies of segregation and isolation.
38 Copies of 'receipt cards' on file with author.
39 In40, 24/09/2018, Balukhali. After the period of field research, following the order of provisional measures by ICJ in 2020, 'receipt cards' could temporarily be used to apply for permission to travel internally within Rakhine State. Movement restrictions were reinstated and increased in 2021 Fortify Rights (2021).
40 This opinion was provided repeatedly in interviews and focus groups. It is also reflected in Fortify Rights (2019). After the research period, more Rohingya accepted the NVC card in order to maintain their livelihoods and continue with their jobs and activism work.
41 The low levels of literacy amongst Rohingya communities mean that many people rely on the colour of the documents to know what they are being issued. As such one participant believed that changing the colour of the cards was a 'trick' by state authorities to get Rohingya to accept the card as it was similar to the 'green' naturalised citizenship card. In21, 29/06/2018, Skype from Australia.
42 Copies of the registration forms on file with the author. They are also referred to in Fortify Rights (2019).
43 Fg6, 26/07/2018, Kutapalong.
44 'Pathway to citizenship' is a common term used in statelessness policy literature and is frequently used to describe a solution for Rohingya in Myanmar. The term is objected to by some Rohingya participants since it was understood to be a slow

process towards citizenship rather than the restoration of a citizenship that had been 'stolen' from them. See Brinham, N. (2021).

45 On arbitrariness and discrimination in citizenship application processes, see de Chickera, Arraiza et al. (2021).

46 See, for example, Center for Diversity and National Harmony (2019). Myanmar's Citizenship Law: An Analysis, Which Was Written Prior to the 2017 Violence but Published Several Years After.

47 The 'Kofi Annan Commission' was also criticised by Rohingya for not using their ethnic name, referring to them instead as 'Muslims.'

48 This approach was favoured by UNHCR in 2014 (conversations with author). Favourable statements about NVCs were also made by the EU Ambassador and by key UN staff. See Burma Campaign UK (2018).

49 No consistent government figures were provided regarding the number of citizenship cards issued to Rohingya under national verification exercises. See Human Rights Watch (2020).

50 Fg1, 13/08/2017, New Delhi; Fg5, 28/04/2018, Kuala Lumpur; In64, 26/06/2019, The Hague. Also Ibid.

51 Fg6, 26/07/2018, Kutapalong.

52 The following is written on the back of NVCs: 'This identity card holder is a person who need (sic) to apply for citizenship in accordance with Myanmar Citizenship Law.' Copies of NVCs on file with author.

53 Fg6, 26/07/2018, Kutapalong.

54 In50, 27/09/2018, extension 4; In53, 27/09/2018, Extension 4; In40, 24/09/2018, Balukhali.

55 'Tricks and lies' were other strong themes from coding.

56 Applications for citizenship were indicated in interviews by the further submission of documents and the submission of biometric data.

57 In40, 24/09/2018, Balukhali.

58 Fg1, 13/08/2017, New Delhi; FG5, 28/04/2018, KL; Fg7, 26/07/2018, Kutapalong.

59 In14, 25/04/2018, Kuala Lumpur.

60 In64, 26/06/2019, The Hague.

61 In65, 26/06/2019, The Hague; Fg1, 13/08/2017, New Delhi; In51, 27/09/2018, extension 4; IN42, 24/09/2018, Balukhali.

62 In52, 27/09/2018, extension 4.

63 In14, 26/04/2018, Kuala Lumpur; In42, 24/09/2018, Balukhali.

64 In51, 27/09/2018, extension 4; In42, 24/09/2018, Balukhali.

65 In14, 26/04/2018, Kuala Lumpur; In64, 26/06/2019, The Hague.

Bibliography

Advisory Commission on Rakhine State (Aug 2017). *Towards a Peaceful, Fair and Prosperous Future for the People of Rakhine: Final Report*. www.rakhinecommission.org/app/uploads/2017/08/FinalReport_Eng.pdf [Accessed 05/06/2018]

Amnesty International (2017). *Caged without a Roof: Apartheid in Myanmar's Rakhine State*. www.amnesty.org/en/documents/asa16/7484/2017/en/ [Accessed 02/12/2018]

Anderson, B. R. (1991). *Imagined Communities: Reflections on the Origin and Spread of Nationalism*. Verso.

Arnold, B. (2002). Justifying Genocide: Archaeology and the Construction of Difference, in Hinton, A. L. (ed), *Annihilating Difference: The Anthropology of Genocide*. University of California Press. 95–116.

Brinham, N. (2018). 'Genocide Cards': Rohingya Refugees on Why They Risked Their Lives to Refuse ID Cards. *OpenDemocracy*. www.opendemocracy.net/

natalie-brinham/genocide-cards-why-rohingya-refugees-are-resisting-id-cards [Accessed 30/01/2019]

Brinham, N. (2019). Looking Beyond Invisibility: Rohingyas' Dangerous Encounters with Papers and Cards. *Tilburg Law Review* 24(2).

Brinham, N. (2021). 'We Are Not Stateless! You Can Call Us What You Like, But We Are Citizens of Myanmar!' Rohingya Resistance and the Stateless Label, in Bloom, T. and Kingston, L. (eds), *Statelessness, Governance, and the Problem of Citizenship*. Manchester University Press. 342–355.

Brinham, N., A. D. Tiwari, J. Field, J. Ealom, J. M. Arraiza and A. de Chickera (2020). *Locked In and Locked Out: The Impact of Digital Identity Systems on Rohingya Populations, Institute on Statelessness and Inclusion and UN Special Rapporteur on Racism.* https://files.institutesi.org/Locked_In_Locked_Out_The_Rohingya_Briefing_Paper.pdf [Accessed 25/05/2021]

BROUK (2015). *Rohingya, the Citizenship Law, Temporary Registration and the Implementation of the Rakhine State Action Plan.* http://burmacampaign.org.uk/media/BROUK-White-Card-Briefing.pdf [Accessed 30/04/2019]

Burma Campaign UK (2018). *Rohingya Citizenship: Now or Never.* https://burmacampaign.org.uk/burma_briefing/rohingya-citizenship-now-or-never/ [Accessed 12/02/2021]

Caplan, J. (2013). 'Ausweis Bitte!' Identity and Identification in Nazi Germany, in About, I., Brown, J. and Lonergan, G. (eds), *Identification and Registration Practices in Transnational Perspective: Papers, People and Practices*. Palgrave. 224–242.

Center for Diversity and National Harmony (2019). *Myanmar's Citizenship Law: An Analysis*. www.cdnh.org/publication/myanmars-citizenship-law-an-analysis/ [Accessed 08/10/2019]

Charney, I. W. (2009). The Definition of Genocide, in Totten, S. and Bartrop, P. R. (eds), *The Genocide Studies Reader*. Routledge. 36–39.

Cox, J. M. (2017). *To kill a People: Genocide in the Twentieth Century*. Oxford University Press.

de Chickera, A., J. Arraiza, Z. Albarazi, G. Field and N. Brinham (2021). *Navigating with a Faulty Map: Access to Citizenship Documents and Citizenship in Myanmar, Institute on Statelessness and Inclusion.* https://files.institutesi.org/Access_to_Citizenship_in_Myanmar_Report.pdf [Accessed 28/12/2021]

European Network on Statelessness & Institute on Statelessness and Inclusion (2019). *Statelessness in Myanmar: Country Position Paper.* https://statelessjourneys.org/wp-content/uploads/StatelessJourneys-Myanmar-final.pdf [Accessed 11/11/2019]

Feierstein, D. (2014). *Genocide as Social Practice: Reorganizing Society under the Nazis and Argentina's Military Juntas*. Rutgers University Press.

Feierstein, D. (2015). Debates on the Criminology of Genocide: Genocide as a Technology for Destroying Identities. *State Crime* 4(2): 115–127.

Fein, H. (1993). *Genocide: A Sociological Perspective*. Sage.

Fein, H. (2009). Defining Genocide as a Sociological Concept, in Totten, S. and Barton, P. R. (eds), *The Genocide Studies Reader*. Routledge. 44–55.

Fortify Rights (2014). *Policies of Persecution: Ending Abusive State Policies Against Rohingya Muslims in Myanmar*. https://fortifyrights.org/downloads/Policies_of_Persecution_Feb_25_Fortify_Rights.pdf [Accessed 03/05/2017]

Fortify Rights (2019). *'Tools of Genocide': National Verification Cards and the Denial of Citizenship of Rohingya Muslims in Myanmar*. www.fortifyrights.org/downloads/Tools%20of%20Genocide%20-%20Fortify%20Rights%20-%20September-03-2019-EN.pdf [Accessed 08/10/2019]

Fortify Rights (2021). *UN Security Council: Take Urgent Action against Myanmar Military Junta*. www.fortifyrights.org/mya-inv-2021-12-06/ [Accessed 30/12/2021]

Frieze, D.-L. and R. Lemkin (2013). *Totally Unofficial: The Autobiography of Raphael Lemkin.* Yale University Press.

Green, P., T. McManus and A. de la Cour Venning (2015). Countdown to Annihilation: Genocide in Myanmar. *International State Crime Initiative.* http://statecrime.org/data/2018/04/ISCI-Rohingya-Report-II-PUBLISHED-VERSION-revised-compressed.pdf [Accessed 29/08/2024]

Green, P., T. McManus and A. de la Cour Venning (2018). Genocide Achieved, Genocide Continues: Myanmar's annihilation of the Rohingya. *International State Crime Initiative.* http://statecrime.org/data/2018/04/ISCI-Rohingya-Report-II-PUBLISHED-VERSION-revised-compressed.pdf [Accessed 29/08/2024]

Harff, B. and T. R. Gurr (1988). Toward Empirical Theory of Genocides and Politicides: Identification and Measurement of Cases Since 1945. *International Studies Quarterly* 32(3): 359–371.

Hayden, R. M. (1996). Imagined Communities and Real Victims: Self-Determination and Ethnic Cleansing in Yugoslavia. *American Ethnologist* 23(4): 783–801.

Hinton, A. L. (2002). Introduction: Genocide and Anthropology, in Hinton, A. L. (ed), *Genocide: An Anthropological Reader.* Blackwell.

Human Rights Watch (2020). *An Open Prison without End: Myanmar's Mass Detention of Rohingya in Rakhine State.* www.hrw.org/report/2020/10/08/open-prison-without-end/myanmars-mass-detention-rohingya-rakhine-state [Accessed 09/10/2020]

International Court of Justice (23 Jan 2020). *Order on Provisional Measures: Application of the Convention on the Prevention and Punishment of the Crime of Genocide (Gambia v. Myanmar).* www.icj-cij.org/public/files/case-related/178/178-20200123-ORD-01-00-EN.pdf [Accessed 06/01/2021]

Leach, E. (1973). *Political Systems of Highland Burma.* Berg.

Lemkin, R. (1944). Axis Rule in Occupied Europe: Law of Occupation, Analysis of Government, Proposals for Redress. *Carnegie Endowment for International Peace, Division of International Law.*

Lemkin, R. (2002). Genocide (Extracts from Axis Rule in Occupied Europe 1944), in Hinton, A. L. (ed), *Genocide: An Anthropological Reader.* Blackwell.

Lieberman, V. B. (1978). Ethnic Politics in Eighteenth-Century Burma. *Modern Asian Studies* 12(3): 455–482.

Longman, T. (2001). Identity Cards, Ethnic Self-Perception, and Genocide in Rwanda, in Caplan, J. and Torpey, J. (eds), *Documenting Individual Identity: The Development of State Practices in the Modern World.* Princeton University Press. 346–348.

Republic of the Union of Myanmar (2013). *Final Report of Inquiry Commission on Sectarian Violence in Rakhine State.* https://meriyadh.org/images/pdf/rakhine-commission-report-en-red.pdf [Accessed 05/09/2017]

Sands, P. (2016). *East West Street: On the Origins of Genocide and Crimes Against Humanity.* Weidenfeld and Nicolson.

Scott, J. C. (1998). *Seeing Like a State: How Certain Schemes to Improve the Human Conditions Have Failed.* Yale University Press.

Scott, J. C. (2009). *The Art of Not being Governed: An Anarchist History of Upland Southeast Asia.* Yale University Press.

Siegelberg, M. L. (2013). Unofficial Men, Efficient Civil Servants: Raphael Lemkin in the History of International Law. *Journal of Genocide Research* 15(3): 297–316.

Siegelberg, M. L. (2020). *Statelessness: A Modern History.* Harvard University Press.

Simon Skjodt Center for the Prevention of Genocide (2020). How the Genocide Convention's Obligation to Prevent Applies to Myanmar, Legal Brief Report 2: The Denial of the Right to Citizenship and the Right to Participate in Public Affairs, United States Holocaust Memorial Museum. https://vault.ushmm.org/adaptivemedia/rendition/id_f4f26d53e72a39aafc94ffc178328d4144b7f8ac [Accessed 30/08/2024]

Stanton, G. H. (1998). The 8 Stages of Genocide. *Working Paper of the Yale Program in Genocide Studies*. www.genocidewatch.com/images/8StagesBriefingpaper.pdf%2C [Accessed 28/03/2017]
Stanton, G. H. (2004). Could the Rwandan Genocide Have been Prevented? *Journal of Genocide Research* 6(2): 211–228.
Stanton, G. H. (2017). *The Ten Stages of Genocide, Genocide Watch*. http://genocidewatch.net/genocide-2/8-stages-of-genocide/ [Accessed 20/01/2021]
Tilly, C. (1995). Citizenship, Identity and Social History. *International Review of Social History* 40(S3): 1–17.
Torpey, J. (2000). *The Invention of the Passport: Surveillance, Citizenship, and the State*. Cambridge University Press.
Totten, S. and P. R. Bartrop, eds (2009). *The Genocide Studies Reader*. Routledge.
UNHRC (Sept 2018). Report of the Independent International Fact-Finding Mission on Myanmar: Report of the 34th Session of the Human Rights Council A/HRC/34/67.
UNHRC (Sept 2019). Detailed Findings of the Independent International Fact-Finding Mission on Myanmar: Report to the 42nd Session of the Human Rights Council, A/HRC/42/CRP.5.

7 'Genocide cards'

IDs, registration, and the phases of Rohingya genocide

Introduction

This chapter frames Rohingya ID narratives within Feierstein's phases of genocide, as outlined in Chapter 6. Drawing on Lemkin and Feierstein's work on genocides that reorganise national identities and social relations, I explore how registration and identity card schemes in Myanmar feature in Rohingya narratives as attempts to destroy Rohingya identities and impose new national identities as part of the objectives of reorganising genocides. I consider how the production of statelessness was a slow process that accompanied and was integral to the phases of genocide. The chapter considers harassment and isolation, policies of systematic weakening, and preparation and extermination. I focus particularly on how the production of statelessness over time contributed to and culminated in 'symbolic enactment' (Feierstein's sixth phase of genocide). This phase was originally described by Lemkin (2002:27–28) as 'the imposition of the national pattern of the oppressor' and is a key element of Feierstein (2014) conceptualisation of genocide, in which the effect and aim of terror are to destroy and reorganise social relations. There were considerable overlaps and intersections between these stages in Rohingya narratives, owing to the ongoing cycles of identity destruction. These overlaps and intersections are noted throughout the chapter.

Stigmatisation

Feierstein's first phase of genocide, 'stigmatisation,' broadly correlates with Stanton's 'classification' and 'symbolisation' stages. He places greater emphasis on the myths and discourses legitimised through such processes. Within this stage, 'those in power draw on symbols in the collective imagination, build new myths and reinforce latent prejudices' to construct 'negative Otherness' (2014:110). In the Myanmar situation, methods of reinforcing exclusionary myths included the enactment of the 1982 citizenship law, the implementation of an associated colour-coded identity card scheme from 1989 onwards, and latterly NVC enforcement. As described in Chapter 4, the citizenship rules lent a historical legitimacy to notions of belonging and

DOI: 10.4324/9781003494539-7
This chapter has been made available under a CC-BY 4.0 license.

ethnicity based on the 'myth of 1824' (Charney 2018). The rules reinforced the re-imagination of the Burma region as a bounded Buddhist nation-state within which were contained a set of fixed indigenous minority groups that pre-existed British colonisation (Charney 2016). Previous chapters have also described how, based on the shifting boundaries between citizens and foreigners, Rakhine Buddhists were re-imagined as the protectors of the 'western gate' preventing the 'illegal' entry of South Asian or Muslim 'others' (see also Zarni and Brinham 2017). These myths of nationhood and citizenship collided with the demographic reality of a large Muslim and heterogeneous 'borderland' community with ancestral links to territory within the modern-day borders of Myanmar. Accordingly, a citizenship regime was produced which was violent or 'pathological,' to use Spiro's (2011) term, in that it did not comport to the organic population on the ground.[1] It was the state ID scheme that gave these myths a material form. The ID cards people held stigmatised them and actualised their experiences of discrimination, segregation, persecution, and harassment based on a reworked ideology.

Within Rohingya narratives, stigmatisation was closely associated with the colour-coded state ID scheme in Myanmar that was implemented in accordance with the 1982 Citizenship law. This ID scheme was first rolled out in 1989 and underwent several changes that further stigmatised Rohingya culminating in the NVCs after 2015. As such, stigmatisation was better characterised not as one that preceded all other stages of genocide but as a slow process that intensified over time and was interspersed with episodes of mass violence and expulsion. ID-associated stigmatisation was often juxtaposed in narratives against nostalgia for the NRCs of the past (see Chapter 5). It was often recounted that NRCs were of the same appearance for everyone across the country and did not display ethnic or religious data. As such, they represented an era free of stigmatisation and underlined Rohingya equal status with others. White cards and NVCs, on the other hand, were noted in narratives as pivotal points of ideological departure from the more inclusive NRC era.[2] Contrastingly, these IDs reinforced and reconstituted the latent prejudices from Myanmar's colonial past that were revived by the 1982 Citizenship Law and contributed to the gradual reorganisation of social relations in ways that 'othered' Rohingya (Zarni and Brinham 2017).

There were four key stigmatising features of the post-1989 ID schemes identified by participants in the fieldwork. First, the colour coding of IDs from 1989 onwards immediately identified the holder as being of lower status, with less of a claim to belong. The hierarchy of belonging was coded on cards from 1989 onwards as pink for full citizens, green for naturalised citizens, and white for Rohingya or those with undecided national status.[3] The white cards were invalidated in 2015 and NVCs issued in their stead. Second, displaying ethnic and religious data on all national IDs, marked Rohingya out for discrimination. There were different and shifting stigma-related meanings attached to ethnic and religious data displayed on cards. Such stigmas included most notably being recorded as 'Bengali' which had connotations of being foreign or 'other';[4] having ethnic identity recorded under the religious category 'Muslim';[5] the absence of ethnic data, which inferred 'Bengali' or foreigner (NVCs post-2016), etc. Third, data contained on registration documents that inferred the place of origin as being in North Rakhine State, used in conjunction with religious identifiers, marked Rohingya out and stigmatised them. For example, those living outside of Rakhine State were required to hide their Rohingya identity in order to function safely in society.[6] Data or issue numbers on ID cards for either themselves or parents could mark them out as originating from North Rakhine State and therefore stigmatised them as 'Bengali.' In such cases, there was a risk of harassment and extortion by state authorities. It could also lead to internal 'deportation' from elsewhere in Myanmar to the areas of North Rakhine State where Rohingya were segregated and contained. Fourth, at certain times, the absence of any individual ID or registration documents stigmatised Rohingya and left them increasingly vulnerable to harassment by both state authorities and the broader populations. This included the period between 1989 and the mid-1990s before white cards were issued and the period after 2015 when white cards were expired. Notably, though, after the white cards were nullified and collected in 2015, most Rohingya participants felt the stigma of holding NVCs was greater than having no IDs.

NVCs were generally understood to indicate an additional step beyond the white cards in the stigmatisation process. White cards and NVCs functioned in a similar way relating to the state and local bureaucracies, as a pre-requisite to applying for multiple permissions and licenses including for travel between townships; marriage and birth registration; as well as temporary permits for fishing, farming, driving, and other livelihood-related activities. However, white cards denoted a temporary status in limbo between citizenship and noncitizenship. Although this limbo became indefinite, the stigma was still considered lesser than the NVCs. For example, 'In 1989. . . Rohingya . . . were given temporary citizenship. Even with the white card, we had citizenship rights—we were voting and in parliament.'[7] NVCs, on the other hand, were understood to permanently cement a noncitizenship status. In this respect, group resistance to NVCs can be understood as a rejection of the stigmatising and 'othering' features of personal identification processes in Myanmar.

Harassment, isolation, and policies of systematic weakening

The stages of harassment, isolation, and policies of systematic weakening outlined in Feierstein's scholarship were reflected in Rohingya narratives. They also developed over time, rapidly intensifying prior to episodes of mass violence/terror and after mass repatriations. These stages did not so much occur one after another, but rather mutually reinforced one another. As such,

I include them in the same section. There is a broad human rights literature documenting how policies enabled the persecution of Rohingya and established a system of isolation, discrimination, and apartheid. Segregation and isolation were systematised under the *NaSaKa* in North Rakhine State from the 1990s onwards.[8] This broadened to other areas of Rakhine, including Sittwe, Kyauktaw, and Kyaukpyu after the violence of 2012, when Rohingya and other Muslims were forced from their homes and lands and detained in camps (Equal Rights Trust 2012; Human Rights Watch 2013, 2020). Extensive human rights abuses were documented as occurring during these periods, including land grab, forced labour, torture, enforced disappearances, sexual exploitation, extortion, mass arbitrary arrests, and detention. Some research from the period placed the abuses within the framework of Crimes against Humanity (NUI Galway 2010; Amnesty International 2017) and genocide (Zarni and Cowley 2014; Green, McManus et al. 2015; Yale Law School and Fortify Rights 2015). Given the volume of existing human rights documentation, this section does not focus on the legal and policy framework. Instead, drawing on the field research, it considers the ways in which state registration and identification processes enabled persecution and weakened societal structures and relations in ways that undermined group identities.

From the 1990s onwards, the colour-coded ID scheme helped to hold in place a system which segregated and isolated Rohingya from the rest of Myanmar society. Rohingya were increasingly contained in geographical pockets in Rakhine State with stigma and harassment resulting from ethnic and religious categorisation as well as geographic location. A separate set of policies was applied to Rohingya in these areas and implemented on the basis of their lower status as white card holders, and their categorisation as 'Bengali' or 'Muslim' on family lists. Rohingya and persons of mixed Muslim heritage often described functioning outside the area of North Rakhine State prior to the 1990s, then being contained, issued with white cards, and treated as noncitizens.[9] Rohingya in these areas were made subject to a broad range of restrictions including restrictions of movement between townships and village tracts; marriage and birth restrictions; and restrictions on access to education, healthcare, and livelihoods (Fortify Rights 2014). White cards became mandatory after the 1990s repatriations. They were a requirement for civil registration (birth, marriage, and marriage permission), access to basic services (healthcare and education) and a wide range of bureaucratic permissions required for everyday life such as travel between townships, and licenses necessary for livelihoods such as fishing and driving.[10] Meanwhile, the family lists functioned as proof of habitual residence in Myanmar. As such, the threat of being struck from the family list or being 'blacklisted' by state authorities underlay many experiences of harassment, extortion, expulsion, arbitrary arrest, and detention. It also became a driver of a steady flow of Rohingya leaving Myanmar from the mid-1990s onwards in between the episodes of mass violence.[11]

For the most part, the bureaucratic violence associated with state-issued documents was described by participants as intense and devastating, but quietly executed. When family members had their residency cancelled, sending them into permanent exile, participants recounted how these acts of extreme violence and consequence were carried out with the mundane act of striking an absent family member's name off the family list with a pen. Reasons for cancellation were written on the edges of the family lists in Burmese. Sometimes the comments were illegible or recorded incorrectly.[12] Likewise, land confiscation was experienced as a bureaucratic formality, sometimes without ever coming face-to-face with the security services responsible. Landowners were mostly informed by Rohingya village chairmen that their properties had been requisitioned. Flags would be placed around the confiscated land. Then, their yearly land registration documents would simply not be renewed.[13]

There was a gendered dimension to experiences of ID-related abuses. Gendered norms underscored by experiences of insecurity and violence meant that Rohingya men were more likely to undertake regular activities in the public sphere including travelling for work, education, or crossing checkpoints. As such, accounts of ID-related discrimination and abuse often featured white cards which were needed for these journeys and economic activities. A common experience was being beaten or humiliated when attempting to travel or obtain permission to travel either within or outside North Rakhine State. Often the perpetrators required them to say that they were Bengali, deny their Rohingya identity, or renounce their Burmese identity.[14]

> I was working with the fire service as a volunteer. When the violence started, they called me to the office and beat me using many techniques. I was blamed—'you may be involved in the ethnic violation against other communities. That's why you must come every day to the office'. . . . They gave me a big drum to fill up with water. They gave me only a spoon. Using the spoon to take the water, I had to fill the drum in 13 hours. If I couldn't fill the drum in 13 hours, I was tortured very seriously. I was told to return home at 6. But it was curfew at 6—the government did not allow us to be in the street. While I was travelling home, I was arrested. They beat me and made me say I am 'Bengali Kalar.'

A larger proportion of women's accounts of harassment and abuse related to the family lists. Often women occupied the private sphere and worked within the home or vicinity.[15] Direct encounters with state authorities, therefore mostly occurred at home and involved either regular household checks of the family lists (generally twice yearly) or spot checks of the family list. Household checks involved armed security forces and sometimes civil administrators. Security forces conducting checks included *NaSaKa* (later BGP), immigration, the police, and sometimes the army. The process was described as intimidating and degrading. For example, one woman described how local informers told the authorities that her husband had left the country. The authorities came to her home and extorted money from her. Unable to pay the 'fines,' he was struck from the family list. She was pregnant at the time and had to conceal her pregnancy as the child could not be registered on the family list if the husband was absent. After the child was born, she paid large bribes to have the child added as a twin to her sister-in-law's family list, to ensure the child was not 'blacklisted.'[16]

From the 1990s onwards, families were gathered by these authorities outside the house and their group photographs were taken by the team in order to scrutinise the family list on the following visits.[17] Harassment and abuse often related to minor errors or infringements on household and property registration documents. These included people on the household list being absent from the home or overstaying their travel permits, additional persons staying in the household who were not recorded on the family list, livestock not being registered according to the regulations, and unregistered home upgrades or repairs.[18] Experiences most often included extortion and threats of arrest. Extortion levels were higher if family members had fled the country—especially if relatives were known to be in Saudi Arabia.[19] For example, a village chairman noted:

> After 1992 the military came for inspection. On the family list, they attached the group picture. They also took pictures of all of the houses and masjids, schools, cows, goats, everything. Then after the next year, if they see that due to the picture that there are changes, like a bamboo fence for example. They will say—'who permitted you to do this?' Every December they came and checked all the boundary of the houses. If one bit is out of the measurements, then they will be fined for the house. If there is anyone absent in the house, then he will be removed.[20]

Where the bribes were refused or could not be paid, it would most often result in household members being crossed off the family list, thus cancelling their right to reside in Myanmar, which in turn caused them to flee from Myanmar. Otherwise, it could result in the arrest of household members on immigration charges.[21] The absence of Rohingya men in a household was often described as a vulnerability for women and girls and for the community as a whole.[22] In these ways, oppressive registration and ID processes changed the gender balance of communities and the make-up of households, producing vulnerabilities, and driving further outward forced migration.[23]

From the 1990s, the restrictions and discriminatory policies were enforced by the *NaSaKa*, replaced in 2013 by the Border Guard Police (BGP). The *NaSaKa* was established and directed by former head of military intelligence, General Khin Nyunt until he was purged in 2004. *NaSaKa* was a hybrid security force that was only deployed in Rohingya areas (International Crisis

Group 2013). Thus, it was not only the laws and policies that produced a system of segregation and isolation but also the methods of enforcement and military intelligence strategies that were developed specifically for Rohingya populations. Khin Nyunt developed a surveillance and informer network that underlay the rights abuses. Participants explained how the informer networks created an environment of intra-communal mistrust, paranoia, and fear. Regular informers populated neighbourhoods and markets. They accrued small financial or other benefits from the information they provided.[24] Abuses relating to household registration often occurred after a row or disagreement with neighbours. Neighbours could inform each other regarding overnight guests, absent family members or children who had been registered incorrectly.[25] This created an insecure environment in which minor disputes with neighbours could result in severe punishment and exile. It also led to mistrust of one another within communities and the breakdown of informal community support networks. For example:

> I had to pay much higher bribes to have my last daughter registered on the family list because my husband was in Saudi Arabia. They charge more. I tried to hide that he was there, but the neighbours informed on me. They were brokers who were working for the authorities, so it was easy for them to inform.[26]

Villages were organised into administrative units that were managed by government township offices. Chairmen were at the top of the hierarchy of village administration. They were generally Rohingya until 2005–10, when they were gradually replaced by non-Muslims.[27] Chairmen provided information to state authorities on the population within their area and provided supporting documentation for additions to the family list, including newborns and spouses. In these ways, they helped the authorities maintain the family lists. They also relayed information from the state authorities to the populations within their district including registration and ID requirements and operations. There was a hierarchy of lower-level Rohingya leaders underneath them in charge of a set number of households, for example, 100 houses and 10 houses. Known as 'in-charges,' these low-level administrators were asked to relay official information to members of these 10 or 100 houses and feedback data on the populations in these houses.[28]

All chairmen and in-charges prior to 2010 were not paid salaries. These were voluntary positions. Nonetheless, benefits were accrued through these roles. There were financial gains, as all forms of registration, permissions, and paperwork involved 'informal' fees or bribery from which the chairmen would benefit.[29] Often chairmen were also able to secure business deals or licenses from state officials that brought financial rewards. Examples from the research include permission to run the jetties and boats that cross to Bangladesh, licenses to oversee market vendors, cross-border trade deals, and negotiating the sale of black-market goods between the Myanmar and Bangladesh security forces.

They were also able to secure travel permissions and other benefits through their government and military contacts. Rohingya in these positions were implicated in systems of endemic corruption and extortion and were open to manipulation by state officials. However, they were also sometimes able to ease the bureaucratic burdens for community members or offer minimal forms of protection from harassment related to state registration by vouching for members of the community or calling in favours on their behalf. One former chairman explained his role as supportive:

> I was chairman when the people returned home from Bangladesh in 1993, then the military called me. So, I had documents that list all the families in my village. So that family when they were in Myanmar, they had seven persons. But after they fled to Bangladesh and were due to return, they became 8 persons. And their son got married with a girl. So, who is she? And where is she from? And where is her village? So, I helped them get the proper documents.[30]

The calibre of the village-in-charges was understood to have diminished over the years. The positions in the past were generally held by educated or high-status people. However, the educated class was often targeted for arrest or enforced disappearance with the impact of weakening social structures in Rohingya areas.[31] As such, chairmen positions were taken up by persons of less status who offered significant bribes to the government officials. This was viewed as a form of investment to secure future income.[32] Participants complained about chairmen and in-charges increasingly being unable to operate effectively with the government power structures in order to protect villagers from registration-related abuses.

> Now, those that are Rohingya—the village-in-charge and head of 100 houses, 10 houses, they all are also corrupted- they have invested the money. There are some good people who really want to give the service for their own community but most of them are corrupted. The village administrators who have the full authorisation to appoint them, they only select the people who will advance their rule. Only the corrupted people are selected—and their intention is to pacify the people. So, this is their system.[33]

Chairmen were thus sometimes spoken about with respect and reverence. In other cases, they were viewed with an intense mistrust and disregard. One woman described spiralling registration costs and extortion from many levels of bureaucracy, including the Rohingya chairman.[34] On the other hand, some chairmen spoke about how they were able to bend the rules or shortcut registration requirements in order to help households in difficulty. For example, following repatriations from Bangladesh, they could assist those who had been left off the family lists due to marriage or births occurring outside Myanmar in the Bangladesh refugee camps.[35] In one case, a former chairman was referred to by others as 'MI' (military intelligence) and openly described the role of other Rohingya MI agents. His narrative was one of the saviour, describing how he had been able to negotiate for the return of lands after Rohingya were repatriated in the 1990s, in 2012 help hide Rohingya victims of violence and, in 2017, when he could no longer protect himself or others inside Myanmar, provided cost-free escape routes across the border through his boat business.[36] Nonetheless, the violence of paperwork, coupled with surveillance practices that pervaded societal structures, dismantled social and familial relations. State registration processes were turned into systems of bureaucratic violence through which Rohingya were implicated in policing and surveillance of their own communities. This left a pervasive sense of mistrust of their own and enabled the destruction of the social fabric within Rohingya communities. These elements of destruction were part of the 'systematic weakening' of social structures identified by Feierstein (2014) as part of a broader genocidal process (see also Green, McManus et al. 2015). Important in some Rohingya narratives was the notion that the system of endemic corruption was deliberately put in place by Khin Nyunt and others to actively enable an environment of extortion and oppression.[37] For example:

> Khin Nyunt was a brilliant strategist and politician. If money could do something, he would do it. If strategy can do something, he will do it. Force was the last option. He only used force if he needed to.[38]

Under this system, the revenue that *NaSaKa* personnel derived from bribery and corruption related to bureaucratic functions and the cross-border black market were understood as perks of the job.[39] This system of corruption was also effective in maintaining a surveillance grid through which abuses continued to occur and drive Rohingya from their lands.

Changes in the administrative and surveillance structures in Rohingya areas brought a further decline in informal social protections. The system of voluntary village chairmen was changed to a more formalised one with a salary around 2010. Since Rohingya, as white card holders were banned from government jobs, they were not allowed to be paid for this role. Most Rohingya village chairmen were replaced by Rakhine or other members of the *taingyintha* even in Rohingya areas. Those Rohingya who worked as chairmen had to do so in a voluntary capacity. This further reduced the function of informal protections from bureaucratic violence that Rohingya chairmen were able to offer in the past. It created another layer of vulnerability of Rohingya communities to bureaucratic violence as the white cards were invalidated and NVCs were imposed.[40]

In the general elections of 2010, Thein Sein's USDP party campaigned in Rohingya areas. During fieldwork, Rohingya showed their USDP membership cards, from this period, which identified them as 'Muslim,' not 'Bengali.' They shared photos from the meetings during the campaign period. They recounted how one of USDP's election pledges was to campaign for citizenship cards for Rohingya. The hope, when the USDP was elected and Thein Sein became president, was that citizenship opportunities for Rohingya would be opened up. Thus, when the state-led violence occurred in 2012, and when white cards and voting rights were revoked by Thein Sein ahead of the 2015 general elections, participants overwhelmingly described feelings of betrayal.[41] This sense of betrayal and the increasing levels of precariousness in Rohingya communities underscored their resistance efforts relating to the state issuance of NVCs.

> Before the 2010 elections, Thein Sein's USDP party came to the village and selected candidates. They committed that within short time they will provide us with nationality cards. 'Don't worry' they said, 'if you work for us, we will provide you after our party is elected with a citizenship card'. . . . Then later in 2015 Thein Sein told us we cannot even vote—they took the white cards and demanded that we need the nationality card.[42]

Following this period, attempts to enforce NVCs began. Important features in Rohingya narratives about NVCs as a part of the genocide process involved articulating who enforced them and by what methods. In focus groups, accounts listed different state entities that were involved. Accounts were structured as such, to build a picture of how, as the process became increasingly coercive, all sectors of government were implicated from civil administration to health and education professionals, from immigration and the border guard police (BGP) to the army. By describing such an extensive and coercive process, participants inferred that the orders for both bureaucratic and genocidal violence were delivered through the same command structures. This 'plan' was understood to have been executed by the military generals at the top of the command structure, and to directly involve the civilian government as well as the security sector. As one participant explained:

> 'Every department tried to force us (to take NVCs) in their own ways. It is not only the immigration department. That is how we can know it is centrally planned and part of the genocide.'[43]

His comment, corroborated by the fieldwork more generally, identified a wide range of actors and methods of coercion. Attempts to forcibly issue NVCs occurred in village meetings, in homes, and also in various settings outside the neighbourhood, impacting all aspects of social and economic life.

Outside of homes and villages, participants described the following attempts to forcibly issue NVCs.[44] Accessing healthcare in hospitals required Rohingya to pass through checkpoints. It was reported that people requiring hospital treatment outside their area, were only allowed to pass through checkpoints if they had registered for an NVC (see also Physicians for Human Rights 2016). Others reported that hospital staff and doctors themselves attempted to force patients to accept NVCs.[45] Students reported that they were told by headteachers that they were not allowed to sit exams, matriculate or enrol in new schools/classes without NVC cards. Parents who refused NVC cards were also told that their children could not continue their education as punishment. Punishing children for parents' refusal to take the NVCs through the education systems, was one of the most emotional issues in interviews because it impacted roles and relationships within the family structure.[46]

The civil administrators in the township offices attempted to enforce NVCs by refusing various forms of registration and permissions for those who did not accept NVCs. This directly impacted family life. Marriage permissions were not issued, effectively illegalising relationships. Parents could not register the births of their children on the family list if they refused NVCs. This led to 'blacklisting' or denying children residence rights in Rakhine on the basis of NVC non-compliance.[47] Blacklisting was described as a driver of forced migration. Further, township administrators refused licenses and permissions required to earn income if applicants did not submit data for NVC registration. Fishermen could not obtain the licenses required to go fishing. Agricultural workers could not obtain products required for their work without travel permission. Shopkeepers could not obtain the required licenses to stay open. Permits to drive cars and bikes were not issued, restricting trade and business. Daily labourers and businessmen could not obtain travel passes to go through checkpoints to earn a living. This severely impacted household-level incomes, leading to shortages of food and basic necessities.

NVCs were enforced at the network of checkpoints between different towns and villages, with reports that Rohingya were no longer allowed to pass checkpoints without NVCs, and those that refused NVCs would be subject to abuse and intimidation at checkpoints. The orders were understood to come from the highest (G1) level.

> 'The G1 ordered the checkpoint officers to pressure us to take the NVC. If I made the journey 12 miles to reach Maungdaw town, I would need to pass through 7 check points. Every single check point would ask me for NVC.'[48]

This was particularly problematic for those who traded in the market towns—for example, buying and selling cattle or agricultural products. Without NVCs, travel through checkpoints was initially still possible with large bribes. The costs of bribery skyrocketed as pressure to issue NVCs increased. As both pressure and resistance to the NVCs mounted, the costs became so high that it rendered businesses unviable. Merchants and traders interviewed reported they had to pass through between 4 and 7 checkpoints to reach the market. At each checkpoint, escalating bribes were required until they had to give up their businesses altogether.[49]

In some accounts, bribes were simply not taken any more at checkpoints. In refusing bribes or extorting money, checkpoint personnel were reportedly acting on orders from above with the purpose of imposing NVCs by further curtailing movement. Thus, the systems of bribery endorsed through the chain of command, which had been utilised out of necessity by Rohingya as a survival mechanism, were closed down in order to enforce the NVC scheme. NVCs were further enforced by prison guards. There were multiple reports that those who had served out prison sentences either could not obtain release or could not travel home from prison without accepting an NVC card. This included those who had been arbitrarily arrested in the past, including following the 2012 violence.[50]

NVCs were also imposed upon those working with UN agencies and some humanitarian INGOs. This was provided as evidence that the international agencies were too close to the perpetrating Myanmar State authorities. Some claimed that their quiet supporting role in state ID card schemes over the years illustrated that they were the 'agents' of the Myanmar government. Rohingya UN/INGO staff were unable to receive their salaries through their bank accounts without NVCs. With banking a requirement for receiving salaries, staff were unable to retain their jobs if they did not comply.[51] A Rohingya man pensioned from a government job, also reported that he was unable to access his pensions without an NVC.[52]

The impact of making so many permissions and licenses contingent on registering for an NVC, combined with the excessive restrictions and the infrastructure of bureaucracy that were already in place, was devastating for Rohingya at the individual, household, and societal levels. Livelihoods, family life, and social life were severely impacted. These intensifying coercive practices left Rohingya increasingly unable to survive on a day-to-day basis without NVCs. In attempts to forcibly issue NVCs, Rohingya were prevented from accessing livelihoods, income and access to nutritional opportunities, healthcare, and other basic services. This impacted Rohingyas' ability to survive in Myanmar. As such, the NVC scheme significantly contributed to the destruction of Rohingya as a group. Whilst the focus of this section is on Feierstein's second to fourth stages of genocide, it is also noteworthy that findings from this research were consistent with those in a Fortify Rights report which suggested that the methods of enforcing NVCs contributed to the following acts of genocide: *causing serious bodily or mental harm to members of the group; deliberately inflicting on the group conditions of life, calculated to bring about its physical destruction in whole or in part* (Article 2, Genocide Convention).

This section has shown how ID cards and registration processes held together a system of bureaucratic violence that enabled harassment, isolation, and a persecutory policy framework. Coupled with the implementation of a pervasive militarised surveillance regime, ID and registration practices that specifically targeted Rohingya populations helped to break down social relations between Rohingya and broader Rakhine and Myanmar society. They also weakened intra-communal social structures and informal protection and survival strategies. The following section continues to focus on NVCs as pressure and tension built towards the mass violence in 2017.

Preparation and extermination

This section considers the connections made in Rohingya narratives between NVCs and the mass killings and violence executed by the Myanmar armed forces in 2016–7. The field research involved participants from across North Rakhine State. As such it built a regional picture. From the field research, the roll-out of the NVC scheme was often considered by participants to be preparation for genocidal violence; and Rohingya resistance to the NVCs was also understood as a significant trigger factor for campaigns of terror. Tensions between state authorities and Rohingya built up over time as attempts to implement the NVC scheme were met with increasing resistance. As such, this section focuses on events that occurred at the village and household levels in 2016 and 2017.[53]

The issuance of NVCs was initially attempted through a series of village-level meetings. At first, these meetings were called by civil administrators. As these attempts failed, further meetings were held involving armed security forces. News spread between the different areas of Maungdaw, Buthidaung, and Rathedaung regarding these meetings. Likewise, warnings that the cards threatened to further destroy Rohingya as a national and ethnic identity circulated between local areas and between Rohingya diaspora and local communities.

Resistance in the form of non-compliance with the NVC scheme grew. Villagers also increasingly refused to attend the meetings or spoke out against the NVC scheme in the meetings as a form of civil disobedience. Government authorities attempted to roll out the ID system through the existing village administrative structures, putting pressure on chairman and in-charges. Latterly, household checks and night-time raids occurred. Army abuses in villages related to 'counter-insurgency' and 'clearance operations' were also linked in narratives with forced issuance of NVCs (also findings in UNHRC 16th Sept 2019; Green, McManus et al. 2018). The following looks in more detail at this process.

Participants described how attempts to issue NVCs first began with village meetings being called. The meetings began with high-ranking members of the civil administration from township/regional level. They were non-Rohingya 'outsiders' and were Rakhine, Bamar, or other *Taingyintha*. When the meetings with these government officials failed to result in NVC registrations, further meetings were organised, with immigration, then with BGP and the military present. There were often three or four meetings in each village. Immigration, BGP, and the military were armed and carried guns in the meetings. Participants reported that high+ranking officers attended and spoke at these meetings. This was understood as an attempt to intimidate villagers into complying with the NVC scheme.[54] It was obligatory for chairmen (Rakhine or Rohingya) and in-charges (Rohingya) to attend the meetings. Other men from the village would be gathered. Men of status, or with government links, were instructed or coerced into joining. Sometimes the purpose of the meetings was obscured in order to gather people. For example, men from a village in Rathedaung explained that they were told the meeting was with NGOs about development projects, only to find it was a meeting about NVCs with no NGOs present.[55]

In the meetings, civil authorities would convey that NVCs were mandatory and without the cards Rohingya would not have the right to remain in Myanmar. Participants from across all areas of North Rakhine State were consistent in saying that if they did not accept NVCs, they would not be permitted to remain in Myanmar. It was repeatedly noted that this was perceived by participants as a threat that they would be forcibly removed. With the hindsight of the atrocities that occurred during the operations of 2017, they believed this threat had been carried out—but in the form of both mass killings/extermination and a campaign of terror to forcibly remove them.[56] The meetings also often involved promises that holders would be given freedom of movement and in the future may be eligible for citizenship. These promises were generally described as 'trickery' or 'lies,' and that the underlying purpose of the cards was to 'make them into foreigners' and destroy Rohingyas' identity as a group belonging to Rakhine.[57] Once again with the benefit of hindsight, participants were able to explain how these were indeed 'lies' since those with NVCs were still subjected to restrictions of movement.[58]

Chairmen (if Rohingya) and in-charges were told by civil and armed authorities that they must ensure the households within their administrative units accept NVCs. They were pressured to register for NVCs as an example to others. They were told that they would be dismissed from their positions if they failed to register, or if they failed to get the households in their units to comply. Additionally, as the pressure mounted, they were also threatened with arrest.[59] Participants described how these meetings with the armed forces became flashpoints of violence. Villagers who spoke out or asked questions in the meetings were threatened, arrested, and beaten or tortured. Often villagers' comments were about the NVCs being for foreigners—and that they were not foreigners.[60] Four interviewees from the same village explained how one such meeting with BGP presence unfolded.[61] One of the in-charges (also interviewed[62]) became frustrated and banged his hand on the table asking what the benefits of the card were and why they had to hold them. The BGP officers pointed their guns at him and escorted him from the room. He was handcuffed to a chair in the school. Meanwhile, tensions in the meeting increased because he had been removed from the meeting. People began to gather outside the school. Verbal protests in the meeting gained momentum. Approximately 30 people were arrested. Those arrested were then forced to register for NVCs in exchange for release. Four of those arrested attempted to run away. One man was too slow and was caught by BGP. He was severely beaten and, as a result, lost his sight in one eye. He was sentenced to six years in prison.[63] He was given early release in 2018 and fled to the Bangladesh camps where he was housed amongst others from his village.[64] He was described as 'severely mentally disturbed' as a result of the recurrent torture he endured during his detention. The other three men managed to escape before being charged. However, following a report from a local informer, BGP forces arrived at one of the men's houses to search for him. His son-in-law saw BGP arriving, panicked, and ran from the house. He was shot dead as he ran. His widow and children were also living nearby in the camp at the time of interview.

Similar patterns of events were described across other villages in northern Rakhine during 2016–7 with both resistance and tensions rising over time. Often it was the chairmen, in-charges, or men of status who were targeted for arrest. Targeting these men was understood as a way to break people's resolve in refusing NVCs. It made people more fearful—since these men were government representatives or had government links. As such they would usually have some protection from arrest and harassment. Their arrests were seen as an indicator that the informal village structures through which villagers sought minimal informal protections from harassment were under assault.[65] Several accounts explained how chairmen and in-charges had accepted the NVCs under pressure. In the public meetings, they would counsel villagers to take the cards, but in private they would counsel them to resist. In this way, they tried to maintain respect amongst the villagers whilst keeping their position.[66] One in-charge also described how he was fearful of the reaction of villagers if he accepted the NVC. He and the other in-charges were forced to register but hid this fact from others.[67]

Increasingly, Rohingya chairmen and in-charges were divided into 'good' and 'bad' for the Rohingya cause, depending predominantly on their response to NVCs.[68]

> In our village, we had a Rohingya chairman. He was a good chairman. He stood firm against the NVCs and did not try to make us take the NVCs. It is not the same in every village. In some villages they have Buddhist leaders that try to force people or otherwise the Rohingya chairmen are pressured first themselves to take it and then to make other people take it.[69]

In 2016 and 2017, there was a build-up of army and *Lon Htein* (riot police) in Rohingya areas. Under their orders, sharp and blunt objects were confiscated from Rohingya homes during this time. This included kitchen knives and implements for cutting firewood, making food preparation difficult. Furthermore, Rohingya were required to dismantle the fences and cut the trees around their properties, with the effect of allowing security forces to see directly into their homes at any given time. Washing facilities were outside, and women were left feeling increasingly vulnerable and exposed (UNHRC 2017b). These instructions were sometimes conveyed through village chairmen, and at other times homes were searched by troops. Whilst these measures were ostensibly for counter-insurgency purposes, Fortify Rights (2018:43) characterised the measures taken as 'preparations for mass atrocities.' This analysis draws on Stanton's ten stages of genocide. 'Preparation' is the seventh stage, in which plans are put in place in order to execute genocidal killings more effectively (Stanton 2017). When participants narrated these events, these preparations were also linked with the forced issuance of NVCs. Some understood that confiscations of sharp objects and the clearance of boundaries around their properties were a form of group punishment for not complying with the NVC schemes—and a response to the rising resistance in Rohingya villages.[70] Some stated that they were told directly by troops that if they accepted NVCs, they could keep their fences.[71] These narratives highlight the idea that, as Rohingya resistance grew, accepting NVCs was understood as a form of collaboration with state authorities. Mass violence, accordingly, was understood as a direct response to NVC resistance.

Another prominent feature of narratives was the notion that the NVC scheme itself was preparation for the mass atrocities that were to follow. Labelling Rohingya as foreigners before subjecting them to campaigns of terror was sometimes understood as a strategy to ensure those who fled the terror, would never be able to return. These notions of the NVCs as preparation for mass atrocities drew on Rohingya oral histories in which Myanmar had, unwillingly, repatriated Rohingya after attempts to expel them en masse. For example:

> We had every kind of document in the past because Rohingya ethnicity was recognised. They drove us away into Bangladesh in 1990s, but we returned . . . . NVC is genocide card for Rohingya people. They are trying to make us as foreigners . . . . The army came to the villages to do the NVC . . . . People were arrested and people were tortured to force them to take NVC . . . . Properties were burned and women were raped, all in the name of NVC.[72]

Indeed, one of the key sticking points to repatriation following the 2017 violence, alongside the absence of security and the return of lands, became whether the NVC or similar ID scheme would continue to be issued. Rohingya contrasting demands were for citizenship to be restored in full.[73]

As tensions and resistance mounted relating to the NVCs in 2016–7, villagers linked the increased presence of armed forces to threats that had been made in the village meetings that they would not be allowed to remain in the country if they did not accept the IDs. News spread from one village to another that troops were expected to enter Rohingya villages and homes. On receiving the news, Rohingya men would leave their homes and hide in forests.[74] Women and children remained in the homes. In the context of previous patterns of registration-related abuses, it was believed that women were less likely to be arrested and subjected to physical violence than men. As homes were increasingly entered by security forces in 2016–7, these assumptions were proved wrong. Sexual violence in the home, including gang rape by soldiers, became a feature of the genocidal violence in 2016.[75] These encounters were associated in many narratives with the enforcement of NVCs. For example, one participant explained that as his brother hid in the forest one night, he was bitten by a snake and died. He said that his brother had 'died for the NVCs.'[76] Although participants did not have evidence to show how the increasingly regular encounters with security forces in their villages and homes were linked with NVC non-compliance, linkages were extremely common in narratives. Many participants asserted that the violence that was to be unleashed in 2017 was mostly because of the NVCs. Some participants explained that they were told if they accepted the NVCs as a group, their villages would be spared from the violence. Yet when the violence was unleashed, it spared no one. For example, one stated:

> They tortured us and killed the people and raped the women—killed and cut the necks of children, burnt children and houses, looted our properties . . . only for one thing—that is the NVC card.[77]

In summary, when the army clearance operations in 2017 swept across Rohingya areas, ostensibly in response to ARSA[78] attacks on police outposts, one of the underlying purposes was understood to be a response to NVC non-compliance (see also UNHRC 16th Sept 2019; Fortify Rights 2019). The military was understood to be acting on the threats made in meetings to ensure that Rohingya would not be allowed to remain or exist in Myanmar. In other words, where legal and bureaucratic measures had failed to erase Rohingya as a part of Myanmar, the military resorted to physical destruction or of their people and communities.[79] In Rohingya descriptions of genocide, the physical destruction of their group was intricately and indelibly linked to the symbolic destruction of their identity. In particular, that symbolic destruction manifested itself in the state ID and registration projects over decades, culminating in the NVCs, from which it morphed into the physical destruction of their group.

Symbolic enactment

As Feierstein (2014, 2015) has shown, the purpose and effect of genocidal terror are to reorganise social relations and identities. In his sixth stage of genocide, symbolic enactment, social relations are reconstituted in such a way as to erase the victim group and re-imagine and reorganise society as one in which they never existed. Symbolic enactment can be achieved by distorting the meaning of events that have occurred as part of the genocide; physically erasing evidence that the victim group ever existed; symbolically erasing or appropriating the histories and narratives of the victim group and the denial of the identity of the victims and the transference of guilt onto members of the victim community (2014:120–126). As such, this stage involves the 'transformation of the victims into "nothing" and the survivors into "nobodies."' He notes that,

> not just their bodies but also the memory of their existence was supposed to disappear, forcing the survivors to deny their own identity, as a synthesis of being and doing defined like any other identity by a particular way of life.
>
> (Feierstein 2014:38)

There are many ways in which notions of symbolic enactment can be applied to the Rohingya genocide, including the decimation of their lands, the targeting of the educated and religious leadership as a way to erase the cultural foundations, and the erasure of Rohingya history and culture through the schooling and censorship systems. Alluding to this stage and purpose of genocide, for example, UNHRC described the campaign of destruction against the Rohingya beginning in August 2017 as follows:

> The destruction by the Tatmadaw of houses, fields, food-stocks, crops, livestock and even trees, render the possibility of the Rohingya returning to normal lives and livelihoods in the future in northern Rakhine almost impossible. It also indicates an effort to effectively erase all signs of memorable landmarks in the geography of the Rohingya landscape and memory in such a way that a return to their lands would yield nothing but a desolate and unrecognizable terrain.
>
> (UNHRC 2017a:1)

This section focuses on symbolic enactment through identity card schemes. It draws on the notion, employed throughout this thesis that state categorisation and identification projects do not simply record neutral facts about people but can also bring identities into being and destroy them (Scott 1998; Torpey 2000; Hull 2012; Sadiq 2016). When national identities are re-imagined, notions of belonging are often written into law—in constitutions or in citizenship rules (Anderson 1991; Hayden 1996). Those re-imaginings are experienced as a set of social realities through ID and registration schemes based on this legal framework (Hull 2012; Sadiq 2016; Chhotray and McConnell 2018). Following the 1962 coup, the Myanmar military's re-imagining of a national identity devoid of the Rohingya as a borderland people with ancestral claims to the lands close to Myanmar's western border did not comport with the demographic reality in Rakhine State. The 1982 citizenship law wrote this erasure into law. Data from the fieldwork reveal how the ID schemes that followed gradually made that symbolic erasure a social reality. The previous section explores how the ID schemes were connected with terror, mass expulsions, and mass killings to permanently erase and destroy Rohingya as a group in Myanmar. This section considers three features of symbolic enactment identified through the fieldwork data: the denial and removal of IDs and civil documentation as a form of identity destruction, the recategorisation of Rohingya as foreigners, and forced assimilation that required survivors to deny their identity.

Civil documentation practices that deny the birth, life, and deaths of victim groups can be a part of the symbolic enactment process.[80] Indeed, the denial and removal of civil registration and ID documents were deeply significant in the fieldwork. As described in this chapter, the absence of documents has enabled Myanmar to claim, following mass expulsions to Bangladesh, that Rohingya never existed as a Myanmar community, and that they migrated from Bangladesh. The very targeted nature of the removal, destruction, and denial of documents, as shown in this chapter, indicates that this was not simply omission or neglect on the part of the state but a deliberate attempt to destroy their identity as nationals of Myanmar.

As Chapter 8 reveals, the repeated assertion within statelessness studies, that the stateless—including Rohingya—are invisible to the state and require identification and documentation to ease their suffering, mischaracterised the nature of the Myanmar State.[81] Rather the wilful and targeted denial and removal of documents is better understood as part of the symbolic enactment process that erases evidence that the Rohingya ever existed as a part of Myanmar. As noted, scholarship on bureaucracy and the state understands IDs to be the artefacts of the state (Hull 2012; Chhotray and McConnell 2018). As noted in Chapter 5, this was in-line with the accounts of Rohingya participants who collected and archived identity documents from the early decades of independence as proof of their identity. As such, the destruction and removal of Rohingya documents can also be understood as an erasure of their histories as part of the national community. Oral histories of Rohingya citizenship in Myanmar do not simply seek to ascertain their pre-colonial presence and indigeneity in Rakhine. They also seek to establish the historical post-colonial relationship between Rohingya and the state. With an innate understanding that state-issued documents are historical artefacts evidencing that relationship, participants drew on the stories of their documents throughout this research to show how their identity as Myanmar had been erased and destroyed. As such, the destruction and removal of ID documents functioned in a similar way to the destruction of cultural symbols such as historical mosque buildings, which has been explored by genocide scholars (Lee and González Zarandona 2019; MacLean 2019). Both erased physical evidence of the existence of Rohingya and, in the process, erased and appropriated their histories and identities.

Re-categorisation of Rohingya as a people has also been a significant factor in this appropriation. Internationally, statelessness is often linked to the ideas of being uncounted, unregistered, or undocumented by the state (Brinham 2019). As we will see in the next chapter, viewed within this paradigm, national verification and documentation exercises which identify, register, and document those entitled to citizenship, and simultaneously provide 'pathways to citizenship' for those who lack legal status, are therefore a logical policy response to the problems of statelessness. The domestic and international support for national verification processes and NVCs in Myanmar has a grounding in mainstream international policy responses to statelessness. However, Rohingya oral histories of the identity documents powerfully challenge this assumption and logic. Their experience is not one of invisibility or state neglect that preceded persecution, but one of hypervisibility and persecution through state ID and registration practices. As described in this chapter, their experience is one of living under an oppressive registration and surveillance regime that destroyed social relations with Myanmar society and tore away at the social fabric within their own communities. Theirs is a story not of being uncounted or undocumented, but being recounted, re-registered, and re-documented as something they were not—'foreigners' or 'Bengalis' or 'migrants' or 'noncitizens.' As Chapter 6 explored, the gradual recategorisation of Rohingya as foreigners began in the 1990s when they were re-recorded on family lists and ID cards as 'Bengali,' and culminated in the NVC scheme, which effectively cemented their recategorisation as 'foreigners' who needed to apply for citizenship. The recategorisation process dramatically changed the ways in which they could interact with and function within Myanmar society on a day-to-day basis. Re-categorisation attempted to destroy their national and ethnic identity as one belonging to Rakhine and Myanmar. Concurrently, it bolstered and lent legitimacy to the re-imagination of Myanmar as a timeless geographically bounded ethnically pure nation-state devoid of shared demographic and cultural linkages with South Asia (Amrith 2013; Zarni and Brinham 2017; Charney 2018). The 1982 Citizenship Law and the ID schemes were framed as the righting of past colonial wrongs (see also Tonkin 2018). According to this myth, the imagined South Asian migrant collaborated with British colonial powers to penetrate the ethnic purity of the ancient nation. The aspects of symbolic enactment that reified exclusionary ethnic identities did not so much occur as a post-genocide restructuring but rather restructured social relations as a central component of an ongoing genocidal process from the 1990s onwards.

The ID schemes attacked and reconstituted two key foundations of Rohingya identity—first as group belonging to Rakhine, which is inferred by the ethnonym, Rohingya (Charney 2005); and second as belonging to the post-colonial state of Myanmar. These aspects of identity destruction and reconstruction in Rohingya narratives echo sociologic and anthropological understandings of state categorisation process as technologies of power. These technologies do not neutrally record populations but rather destroy and bring identities into being (Longman 2001; Navaro-Yashin 2007; McConnell 2013; Reddy 2015; Chhotray and McConnell 2018). As the next chapter charts, understanding state ID and registration schemes as a technology of state power that can be utilised in genocides can challenge international policy approaches that promote 'pathways to citizenship' and 'legal identities for all' as a gateway to human rights (see also Brinham 2019).

The third way in which state ID schemes can be understood as part of a symbolic enactment process is the forced assimilation of victim populations. This process can force survivors to deny or hide their group membership in order to survive or function effectively in society. In Feierstein's work (2014:14), a central component of the symbolic enactment stage of genocide is that survivors are forced to deny their own identity. This was part of the dualistic process of genocide that Lemkin described in his original work, whereby genocide not only destroys 'the national pattern' of the victim group but also imposes 'the national pattern of the oppressor' (2002:27–28). In the Rohingya situation, this forced assimilation has increasingly become a part of the Rohingya experience for those living or functioning outside of North Rakhine State. As with the other aspects of symbolic enactment, the forced assimilation process began in the 1990s after the implementation of the colour-coded ID scheme based on the 1982 citizenship law and intensified throughout that period, culminating in the moves to formalise and digitise ID systems in Myanmar, which occurred alongside the implementation of NVCs from 2015 onwards (see also Brinham, Tiwari et al. 2020).

As this chapter describes, the segregation and isolation of the Rohingya in North Rakhine State were implemented and held in place through the post-1989 colour-coded ID scheme. Since then, Rohingya living outside of these areas were forced to hide their identities. Hiding or denying their identities not only did involve avoiding the term Rohingya but could also require them to hide their linguistic and geographic origins that were a core aspect of group identity (see also Habiburahman and Ansel 2018; Ealom 2021). In many areas of Myanmar, it was possible to function and operate in society using a variety of documents to access education, work, and move freely within some areas of Myanmar. For example, in Yangon and many other areas, it was possible to use NRCs issued under previous registration rules as the primary form of identification. This did not just apply to Rohingya but to a significant proportion of the Myanmar population who struggled to obtain IDs under the post-1982 system, for example, people from rural or ethnic minority areas or members of the political opposition (European Network on Statelessness and Institute on Statelessness and Inclusion 2019; de Chickera, Arraiza et al. 2021).[82] Additionally, due to the combination of administrative barriers and endemic corruption in bureaucratic processes throughout the country, it was possible to secure various documents through irregular means if large amounts of money were paid. Due to the costs of bribery to obtain documents and permissions or to function with limited documents in Yangon or other urban centres, those in Yangon or other areas of central Myanmar were often described as elite, educated, or wealthy Rohingya.[83] These Rohingya, due to the segregation of North Rakhine State, were most often unable to travel back and stay connected with their communities. This severing of geographic and social ties also functioned to divide Rohingya along class lines, whereby many of the 'elite' were forced to assume Myanmar identities whilst downplaying their cultural, linguistic, and familial ties in northern Rakhine.[84]

Both bureaucratic and social pressures required Rohingya outside of Rakhine to hide their ethnic identities. They largely identified as Myanmar Muslim to society at large, whilst their IDs would generally carry alternative ethnic terms imposed by the state, including but not limited to the contentious term 'Bengali.' Identifying as Myanmar Muslim was not described by participants in the research as problematic in itself, as it reflected an important aspect of their identity. Nonetheless, as the significance of Rohingya identity as a form of resistance to group destruction and genocide grew, other identities became increasingly divisive in the context of Myanmar's ID schemes. In narratives, there was sometimes a resentment of the decisions these Rohingya had made in terms of ethnic identification. This underscored the underlying tensions between Rohingya in northern Rakhine and Rohingya in Yangon and diaspora, which were an inevitable part of the restructuring of social relations, which severed Rohingya communities along geographic and class lines.[85]

This was further exacerbated by Yangon Rohingyas' inabilities to 'speak up' or 'speak out' against the discrimination and persecution of their communities in northern Rakhine. Their voices were limited by their own insecurities. In field research, Rohingya who lived in Yangon and other areas spoke of harassment and extortion that occurred if their ethnic and geographic origins were discovered by state authorities. Many lived under the pervasive fear that their ethnic origins would be discovered, or their documents, even if valid and legal, would be considered 'fraudulently obtained.' Being found out or discovered could result in either imprisonment on immigration changes or being forcibly transferred back to North Rakhine State (see also Ealom 2021). This was described in narratives as internal 'deportation.'[86] There were notable individual exceptions amongst Rohingya in Yangon, but for the majority the pervasive insecurities and fears were experienced as the public denial of their identities and forced assimilation.

This process of identity denial and forced assimilation that occurred for Rohingya living across Myanmar was understood to have been copied and adapted for use in Rakhine through the national verification process.

> Even you know the activists from Yangon, they say you know, we have citizenship. That's sounds very funny to me, because unless you are recognised as a Rohingya, you cannot say that you have citizenship. You know, you are denying, they don't recognise you as Rohingya you know (laughing). Now they are trying to force everyone to take Bengali identity.[87]

As noted earlier in this chapter, national verification required Rohingya to forsake their identities. In return, they could obtain small benefits if they were able to prove their entitlement to one of Myanmar's colour-coded citizenship IDs. Nonetheless, the practices of segregation and isolation were held in place by geo-location as well as the ID card scheme, meaning in practice citizenship rights and benefits could not be accessed effectively.

The broader impact on the group of the ID regime—in both Rakhine and the rest of Myanmar—was the erasure of Rohingya as a national group through forced assimilation and identity denial. The identity denial was broader than whether individuals recorded and spoke about themselves using the term Rohingya. The process of destruction also required them to deny their linguistic, cultural, and geographic origins. This had the impact of destroying evidence of Rohingyas' historical existence as a people of Rakhine and Myanmar. It forced survivors to be implicated in the erasure of their own group identity and history. Simultaneously it reinforced the re-imagination of Myanmar as an ethnically defined nation-state that pre-dated Rohingya and Arakanese belonging.

This section has shown how ID schemes erased and appropriated Rohingya identities and histories in Myanmar through the targeted denial of civil documentation; the recategorisation of Rohingya as foreign and 'other'; and through forced assimilation. ID cards were an integral aspect of turning the re-imagination of Myanmar as ethnically and geographically separate from the Indian sub-continent, into a social reality. This social reality was experienced as the physical and symbolic destruction and erasure of Rohingya as a group.

Conclusion

This chapter has shown how Rohingya narratives of their ID cards correlated with academic analyses of genocide as a sociological process (Fein 1993; Arnold 2002; Hinton 2002; Mukimbiri 2005; Feierstein 2015; Green, McManus et al. 2015; Stanton 2017). In particular, the narratives revealed understandings that symbolic and physical destructions of their group occurred in tandem and were intrinsically connected. The narratives explained how Rohingya belonging in Myanmar was unmade through ID schemes and how that process radically reorganised social relations to produce exclusion, isolation, and group vulnerabilities to mass atrocities. Myanmar's ID schemes across all the interviews and focus groups were understood as core components of the genocide that led to the symbolic and physical destruction of their group. This understanding finds support in sociological and historical studies that analyse IDs as key technologies of power, which can ultimately be deployed as part of genocides (Longman 2001; Torpey 2001; Caplan 2013). Statelessness was not understood to precede or be a causal factor for human rights violations; rather the production of Rohingya noncitizenship in Myanmar was understood as a slow process that was a key aspect of the broader genocidal processes. Rohingya narratives revealed that experiences of genocide, as related through oral histories of IDs, broadly correlated to the stages of genocide identified in genocide scholarship. They did not, however, occur in an even linear series of events but rather in pattern of uncompleted cycles that repeated (Feierstein 2014:117). Building on these findings, the following chapter compares the way in which Rohingya explained Myanmar's ID schemes as an intrinsic part of the genocidal destruction of their group, with international approaches to legal identities and the reduction of statelessness that promoted 'legal identities for all' and the provision of registration and IDs as 'pathways to citizenship.'

Notes

1 Spiro describes denationalisations that redefine national identity in ways that do 'not comport with the organic community on the ground' as fundamentally 'pathological' Spiro (2011:711).

2 Fg2, 22/04/2018, Kuala Lumpur; Fg5, 28/04/2018, Kuala Lumpur; Fg6&7, 26/07/2018, Kutapalong; Also see Greg Constantine's photo exhibition at US Holocaust Museum, Burma's Path to Genocide Available at: https://exhibitions.ushmm.org/burmas-path-to-genocide (accessed 25/03/2021).

3 There is also a blue citizenship card for 'Associate Citizens' which was issued to those who applied before the 1982 Citizenship Law was enacted. However, this card was not referred to at all in fieldwork.

4 E.g. on white cards issued after the initial 2–3 years, family cards filled in after mid-1990s onwards, green cards.

5 E.g. on early issues of white cards, family lists prior to mid-1990s, political party membership cards from 2010. NB: 'Muslim' was not always stigmatising. It depended on the context.

6 In64&65, 26/06/2019, The Hague.

7 Fg6, 26/07/2018, Kutapalong.

8 *NaSaKa* (border control forces) was an inter-agency web of security/intelligence-administrative organizations that had control and power over all aspects of life for Rohingya, from livelihoods, physical movements, and family life including marriage and birth control. It was established in 1992 and was in control during the second wave of mass repatriation in 1994–5 in the Rohingya areas of Northern Rakhine towns and villages.

9 Fg1, 13/08/2018, New Delhi; In21, 28/06/2018, Skype from Australia; Fg8, 26/09/2018, Hakimpara.

10 White cards featured heavily across all field research. They were mostly associated with the broad themes of restrictions, persecution, and state surveillance.
11 Cancellation of residence on the family list was frequently noted as a reason for family members fleeing Myanmar, particularly those who prior to the 2016–7 violence.
12 In30, 28/07/2018, Balukhali; In31, 28/07/2018, Balukhali; In40, 24/09/2018, Balukhali.
13 Fg2–5, 22–28/04/2018, Kuala Lumpur.
14 In4, 15/08/2017, New Delhi; In45, 26/09/2018, Hakimpara. Also see Habiburahman and Ansel (2018).
15 For example, Only 36% of women in Myanmar went outside the home according to study by Asia Foundation and Centre for Peace and Justice, B. U. (2020). Navigating the Margins: Family, Mobility and Livelihoods amongst Rohingya Refugees in Bangladesh.
16 In19, 27/04/2018, Kuala Lumpur
17 In13, 23/04/2018, Kuala Lumpur; In14, 25/04/2018, Kuala Lumpur; In43, 25/09/2018, Jolatoli.
18 In43, 25/09/2018, Jolatoli; In14, 26/04/2018, Kuala Lumpur; Fg7, 26/08/2018, Kutapalong. Also see Human Rights Watch (2020).
19 In19, 27/04/2018, Kuala Lumpur.
20 In43, 25/09/2018, Jolatoli
21 In19, 27/04/2018, KL; IN30, 28/07/2018, Balukhali; IN31, 28/07/2018, Balukhali.
22 Fg2, 22/04/2018, KL; Fg4, 27/04, 2018, KL; Fg7, 26/07/2018, Kutapalong.
23 See also p16–27 Family separation in Asia Foundation and Centre for Peace and Justice (2020).
24 In64, 26/06/2019, The Hague (cross-checked against other interviews).
25 In19, 27/04/2018, KL; In47, 26/09/2018, Camp 4.
26 In19, 27/04/2018, Kuala Lumpur.
27 One chairman interviewed stated Muslims were gradually replaced from 2006 onwards. Salaries for this role were brought introduced in 2010. In43, 23/09/2018, Jamtoli. This information was cross-checked. In64, 26/06/2019, The Hague.
28 Information obtained and cross-checked across all interviews, including interviews with chairmen, 100 house and 10 house in-charges.
29 For more information on informal fees and corruption, see de Chickera, Arraiza et al. (2021).
30 In43, 25/09/2018, Jamtoli.
31 In14, 18/04/2018, Kuala Lumpur.
32 In64&In65, 26/06/2019, The Hague.
33 In64, 26/06/2019, The Hague.
34 In19, 27/04/2018, Kuala Lumpur.
35 In30, 28/07/2018, Balukhali; In43, 25/09/2018, Jolatoli.
36 In44, 25/09/2018, Thayingkhali.
37 In50, 27/09/2018, Extension 4; In65, 26/06/2019, The Hague.
38 In35, 02/08/2018, Chittagong.
39 For further information on corruption and bribery, see de Chickera, Arraiza et al. (2021).
40 In31, 28/07/2018, Balukhali; In43, 25/09/2018, Jolatoli; In44, 25/09/2018, Thayingkhali.
41 In40, 24/09/2018, Balukhali; In46–48, 26/09/2018, Camp 14.
42 In40, 24/09/2018, Balukhali.
43 Fg6, 26/07/2018, Kutapalong.

44 The following examples are collated from across the fieldwork data. Information was also cross-checked against other interviews. These examples also broadly correlate with findings in UNHRC (Sept 2018) and Fortify Rights (2019).
45 Some participants reported that from their areas it was still possible to obtain permission for accessing emergency hospital care.
46 In49, 26/09/2018, camp 14.
47 In28, 27/07/2018, Unchiprang.
48 In31, 28/07/2018, Balukhali.
49 In50, 27/09/2018, extension 4; In51, 27/09/2018, extension 4; In31, 28/07/2018, Balukhali.
50 In41&42, 24/09/2018, Balukhali.
51 Fg7, 26/07/2018, Kutapalong; In14, 26/04/2018, Kuala Lumpur. This was consistent with findings in Fortify Rights (2019).
52 Fg6, 26/07/2018, Kutapalong.
53 Findings from this section draw primarily from the narratives of those who were directly affected by the violence of 2016–7 as such they compared interviews and focus group conducted in the camps in Bangladesh during 2017–8. They are also cross-checked against information provided by Rohingya activists and researchers living in diaspora in 2019.
54 In30–31, 28/07/2018, Balukhali; In34–5, 02/08/2018, Chittagong; In46–49, 26/09/2018, Camp14; In45, 26/09/2018, Hakimpara.
55 In46–49, 26/09/2018, Camp14.
56 In45, 26/09/2018, Hakimpara; FG6&FG7, 26/07/2018, Kutapalong; In50–54, 27/09/2018, extension 4.
57 Trickery and lies in relation to IDs and citizenship promises was a key theme identified in the coding that ran throughout narratives from Bangladesh, India, and Malaysia.
58 Fg8,26/09/2018, Hakimpara.
59 In46, 26/09/2018, Camp 14; In51, 27/09/2018, extension 4; In27–29, 27/07/2018, Unchiprang.
60 In46–49, 26/09/2018, Camp 14; In19, 27/04/2018, Kuala Lumpur; In30&31, 28/07/2018, Balukhali.
61 In46–49, 26/09/2018, Camp 14. Information cross-checked between interviews.
62 In48, 26/09/2018, Camp 14.
63 It is believed the charges related to immigration, but this could not be verified.
64 Participants believed he was released in an amnesty but were unable to verify.
65 In31, 28/07/2108, Balukhali; In44, 25/09/2018, Thayingkhali.
66 In43, 25/09/2018, Jamtoli; In51, 27/09/2018, extension 4; In30, 28/07/2018, Balukhali.
67 In51, 27/09/2018, extension 4.
68 In65, 26/06/2018, The Hague.
69 In28, 27/07/2018, Unchiprang.
70 In51, 27/09/2018, Extension 4; In24, 26/07/2018, Teknaf.
71 In43, 25/09/2018, Jamtoli.
72 Fg, 26/07/2018, Kutapalong.
73 Fg6–8, Jul&Aug 2018, camps of Bangladesh.
74 In43, 25/09/2018, Jamtoli; In51, 27/09/2018, Extension 4.
75 Cross-checked in Kalandan Press (2018).
76 In51, 27/09/2018, extension 4.
77 In40, 24/09/2018, Balukhali.
78 Arakan Rohingya Salvation Army.
79 In Hayden's work on the former Yugoslavia, he also describes how when bureaucratic measures failed to remove the ethnic 'other,' physical force, and destruction was used instead. See Hayden (1996).

80 The Question of 'Intent' in Genocide: A Public Dialogue, Free Rohingya Coalition livecast with Gregory Stanton and Daniel Feierstein, 25/01/2021.
81 For example: 'Most of these people are stateless and most of these people have not had any form of identification document, so for the vast majority of the Rohingya refugees, this is the first ID, a first proof of identity that they have,' UN Refugee Agency spokesperson Andrej Mahecic told journalists in Geneva. UN News, 2019, More than Half a Million Rohingya in Bangladesh Get ID Cards for First Time: UN Refugee Agency Available at: https://news.un.org/en/story/2019/08/1044041 (accessed 26/03/2021).
82 In the research, it was frequently brought up that this included Aung San Suu Kyi, whose main ID card was the NRC until after her release from house arrest in 2012. See also Ealom (2021).
83 In64&65, 26/06/2019, The Hague. Also interviews conducted for Brinham, Tiwari et al. (2020).
84 In64&65, 26/06/2019, The Hague.
85 For example, during the fieldwork, there were accusations that Rohingya who had taken Bangladeshi IDs had 'sold out' or were 'Bangladeshi' and not Rohingya. e.g. In22&23, 25/07/2018, Coxes Bazar.
86 In64&65, 26/06/2019, The Hague. Also interviews conducted for Brinham, Tiwari et al. (2020).
87 In64, 26/06/2018, The Hague.

Bibliography

Amnesty International (2017). *Caged without a Roof: Apartheid in Myanmar's Rakhine State*. www.amnesty.org/en/documents/asa16/7484/2017/en/ [Accessed 02/12/2018]

Amrith, S. S. (2013). *Crossing the Bay of Bengal: The Furies of Nature and the Fortunes of Migrants*. Harvard University Press.

Anderson, B. R. O. G. (1991). *Imagined Communities: Reflections on the Origin and Spread of Nationalism*. Verso.

Arnold, B. (2002). Justifying Genocide: Archaeology and the Construction of Difference, in Hinton, A. L. (ed), *Annihilating Difference: The Anthropology of Genocide*. University of California Press. 95–116.

Asia Foundation and Centre for Peace and Justice (2020). *Navigating the Margins: Family, Mobility and Livelihoods amongst Rohingya Refugees in Bangladesh*. https://asiafoundation.org/wp-content/uploads/2020/09/Navigating-the-Margins_Family-Mobility-and-Livelihoods-Amongst-Rohingya-in-Bangladesh.pdf [Accessed 25/03/2021]

Brinham, N. (2019a). Looking Beyond Invisibility: Rohingyas' Dangerous Encounters with Papers and Cards. *Tilburg Law Review* 24(2): 156–169.

Brinham, N. (2019b). When Identity Documents Produce Exclusion: Lessons from Rohingya Experiences in Myanmar. https://blogs.lse.ac.uk/mec/2019/05/10/when-identity-documents-and-registration-produce-exclusion-lessons-from-rohingya-experiences-in-myanmar/ [Accessed 20/02/2020]

Brinham, N., A. D. Tiwari, J. Field, J. Ealom, J. M. Arraiza and A. de Chickera (2020). Locked In and Locked Out: The Impact of Digital Identity Systems on Rohingya Populations. *Institute on Statelessness and Inclusion and UN Special Rapporteur on Racism*. https://files.institutesi.org/Locked_In_Locked_Out_The_Rohingya_Briefing_Paper.pdf [Accessed 25/05/2021]

Caplan, J. (2013). 'Ausweis Bitte!' Identity and Identification in Nazi Germany, in About, I., Brown, J. and Lonergan, G. (eds), *Identification and Registration Practices in Transnational Perspective: Papers, People and Practices*. Palgrave. 224–242.

Charney, M. (2005). Buddhism in Arakan: Theories and Histiographies of the Religious Basis of Ethnonyms. Paper presented at 'Arakan History Conference, Institute of Asian Studies, Chulalongkorn University [Accessed 23/11/2016]

Charney, M. (2016). State and Society in Arakan from the Fourteenth Century: From Inclusion to Polarisation and Exclusion. Paper presented at Myanmar's Democratic Transition and the Rohingya Persecution, Wolfson College, Oxford University [Accessed 11/05/2016]

Charney, M. (2018). A State Myth of 'National Race' and the Tatmadaw's War on the Rohingya and other Myanmar Ethnic Groups. Berlin Conference on Genocide [Accessed 26/02/2018]

Chhotray, V. and F. McConnell (2018). *Certifications of Citizenship: The History, Politics and Materiality of Identity Documents in South Asian States and Diasporas*. Taylor & Francis.

de Chickera, A., J. Arraiza, Z. Albarazi, G. Field and N. Brinham (2021). *Navigating with a Faulty Map: Access to Citizenship Documents and Citizenship in Myanmar, Institute on Statelessness and Inclusion*. https://files.institutesi.org/Access_to_Citizenship_in_Myanmar_Report.pdf [Accessed 28/12/2021]

Ealom, J. (2021). *Escape from Manus: The Untold True Story*. Penguin Viking.

Equal Rights Trust (2012). *Burning Homes, Sinking Lives: A Situation Report of the Violence against Rohingya in Myanmar and Their Refoulement from Bangladesh*. www.equalrightstrust.org/ertdocumentbank/The%20Equal%20Rights%20Trust%20-%20Burning%20Homes%20Sinking%20Lives.pdf [Accessed 21/05/2019]

European Network on Statelessness & Institute on Statelessness and Inclusion (2019). *Statelessness in Myanmar: Country Position Paper*. https://statelessjourneys.org/wp-content/uploads/StatelessJourneys-Myanmar-final.pdf [Accessed 11/11/2019]

Feierstein, D. (2014). *Genocide as Social Practice: Reorganizing Society under the Nazis and Argentina's Military Juntas*. Rutgers University Press.

Feierstein, D. (2015). Debates on the Criminology of Genocide: Genocide as a Technology for Destroying Identities. *State Crime* 4(2): 115–127.

Fein, H. (1993). *Genocide: A Sociological Perspective*. Sage.

Fortify Rights (2014). Policies of Persecution: Ending Abusive State Policies Against Rohingya Muslims in Myanmar. https://fortifyrights.org/downloads/Policies_of_Persecution_Feb_25_Fortify_Rights.pdf [Accessed 03/05/2017]

Fortify Rights (2018). *'They Gave Them Long Swords': Preparations for Genocide and Crimes against Humanity against Rohingya Muslims in Rakhine State, Myanmar*. www.fortifyrights.org/downloads/Fortify_Rights_Long_Swords_July_2018.pdf [Accessed 26/03/2017]

Fortify Rights (2019). *'Tools of Genocide': National Verification Cards and the Denial of Citizenship of Rohingya Muslims in Myanmar*. www.fortifyrights.org/downloads/Tools%20of%20Genocide%20-%20Fortify%20Rights%20-%20September-03-2019-EN.pdf [Accessed 08/10/2019]

Green, P., T. McManus and A. de la Cour Venning (2015). Countdown to Annihilation: Genocide in Myanmar. *International State Crime Initiative*. http://statecrime.org/data/2015/10/ISCI-Rohingya-Report-PUBLISHED-VERSION.pdf [Accessed 29/08/2024]

Green, P., T. McManus and A. de la Cour Venning (2018). Genocide Achieved, Genocide Continues: Myanmar's Annihilation of the Rohingya. *International State Crime Initiative*. http://statecrime.org/data/2018/04/ISCI-Rohingya-Report-II-PUBLISHED-VERSION-revised-compressed.pdf [Accessed 29/08/2024]

Habiburahman and S. Ansel (2018). *First, They Erased Our Name: A Rohingya Speaks*. Scribe.

Hayden, R. M. (1996). Imagined Communities and Real Victims: Self-Determination and Ethnic Cleansing in Yugoslavia. *American Ethnologist* 23(4): 783–801.

Hinton, A. L. (2002). Introduction: Genocide and Anthropology, in Hinton, A. L. (ed), *Genocide: An Anthropological Reader*. Blackwell. 1–24.
Hull, M. S. (2012a). Documents and Bureaucracy. *Annual Review of Anthropology* 41: 251–267.
Hull, M. S. (2012b). *Government of Paper: The Materiality of Bureaucracy in Urban Pakistan*. University of California Press.
Human Rights Watch (2013). *All You Can Do It Pray: Crimes against Humanity and Ethnic Cleansing of Rohingya Muslims in Burma's Arakan State*. www.hrw.org/reports/burma0413_FullForWeb.pdf [Accessed 16/03/2017]
Human Rights Watch (2020). *An Open Prison without End: Myanmar's Mass Detention of Rohingya in Rakhine State*. www.hrw.org/report/2020/10/08/open-prison-without-end/myanmars-mass-detention-rohingya-rakhine-state [Accessed 09/10/2020]
International Crisis Group (2013). *Myanmar's 'NaSaKa': Disbanding an Abusive Agency*. www.crisisgroup.org/asia/south-east-asia/myanmar/myanmars-nasaka-disbanding-abusive-agency [Accessed 25/03/2021]
Kalandan Press (2018). *Rape by Command: Sexual Violence as a Weapon against the Rohingya*. www.kaladanpress.org/images/document/2018/RapebyCommandWeb3.pdf [Accessed 17/12/2018]
Lee, R. and J. A. A. González Zarandona (2019). Heritage Destruction in Myanmar's Rakhine State: Legal and Illegal Iconoclasm. *International Journal of Heritage Studies* 26(5): 519–538.
Lemkin, R. (2002). Genocide (Extracts from Axis Rule in Occupied Europe 1944), in Hinton, A. L. (ed), *Genocide: An Anthropological Reader*. Blackwell.
Longman, T. (2001). Identity Cards, Ethnic Self-Perception, and Genocide in Rwanda, in Caplan, J. and Torpey, J. (eds), *Documenting Individual Identity: The Development of State Practices in the Modern World*. Princeton University Press. 346–348.
MacLean, K. (2019). The Rohingya Crisis and the Practices of Erasure. *Journal of Genocide Research* 21(1): 83–95.
McConnell, F. (2013). Citizens and Refugees: Constructing and Negotiating Tibetan Identities in Exile. *Annals of the Association of American Geographers* 103(4): 967–983.
Mukimbiri, J. (2005). The Seven Stages of the Rwandan Genocide. *Journal of International Criminal Justice* 3(4): 823–836.
Navaro-Yashin, Y. (2007). Make-Believe Papers, Legal Forms and the Counterfeit: Affective Interactions between Documents and People in Britain and Cyprus. *Anthropological Theory* 7(1): 79–98.
NUI Galway (2010). *Crimes against Humanity in Western Burma: The Situation of the Rohingyas*. www.nuigalway.ie/media/intranet/Crimes-Against-Humanit-in-Western-Burma.pdf [Accessed 03/05/2017]
Physicians for Human Rights (2016). *Where There Is Police, There Is Persecution: Government Security Forces and Human Rights Abuses in Myanmar's Northern Rakhine State*. https://phr.org/wp-content/uploads/2016/10/Burma-Rakhine-State-Oct-2016.pdf [Accessed 12/05/2017]
Reddy, M. (2015). Identity Paper/Work/s and the Unmaking of Legal Status in Mae Sot, Thailand. *Asian Journal of Law and Society* 2(2): 251–266.
Sadiq, K. (2016). Limits of Legal Citizenship: Narratives from South and Southeast Asia, in Lawrance, B. N. and Stevens, J. (eds), *Citizenship in Question: Evidentiary Birthright and Statelessness*. Duke University Press. 165–176.
Scott, J. C. (1998). *Seeing Like a State: How Certain Schemes to Improve the Human Conditions Have Failed*. Yale University Press.
Spiro, P. J. (2011). A New International Law of Citizenship. *American Journal of International Law* 105(4): 694–746.

Stanton, G. (2017). *The Ten Stages of Genocide, Genocide Watch*. http://genocidewatch.net/genocide-2/8-stages-of-genocide/ [Accessed 20/01/2021]
Tonkin, D. (2018). Exploring the Issue of Citizenship in Rakhine State, in South, A. and Lall, M. (eds), *Citizenship in Myanmar: Ways of Being in and from Burma*. ISEAS. 222–263.
Torpey, J. (2000). *The Invention of the Passport: Surveillance, Citizenship, and the State*. Cambridge University Press.
Torpey, J. (2001). The Great War and the Birth of the Modern Passport System, in Caplan, J. and Torpey, J. (eds), *Documenting Individual Identity: The Development of State Practices in the Modern World*. Princeton University Press. 269–270.
UNHRC (2017a). Mission Report of OHCHR Rapid Response Mission to Coxes Bazar, Bangladesh. https://www.ohchr.org/sites/default/files/Documents/Countries/MM/CXBMissionSummaryFindingsOctober2017.pdf [Accessed 30/08/2024]
UNHRC (2017b). Report of the Special Rapporteur on the Situation of Human Rights in Myanmar, Thirty-fourth session, Feb to March 2027. A/HRC/34/67.
UNHRC (Sept 2018). Report of the Independent International Fact-Finding Mission on Myanmar. Thirty-Ninth Session. A/HRC/39/64.
UNHRC (Sept 2019). Detailed Findings of the Independent International Fact-Finding Mission on Myanmar: Report to the 42nd Session of the Human Rights Council, forty-second session, A/HRC/42/CRP.5.
Yale Law School and Fortify Rights (2015). *Persecution of Rohingya Muslims: Is Genocide Occurring in Myanmar's Rakhine State?* www.fortifyrights.org/downloads/Yale_Persecution_of_the_Rohingya_October_2015.pdf [Accessed 25/05/2018]
Zarni, M. and N. Brinham (2017). Reworking the Colonial Era Indian Peril: Myanmar's State-Directed Persecution of Rohingyas and Other Muslims. *Brown Journal of World Affairs* 24(1): 53–76.
Zarni, M. and A. Cowley (2014). The Slow-Burning Genocide of Myanmar's Rohingya. *Pacific Rim Law & Policy Journal* 23(3): 681–754.

8 IDs and international approaches to Rohingya statelessness

Towards social inclusion or identity destruction?

Introduction

This chapter considers where Rohingya experiences and understandings of statelessness diverge from international discourses relating to the prevention of statelessness. In doing so, it also explores how the voice and experiences of survivors influence and inform international approaches to statelessness. It builds on and analyses the findings from Chapters 3 to 7. In Chapters 6 and 7, Rohingya oral histories told a story of how state identification and categorisation practices were central to the genocidal process. They explained that intrinsic to experiences of citizenship loss was the annihilation of their identity as a group belonging to Rakhine, Myanmar—in addition to the deprivation of their individual legal status and associated rights. State IDs did not just record sets of biodata but rather destroyed their group identity and restructured Myanmar national identity and social relations based on notions of racial purity and exclusivity. Further, IDs and state-issued documents were understood as the material objects of state law and policy that could be removed and denied as part of a broader erasure of Rohingya history and identity. Chapter 3 explored understandings of the state within international approaches to reducing and preventing statelessness, in which the abuses of the state were largely by-passed and the stateless person was conceived of as administratively 'invisible' to state and international bureaucracies. Thus, in order to lift them out of a state of invisibility, the international sphere promoted state registration and IDs. In this chapter, I explore IDs within international governance in more detail. Chapter 3 also showed how identity was conceived of as the third element of a trinity of citizenship: status, rights, and belonging/identity (Tilly 1995; Yuval-Davis 2006; Joppke 2007) and that approaches to reducing statelessness have largely privileged the first aspect, focusing on individual access to legal status under state laws. Legal status was understood to have a bundle of rights attached, with belonging and group identity also assumed to flow from the attainment of legal status. As such, establishing an individual's legal identity, or set of facts about his/

DOI: 10.4324/9781003494539-8
This chapter has been made available under a CC-BY 4.0 license.

her characteristics such as name, sex, date, and place of birth, was prioritised in attempts to reduce human rights deficits.[1] With the harmful aspects of state bureaucracies largely by-passed, state-issued IDs and registration were understood within this paradigm to neutrally record a set of pre-existing facts about individuals that would contribute towards evidence of citizenship. Accordingly, advocating for state-issued IDs and registration for individuals under national laws, as evidence of citizenship, became the mainstay of approaches to reducing statelessness.

This chapter draws on Rohingya understandings of genocide and ID schemes to interrogate international approaches to citizenship and statelessness in Myanmar. The purpose is to identify where international policy logic departed from Rohingya understandings and experiences. In doing so, this chapter attempts to highlight the implications of the ongoing production and reproduction of Rohingya statelessness in Myanmar for broader international and global approaches to legal identities and statelessness.

International approaches to Rohingya statelessness in historical perspective

The role of international agencies in addressing Myanmar's production of statelessness and the deprivation of Rohingya citizenship in Myanmar frequently came up in Rohingya narratives. Statelessness was generally not only understood as being produced by the Myanmar militarised state but also reinforced within the international state system through processes outlined in this chapter. As noted, academic research has outlined how state-issued documents provide a lens through which to explore how individuals experience and interact with the state—a way to understand both the structures and subjectivities that frame identities and power relations (Navaro-Yashin 2007; Sadiq 2009; Hull 2012; Reddy 2015; Williams 2019). Following the expulsion of Rohingya outside of Myanmar in the 1990s and the subsequent mass repatriations, UN agencies and INGOs featured frequently in Rohingya ID narratives. Thus, ID histories and narratives enabled an additional exploration of how the international sphere framed Rohingya experiences—how power and structures relating to the international political order framed their experiences of genocide and citizenship deprivation.

International agencies were often characterised as having failed to protect Rohingya over decades. Often approaches that pragmatically engaged in 'quiet diplomacy' with Myanmar on issues of registration and IDs were understood to have resulted in the legitimisation of an exclusionary citizenship regime and identity erasure, as explored in this chapter.[2] The international agency referred to most frequently in oral histories was UNHCR, due to its long-term presence in Myanmar and the camps in Bangladesh, and its mandates on both statelessness and the repatriation of refugees. However, other agencies also featured in ID narratives including humanitarian INGOs working in Myanmar, and other UN, government, and inter-governmental organisations involved in development projects or conflict resolution efforts in Myanmar.[3] The fieldwork included interviews with Rohingya who had previously worked for UNHCR and partner NGOs in North Rakhine State,[4] as well as Rohingya activists. Together the interviews and focus groups presented a nuanced but critical picture of international approaches towards registration and IDs.

This chapter identifies from the fieldwork data key periods in which international agencies were associated with state registration and IDs in Myanmar. It contextualises these key moments in broader global approaches to statelessness and legal identities. These were periods in which Rohingya experiences and understanding of ID schemes as part of a genocidal process collided with the approaches taken internationally towards state identification processes. The periods were the issuance of white cards to the Rohingya in North Rakhine State after mass repatriations from the mid-1990s onwards; state registration and verification processes after the 2012 violence and displacement; the issuance of NVCs from 2015 onwards; and lastly approaches and plans for future repatriation from Bangladesh in the wake of the mass expulsions of 2016–7.

Drawing on Chapter 3, this section places international approaches to IDs and registration within the broader historical shifts in the significance and meanings attached to the term statelessness. The concept of statelessness and related international policy approaches is understood within the section as constantly evolving with world events and the shifting concepts of statehood, international society, and law (Mamdani 1996; Benton 2002; Sharma and Gupta 2006). It also understands that statelessness is produced not only within the boundaries of state territory and membership but also in the boundaries between state sovereignty and international law (Siegelberg 2020). This section provides some background to the international approaches to statelessness that are most relevant to the Rohingya situation. It shows how state-issued IDs became increasingly prominent in international approaches to statelessness and considers the implications of this.

From group identities to individual legal status and state registration

Chapter 3 explored how in the interwar years, concerns about statelessness arose as a result of the break-up of empire (including Habsberg, Ottoman, Romanov), and the emergence of new states. The problem of statelessness was largely dealt with through the minority treaties which focused on attempting to provide state protections to national groups and minorities (Fink 1994; Siegelberg 2020). The chapter also plotted how in the post-WWII years and beyond, individual rights took precedence over the group in reducing and preventing statelessness. Conceptions of group and ethnic identity linked to citizenship became sidelined in the international sphere, which increasingly focused on citizenship status and the reduction of the overall numbers of *de jure* stateless persons, as statist interests were balanced with human rights approaches. Chapter 4 showed how group and ethnic identity in Burma, gained significance in the independence movement of the 1920s and 1930s in the lead-up to separation from India in 1937. Whilst ethnicity remained salient in Myanmar's post-independence citizenship framework, this was initially balanced in post-WWII independent Burma by other ways to other ways to acquire citizenship through residence, birth on the territory, marriage, and other criteria (de Chickera, Arraiza et al. 2021). Following the military coup of 1962, these balances were stripped away, largely reducing citizenship identities to membership of a state-assigned ethnicity (Cheesman 2017; Nyi Nyi Kyaw 2017). Chapters 5 and 6 showed how, within this context, Rohingya experienced the denial of citizenship in Myanmar as part of a genocidal process which sought to physically and symbolically destroy them as a group belonging to the Rakhine region of Myanmar. Accordingly, approaches which formed the mainstay of international policy solutions to statelessness, including the provision of IDs as pathways to citizenship, or expanding naturalisation provisions and reducing administrative barriers, were often rejected by Rohingya participants (see Advisory Commission on Rakhine State Aug 2017). State-issued IDs which were devoid of rights and identity, or approaches that aimed to provide some individuals with access to a formal citizenship status whilst forsaking their ethnic identity (such as through the 'naturalisation' provisions within the existing Citizenship Law), were largely rejected and resisted. As survivors of genocide, a crime against the group, Rohingya pursuits for justice did not predominantly focus on securing individual citizenship status but rather sought citizenship restitution and recognition for the group. These concepts are explored further throughout this chapter.

Chapter 3 showed how, since the interwar and post-WWII years when the state slowly emerged as the sole legitimate unit of political organisation (Siegelberg 2020:6), international policy on preventing and reducing statelessness increasingly relied on state ID schemes as evidence of citizenship as a legal status bestowed by states. Chapters 6 and 7 revealed how successive state regimes in Burma/Myanmar—from the British colonial state to the militarised state in Myanmar—utilised state registration and identification procedures not only as technologies to embrace their membership but also as tools of surveillance and oppression. Through their ID schemes, these regimes established and maintained their power and legitimacy by embracing some and excluding others. Chapter 3 explored how international discourses on statelessness tended to by-pass the oppressive and destructive powers of state bureaucracies in this regard, constructing 'the stateless person' as a person who could be lifted out of a state of administrative and legal invisibility by more documentation. Rohingya narratives revealed how IDs from the early decades of independence had emancipatory qualities that provided them with status, rights, and belonging. Yet under the militarised state, ID schemes and state implementation were utilised to persecute them and erase their histories and identities. Meanwhile, Rohingya expressed how within the international sphere, their legal condition had been reduced to the question of which state-issued documents they were able or not able to produce.[5]

White cards: reducing or producing statelessness?

This section outlines how UNHCR's increasing global focus on its statelessness mandate coincided with the establishment of its presence in Rakhine State to oversee Rohingya repatriations from Bangladesh. It considers the engagement of UNHCR with Myanmar's state registration and identification procedures during this period. It examines where Rohingya narratives from the fieldwork challenged the foundations of these approaches through claims that state ID schemes produced rather than reduced statelessness. Chapter 3 explained how in the 1990s, in response to the large-scale state secession following the break-up of the Soviet bloc and Yugoslavia, UNHCR's mandate on statelessness was strengthened and become a renewed focus within the organisation. In 1995, the UNGA formally entrusted the UNHCR with a global mandate to 'identify, prevent and reduce' statelessness[6] with a focus on the provision of technical and advisory services to states.[7] This focus on engaging with the state and the provision of technical legal services as well as identification of stateless persons and ID systems was to characterise their initial approach to Rohingya citizenship in Myanmar in the 1990s.

Rohingya first encounters with the UNHCR in relation to the provision of state-issued IDs in Myanmar occurred around the same time as this revival of statelessness as a focus within the organisation. International agencies were first referred to in fieldwork in relation to the provision of white cards in the mid-1990s which followed mass repatriations from Bangladesh. 250,000 Rohingya had fled to Bangladesh in 1991 and 1992 (Crisp 2018) citing extensive human rights abuses as part of 'operation *pyi thaya*' or 'operation clean and beautiful nation' designed to expel 'foreigners' and flush out Rohingya insurgents. Other human rights abuses from the period included forced labour, land confiscation, arbitrary arrest, and torture (Human Rights Watch 1996; Lewa 2008; NUI Galway 2010). This occurred in tandem with the increased militarisation of border areas after the 1990 elections, and the withdrawal of NRCs and denial of new IDs for Rohingya when the new colour-coded ID scheme was rolled out in 1989 (see Chapter 5). The mass repatriations were largely forced and UNHCR attempted to secure a monitoring role in Rakhine. UNHCR came under international scrutiny and criticism for their failure to ensure the voluntariness of the repatriations in Bangladesh and safe conditions of return in Myanmar (Pittaway 2016; Crisp 2018). Against this backdrop, UNHCR established their presence in North Rakhine State in 1994, not formally under a statelessness mandate, but with an initial mandate to monitor the repatriations from Bangladesh. The MoU between UNHCR and Myanmar stipulated that, 'returnees will be issued with the appropriate identification papers and that the returnees will enjoy the same freedom of movement as all other nationals.'[8] This placed further emphasis on ID documents as central to UNHCRs advocacy efforts in Myanmar. The mandate for the UN Special Rapporteur (UNSR) on the human rights situation in Myanmar also began in 1993. The UNSR reports highlighted the discriminatory aspects of the citizenship law and, in 1994, called for efforts to reduce statelessness (UNHRC 1994:74h).[9] His reports first referred to Muslims from Rakhine in the context of documenting stateless persons in 1996 (UNHRC 1996:163–164). This period marked the increased use of the term 'stateless' to describe Rohingya in broader international discourses. As noted in Chapter 4, many Rohingya rejected that they had been made stateless before or during the mid-1990s, instead seeing the state's production of their statelessness as a long and ongoing process. Many Rohingya participants felt that the international labelling them as stateless during this period undermined their claims to belong and to full citizenship (Brinham 2021). For example, in a focus group, one Rohingya participant received many expressions of agreement when she stated, 'I hate the UN started calling us stateless in the 1990s. It started from UNHCR. It is wrong. We are citizens.'[10]

Many also understood that the issuance of white cards a few years after the initial repatriations gave a material form to state claims of their foreignness and noncitizenship. The provision of white cards themselves was understood by participants to have contributed to making them stateless, not the 1982 citizenship law alone. This echoes notions from within academic work that IDs and documents do not only reflect identities but actually make and break identities (Navaro-Yashin 2007; Hull 2012; McConnell 2013; Chhotray and McConnell 2018). International support for the issuance of white cards was often viewed within this paradigm (see Chapter 5). As one participant stated:

> white cards made us stateless. White cards did not make us safe . . . Because we were demanding [rights] from UN, UN gave us white cards—the reason was for safety.[11] But there is no safety yet. So, we are asking the UN—where is your safety? The UN made us stateless.[12]

In the early part of the 1990s during the mass expulsions and mass repatriations, the Myanmar State did not issue any individual IDs to Rohingya. The old NRCs were effectively invalidated—and many had been submitted as part of an application for new citizenship cards from 1989 onwards. Instead, the state maintained detailed records of the population, including permanent residency, through the household registration documents (see Chapter 7). A key aspect of UNHCR's advocacy for Rohingya in NRS, then, related to the provision of individual IDs. These were seen as central to ensuring that Rohingya, particularly those who had been returned from Bangladesh had a continued legal right to remain. Unable to intervene in matters of citizenship in the difficult operating environment in Myanmar, recognition of Rohingyas' permanent residence was sought instead, and the provision of white cards to Rohingya was thus seen as a positive move in evidencing individual permanent residency. UNHCR described their reasoning for supporting the scheme as such:

> The issuance of TRCs, although not giving rise to citizenship rights, represents a step towards the regularisation of the current legal status of the NRS population . . . . TRCs have no time limit, despite their name, and constituted proof of legitimate residence in Myanmar for the bearers . . . . Attempts to issue more of these cards serve, in our view, to enhance the current legal status of the NRS population and not to weaken it. TRCs are an additional document proving the legitimate presence of the holders in NRS . . . . UNHCR continues to actively advocate for the citizenship status of the population of NRS . . . . Authorities have assured UNHCR that the TRCs were a first step in that direction.[13]

Fitting in with broader global approaches to statelessness focusing on legal status and state recognition, white cards, then, from UNHCR perspective were considered as a step or pathway towards citizenship in a way that did not directly undermine Myanmar's legitimacy or sovereign right to determine their own citizenship. As such, according to the fieldwork and other Rohingya-authored documents at the time, UNHCR lent the white card scheme their support, expressing their public support for it and, according to many participants, encouraging Rohingya to accept the cards.[14] Rohingya participants also related how UNHCR helped provide equipment for the government offices to issue white cards.[15]

Meanwhile, the white cards in the views expressed by many Rohingya participants were not a step towards, but a step away from, citizenship—they helped produce statelessness by giving material form to a new legal condition of noncitizenship deliberately produced by the state. According to the narrative research, objections to their issuance were raised by Rohingya at the time with some attempting to reject or refuse to accept the cards.[16] However, the resistance was largely muted. This was put down to four factors in Rohingya narratives. First, the white cards were formally described as a 'temporary' measure and held a promise for many that they would lead to citizenship; second in the first few years of issuance, they mostly held the term 'Muslim' rather than the term 'Bengali,' deflecting objections; third the establishment of the *NaSaKa* in north Rakhine and the new tightening of restrictions and control over Rohingya population struck fear into Rohingya populations and quelled dissent; fourth UNHCR's formal support for the white cards encouraged and reassured Rohingya populations that they would be beneficial in the longer term.[17] In a letter written to UNHCR Myanmar in 2002, a Rohingya group in exile in Japan expressed their concerns regarding the UNHCR's support for the white card scheme as follows:

> authorities had issued Temporary Registration Cards (TRCs) known as 'white cards' to some Rohingyas against their wish. It is nothing but a design to degrade their national status and put them in a state of uncertainty. The withholding of citizenship has become a mechanism for discrimination and persecution on the basis of ethnicity. Surprisingly, the UNHCR, who was mandated by UNGA to protect stateless people welcomed and supported this action of the SPDC in utter disregard of the previous indigenous status of the Rohingya in Arakan, hence Burma.[18]

Within the fieldwork, the dynamics between UNHCR and the Myanmar government relating to white cards were characterised in two broad ways. First, the Myanmar military government was understood to have 'tricked' UNHCR, pretending the white cards were a pathway to citizenship whereas they were in fact 'a tool' to undermine Rohingyas' indigenous identity. As such, in supporting the white cards, UNHCR had inadvertently supported bureaucratic forms of state violence. Second, by working on a state registration scheme implemented under such abusive conditions, UNHCR was characterised as colluding with the Myanmar regime or by-standing the regime's crimes.[19] As one participant phrased it, 'UNHCR is working with perpetrators—a thief will never admit that he stole things. And the Burmese government will never admit that they stole our citizenship.'[20]

UNHCR's focus on the state issuance of individual IDs that proved long-term residence—as opposed to more contentious issues of citizenship—served a dual purpose that fitted within global approaches to statelessness. First, ID documents were viewed in global contexts as evidence of residence and thus a potential pathway to citizenship. Second, this focus enabled them to provide technical assistance for mediating between states in citizenship disputes. Even after Myanmar agreed in principle to the return of refugees from Bangladesh in the 1990s disputes over the number of Rohingya with the right to return remained. Accordingly, the MoU between Myanmar and Bangladesh on repatriations also had a focus on 'evidence' of residence.[21] So the focus on registration and IDs also served the interests of Bangladesh in securing repatriations. Nonetheless, from Rohingya's perspectives, the emphasis on documenting residence, which was anyway recorded on the 'family lists,' alarmingly side-stepped state abuses relating to the 1982 citizenship law as well as state registration and documentation processes. The focus on documenting residence in global approaches to legal identity and side-stepping the more fundamental issues of citizenship and group identity, as we will see in the sections that follow, remained a key critique of international approaches to statelessness and the 'Legal Identities for All' agenda (Sustainable Development Goal 16.9).

Post-violence registration and documentation: 'pathways to citizenship' or legitimising citizenship exclusions?

The next critical moment in Rohingya narratives relating to international organisations and state registration and IDs was the period that followed the violence of 2012. This section considers how the increasing global focus on IDs and statelessness combined with international approaches in Myanmar that prioritised 'strategic' economic and diplomatic engagement with Myanmar during a period of political 'reform.' This resulted in downplaying the role of the state in the abuses occurring in Rakhine State including in their registration and enumeration processes.

Waves of violence hit Rakhine in June and October 2012, permanently displacing approximately 130,000 Rohingya and other Muslims in Rakhine State from their homes and lands, most of whom remained contained in camps (Human Rights Watch 2020). Between 2012 and 2015, an estimated 170,000 Rohingya boarded boats from Rakhine and Bangladesh and made perilous journeys across the sea to Southeast Asia (UNHCR 2016). Those displaced by the violence and living in camps, were restricted from moving or working outside the camps, and international agencies became involved in aid distribution and broader development in Rakhine (United Nations 2012). In the wake of the displacement that saw the destruction of many people's properties and documents, several different enumeration and registration exercises were initiated. These included nationality verification and assessing applications for replacement document, registration of camp residents for the purposes of aid delivery, and Myanmar's national census of 2014.[22] In Rohingya narratives, these three processes were often linked and overlapping. However, due to the scope of this thesis, this section focuses on international approaches to citizenship verification and the replacement of documents.

As explored in Chapter 3, the 2010s also saw the further revival of interest and concern with statelessness within UNHCR and internationally, termed the 'rediscovery' of statelessness (Kingston 2013; Blitz 2017). This time, there were both an increased internal focus within UNHCR on statelessness and outward-facing public campaigns involving coalitions of NGOs. The renewal of interest drove a 2014 global campaign to eliminate statelessness by 2024, called the IBelong campaign. As explored in Chapter 3, the messaging behind public campaigns established the significance of statelessness as a human rights issue but at the same time reduced the framing of statelessness to 'invisibility'—a notion that sat comfortably within the approaches to statelessness that largely by-passed the violence of state bureaucracies and framed citizenship deprivation as state oversight. As the violence in Rakhine in 2012 hit the international headlines, the term stateless was included in many media articles to describe Rohingya. This process which labelled Rohingya 'stateless' in the popular global consciousness was a source of frustration for participants in the fieldwork. Rohingya participants argued passionately that the label 'stateless,' without reference to the military's role in arbitrarily stripping them of their citizenship, further undermined their identity and legitimised state discourses that they had never belonged to Myanmar (for further explanation, see Brinham 2021).

Statelessness during this period was reasserted internationally as a fundamental human rights issue—expanding beyond the 1990s focus on state succession and legal technical solutions addressing gaps between nationality laws (Spiro 2011; Foster and Lambert 2016). However, in Myanmar directly addressing racial discrimination in the citizenship law was put on hold with UN agencies, in favour of the softer approaches engaging with the state. Policy approaches that were put forward to address statelessness in Myanmar, became divided. As noted in Chapter 7, on the one hand, some advocated for fundamental changes to the Citizenship Law, and on the other some advocated for softer administrative approaches relating to state registration and the provision of individual documents and civil registration.[23] In line with these softer approaches, the individual documentation of Rohingya was viewed as integral to reducing statelessness. First, it would assist with 'naturalisation' applications of some individuals who still held historical identity documents, thereby expanding individual rather than group access to citizenship.[24] Second, documents were considered a way to potentially plot a pathway towards citizenship for larger numbers in the future by providing additional evidence of permanent residency (Center for Diversity and National Harmony 2019; Advisory Commission on Rakhine State Aug 2017). This was understood in international policy circles to potentially increase the number of people who could acquire citizenship in the future under the 'naturalisation' provisions in the citizenship law if administrative and evidentiary burdens were relaxed. However, from most Rohingya perspectives expressed in fieldwork, attempts to expand state registration and documentation processes without reforming the citizenship law, lent legitimacy to a scheme that had been utilised to destroy their identities and increased the risks of violence and expulsion (Brinham 2019). Whilst the international agencies perceived registration and IDs to be promoting 'pathways to citizenship' for more individuals through 'naturalisation,' many Rohingya understood the state was producing and reproducing a noncitizenship status as part of a process that violently attacked group belonging (see Chapter 6). In international circles, directly tackling discrimination in the citizenship law in the context of increasing anti-Rohingya rhetoric at both the state and societal levels was viewed as potentially igniting further conflict (see, e.g. Republic of the Union of Myanmar 2013). However, the context in which fundamental human rights and discrimination issues went unaddressed by international agencies working in Myanmar also occurred in the context of their political and economic reform process which saw pragmatic engagement with the Myanmar government prioritised as an international approach (Mahony 2018; Rosenthal 2019).

Prior to this period, the Myanmar military leadership began implementing what they called the 'road map to discipline flourishing democracy.'[25] It was a political and economic reform process marked by a new constitution in 2008 and general elections in 2010. This changed the dynamics in international relations between Myanmar and the global north, with a shift from the economic and political isolation of Myanmar to engagement. Sanctions were lifted, financial investment and international trade resumed, and development aid increased (Hlaing 2012). With the increase of development aid, came an increased international focus on the need to enumerate and document populations in the country. The 2014 census, for example, was seen as a vital pre-requisite to the effective delivery of development projects (The Republic of the Union of Myanmar 2014; Ferguson 2015). International diplomatic relations focused on 'constructive engagement' (Razak 2012). Human rights issues were approached through 'quiet diplomacy' so as not to endanger the 'fragile reform process' or damage the 'fledgling democracy' (Rosenthal 2019). In retrospect, the pragmatic prioritisation of securing access and state engagement for UN agencies in Myanmar came at the expense of a stronger human rights approach. This approach was to be widely criticised following the genocidal violence against Rohingya in 2017. Parallels were drawn between the UN's failure to prevent atrocity crimes against Tamil populations in Sri Lanka, and their failures to prevent atrocities against Rohingya in Myanmar (Mahony 2018; Rosenthal 2019). Within this context, the term 'Rohingya' was not used by international agencies in meetings and documents accessed by Myanmar government officials—their historic claims to belong to Myanmar were largely ignored (UNHCR Feb 2012). This contributed to the insecurities and mistrust of UN agencies expressed by Rohingya in the fieldwork.[26]

Prior to the violence of 2012, in the context of renewed international political and economic engagement in Myanmar, UNHCR Rohingya staff in NRS had compiled extensive documentation of abuses relating to household registration and blacklisting. In the fieldwork, participants reported feeling hopeful that this information would be used more effectively by international staff in the organisation to push for change.[27] In the immediate wake of the first round of violence in June 2012, there were mass arbitrary arrests of Rohingya, accused of instigating violence. Those who worked for international agencies and NGOs were targeted for arrest, with Muslim staff members detained and some charged (Lavelo 2012).[28] Access for international organisations to NRS and other areas was further restricted by the Myanmar government—they were accused of prioritising Muslim over Buddhist populations in their relief operations (Fan and Saleen 2012). UNHCR's Muslim staff in Maungdaw were told to reapply for their jobs and most were replaced by other candidates. Buddhist staff were retained without application. This was understood to be a result of interference from the Myanmar government and designed to prevent further uncovering of abuses.[29] In fieldwork narratives, the events of 2012 were also drawn on as further evidence that UNHCR had misread the nature of the militarised state in Myanmar and had been 'tricked' by the government in Myanmar.[30]

The violence of 2012 was characterised by Rohingya participants in the research as pre-planned, state-led and coordinated between state-sponsored and anti-Muslim Rakhine groups. Several international human rights groups characterised the violence similarly (Equal Rights Trust 2012; Human Rights Watch 2013; Green, McManus et al. 2015). Domestically in Myanmar and amongst UN and aid agencies, the violence was generally characterised as 'inter-community conflict' with the role of the state largely downplayed (United Nations 2012:1; Republic of the Union of Myanmar 2013). This terminology characterised the situation as a two-way conflict between Buddhists and Muslims in Rakhine, without addressing the role of the central state in the violence. Debates over the role of the state in the 2012 violence ensued in human rights and academic literature (Cheesman 2017). Nonetheless, the characterisation of the violence in international policy circles as predominantly 'inter-communal' profoundly influenced international approaches to registration and identification policy in Myanmar. International agencies supported government registration and verification efforts and engaged in trust and 'confidence-building' exercises at the community level where conflict between the state and the community over registration occurred (UNHCR 2014). Meanwhile, Rohingya increasingly resisted registration and enumeration processes understanding them as persecutory (Fortify Rights 2019; Human Rights Watch 2020). Rohingya's underlying concerns went largely unaddressed as international approaches focused on 'confidence-building' (UNHCR 2014). As such, international efforts to support the state in these processes were sometimes characterised in fieldwork as indicating international complicity in state crimes.[31] As one community leader in Bangladesh stated on international agencies' approach to registration during this period, 'They were supporting the violence of the government.'[32] Another focus group participant stated of the period, 'UNHCR sponsored the government . . . It is a clear policy of UNHCR to closely work with the Burmese government.'[33]

By the end of 2012 in the aftermath of the violence, 'intimidation' by state authorities was being reported in nationality verification processes (United Nations 2012:26). The UN-coordinated response plan for international agencies working in Rakhine, recommended addressing this and the 'lack of citizenship' in Rakhine through further international involvement:

> involvement in citizenship verification exercises undertaken by the Government, work[ing] with authorities to restore personal documentation lost by individuals in the context of the recent displacement, and appropriate interventions and advocacy at the Government level to support initiatives to adopt citizenship legislation which promotes rights to citizenship and prevents and reduces situations where individuals do not have any citizenship.
>
> (United Nations 2012:11)

The approach then sought to publicly engage with government in verification and identification exercises. Meanwhile, 'quiet diplomacy' on citizenship questions was advocated. However, in providing technical support to government on IDs and registration, some fundamental issues were largely sidelined including the role of the militarised state in establishing and maintaining legal frameworks and state documentation practices that institutionalised discrimination and persecution. Further, the focus on individual over group access to citizenship overlooked the issue that Rohingya understood as absolutely fundamental to their experiences of violence—their membership of a group that the state had singled out for destruction (see Chapter 6). Associated approaches prioritised naturalisation over the automatic right to citizenship, relaxing administrative requirements within the existing law over reform of the discriminatory provisions in the citizenship law and individual over group access to citizenship. Such approaches continued to be advocated for in international policy circles, even as the genocidal violence of 2016–7 unfolded (Advisory Commission on Rakhine State Aug 2017). Increased registration and issuance of IDs were viewed as fundamental to these approaches in reducing statelessness. As the global development agenda began to prioritise 'legal identities for all' (SDG 16.9), the focus on state ID schemes as a foundation of inclusive development was further consolidated.

NVCs: promoting inclusive development or consolidating the state's power to exclude?

This section considers how the focus within the global development agenda on 'legal identities for all' influenced international approaches in Myanmar that viewed universal IDs and verification of legal status as desirable from development, human rights, and governance perspectives. It considers how Rohingya experiences and understandings of state power in Myanmar interrupted these notions.

As noted in Chapter 3, the inclusion of legal identities within the Sustainable Development Goals (SDGs) in 2015 was viewed within the statelessness field as a significant opportunity to ensure that the issue of statelessness was addressed within the global development agenda (UNHCR 2017; Bloom, Manby et al. 2019). Linked to the guiding principle of the SDGs, 'leave no one behind' (United Nations System 2017), the notion that stateless people are 'invisible' to states and to international development agencies; that being left out of national data and statistics results in being excluded from national development initiatives (UN Sustainable Development Group 2019). The inclusion of SDG target 16.9, 'to provide legal identity for all, including birth registration,' by 2030 was significant for those seeking to raise the international profile of the issue. Within the statelessness movement, this SDG was viewed as an opportunity to build more momentum to address the global problem of statelessness and its impacts (UNHCR 2017; Bloom, Manby et al. 2019; UN Sustainable Development Group 2019).

Nonetheless, the framing of legal identities within the SDGs was also debated and critiqued from within statelessness studies (Oppenheim and Powell 2015; Institute on Statelessness and Inclusion, line-height: normal et al. 2017; Institute on Statelessness and Inclusion 2019; Manby 2021). Critiques focused on three factors. First, the lack of definition of the term 'legal identity' made it easy for states to focus on recording the basic characteristics of identity such as name, sex, and place of birth without incorporating some of the underlying human rights principles relating to legal identities such as equality before the law, and the right to nationality (Institute on Statelessness and Inclusion 2017; UN Legal Identity Expert Group 2019). Second, the indicator for the legal identity target, 'proportion of children under 5 years of age whose births have been registered with a civil authority,' was critiqued as being neither broad enough nor nuanced enough to account for the deprivation of legal identities across all ages and minority groups (Institute on Statelessness and Inclusion 2019). Third, the focus on the right to a legal identity rather than the right to nationality within the development agenda was critiqued. It was noted that state registration did not always equate to social inclusion, access to services, or steps towards citizenship and as such did not have a strong enough human rights focus (Institute on Statelessness and Inclusion 2019; Manby 2021). Examples of these three critiques came from various countries in Africa (Manby 2018), the Dominican Republic (Hayes de Kalaf 2020), and India (Chaudhuri and König 2018), amongst others. Concepts of 'legal identity,' then, within this agenda became increasingly fused and confused with 'legal IDs' (van Waas 2015). This undermined the links between legal identities and the 'right to nationality,' instead focusing on state approaches to registration and identification that did not necessarily link to the promotion of human rights.

The incorporation of legal identities within the SDGs, then, was to promote social protection and social inclusion based on the understanding that IDs and registration benefitted invisible and marginalised persons (UN Sustainable Development Group 2019). Building on the goals and language of the SDGs, the World Bank developed a global programme promoting IDs for development, or the ID4D programme.[34] ID4D established national digital ID systems as a tool and pre-requisite for broader national development and investment projects (World Bank Group 2016). Digital ID systems involved large, often multi-national tech companies in public–private partnerships that digitised national databases relating to civil documentation and vital statistics, incorporated biometric technologies, and established a Single Source of Truth (SSOT) as to individual identities, thereby cutting out any irregularities in recording of people's details (Manby 2020). Biometrics, Unique ID numbers, and 'smart' ID cards often provided a single access point to services and benefits. Such systems were promoted as reducing paperwork, bureaucracy, and administrative inefficiencies (World Bank Group 2018). As such they were hailed by development agencies and the tech sector as relieving the problems of those who had lost or lacked adequate state documentation to prove their identity (Chaudhuri and König 2018). Digital ID systems and biometric IDs were seen as reducing corruption and preventing the production of fraudulent documents. As such, legal identities—or IDs—for all became established as a tool to enhance development approaches to 'digital development, social protection, health, financial inclusion, governance, gender, and legal issues' (World Bank Group 2016). Digital IDs became a massive growth industry, particularly in the global south. Within the industry, they were described as tools of freedom and liberation, the point at which tech, development, and human rights converged (Gelb and Manby 2016; Manby 2020).

Three key critiques of the promotion of digital ID systems from academics and rights groups emerged. First, they noted that private tech companies involved in the development of ID systems were largely unregulated and unaccountable to the end users, or the general population (Institute on Statelessness and Inclusion 2019). Further concerns were raised about intrusive state surveillance through ID systems, as well as privacy and data protection (Bennet and Lyon 2008; Breckenridge 2008; Privacy International 2019; Privacy International 2020). Of particular concern to statelessness scholars was the potential for ID systems to exclude those with precarious or uncertain citizenship status, by cementing their lack of legal status. This made it harder for those not included to access services and to use informal strategies to survive as undocumented or under-documented people. Hence, critiques described how digital ID systems could 'lock in' statelessness and 'lock out' noncitizens from the formal economy and government services (Manby 2018; Brinham, Tiwari et al. 2020). Examples of how digital ID systems could produce exclusions came from the Dominican Republic, where the legal identity agenda supported by the World Bank resulted in birth records for Dominicans of Haitian descent being transferred to a 'foreign' register. This effectively excluded them from equal access to education, employment, and social welfare and undermined their citizenship claims by 'making them foreign' (Hayes de

Kalaf 2020). Also in Kenya, the planned National Integrated Identity Management System (NIIMS) registration would be required to register as a voter, apply for a passport driving licence, register a mobile phone number, pay taxes, open a bank account, access healthcare, and more. This had a potentially devastating impact on those who had struggled to secure citizenship documentation. In January 2020, the court ruled to stop the scheme until a regulatory framework was in place to address data privacy and exclusions (Open and Society Justice Initiative 2020; Privacy International 2020).

Despite the principles of inclusion that underlay the SDG 16.9, state registration and IDs were not always benevolent tools of development. As shown in Chapters 6 and 7, they could also be tools of oppression and persecution. Further, from statist perspectives, providing IDs served another function beyond inclusive development. IDs 'for all' also bolstered border controls by enabling better identification of irregular migrants and facilitating deportations. Chapter 3 described how, from a border enforcement perspective, statelessness had long been viewed as a problem since stateless people most often could not be removed or deported (de Chickera 2010). Statelessness was thus viewed within 'the international order' as 'an administrative anomaly in the global filing system' that failed to provide a return address (Macklin 2007:340). Thus, the legal identity agenda served the interests not only of states noted for oppressive or intrusive surveillance practices but of all states in border control. Sometimes using digital IDs as bordering practices resulted in discrimination and racism (UNHRC Nov 2020). Ultimately then, the promotion of the 'legal identities for all' agenda became the point at which state interests in border and population control married with the global development agenda and human rights approaches to the right to nationality that promote pathways to citizenship. Both state and human rights approaches converged in considering that universal state registration and identification was desirable (see also Brinham 2019).

Digital national ID systems followed two different models, those that provided IDs on the basis of citizenship and those that provided IDs on the basis of residency. The Aadhaar scheme in India was hailed as a model for the latter, whereby IDs based on residency aimed to provide more inclusive access to services whilst by-passing questions of citizenship. Nonetheless, in India, the citizenship card scheme was experienced in some communities, including the Rohingya, as a tool of exclusion. Whilst the Aadhaar ID scheme was being rolled out, simultaneously refugee protections eroded, and national databases—the National Population Register (NPR) and the Nation Register of Citizenship (NRC)—increasingly differentiated between citizens and noncitizens. Further, the Citizen Amendment Act (CAA) of 2019 reframed access to naturalised citizenship for people escaping persecution on the basis of religion and country of origin. These factors combined with the use of the Aadhaar card as a single access point for services and benefits to produce further marginalisation of Muslim refugees and noncitizens (Brinham,

Tiwari et al. 2020; Chapparban 2020; Tiwari and Field 2020). Focusing on residency rather than citizenship enabled international agencies to continue to by-pass the sticky and contentious issues of citizenship laws without encroaching on sovereignty (Manby 2021).[35] This echoed past approaches to IDs in Myanmar, as we saw in the last section, whereby documentation and registration of residency became an end in itself—it did not lead to a more stable legal status but rather, in the context of broader national ID schemes, cemented a noncitizen status (Brinham 2019; Tiwari and Field 2020).

This global momentum that spurred forwards universal identification and registration globally also set the context for both direct and indirect international support for the registration and national verification of Rohingya and others in Myanmar under the NLD government from 2016 onwards (Brinham 2018; Fortify Rights 2019). Within this paradigm, registration and individual IDs for Rohingya were promoted as key to inclusive development and as a 'pathway to citizenship' (see, e.g. United Nations 2012; Republic of the Union of Myanmar 2013; Center for Diversity and National Harmony 2019; Advisory Commission on Rakhine State Aug 2017). In 2016, the World Bank began the 'diagnostic stage' of the ID4D programme in Myanmar with a view digitising registration systems and introducing biometrics to national ID systems (World Bank Group 2018). A digital ID system was envisaged as accompanying and complementing broader development and infrastructure projects in the country. The state violence against Rohingya in 2017 put ID4D and other World Bank projects on hold indefinitely with the risks being ascertained as too high. However, international banks and tech companies offered loans and potential partnership with Myanmar government Ministries for the digitisation of Myanmar's national ID system (Brinham, Tiwari et al. 2020).[36] Rather than an ID scheme based on residency, the Myanmar Government stated explicitly that a digital ID system would be implemented under the existing 1982 Citizenship Law, referring directly to national verification in Rakhine State (Ministry of Information (Myanmar) 23 Jan 2020).

Further, within Myanmar government discourses, citizenship verification under the 1982 Citizenship Law was framed as part of the broader national project of transitioning to a 'rule of law'-based society. International policy circles sometimes echoed this notion that sorting Myanmar's citizens from foreigners, even if that meant doing it under the 1982 Citizenship Law as an interim measure before tackling discrimination within the law, could help contribute to 'peace,' 'development,' and 'rule of law' (Advisory Commission on Rakhine State Aug 2017:27). Key international actors indicated their support for the NVC scheme (explored in Chapter 7) as part of broader development proposals. Most significant was the 'Kofi Annan report' (Advisory Commission on Rakhine State Aug 2017), which was published on the eve of the campaigns of genocidal violence on 24 August 2017. The report, which called for reform of the 1982 Citizenship Law, also included recommendations on implementing national verification and proceeding with NVCs, as well as expanded naturalisation under the existing 1982 citizenship law as an initial step (recommendations 11–16, pp. 27–28). The report did not use the term Rohingya but rather referred to 'Muslims,' a term which participants felt in this context undermined their identity and belonging (see Chapter 5). After the violence of 2017, the recommendations of the Kofi Annan report continued to be drawn on by international governments and agencies as a system of benchmarks that should be met in establishing conditions of return for Rohingya who had been forcibly displaced by violence and living in camps both within Myanmar and in Bangladesh (Reuters 28th Jan 2019). Other public remarks were made by key international figures that appeared to support national verification and NVCs after the violence of 2017. These remarks were referred to by participants during the fieldwork as grievances. These included photos and Twitter remarks posted by the EU ambassador to Myanmar, Kristian Shmidt, that appeared to endorse NVCs as a step towards freedom of movement for Rohingya (Coconuts Yangon 14th Feb 2018), and remarks made by UN Special Envoy on Myanmar, Christine Schraner Burgener, which encouraged Rohingya to accept and trust the NVC process as 'a step towards citizenship' (Burma Campaign UK Jan 31st 2019).

Whilst UNHCR was associated in interviews and focus groups with supporting the issuance of white cards, their public response to NVCs was muted. They neither condemned nor endorsed the process.[37] Nonetheless, participants expressed concern that UNHCR may be tacitly supporting Myanmar's NVC scheme, noting that Rohingya working for UNHCR in Myanmar had to accept NVCs to have their salaries processed through the Myanmar banking system (see Chapter 7).[38] Further, a Fortify Rights report found that five different international humanitarian organisations were 'coercing' Rohingya to accept NVCs for these purposes (Fortify Rights 2019:63). There was also an underlying mistrust of UNHCR that fed into concerns that they may support future government verification schemes in Myanmar. This was due to a number of factors including UNHCR's support for white cards in the past; not using the term 'Rohingya' in their written and verbal interactions with the Myanmar government or Myanmar reports and statistics; their closed-door as opposed to public approach to advocacy on Rohingya human rights and citizenship issues; and their lack of consultation with Rohingya populations and the lack of transparency regarding the MOU on repatriations between Myanmar and UNHCR and UNDP (see also Brinham 2018; Fortify Rights 2019).[39]

More and more abuses relating to the NVCs came to light in human rights reports relating to the period of 2016–7 during the process of this research (Green, McManus et al. 2018; Potter and Kyaw Win 2019; UNHRC Sept 2018). As this occurred, international support for NVCs waned. Nonetheless, support for universal ID schemes, 'verification' of Rohingya, and promotion of naturalisation under the existing law, all continued to be advocated in international circles and reports. As described in the last chapter, these were aspects of Myanmar's citizenship rules and ID schemes that were all contested and resisted by Rohingya as part of identity destruction and the genocidal process. Two key examples of continued support for these processes in Myanmar that were provided in the fieldwork were talked about with raised voices expressing anxiety and frustration. They were first the references to 'verification' and provision of IDs on return to Myanmar in the MOU on repatriations between Myanmar, UNHCR and UNDP (Jun 2018); and the biometric verification cards referred to throughout an ASEAN report on repatriation (ASEAN-ERAT 2019). The ASEAN-ERAT (2019:32) report proposed returnees immediately on arrival would:

> receive an NVC with a barcode and will further proceed to Biometric Registration. The NVC serves as a guarantee by the Government of Myanmar for the returnees to be able to access livelihood opportunities and basic needs such as health and education services in Maungdaw and serves as evidence that the person is a resident of Myanmar . . . . The recording of personal information of returnees 18 years old and above and the immediate issuance of their NVCs at the Reception Centre also supports the enhancement of the security process such that every person processed through the Centres is recorded and accounted for.

The next section contrasts this ongoing support for verification and state ID schemes with articulations within Rohingya narratives from the fieldwork relating to Rohingya futures in Myanmar, the right of return and repatriations.

IDs and the right of return: sustainable futures or depleted rights and security?

This section considers how, as Myanmar expelled Rohingya on mass in 2017, the 'legal identities for all' agenda was being further consolidated within global governance of refugees and migrants marking a lean towards the prioritisation of state interests in border control and 'migration management' over the human rights and protection of refugees and stateless persons. The historical context of the continued cycles of forced expulsions and repatriations of Rohingya from Bangladesh combined with the global push for universal IDs to make Myanmar's IDs desirable in securing 'sustainable' repatriations. This approach collided with Rohingya experiences and perspectives on the violence and coercion inherent in registration and documentation processes and produced further frustration and resistance from Rohingya communities in the camps in Bangladesh.

In 2016, guided by the Sustainable Development Goals, the UNGA adopted the New York Declaration on Refugees and Migrants.[40] This initiated the development of two global compacts on refugees (GCR) and Safe, Orderly and Regular Migration (GCM) in 2017 and 2018.[41] These were non-binding agreements which established a set of principles and objectives for the governance of refugees and migration (Guild and Basaran 2018). Whilst the New York declaration brought the issues of refugees and migrants together and called for inter-agency coordination on 'mixed flows' of migrants and refugees, the two compacts developed separately and reflected the different mandates of the overseeing agencies—UNHCR for the GCR on refugees and the International Organisation for Migration (IOM) for the GCM on migration. The GCM saw the incorporation of IOM into the UN system, raising a number of concerns within the human rights field that their mandate was not compatible with the normative framework of the UN system (Guild, Grant et al. 2017; Geiger and Koch 2018; Moretti 2021). Whilst UNHCR's mandate was based on norms relating to the protection of refugees, IDPs, and stateless persons,[42] IOM was established and developed to 'strengthen inter-state cooperation' on migration and thus predominantly represented statist interests rather than the rights and interests of refugees and stateless individuals.[43] Moretti (2021) suggested that the development of two separate compacts was related to the differing mandates and the pre-existing inter-agency 'competition' between UNHCR and IOM.

In the GCR, addressing statelessness was mentioned in four different paragraphs, with a clear focus on supporting states to strengthen 'data collection' (46), 'identification' processes and procedures (60), and 'civil registration' (82).[44] The stated purpose of these measures, in line with UNHCR's mandate, was 'protection and solutions' for refugees, stateless persons, and those at risk of statelessness (82). The document clearly attempted to balance the protection needs of individuals with providing support for states hosting refugee populations. Nonetheless, state registration and identification were not problematised as potentially harmful processes and practices, and no risk assessments were recommended. On civil registration, for example, the document notes that whilst it does not necessarily lead to conferral of nationality, it 'helps establish legal identity and prevent the risk of statelessness' (82). In the Rohingya refugee context in Bangladesh, it was in the interests of UNHCR and the Government of Bangladesh to ensure that Myanmar registered and documented Rohingya in Myanmar to ensure that repatriations were more sustainable this time around. Against the backdrop of the abuses that had taken place in Myanmar in relation to registration and ID schemes, identification processes in the camps were predominantly in the interests of Bangladesh in providing evidence of who originated in Myanmar. This was based on past experiences in the 1970s and 1990s. Repatriations could only be sustainable if documents could prove Rohingyas' right to reside permanently in Myanmar.[45] Further, it was understood that digital databases could help ensure that civil registration and IDs could not be destroyed or lost as they had been in the past (Brinham, Tiwari et al. 2020). Nonetheless, Bangladesh did not integrate birth, marriage, and death registration for Rohingya refugees with the procedures available to Bangladesh nationals. A separate approach was taken for refugees, which helped to ensure that civil documentation processes did not provide avenues for Rohingya refugees to naturalise as Bangladeshi nationals under their citizenship law (Hoque 2016).

The GCM text on legal identity was more focused on state interests and did not attempt the same balance between human rights and state interests of the GCR. Objective 4 of the GCM was to 'ensure that all migrants have proof of legal identity and adequate documentation.' This objective put legal identities and universal ID documents at the centre of international governance of migration. Objective 4 was broken down into seven sub-paragraphs or specific actions to be taken. One of the Actions (20e) related directly to reducing statelessness. This made explicit the link between state registration and ID documents and international approaches to reducing statelessness. Whilst the inclusion of statelessness within the GCM was viewed as a positive step for raising the profile of the issue internationally, critiques focused on how GCM reflected the interests of states over the protection of stateless persons and migrants (de Chickera 2018; Guild and Basaran 2018; Moretti 2021). Amal de Chickera and others writing for the Refugee Law Initiative noted how the evolution of the GCM from 'zero draft' to 'final draft' represented a 'watering down' of the text to represent state interests relating to border control and 'migration management' over the protection of individuals (de Chickera 2018; Guild and Basaran 2018). The wording of the action relating to statelessness was significant in setting the parameters for tackling statelessness.

> Strengthen measures to reduce statelessness, including by registering migrants' births, ensuring that women and men can equally confer their nationality to their children, and providing nationality to children born in another State's territory, especially in situations where a child would otherwise be stateless, fully respecting the human right to a nationality and in accordance with national legislation (20e).

The text avoided any emphasis on discriminatory citizenship laws, stating that providing nationality should take place in accordance with national legislation. It also placed the responsibility on the country of origin to register and document, thereby further narrowing approaches to tackling statelessness. Amal de Chickera (2018) summarised this action's limitations as being based on the dual assumption that 'providing migrants with documentation alone will resolve their statelessness' and that responsibility to address statelessness through documentation 'lies with the country of origin.' In the case of Myanmar, this would still leave the responsibility to document and identify Rohingya with the perpetrating state that, in the views of participants, had used registration and IDs as tools in the process of genocide and the production of statelessness.

As the Global compacts were being negotiated, developed, and divided between UNHCR and IOM, in 2017, Rohingya fled across the border from Myanmar into Bangladesh. Bangladesh had not allowed UNHCR to register Rohingya refugees since the early 1990s, and, without having signed the 1951 Refugee Convention, officially categorised Rohingya who arrived after this time as 'illegal migrants' (Pittaway 2016; Crisp 2018). The Government of Bangladesh (GoB) initially raised concerns that UNHCR refugee registration and involvement would lock them into international obligations relating to refugees that would make the repatriation of Rohingya more difficult. Instead, IOM with their mandate on 'migration' as opposed to 'refugees' initially coordinated with the Bangladeshi government in registering new arrivals. Concerns that the new role of IOM globally could undermine UNHCR's role and the focus on refugee protection were reflected in concerns raised regarding the situation in Bangladesh. IOM together with Government of Bangladesh provided refugees with digital ID cards on arrival that recorded them as 'Forcibly Displaced Myanmar Nationals' (FDMNs), not 'refugees.'[46] It was not until a year after the arrivals, that UNHCR and the Government of Bangladesh rolled out a new digital and biometric ID system for Rohingya refugees in the camps (see also The Engine Room 2020). UNHCR had to operate within parameters of engagement set by the Government of Bangladesh. As such, the new IDs also did not include the term 'refugee' (Brinham 2018; The Engine Room 2020). According to UNHCR (2018), 'smart cards' served the purpose of 'protection, identity management, documentation, provision of assistance, population statistics and ultimately solutions for an estimated 900,000 refugees.' The Refugee Relief and Repatriation Commission (RRRC), the Bangladesh government partner in data collection and identification, frontloaded the 'smart cards' used in repatriations to sort Rohingya from Bangladeshis, detracting from UNHCR's distancing of smart cards from repatriation (The Engine Room 2020).

UNHCR's role in implementing this digital ID system for camp-based Rohingya, and their increased role and visibility in the camps in Bangladesh, occurred within the same time period as the signing of an MoU on repatriations between the Government of Myanmar, UNHCR and UNDP.[47] This MoU paved the way for UNHCR to oversee repatriations when conditions allowed, and to secure access to Rakhine State to monitor and establish these conditions.[48] This MoU built on and referred to another bilateral MoU on repatriations between Bangladesh and Myanmar which set out the arrangement regarding the verification of returnees and the provision of IDs on return.[49] The UNHCR/UNDP/Myanmar MoU met extensive criticism amongst refugees in Bangladesh on the basis that they had not been consulted in the terms and the document had not been made available to them (Zarni and Brinham Jun 2019). During fieldwork, in the community meeting room, a large banner was displayed that read:

> 1. Include Rohingya in meetings about Rohingya; 2. Dignified Repatriation must include full citizenship right as Rohingya ethnic group; 3. UNHCR please talk to us about MOU.[50]

The underlying concern for Rohingya was that the two repatriation agreements referred to 'verification' processes and 'identification documents' to be issued by Myanmar on return, which they believed paved the way for the continued use of coercion in the issuance of NVCs on return to Myanmar.[51] This they understood would further cement their 'foreignness' under Myanmar's national verification processes. Instead, they sought the immediate restitution of their citizenship in Myanmar as a guarantee against further group persecution.[52]

Rohingya resistance to the smart cards in the Bangladesh camps grew (Rahman 18th Feb 2020; Brinham 2018; Brinham, Tiwari et al. 2020; The Engine Room 2020). This related predominantly to their unacknowledged demands for full citizenship in Myanmar and ethnic recognition on return as a form of inclusion and protection against future atrocities. For a period of time during the field research, many Rohingya refused to register for the new UNHCR/GoB smart cards. There was talk in focus groups of shadowy organisations offering bribes to families to take the ID cards and rumours of scuffles and beatings by Bangladesh soldiers outside the UNHCR offices.[53] Rohingya also engaged in a series of 'strikes' in the camps to highlight their objections and demands. Their demands included being termed 'refugees,' being recorded as 'Rohingya' and having assurances over the protection of their data from the Myanmar government and cross-border intelligence agents.[54] Ultimately, participants in the research understood the smart cards to be associated with repatriations and their futures in Myanmar, rather than just access to refugee services in the Bangladesh camps. In that respect, they drew on oral histories of forced repatriations from Bangladesh in which UNHCR had been indirectly involved through their working relationships with both Bangladesh and Myanmar (Pittaway 2016; Crisp 2018). Unable to effectively voice their concerns over being excluded from the MoU processes and decisions about their futures, Rohingyas' refusal to submit their biometrics and be issued with smart cards became a way in which they could express their demands about data collection and state registration processes related to repatriation and their futures.[55] UNHCR and RRRC responded to the Rohingya strikes and resistance by improving their messaging about smart cards and engaging more directly with refugees' concerns. This led to the almost universal issuance of smart cards to refugees a year later. Since the period of research, Human Rights Watch published a report documenting how data collected by UNHCR as part of the process of issuing smart cards had been shared with Myanmar for the purposes of repatriation. The refugees concerned as consequently gone into hiding fearing forced repatriation (Human Rights Watch 2021).

The UNHCR/GoB ID scheme then was associated in Rohingya narratives with biometric and biographic data collection that in future may be utilised not just within Bangladesh but also in managing their repatriations to Myanmar. Meanwhile, agreements between states and international agencies, which they had no influence over, left them feeling powerless. UNHCR/GoB data collection and the ID system in the Bangladesh camps were understood by Rohingya in the fieldwork as representing the combined interests of states and international agencies in the 'management' of Rohingya displacement but not as a tool that could enable them to access rights, protections, safety, or inclusion. In that respect, Rohingya feelings towards the smart cards and their notions of the underlying state/international interests behind the cards reflected academic critiques of the global refugee governance and legal identity agenda in two respects. First, they reflected concerns about the move within global refugee and migration governance away from individual human rights towards a focus on state interests outlined in the critiques of the global compacts (Guild, Grant et al. 2017; de Chickera 2018; Geiger and Koch 2018; Moretti 2021). Second, they reflected academic critiques of the 'legal identity for all' agenda that understood the right to nationality as being reduced in global campaigns to the right to a state ID (Van Waas 2015; Manby 2018; Institute on Statelessness and Inclusion 2019; Manby 2021).

Conclusion

This chapter has explored how international approaches to statelessness evolved, to become increasingly focused on state registration and ID schemes as solutions. Whilst such approaches were understood to address statelessness as a human rights issue, they simultaneously worked in the interests of states and their bordering projects that sometimes served to exclude. The increasing focus on state registration and ID schemes influenced the way in which Myanmar's registration and ID schemes were perceived internationally as a solution to Rohingya statelessness in Myanmar, and as a necessary pre-requisite for development, peace, and rule of law. However, Rohingya experiences of identity destruction and genocide disrupted assumptions behind these approaches and suggested that the legitimacy lent to Myanmar through international support for ID schemes ultimately resulted in harm.

This chapter has shown how approaches to statelessness have shifted over time to focus on individual access to citizenship over group rights. For Rohingya participants, in a situation of genocide which sought to physically and symbolically destroy them as a national group, the sidelining of their group identity in Myanmar was experienced as divisive and harmful. International approaches often prioritised the expansion of the naturalisation provisions within existing persecutory laws as an interim measure, and this prioritisation was thereby understood by participants as supporting and legitimising the state's processes of identity destruction.[56] From Rohingya perspectives, approaches such as these that avoided issues of group identity—specifically Rohingya group identity—legitimised the state discourses that attempted to erase Rohingya from Myanmar's history and identity.

State registration and IDs increasingly became a mainstay of approaches to reducing statelessness. The consolidation of 'legal identities for all' within the development, human rights, and migration management agendas produced an almost universal desirability for state registration and IDs within global governance agendas. Legal identities were promoted as a way to prevent exclusions and alleviate the deficit of human rights experienced by noncitizens. However, this approach failed to effectively factor in the ways in which ID systems were also used by states to persecute and exclude. Rohingya experiences showed how Myanmar's ID schemes produced statelessness and violence. Whilst IDs were largely described in international policy approaches as supporting 'pathways to citizenship,' contrastingly for Rohingya participants state-issued IDs set them on a trajectory away from citizenship and belonging in Myanmar. Their narratives disrupted notions that state ID systems were benevolent or neutral purveyors of facts about individuals, instead revealing how these categorisation processes were utilised by the state to destroy Rohingya identities and make new exclusive national identities. Furthermore, these processes were inextricable from their broader experiences of genocide.

Finally, this chapter described how the 'legal identities for all' agenda that sought to 'leave no one behind' in international development initiatives also served the interests of the international state system that filed people according to the return addresses on their IDs. As such the universal IDs agenda bolstered international cooperation in border controls and further enabled the cross-border management of migration and refugees. In doing so, it made the lives of the undocumented more difficult, by reducing their access to informal mobility and survival strategies (see also Brinham, Tiwari et al. 2020). For Rohingya refugees in Bangladesh who sought to ensure their right of return to Myanmar, citizenship restitution and group recognition by Myanmar were central to notions of safety and justice. Meanwhile, international approaches to repatriation sought Myanmar-issued legal identities and IDs that established residency and by-passed discriminatory citizenship laws. This reflected state interests in returning them to Myanmar, without effectively incorporating Rohingya understandings, experiences, and grievances regarding Myanmar's ID systems and citizenship regime. The promotion of IDs as evidence of a legal status without guarantees of substantive rights and recognition of their national identity was understood by Rohingya as undermining their safety, security, and group recognition. These factors illustrated how IDs were utilised within global governance and international political structures to consolidate state interests over and above the protection and rights of individuals and non-state groups.

Notes

1 UN Legal Identity Expert Group (2019). United Nations Strategy for Legal Identity for All. paras 12 & 13, available at: https://unstats.un.org/legal-identityagenda/documents/UN-Strategy-for-LIA-draft.pdf (accessed 21/12/2021). Whilst the Sustainable Development Goals did not define the term 'legal identity,' a subsequent operational definition was agreed upon by UN Legal Identity Expert Group. Accordingly, 'Legal identity is defined as the basic characteristics of an individual's identity. e.g. name, sex, place and date of birth conferred through registration and the issuance of a certificate by an authorized civil registration authority following the occurrence of birth . . . In the case of refugees, Member States are primarily responsible for issuing proof of legal identity. The issuance of proof of legal

identity to refugees may also be administered by an internationally recognized and mandated authority.' This definition provides useful insight into how UN entities approached SDG 16.9. However, wider human rights-based positions drew on other principles. For a deeper critique, see Institute on Statelessness and Inclusion (2017).

2 UN approaches in Myanmar that place 'quiet diplomacy' and 'constructive engagement' over a human rights approach have been critiqued in Mahony (2018) and Rosenthal (2019).

3 Those mentioned included UNFPA, UNDP, WFP, UNICEF, ASEAN, etc.

4 Names of NGOs excluded to ensure anonymity of participants.

5 Fg5, 28/04/2018, Kuala Lumpur.

6 General Assembly Resolution 50/152 of 21 Dec 1995

7 *Ibid*

8 UNHCR Information Services, Nov 11, 1993, 'Burma Memorandum of Understanding on Repatriation' Available at: www.burmalibrary.org/reg.burma/archives/199401/msg00058.html (accessed 25/04/2021).

9 This report self-admittedly drew predominantly on conversations with state officials during this period to ascertain the legal status of Rohingya. These officials claimed that Rohingya had uncertain status under the 1948 citizenship law. The UN Special Rapporteur noted that this was disputed by Muslim refugees that he interviewed in the Bangladesh refugee camps.

10 Fg9, 02/10/2018, New Delhi.

11 It should be clarified that in fact the white cards were state issued, but participants explained that the state provision of white cards was supported and advocated for by UN agencies working in Myanmar, leading to the assertion that UN 'gave' us white cards. This was not meant to be taken literally.

12 Fg7, 26/08/2018, Kutapalong.

13 Extract from a letter written by the UNHCR in Geneva to BRAJ dated 12/02/2002. Letter republished in Zaw Min Htut (2003). Human Rights Abuses and Discrimination on Rohingya.

14 Correspondence between UNHCR and BRAJ refer to the following article which cited Ms Erika Feller, Director of International Protection at UNHCR expressing her 'satisfaction' at the issuance of white cards Myanmar Times, 7/11/2002, 'Issuance of residence certificates and discussion on repatriations of refugees' (see Ibid).

15 Fg6&7, 26/07/2018, Kutapalong.

16 Also, these objections were referred to and letters of complaint to UNHCR published in Zaw Min Htut (2003).

17 Fg6&7, 26/07/2018, Kutapalong; In12, 24/04/2018, KL; In29. 27/07/2018, Unchiprang; In30, 28/07/2018, Balukhali; IN35, 02/08/2018, Chittagong; In40, 24/09/2018, Balukhali; In45, 26/09/2018, Hakimpara.

18 Letter from BRAJ to UNHCR dated 6/12/2002, republished in Zaw Min Htut (2003).

19 In coding focus groups and interviews, these three key themes emerged in relation to Myanmar's approach to international organisations.

20 Fg6, 26/07/2018, Kutapalong.

21 Joint Statement by the Foreign Ministries of Bangladesh and Myanmar issued at the conclusion of the official visit of the Myanmar Foreign Minister to Bangladesh from 23 to 28 Apr 1992 (on file with author): 7(iv).

22 The census was supported by international agencies—significantly UNFPA—and international governments with the aim of promoting national and regional development (The Republic of the Union of Myanmar 2014).

23 See, for example, the two different approaches in recommendations in on the one hand Republic of the Union of Myanmar (2013) and Center for Diversity and National Harmony (2019), which recommend citizenship verification and

naturalisation approaches whilst refraining from using the term Rohingya, and Burma Campaign UK (2018), which advocates for the immediate restitution and overhaul of citizenship.

24 'Naturalisation' in the context of Myanmar's 1982 Citizenship Law does not enable individuals to naturalise through marriage or long-term residence alone. Instead, it is a process that involves combinations of residence and citizenship over two generations (see Arraiza and Vonk (2017)).

25 The seven-step road map to discipline flourishing democracy was announced on state media in 2003 by General Khin Nyunt, then Prime Minister.

26 This was noted throughout the fieldwork. One example is that Rohingya in the Bangladesh camps in 2018 campaigned for UNHCR to record them as Rohingya on UNHCR/Government of Bangladesh issued 'smart' ID cards. One of their main lobbying points was that UN agencies working in Myanmar had not used the term Rohingya in the country.

27 In30&In31, 28/07/2018, Balukhali.

28 Also, In30&In31, 28/07/2018, Balukhali; In13, 23/04/2018, Kuala Lumpur; In14, 26/04/2018, Kuala Lumpur.

29 In30&In31, 28/07/2018, Balukhali.

30 Fg7, 26/07/2018, Kutapalong; Fg8, 26/09/2018, Hakimpara.

31 Fg6, 26/07/2018, Kutapalong.

32 Fg6, 26/07/2018, Kutapalong.

33 Fg6, 26/07/2018, Kutapalong.

34 The ID4D Website is available at https://id4d.worldbank.org/ (accessed 12/05/2021).

35 Ibid.

36 Austrian bank Unicredit, Austrian company OeSD, and French multinational Thales.

37 UNHCR internal documents from this period documented concerns raised over force and coercion used in relation to issuing NVCs by Myanmar forces. See Fortify Rights (2019).

38 Interviews included eight persons who had previously worked for humanitarian agencies in Rakhine. Also referred to in Fg6, 26/09/2018; FG8, 26/09/2018, Hakimpara.

39 These factors were drawn from all focus groups and interviews. They were a particular focus in Fg6&7, 26/07/2018, Kutapalong; Fg8, 26/09/2018, Hakimpara.

40 UN General Assembly (3 Oct 2016). Resolution adopted by the General Assembly on 19 Sept 2016, 71/1. New York Declaration for Refugees and Migrants.

41 GCR: United Nations (2 Aug 2018). Report of the UNHCR: Part II Global Compacts, A/73/12. GCM: UN General Assembly (11 Jan 2019). Resolution adopted by the General Assembly on 19 Dec 2018, 73/195. Global Compact for Safe, Orderly and Regular Migration.

42 UNHCR Mandate of the High Commissioner for Refugees and his Office Available at: www.unhcr.org/5a1b53607.pdf (accessed 15/05/2021).

43 IOM. Mandate Available at: www.iom.int/mandate (accessed 15/05/2021).

44 There are no other specific mentions of approaches to statelessness, but there is reference to UNHCR's broader 'Action Plan' on statelessness as part of the I Belong campaign.

45 Two participants interviewed had already been repatriated twice and expelled for a third time.

46 Ob4, 17/11/2017. During fieldwork trips between Jul and Sept 2018, refugees showed me their ID cards issued under this process as an example of (a) how the earliest ones carried the term 'Rohingya' and (b) how they already had refugee registration cards and therefore did not need UNHCR registration cards. Photos of cards on file with author.

47 Government of the Union of Myanmar, UNHCR and UNDP (Jun 2018). Memorandum of Understanding between GoM and UNDP and UNHCR (leaked copy).
48 During my first fieldwork trip in Nov 2017, the camps were covered in IOM branding—from buildings to umbrellas to tarpaulins. By the time of my fieldwork trips from Jun 2018, UNHCR branding was dominant in the camps, and IOM branding had been reduced.
49 Government of Bangladesh and Government of Myanmar (23 Nov 2017). Arrangement on Return of Displaced Persons from Rakhine State between GoB and GoM (Leaked Copy on File with Author). Nay Pyi Taw.
50 Photos of banner on file with author. Ob8, 26/07/2018.
51 Para 2 of Government of Bangladesh and Government of Myanmar (23 Nov 2017). Arrangement on Return of Displaced Persons from Rakhine State between GoB and GoM (Leaked Copy on File with Author). Nay Pyi Taw states: 'Myanmar will issue returnees with identity cards for national verification immediately on return.' Para 15 of Government of the Union of Myanmar, UNHCR and UNDP (Jun 2018). Memorandum of Understanding between GoM and UNDP and UNHCR (Leaked Copy) echoes this stating: 'After the necessary verifications, the MoLIP will issue to all returnees the appropriate identification papers and ensure a clear and voluntary pathway to citizenship to those eligible.'
52 'Full citizenship' and 'ethnic recognition' were central to all focus group discussions and interviews relating to future repatriations as well as those relating to justice and restitution. It was also central to all written demands on banners in the camps during field visits in 2018. Photos on file.
53 Fg6, 26/07/2018, Kutapalong; Fg8, 26/09/2018, Hakimpara. See also Rahman (2020).
54 Strike notices and demands on file with author.
55 Fg6&7, 26/07/2018, Kutapalong; Fg8, 26/09/2018, Hakimpara. In Fg6, participants also expressed their concerns about para 27 of Government of the Union of Myanmar, UNHCR and UNDP (Jun 2018). Memorandum of Understanding between GoM and UNDP and UNHCR (Leaked Copy), which states that the sharing of confidential personal data of returnees will be in conformity with the laws and regulations of Myanmar. Myanmar has extremely weak privacy laws, which raised further alarm. See Brinham, Tiwari et al. (2020).
56 Similar findings on objections to naturalisation as a solution to statelessness amongst Kurdish populations in Syria are outlined in Bahram (2021).

Bibliography

Advisory Commission on Rakhine State (Aug 2017). *Towards a Peaceful, Fair and Prosperous Future for the People of Rakhine: Final Report*. www.rakhinecommission.org/app/uploads/2017/08/FinalReport_Eng.pdf [Accessed 05/06/2018]

Arraiza, J. M. and O. Vonk (2017). Report on Citizenship Law: Myanmar. *GlobalCit 14*. European University Institute. https://cadmus.eui.eu/bitstream/handle/1814/48284/RSCAS_GLOBALCIT_CR_2017_14.pdf?sequence=1&isAllowed=y [Accessed 05/06/2019]

ASEAN-ERAT (2019). *The Preliminary Needs Assessment for Repatriation*. https://asean.org/storage/2020/03/13.-June-2019-Preliminary-NeedsAssessment-for-Repatriation-in-Rakhine-State-Myanmar-ad-hoc-AHA-Ctr.pdf [Accessed 13/11/2020]

Bahram, H. (2021). Too Little too Late? Naturalisation of Stateless Kurds and Transitional Justice in Syria, in Bloom, T. and Kingston, P. (eds), *Statelessness, Governance, and the Problem of Citizenship*. Manchester University Press. 264–275.

Bennet, C. and D. Lyon (2008). *Playing the Identity Card: Surveillance, Security and Identification in Global Perspective*. Routledge.
Benton, L. A. (2002). *Law and Colonial Cultures: Legal Regimes in World History, 1400–1900*. Cambridge University Press.
Blitz, B. (2017). The State and the Stateless: The Legacy of Hannah Arendt Reconsidered, in Bloom, T., Tonkiss, K. and Cole, P. (eds), *Understanding Statelessness*. Routledge. 70–84.
Bloom, T., B. Manby and B. Khadija (2019). Why Citizenship Is Relevant to Sustainable Development: Considerations for the 2019 High Level Political Forum. *European Network on Statelessness*. www.statelessness.eu/sites/default/files/2020-09/ENS-Citizenship-SDGs-High_Level_Political_Forum_2019-briefing.pdf [Accessed 12/05/2021]
Breckenridge, K. (2008). The Elusive Panopticon: The HANIS Project and the Politics of Standards in South Africa, in Bennett, C. J. and Lyon, D. (eds), *Playing the Identity Card: Surveillance and Identity in Global Perspective*. Routledge. 39–56.
Brinham, N. (2018). 'Genocide Cards': Rohingya Refugees on Why They Risked Their Lives to Refuse ID Cards. *OpenDemocracy*. www.opendemocracy.net/natalie-brinham/genocide-cards-why-rohingya-refugees-are-resisting-id-cards [Accessed 30/01/2019]
Brinham, N. (2019a). Looking Beyond Invisibility: Rohingyas' Dangerous Encounters with Papers and Cards. *Tilburg Law Review* 24(2): 156–169.
Brinham, N. (2019b). When Identity Documents Produce Exclusion: Lessons from Rohingya Experiences in Myanmar. *LSE Blogs*. https://blogs.lse.ac.uk/mec/2019/05/10/when-identity-documents-and-registration-produce-exclusion-lessons-from-rohingya-experiences-in-myanmar/ [Accessed 20/02/2020]
Brinham, N. (2021). 'We Are Not Stateless! You Can Call Us What You Like, But We Are Citizens of Myanmar!' Rohingya Resistance and the Stateless Label, in Bloom, T. and Kingston, L. (eds), *Statelessness, Governance, and the Problem of Citizenship*. Manchester University Press. 342–355.
Brinham, N., Tiwari, A. D., Field, J., Ealom, J., Arraiza, J. M. and de Chickera, A. (2020). Locked in and Locked Out: The Impact of Digital Identity Systems on Rohingya Populations. *Institute on Statelessness and Inclusion and UN Special Rapporteur on Racism*. https://files.institutesi.org/Locked_In_Locked_Out_The_Rohingya_Briefing_Paper.pdf [Accessed 25/05/2021]
Burma Campaign UK (2018). *Rohingya Citizenship: Now or Never*. https://burmacampaign.org.uk/burma_briefing/rohingya-citizenship-now-or-never/ [Accessed 12/02/2021]
Burma Campaign UK (31 Jan 2019). *UN Special Envoy Should Drop 'Appalling' Support for NVC Process*. https://burmacampaign.org.uk/rohingya-crWoSs-un-special-envoy-should-drop-appalling-support-for-nvc-process/ [Accessed 13/05/2021]
Center for Diversity and National Harmony (2019). *Myanmar's Citizenship Law: An Analysis*. www.cdnh.org/publication/myanmars-citizenship-law-an-analysis/ [Accessed 08/10/2019]
Chapparban, S. N. (2020). Religious Identity and Politics of Citizenship in South Asia: A Reflection on Refugees and Migrants in India. *Development* 63(1): 52–59.
Chaudhuri, B. and L. König (2018). The Aadhaar Scheme: A Cornerstone of a New Citizenship Regime in India? *Contemporary South Asia* 26(2): 127–142.
Cheesman, N. (2017a). How in Myanmar 'National Races' Came to Surpass Citizenship and Exclude Rohingya. *Journal of Contemporary Asia* 47(3): 461–483.
Cheesman, N. (2017b). Introduction: Interpreting Communal Violence in Myanmar. *Journal of Contemporary Asia* 47(3): 335–352.

Chhotray, V. and F. McConnell (2018). *Certifications of Citizenship: The History, Politics and Materiality of Identity Documents in South Asian States and Diasporas*. Taylor & Francis.

Coconuts Yangon (14 Feb 2018). *EU Ambassador Takes Heat over Rohingya Verification Tweet*. https://coconuts.co/yangon/news/eu-ambassador-takes-heat-rohingya-verification-tweet/ [Accessed 14/02/2018]

Crisp, J. (2018). *'Primitive People': The Untold Story of UNHCR's Historical Engagement with Rohingya Refugees, Humanitarian Exchange*. 732018. https://odihpn.org/magazine/primitive-people-the-untold-story-of-unhcrs-historical-engagement-with-rohingya-refugees/ [Accessed 17/12/2018]

de Chickera, A. (2010). *Unravelling Anomaly: Detention, Discrimination and the Protection Needs of Stateless Persons*. Equal Rights Trust.

de Chickera, A. (2018). *GCM Commentary: Objective 4: Ensure That All Migrants Have Proof of Identity and Adequate Documentation*. https://rli.blogs.sas.ac.uk/2018/11/08/gcm-commentary-objective-4/ [Accessed 14/05/2021]

de Chickera, A., J. Arraiza, Z. Albarazi, G. Field and N. Brinham (2021). *Navigating with a Faulty Map: Access to Citizenship Documents and Citizenship in Myanmar, Institute on Statelessness and Inclusion*. https://files.institutesi.org/Access_to_Citizenship_in_Myanmar_Report.pdf [Accessed 28/12/2021]

The Engine Room (2020). *Understanding the Lived Effects of Digital ID: A Multi-Country Study*. https://digitalid.theengineroom.org/assets/pdfs/200123_FINAL_TER_Digital_ID_Report+Annexes_English_Interactive.pdf [Accessed 17/05/2021]

Equal Rights Trust (2012). *Burning Homes, Sinking Lives: A Situation Report of the Violence against Rohingya in Myanmar and Their Refoulement from Bangladesh*. www.equalrightstrust.org/ertdocumentbank/The%20Equal%20Rights%20Trust%20-%20Burning%20Homes%20Sinking%20Lives.pdf [Accessed 21/05/2019]

European Network on Statelessness & Institute on Statelessness and Inclusion (2019). *Statelessness in Myanmar: Country Position Paper*. https://statelessjourneys.org/wp-content/uploads/StatelessJourneys-Myanmar-final.pdf [Accessed 11/11/2019]

Fan, L. and A. Saleen (2012). *Rakhine Crisis: Restricted Humanitarian Access and Risk of Radicalisation. Al Jazeera* www.aljazeera.com/opinions/2012/11/10/rakhine-crisis-restricted-humanitarian-access-and-risk-of-radicalisation [Accessed 04/05/2021]

Ferguson, J. M. (2015). Who's Counting? Ethnicity, Belonging, and the National Census in Burma/Myanmar. *Journal of the Humanities and Social Sciences of Southeast Asia* 171(1): 1–28.

Fink, C. (1994). The League of Nations and the Minorities Question. *World Affairs* 157: 197.

Fortify Rights (2019). *'Tools of Genocide': National Verification Cards and the Denial of Citizenship of Rohingya Muslims in Myanmar*. www.fortifyrights.org/downloads/Tools%20of%20Genocide%20-%20Fortify%20Rights%20-%20September-03-2019-EN.pdf [Accessed 08/10/2019]

Foster, M. and H. Lambert (2016). Statelessness as a Human Rights Issue: A Concept Whose Time Has Come. *International Journal of Refugee Law* 28(4): 564–584.

Geiger, M. and M. Koch (2018). World Organizations in Migration Politics: The International Organization for Migration. *Journal of International Organizations Studies* 9(1): 25–44.

Gelb, A. and B. Manby (2016). Has Development Converged with Human Rights? Implications for the Legal Identity SDG. *Center for Global Development*. www.cgdev.org/blog/has-development-converged-human-rights-implications-legal-identity-sdg [Accessed 17/12/2018]

Government of Bangladesh and Government of Myanmar (23 Nov 2017). Arrangement on Return of Displaced Persons from Rakhine State between GoB and GoM (leaked copy on file with author). *Nay Pyi Taw*.

Government of the Union of Myanmar, UNHCR and UNDP (Jun 2018). *Memorandum of Understanding between GoM and UNDP and UNHCR* (leaked copy).

Green, P., T. McManus and A. de la Cour Venning (2015). Countdown to Annihilation: Genocide in Myanmar. *International State Crime Initiative*.

Green, P., T. McManus and A. de la Cour Venning (2018). Genocide Achieved, Genocide Continues: Myanmar's Annihilation of the Rohingya. *International State Crime Initiative*.

Guild, E. and T. Basaran (2018). The UN's Global Compact for Safe, Orderly and Regular Migration: Analysis of the Final Draft and Monitoring Implementation. *RefugeeLawInitiative*.https://rli.blogs.sas.ac.uk/themed-content/global-compact-for-migration/ [Accessed 14/05/2021]

Guild, E., S. Grant and K. Groenendijk (2017). IOM and the UN: Unfinished Business. Queen Mary School of Law Legal Studies Research Paper No. 255/2017. https://papers.ssrn.com/sol3/papers.cfm?abstract_id=2927414 [Accessed 17/05/2021]

Hayes de Kalaf, E. (2020). Making Foreign: Legal Identity, Social Policy and the Contours of Belonging in the Contemporary Dominican Republic, in Cruz-Martinez, G. (ed), *Welfare and Social Protection in Contemporary Latin America*. Routledge. 101–117.

Hlaing, K. Y. (2012). Understanding Recent Political Changes in Myanmar. *Contemporary Southeast Asia* 34(2): 197–216.

Hoque, R. (2016). Report on Citizenship Law: Bangladesh. *Globalcit 14*. European University Institute. https://cadmus.eui.eu/bitstream/handle/1814/44545/EudoCit_2016_14Bangladesh.pdf [Accessed 2016]

Hull, M. S. (2012a). Documents and Bureaucracy. *Annual Review of Anthropology* 41: 251–267.

Hull, M. S. (2012b). *Government of Paper: The Materiality of Bureaucracy in Urban Pakistan*. University of California Press.

Human Rights Watch (1996). *The Rohingya Muslims: Ending a Cycle of Exodus?* www.hrw.org/reports/pdfs/b/burma/burma969.pdf [Accessed 21/10/2018]

Human Rights Watch (2013). *All You Can Do It Pray: Crimes against Humanity and Ethnic Cleansing of Rohingya Muslims in Burma's Arakan State*. www.hrw.org/reports/burma0413_FullForWeb.pdf [Accessed 16/03/2017]

Human Rights Watch (2020). *An Open Prison without End: Myanmar's Mass Detention of Rohingya in Rakhine State*. www.hrw.org/report/2020/10/08/open-prison-without-end/myanmars-mass-detention-rohingya-rakhine-state [Accessed 09/10/2020]

Human Rights Watch (2021). *UN Shared Rohingya Data without Informed Consent: Bangladesh Provided Myanmar Information That the Refugee Agency Collected*. www.hrw.org/news/2021/06/15/un-shared-rohingya-data-without-informed-con sent [Accessed 21/12/2021]

Institute on Statelessness and Inclusion (2017). *Statelessness, Human Rights and the Sustainable Development Agenda: A Working Paper*. https://files.institutesi.org/SDG_working-paper2017.pdf [Accessed 12/05/2021]

Institute on Statelessness and Inclusion (2019). *Making SDG 16.9 Work for the Wider Sustainable Development Agenda*. https://files.institutesi.org/legal_identity_policy_brief.pdf [Accessed 12/05/2021]

IOM, UN Migration, Mandate. www.iom.int/mandate [Accessed 15/05/2021]

Joppke, C. (2007). Transformation of Citizenship: Status, Rights, Identity. *Citizenship Studies* 11(1): 37–48.

Kingston, L. N. (2013). A Forgotten Human Rights Crisis: Statelessness and Issue (Non)Emergence. *Human Rights Review* 14: 73–87.

Lavelo, J. L. (2012). *UN Staff Members Detained in Rakhine*. www.devex.com/news/un-staff-members-detained-in-rakhine-78568 [Accessed 04/05/2021]

Lewa, C. (2008). North Arakan: An Open Prison for the Rohingya in Burma. *Forced Migration Review* 32: 11–13.

Macklin, A. (2007). Who Is the Citizen's Other? Considering the Heft of Citizenship. *Theoretical Inquiries in Law* 8(2): 333–366.

Mahony, L. (2018). Time to Break Old Habits: Shifting from Complicity to Protection of Rohingya in Myanmar. *Fieldview Solutions*. www.fieldviewsolutions.org/fv-publications/Time_to_break_old_habits.pdf [Accessed 11/11/2019]

Mamdani, M. (1996). *Citizen and Subject: Contemporary Africa and the Legacy of Late Colonialism*. Princeton.

Manby, B. (2018). 'Legal Identity' and Biometric Registration in Africa. *Newsletter of the American Political Science Association's Organized Section on Migration and Citizenship* 6(2).

Manby, B. (2020). Legal Identity for All and Statelessness: Opportunity and Threat at the Junction of Public and Private International Law. *Statelessness and Citizenship Review* 2(2): 248–271.

Manby, B. (2021). The Sustainable Development Goals and 'Legal Identity for All': 'First, Do No Harm'. *World Development* 139: 105343.

McConnell, F. (2013). Citizens and Refugees: Constructing and Negotiating Tibetan Identities in Exile. *Annals of the Association of American Geographers* 103(4): 967–983.

Ministry of Information Myanmar (23 Jan 2020). E-IDs Fundamental to E-Governance: U Thein Shwe. www.moi.gov.mm/moi:eng/news/362 [Accessed 13/05/2020]

Moretti, S. (2021). Between Refugee Protection and Migration Management: The Quest for Coordination between UNHCR and IOM in the Asia-Pacific Region. *Third World Quarterly* 42(1): 34–51.

Navaro-Yashin, Y. (2007). Make-Believe Papers, Legal Forms and the Counterfeit: Affective Interactions between Documents and People in Britain and Cyprus. *Anthropological Theory* 7(1): 79–98.

NUI Galway (2010). *Crimes against Humanity in Western Burma: The Situation of the Rohingyas*. www.nuigalway.ie/media/intranet/Crimes-Against-Humanit-in-Western-Burma.pdf [Accessed 03/05/2017]

Nyi Nyi Kyaw (2017). Unpacking the Presumed Statelessness of Rohingyas. *Journal of Immigrant and Refugee Studies* 15(3): 269–286.

Open and Society Justice Initiative (2020). *Kenyan Court Puts Hold on Digital Identity Scheme*. www.justiceinitiative.org/newsroom/new-kenya-high-court-judgment-sets-important-precedent-for-digital-id-privacy-protections-and-processes [Accessed 12/12/2021]

Oppenheim, B. and B. M. Powell (2015). *Legal Identity in the 2030 Agenda for Sustainable Development: Lessons from Kibera, Kenya*. Open Society Foundation.

Pittaway, E. (2016). Rohingya Refugees in Bangladesh: A Failure of the International Protection Regime, in Adelman, H. (ed), *The Protracted Displacement in Asia: No Place to Call Home*. Routledge.

Potter, R. and Kyaw Win (2019). National Verification Cards—a Barrier to Rohingya Repatriation. *Burma Human Rights Network*. www.bhrn.org.uk/en/report/1090-national-verification-cards-a-barrier-to-rohingya-repatriation-full-report.html [Accessed 08/10/2019]

Privacy International (2019). *Myanmar: Dangerous Plans for Biometric SIM Card Registration Must Be Scrapped*. https://privacyinternational.org/newsanalysis/3303/myanmar-dangerous-plans-biometric-sim-card-registration-must-be-scrapped [Accessed 13/05/2021]

Privacy International (2020). *A Guide to Litigating Identity Systems*. https://privacyinternational.org/sites/default/files/2020-09/PI_A%20Guide%20to%20Litigating%20Identity%20 [Accessed 13/05/2021]

Rahman, S. (18 Feb 2020). For Rohingya Refugees, ID Systems Have Brought Coercion, Violence and Denial of Their Ethnic Identity. *Global Voices*. https://globalvoices.org/2020/02/18/for-rohingya-refugees-id-systems-have-brought-coercion-violence-and-denial-of-ethnic-identity/ [Accessed 17/05/2021]

Razak, N. (2012). The ASEAN Way Won Burma Over. *Wall Street Journal*. www.wsj.com/articles/SB10001424052702303816504577321242628750250 [Accessed 04/05/2021]

Reddy, M. (2015). Identity Paper/Work/s and the Unmaking of Legal Status in Mae Sot, Thailand. *Asian Journal of Law and Society* 2(2): 251–266.

Republic of the Union of Myanmar (2013). *Final Report of Inquiry Commission on Sectarian Violence in Rakhine State*. https://meriyadh.org/images/pdf/rakhine-commission-report-en-red.pdf [Accessed 05/09/2017]

Republic of the Union of Myanmar (2014). Housing and Population Census. *The Union Report*.

Reuters (2019). *UNICEF Boss Urges Myanmar to Enact Kofi Annan Recommendations on Rohingya Crisis*. www.reuters.com/article/us-myanmar-rakhine-idUSKCN1PM15R [Accessed 13/05/2021]

Rosenthal, G. (2019). A Brief and Independent Inquiry into the Involvement of the United Nations in Myanmar from 2010 to 2018. *United Nations*. www.un.org/sg/sites/www.un.org.sg/files/atoms/files/Myanmar%20Report%20-%20May%202019.pdf [Accessed 11/11/2019]

Sadiq, K. (2009). *Paper Citizens: How Illegal Immigrants Acquire Citizenship in Developing Countries*. Oxford University Press.

Sharma, A. and A. Gupta (2006). *The Anthropology of the State: A Reader*. Blackwell.

Siegelberg, M. L. (2020). *Statelessness: A Modern History*. Harvard University Press.

Spiro, P. J. (2011). A New International Law of Citizenship. *American Journal of International Law* 105(4): 694–746.

Tilly, C. (1995). Citizenship, Identity and Social History. *International Review of Social History* 40(S3): 1–17.

Tiwari, A. D. and J. Field (2020). *Bureaucratic Gaps and Exclusions: The Limits of Documentary 'Protection' for Rohingyas in India, Kaldor Centre, University of New South Wales*. www.kaldorcentre.unsw.edu.au/publication/bureaucratic-gaps-and-exclusion-limits-documentary-%E2%80%98protection%E2%80%99-rohingyas-india [Accessed 13/05/2021]

UN General Assembly (3 Oct 2016). Resolution Adopted By the General Assembly on 19 September 2016, 71/1. *New York Declaration for Refugees and Migrants*.

UN General Assembly (11 Jan 2019). Resolution Adopted By the General Assembly on 19 December 2018, 73/195. *Global Compact for Safe, Orderly and Regular Migration*.

UNHCR (Feb 2012). *UNHCR Style Companion*. www.refworld.org/docid/4fe30f9a2.html [Accessed 21/05/2017]

UNHCR (2014). *2014–2015 Global Appeal: Myanmar*. www.unhcr.org/uk/528a0a32b.pdf [Accessed 04/05/2021]

UNHCR (2016). *Mixed Maritime Movements*. https://reporting.unhcr.org/sites/default/files/UNHCR%20-%20Mixed%20Movements%20in%20South-East%20Asia%20-%202016%20--%20April%202017_0.pdf [Accessed 09/10/2020]

UNHCR (2017). The Sustainable Development Goals and Addressing Statelessness. www.refworld.org/pdfid/58b6e3364.pdf [Accessed 12/05/2021]

UNHCR (2018). *Joint Bangladesh/UNHCR Verification of Rohingya Refugees Gets Underway*. www.unhcr.org/en-us/news/%20briefing/2018/7/5b3f2794ae/

joint-bangladeshunhcr-verificationrohingya-refugees-gets-underway.html [Accessed 17/05/2021]

UNHCR Mandate of the High Commissioner for Refugees and His Office. www.unhcr.org/5a1b53607.pdf [Accessed 15/05/2021]

UNHRC (1994). Report on the Situation of Human Rights in Myanmar, prepared by Mr. Yozo Yokota, Special Rapporteur, E/CN.4/1994/57.

UNHRC (1996). Report on the Situation of Human Rights in Myanmar, prepared by Mr. Yozo Yokota, Special Rapporteur, E/CN.4/1996/65.

UNHRC (Sept 2018). Report of the Independent International Fact-Finding Mission on Myanmar: Report of the 34th Session of the Human Rights Council, A/HRC/34/67.

UNHRC (Nov 2020). Report of the Special Rapporteur on Contemporary Forms of Racism, Racial Discrimination, Xenophobia and Related Intolerance, A/75/590.

United Nations (2012). *Rakhine Response Plan: June 2012–June 2013.* https://reliefweb.int/sites/reliefweb.int/files/resources/Revised%20Rakhine%20Response%20Plan%20%28amended%29.pdf [Accessed 28/04/2021]

United Nations (2 Aug 2018). Report of the UNHCR: Part II Global Compacts, A/73/12.

United Nations System (2017). *Leaving No One Behind: Equality and Non-Discrimination at the Heart of Sustainable Development.* https://unsceb.org/sites/default/files/imported_files/CEB%20equality%20framework-A4-web-rev3.pdf [Accessed 12/05/2021]

UN Legal Identity Expert Group (2019). *United Nations Strategy for Legal Identity for All.*

UN Sustainable Development Group (2019). *Leaving No One Behind: An UNSDG Operational Guide for UN Country Teams.*

van Waas, L. (2015). The Right to Legal Identity or the Right to Legal ID? *European Network on Statelessness.* www.statelessness.eu/blog/right-legal-identity-or-right-legal-id [Accessed 17/12/2018]

Williams, P. (2019). Emigration State Encounters: The Everyday Material Life of a Diaspora Technology. *Political Geography* 68: 1–11.

World Bank Group (2016). *Identification for Development (ID4D).* https://id4d.worldbank.org/sites/id4d.worldbank.org/files/2019-10/ID4D%20Program%20Brochure%2010152019.pdf [Accessed 12/05/2021]

World Bank Group (2018). *Identification for Development: ID4D Annual Report 2018.* https://id4d.worldbank.org/sites/id4d.worldbank.org/files/2018_ID4D_Annual_Report.pdf [Accessed 20/03/2019]

Yuval-Davis, N. (2006). Belonging and the Politics of Belonging. *Patterns of Prejudice* 40(3): 197–214.

Zarni, M. and N. Brinham (Jun 2019). New Secretive Deal Between UN, Myanmar Smells Foul. *Anadolu Agency.* www.aa.com.tr/en/analysis-news/new-secretive-deal-between-un-myanmar-smells-foul-/1171661 [Accessed 16/10/2019]

Zaw Min Htut (2003). *Human Rights Abuses and Discrimination on Rohingyas.* Burmese Rohingya Association Japan.

9 Conclusion

Seeing the state and criminality in statelessness

Introduction

Through the research for this book, I have sought to understand how Rohingya survivors of state crime disrupted and contributed to international framings of their statelessness. In doing so, I explored Rohingya experiences and understandings of citizenship and statelessness through ID narratives and oral histories of their IDs. In Chapters 6 and 7, I showed that these ID narratives told a story of how Rohingya statelessness had been produced as part of a broader genocidal process. ID narratives explained how the Myanmar State had attempted to destroy Rohingya's group identity and erase their histories in Myanmar through registration and ID schemes. Identification and registration processes were also intricately bound up with the experiences of the physical destruction of Rohingya people and communities. Participants also highlighted their mistrust of UN agencies working in Myanmar, which had sought to address their statelessness in Myanmar through engagement with the state and its registration and ID schemes. In Chapters 3 and 8, I examined how the approaches of UN agencies to resolving Rohingya statelessness in Myanmar had been developed within the shifting international policy approaches, mandates, and action plans. Latterly this included UNHCR's IBelong Campaign and target 16.9 of the Sustainable Development Goals which sought to provide 'legal identities to all.' I found that international approaches increasingly tended to support solutions to statelessness that engaged with states to provide IDs to all, assuming that this would promote human rights without effectively assessing the more harmful impacts of certain state ID schemes. International framings of statelessness that sought to resolve statelessness as an issue of state oversight by increasing the efficiency of state bureaucracies, combined with strategies in Myanmar that pragmatically engaged with the Myanmar State despite continuing serious human rights abuses. This combination produced approaches to preventing and reducing statelessness that either promoted or tacitly accepted Myanmar's registration and identification schemes within the existing discriminatory citizenship law. These approaches were challenged and often rejected by many Rohingya

DOI: 10.4324/9781003494539-9
This chapter has been made available under a CC-BY 4.0 license.

communities who were supposed to be the beneficiaries of such initiatives on the basis that the ID schemes were destroying their identities and undermining their citizenship claims.

In Chapter 8, I considered where Rohingya experiences and understandings of the production of statelessness diverged from international framings and approaches to statelessness. In doing so, the chapter also considered how the voices and experiences of Rohingya survivors could inform international policy approaches to statelessness. The chapter highlighted three specific areas of divergence: group identity, registration and ID schemes, and notions of the state. First, there were fundamental differences in the way group identity as part of citizenship was conceived. International approaches to preventing and reducing statelessness largely sought to increase the number of individuals able to access Myanmar citizenship in the long term by promoting legal identities and expansion of access to citizenship through the 'naturalisation' provisions within the existing citizenship law. Rohingya genocide survivors largely understood this approach as undermining their citizenship and group identity as they sought justice and security in the restitution of their automatic right to citizenship[1] and recognition of their history and identity in Myanmar. Second, there were fundamental differences between Rohingya and international understandings of the way state registration and identification schemes could either enable or hinder access to citizenship. Whilst international organisations tended to approach state registration and documentation processes as the main solution to statelessness over the longer term in that they strengthened legal identities that should provide access to citizenship over time, Rohingya understood the same bureaucratic processes as producing statelessness as part of a broader process of identity destruction and genocide. Whilst international agencies attempted to lift Rohingya out of a state of invisibility through provision of registration and IDs, Rohingya themselves experienced forms of hypervisibility as a result of the state ID and registration schemes that left them vulnerable and exposed to genocide. Third, understandings of the nature of the state itself diverged. Whilst international bodies largely evaded questions of state crime and sought to pragmatically engage with the state to reduce and prevent statelessness, Rohingya understood the state as the 'perpetrators' of a slow-burning genocide; the 'thieves' that stole their citizenship; and the 'destroyers' of their identities, communities, and lands.

At the time of my research, many Rohingya were going through the difficult process of coming to terms with the failure at the international level to prevent genocide and other atrocity crimes. Following the events of 2017, there was the hope and expectation of international intervention that would help them return to their homelands in security, with their full citizenship rights and recognition of their ethnicity and national identity. These hopes never materialised. Within this context, there were two, often overlapping, ways in which the roles of international agencies were described in Rohingya ID narratives. First, they described how state authorities had 'played' international agencies in matters of their citizenship, simultaneously erasing Rohingya histories and identities whilst making false promises about providing access to citizenship that they never intended to deliver. In these narratives, UN agencies had fallen hook, line, and sinker for these 'tricks.' Second, Rohingya participants often expressed opinions that Myanmar had created and entrenched the conditions of genocide in full view of UN agencies working in Rakhine. In particular, they drew on ID narratives to explain the stripping of their citizenship and erasure of their group identity as evidence of both the state intent to destroy Rohingya as a group and the by-standing of the international community. In these narratives, it was impossible for UN agencies not to see both the state abuses that took place on their watch and evidence of identity destruction and citizenship stripping. As such, the by-passing of the violence inherent in state bureaucracies by international agencies was construed as wilful blindness. In one focus group[2] in the Bangladesh refugee camps, which was focused on the role of state IDs, not international agencies, the following historical examples were provided of wilful blindness.

Participant 1: 'From 1995 UNHCR was supporting the white cards. They provided equipment to government—computers, plastic machine. They held up this white card for us. They told us, "You should have this card. It is important for you". At that time people took it. UNHCR were supporting the violence of the government.'

Participant 2: 'Since the 1990s, UNHCR had a duty to monitor the situation. They have got to be fair, but they have done nothing for us. When the government and the army were torturing us, they did nothing for us. They did not even report it. They are working with the perpetrators.'

Participant 3: '1982 Citizenship Law was the genocidal law. But it was the UNHCR who were describing us as stateless. We are not stateless, we are citizens.'

These retrospective examples from the past were drawn on by Rohingya participants to explain their fears about premature repatriation and to justify the suspicion and concern they felt towards some international agencies at the time of the research. For example, from the same focus group:

Participant 4: 'The MOU (between the Government of Myanmar, UNHCR and UNDP on repatriation arrangements[3]) is totally denying us our rights because they are not consulting with us. MOU is for the repatriation. Repatriation means OUR home. Home is OUR right.

> But they are not concerned with us . . . . In the MOU, there is no term Rohingya. We are suffering inside the country only for the Rohingya identity and for the NVC. In the MOU they are going by the existing law and regulation. Travelling one place to another place, we still must take the form 4. Like foreigners travelling in our own land.'

Since this research set out to understand the divergences between the Rohingya narratives and international approaches and to establish how these divergences were experienced, understood, and perceived, it is beyond the scope of this research to effectively assess the role of the international agencies, or to build an evidence base to indicate complicity or by-standing. However, it would be remiss of me to ignore this important thread in Rohingya analysis of their experiences relating to their IDs. Many Rohingya felt their views were ignored as discussions surrounding their 'forced displacement' and futures in Myanmar became the subject of negotiations between states and international agencies tasked with refugee and migration management (see Chapter 8).

Identities and experiences of identity destruction were absent or sidelined in these assessments which focused predominantly on providing documents to establish the facts of their residence to resolve the dispute between Bangladesh and Myanmar. But the negotiations and the MOUs or other repatriation arrangements did not effectively factor in the risks of identity destruction and further harm inherent in these documentation processes.[4]

Bridging silos in studies of legal identities

In his seminal work, 'Seeing like a State: How certain schemes to improve the human condition have failed' James C. Scott (1998) explored from a historical and global perspective how state categorisation, classification, the standardisation of language and registration schemes were utilised to make populations visible, legible, and governable. He provided examples of how state categories and documents did not only categories and documents did function not to the benefit of society but also to its detriment. They enabled state control that in some regards was welcomed in terms of efficiency, but in others was ultimately harmful. Scott argued that the ways, in which states categorised people, were 'over-simplifications' or 'artificial inventions' (Scott 1998:83). However, states ultimately 'make categories stick' by 'treating people according to their schemata' (Scott 1998:82). The categories, embedded in state-created institutions, then organise people's daily experience and structure social relations. As he phrased it,

> If you wish to have a standing in law, you must have a document that officials accept as evidence of citizenship, be that document a birth

> certificate, passport or identity card. The categories created by state agents are not merely the means to make their environment legible; they are the authoritative tune to which most of the population must dance.
> (Scott 1998:83)

In the case of Rohingya in Myanmar, registration and ID schemes that were not based on historical or demographic reality were used to re-categorise Rohingya as foreigners or noncitizens. As such, they were utilised by the state to erase Rohingya histories and destroy their identity as a group belonging to Rakhine State Myanmar. These categories, materialised through ID card schemes, became the authoritative tune to which the populations of Myanmar had to dance. Moreover, they became the tune to which international agencies also danced as they attempted to secure legal identities for all in order to make Rohingya populations more legible to state entities.

Torpey (2000) explored how, through passport and ID systems, states monopolised the means of movement. ID schemes were powerful tools to legitimise and consolidate state power resulting in both 'emancipatory' and 'repressive' practices. More recent literature has built on this concept and argued that state ID schemes are not only purveyors of rights and protections but critically sites through which surveillance, exclusion, and even genocide take place (Caplan and Torpey 2001; Longman 2001; Lyon and Bennett 2008; Caplan 2013). However, these studies that link registration and ID schemes with bureaucratic violence have not informed international policy approaches to statelessness, which instead have tended to treat state bureaucracies as neutral entities, and registration schemes solely as a way to improve efficiency. This research begins to bridge this gap by considering both experiences of genocide and the ways in which Rohingya statelessness has been framed in international discourses.

There are limited attempts in planning ID schemes to incorporate the concerns of those that stand to be excluded in their implementation. Many of the Rohingya participants in this research were of the opinion that international agencies engaging with the Myanmar State were by-passing Rohingya objections, desires, and experiences of bureaucratic violence (see also Brinham and Johar 2021). In this regard, my research demonstrates that listening to stateless peoples' own analyses of their legal condition necessarily involves examining states from the perspectives of unrecognised citizens and other stateless people. It means understanding the diversity of experiences of stateless people and recognising the homogenising aspects of prescriptive global action plans. Approaches that are appropriate in situations in which people become stateless as a result of state succession, state oversight, or state neglect are not necessarily appropriate to situations of ongoing human rights abuses or genocide. In practice, the promotion at the international level of state ID schemes has not only reduced human rights deficits for undocumented and stateless people but also actually produced exclusions (see also Hayes de Kalaf 2023; Manby 2021).

This study considered some of the harms ID schemes and registration have caused Rohingya in Myanmar. A growing body of work has also looked critically at the role of registration and IDs schemes in producing exclusions in other contexts. In the Dominican Republic, birth registration processes that recorded Dominicans separately from 'foreigners' contributed to a system that increasingly marked out people of Haitian descent and labelled them as noncitizens or 'stateless.' At the same time, accessing services and rights for those not recognised as citizens became increasingly difficult (Petrozziello 2019; Hayes de Kalaf 2023). Some studies focused on the role of the World Bank Group in supporting ID systems in the Dominican Republic context (Hayes de Kalaf 2023). In India, the digital ID scheme known as Aadhaar was heralded as a way to promote social inclusion. It was construed as a way to cut through cumbersome bureaucratic processes and provide easy access to a wide range of services and benefits (Chaudhuri and König 2018). In practice, however, those not deemed permanent residents, for example, refugees and undocumented people, found it increasingly difficult to access vital services and survive within the informal economy (Brinham, Tiwari et al. 2020; Tiwari and Field 2020). Meanwhile, the National Register of Citizens (NRC) in India has increasingly differentiated between those who had the correct documents to evidence their citizenship, and those who did not. In Assam, a large number of people were unable to produce the correct documents to evidence their Indian citizenship and were excluded from the NRC placing their citizenship status at risk. This disproportionately affected those of Muslim or Bengali origin (Arraiza, Aye et al. 2020). Additionally, Manby's (2018; Manby 2021) work on multiple contexts in Africa where national registration processes and new ID systems were in the process of being implemented revealed how, in many situations, there was a danger of producing exclusions. The increased importance placed on state-issued documents in order to access rights and benefits, created barriers for those without documents. For example, in Uganda and Tanzania those previously described as being 'at risk of statelessness' found that their statelessness was 'locked in' as a result of universal ID schemes. Undocumented people faced increasing difficulty in accessing health and education services under the new registration schemes (Manby 2018). Manby argued that in Sudan and Mauritania, new national registration processes were utilised as tools to denationalise particular groups of people. Non-Arabic speaking populations in Mauritania were excluded from the digital national register in a move described by activists as 'biometric genocide' (Minority Rights Group 2017). In Kenya, researchers warned of the harmful impact new ID systems introduced in 2019 could have on Nubian populations who struggled to prove their right to citizenship (Balaton-Chrimes 2014; Oppenheim and Powell 2015; Mwangi 2017). In 2021, a High Court Judgement in Kenya delayed data collection and the roll-out of biometric ID cards until after a regulatory framework was put in place regarding data privacy (Open Society Justice Initiative 2021). Civil society organisations had also petitioned the court in 2020 on the basis that the digital ID scheme, known as 'Huduma Namba,' discriminated against the Nubians and other marginalised communities who faced barriers in accessing identity documents. The judgement held that although there was the potential for exclusion from access to government services through the ID scheme, this was not 'unconstitutional' (Cullen 2020). Nonetheless, the case highlighted the need for both ID systems in Kenya and around the world to curb intrusive state powers and to be more responsive to the objections and concerns of both citizens and those with more precarious legal status (Open Society Justice Initiative 2021).

It is clear then that Rohingya experiences of state registration and ID schemes producing harm and exclusions are not an exception. Other marginalised communities around the world have also found that state registration and ID schemes can undermine their national identity and make it more difficult to access rights. Despite other work in this area, as global policies increasingly prescribe ID schemes, they are yet to effectively incorporate these critiques. Risk assessments relating to the role out of ID schemes typically focus on analysis of the regulatory frameworks relating to the right to privacy (Privacy International 2020). These assessments continue to by-pass the more fundamental issues of how ID schemes produce noncitizenship and rights deficits, opting for the 'neutral stance' of providing technical expertise relating to the universal provision of IDs. They recommend consultation with civil society groups, but this rarely incorporates the views of those most affected (e.g. World Bank Group 2018). There is a need for joining up the dots on how these universal documentation and ID schemes impact stateless, undocumented, and wrongly documented people in different country contexts.

Developing interdisciplinary methods in critical statelessness studies

As this thesis has explored, the provision of IDs and legal identities is central to international policy work that aims to prevent and reduce statelessness. As such, employing ID narratives within statelessness research can provide important insights into how individuals experience the state. They provide a counterbalance to state narratives that often promote or advocate for more comprehensive or 'efficient' ID systems. Drawing on different approaches within academic research, I have explored Rohingya ID narratives from different angles.

In Chapter 2, I introduced ID narratives as a research method and provided background as to how IDs could give insights into Rohingya identity as an ethnic group belonging to Myanmar. In Chapter 3, I considered the powerful discourses within statelessness that has driven the seemingly insatiable desire for state forms of identification. In Chapter 4, I considered how categorisation and identification schemes were drawn on by states to legitimise and consolidate their power. During the British colonial era, identification schemes entrenched race and class hierarchies and established monopoly control over the freedom of movement in ways that consolidated colonial British power and controlled external and internal threats. The registration of foreigners and registration documents likewise became an important aspect of state-building in Burma's independence movement from the 1930s onwards as part of a move to evolve as a nation entirely separate from India/Pakistan. Chapter 5 explored how IDs in the early decades of independence were understood as possessing emancipatory qualities that could deliver peace, inclusiveness, and ethnic and religious equality in newly independent Myanmar. Furthermore, individual and group collections of IDs were treasured as artefacts of the state, which evidenced Rohingya bonds to the central state and their identity and history as citizens in Myanmar. They were also used as evidence of state crime—to plot a trail of the identity destruction and citizenship stripping from the 1970s onwards. Chapters 6 and 7 explored how ID schemes were utilised to oppress and destroy. ID narratives were drawn on to explain citizenship stripping and identity destruction as an intrinsic part of a broader genocidal process which sought to symbolically and physically erase Rohingya and remake a more exclusive Myanmar identity. In Chapter 8, I explored how ID narratives could expose the cracks in the logic of international policy approaches to Rohingya statelessness in Myanmar. It showed how ID narratives offer a window not only into the interactions between individual subjectivities and the state but also into the power relations between individuals and the international sphere.

ID narratives, then, warn us of the potential harm that the 'legal identities for all' agenda can cause when there is little accountability to the individuals and communities that are impacted. Whilst the principle of 'do no harm' is a foundation of international development agendas, it has yet to be effectively incorporated into global governance (Brinham 2019; Manby 2021). Nonetheless, there is a growing evidence base that suggests the 'legal identities for all' agenda, when implemented at its current pace, can actually 'lock in' statelessness and exacerbate the issues of social, financial, and political exclusion for undocumented and stateless communities (Oppenheim and Powell 2015; Institute on Statelessness and Inclusion 2019; Hayes de Kalaf 2023; Manby 2020). The momentum driven by statist border control interests, the international human rights agenda, the international development and finance sectors, and the corporate technology sector has reached a critical point at which there is no turning back or slowing down. The brakes are no longer effective, even as the agenda collides with the very people it was purported to help—the undocumented and the wrongly documented.

ID narratives also tell us that the homogenisation of statelessness as invisibility and a product of state neglect has created yet more barriers to seeing, hearing, and actively listening to the voices of those worst affected by statelessness, and to supporting their pursuit of justice and restitution. As one Rohingya refugee in Bangladesh wrote:

> We complain sometimes. We feel outrage. And then we are cowed. We often ask ourselves. 'Do the things that happen to us outrage the world?' We never get a clear answer. And so for many of us, silence has become a way of life. This is how we deal with the daily injustices and this is how we surface our pain and even our rage.
>
> (Salim Ullah Armany 2022)

Statelessness research, as an offshoot of refugee law, had a tendency to focus predominantly on state law and international policy documents both in analysing problems and in articulating solutions (Recalde-Vela, Jaghai-Bajulaiye et al. 2019). As statelessness studies grow increasingly interdisciplinary, the field searches for methodologies that enable researchers to navigate the conceptual distances between law and broader social science disciplines. ID narratives provide windows into citizenship frameworks, identities and subjectivities, state practices, and the power relations been states and the stateless. This research adds to a growing body of work that attempts to look critically at international governance in the area of statelessness and legal identities.[5] There remains a huge diversity of experiences of unrecognised citizenship, precarious citizenship, and statelessness that remains to be explored in academic research. Such research can help break down the dominant discourses and assumptions that simultaneously inform, and are constructed by, prescriptive international action plans and policy approaches.

Examining ID systems from within a state crime framework

At the heart of the divergences between Rohingya participants and international concepts and practices relating to ID schemes and registration were differing notions about the power and intent of the state behind the use of state registration and ID systems. For Rohingya participants, the ID and registration systems had been weaponised by a state that was intent on destroying their group physically and symbolically. In their views, the state had attempted to secure international legitimacy for these schemes. Inherent in many international approaches to ID schemes were notions that registration and IDs were neutral purveyors of a set of facts about human beings. As such, these processes were promoted as providing evidence that could plot pathways towards citizenship as well as facilitate migration and refugee management. Within these paradigms, the nature of state power and, significantly, the criminality of the state in Myanmar were by-passed. This resulted in the state also being conceptualised as a largely neutral entity in the provision of registration and IDs. This approach did not reflect the experiences of those impacted.

Siegelberg (2020) has shown, through plotting the evolution of the concept of statelessness in international law and political philosophy, that in the 20th century, the state gradually emerged as the 'sole legitimate organising unit of global politics' (2020:6). Accompanying this was a world order that was premised on the formal equality between sovereign states. This system lent an equal legitimacy to the citizenship laws of all states regardless of the way they were politically organised. An international system, built on the premise that all state citizenship laws and consequently their national ID schemes have equal legitimacy, evades and ignores the criminality of states as it relates to the production of statelessness. This international order has also contributed to impunity for states relating to abuses in both citizenship exclusions and persecutory ID schemes. Based on the premises of neutrality, ID schemes in Myanmar were promoted or given tacit support in ways that by-passed survivors' conceptualisations of justice, restitution, security, and citizenship. Until state ID schemes are conceptualised within international governance approaches as a set of state tools that can bring harm as well as benefits, the 'legal identities for all' agenda will ultimately benefit states and the international state system over stateless individuals and groups on the margins.

In attempting to implement the 'legal identities for all' agenda, then, some international organisations in Myanmar by-passed discriminatory citizenship laws in the provision of IDs, by basing legal identities and IDs on existing citizenship laws or residency. The categories attributed through these identification processes, however, were also not neutral. As the Rohingya narratives show, they too were used to destroy group identities and remake new exclusionary national identities. This book has shown how ID schemes function through power relations and profoundly impact social realities. It also demonstrates that state documents are mediators between individuals and the state, through which individuals can negotiate, resist, subvert, or strategically align and position themselves (Hull 2012). The meanings attached to IDs are multi-faceted and aligned to notions of shifting and fluid identities. As such ID schemes can only be a part of sustainable solutions to displacement, conflict, or mass atrocities, when the meanings that survivors attach to both state-issued documents and the state itself are properly factored in. Whilst various social science approaches have understood the centrality and materiality of IDs and state-issued documents (Navaro-Yashin 2007; Hull 2012; McConnell 2013; Reddy 2015; Sadiq 2016; Chhotray and McConnell 2018), it remains for statelessness scholarship to develop more rigorous interdisciplinary approaches, explore how international approaches to statelessness and legal identities can factor in the risks inherent in ID schemes, and account for the potential for state criminality. Seeing the state in 'statelessness requires factoring in the perspectives not only of citizens and international agencies but also of the stateless.'

Notes

1 As opposed to the cumbersome application processes for citizenship that those who do not belong to one of the *Taingyintha* must complete.
2 Fg6, 26/07/21018, Kutapalong.
3 My addition for clarity.
4 Government of the Union of Myanmar, UNHCR and UNDP (Jun 2018). Memorandum of Understanding between GoM and UNDP and UNHCR (Leaked Copy).
5 The Peter McMullin Centre on Statelessness at University of Melbourne has been Expanding 'Critical Statelessness Studies' Available at: https://law.unimelb.edu.au/centres/statelessness/research/research-projects/the-critical-statelessness-studies-project (accessed 21/11/2021).

Bibliography

Arraiza, J., Phyu Zin Aye, and M. Shakirova (2020). Fighting Imagined Invasions with Administrative Violence: Racism, Xenophobia and Nativism as a Cause of Statelessness in Myanmar, the Dominican Republic and Assam (India). *Statelessness & Citizenship Review* 2(2): 195–221.

Balaton-Chrimes, S. (2014). Statelessness, Identity Cards and Citizenship as Status in the Case of the Nubians of Kenya. *Citizenship Studies* 18(1): 15–28.

Brinham, N. (2019). When Identity Documents Produce Exclusion: Lessons from Rohingya Experiences in Myanmar. *LSE Blogs*. https://blogs.lse.ac.uk/mec/2019/05/10/when-identity-documents-and-registration-produce-exclusion-lessons-from-rohingya-experiences-in-myanmar/ [Accessed 20/02/2020]

Brinham, N. and A. Johar (2021). Lending Legitimacy to a Murderous Military: What's in the 'Stateless' Label for Rohingyas? *Critical Statelessness Studies*, University of Melbourne. https://law.unimelb.edu.au/centres/statelessness/resources/critical-statelessness-studies-blog/lending-legitimacy-to-a-murderous-military-what-is-in-the-stateless-label-for-rohingyas [Accessed 08/10/2021]

Brinham, N., A. D. Tiwari, J. Field, J. Ealom, J. M. Arraiza and A. de Chickera (2020). Locked in and Locked out: The Impact of Digital Identity Systems on Rohingya Populations, Institute on Statelessness and Inclusion and UN Special Rapporteur on racism. https://files.institutesi.org/Locked_In_Locked_Out_The_Rohingya_Briefing_Paper.pdf [Accessed 25/05/2021]

Caplan, J. (2013). 'Ausweis Bitte!' Identity and Identification in Nazi Germany, in About, I., Brown, J. and Lonergan, G. (eds), *Identification and Registration Practices in Transnational Perspective: Papers, People and Practices*. Palgrave. 224–242.

Caplan, J. and J. C. Torpey (2001). *Documenting Individual Identity: The Development of State Practices in the Modern World*. Princeton University Press.

Chaudhuri, B. and L. König (2018). The Aadhaar Scheme: A Cornerstone of a New Citizenship Regime in India? *Contemporary South Asia* 26(2): 127–142.

Chhotray, V. and F. McConnell (2018). *Certifications of Citizenship: The History, Politics and Materiality of Identity Documents in South Asian States and Diasporas*. Taylor & Francis.

Cullen, D. (2020). High Court of Kenya Suspends Implementation of Biometric ID System, *Oxford Human Rights Hub Blog*. https://ohrh.law.ox.ac.uk/high-court-of-kenya-suspends-implementation-of-biometric-id-system/ [Accessed 25/11/2021]

Government of the Union of Myanmar, UNHCR and UNDP (Jun 2018). *Memorandum of Understanding between GoM and UNDP and UNHCR* (leaked copy).

Hayes de Kalaf, E. (2023). Legal Identity, Race and Belonging in the Dominican Republic: From Citizen to Foreigner, Anthem.

Hull, M. S. (2012a). Documents and Bureaucracy. *Annual Review of Anthropology* 41: 251–267.
Hull, M. S. (2012b). *Government of Paper: The Materiality of Bureaucracy in Urban Pakistan*. University of California Press.
Institute on Statelessness and Inclusion (2019). *Making SDG 16.9 Work for the Wider Sustainable Development Agenda*. https://files.institutesi.org/legal_identity_policy_brief.pdf [Accessed 12/05/2021]
Longman, T. (2001). Identity Cards, Ethnic Self-Perception, and Genocide in Rwanda, in Caplan, J. and Torpey, J. (eds), *Documenting Individual Identity: The Development of State Practices in the Modern World*. Princeton University Press. 346–348.
Lyon, D. and C. J. Bennett (2008). Playing the Identity Card: Understanding the Significance of Identity Card Systems, in Bennet, C. J. and Lyon, D. (eds), *Playing the Identity Card: Surveillance and Identification in Global Perspective*. Routledge. 3–20.
Manby, B. (2018). 'Legal Identity' and Biometric Registration in Africa. *Newsletter of the American Political Science Association's Organized Section on Migration and Citizenship* 6(2).
Manby, B. (2020). Legal Identity for All and Statelessness: Opportunity and Threat at the Junction of Public and Private International Law. *Statelessness and Citizenship Review* 2(2): 248–271.
Manby, B. (2021). The Sustainable Development Goals and 'Legal Identity for All': 'First, Do No Harm'. *World Development* 139: 105343.
McConnell, F. (2013). Citizens and Refugees: Constructing and Negotiating Tibetan Identities in Exile. *Annals of the Association of American Geographers* 103(4): 967–983.
Minority Rights Group (2017). *World Directory of Minorities and Indigenous Peoples—Mauritania: Black Africans*. www.refworld.org/docid/49749ce7a.html [Accessed 13/12/2021]
Mwangi, O. G. (2017). Statelessness, Ungoverned Spaces and Security in Kenya, in Bloom, T., Tonkiss, K. and Cole, P. (eds), *Understanding Statelessness*. Routledge. 117–134.
Navaro-Yashin, Y. (2007). Make-Believe Papers, Legal Forms and the Counterfeit: Affective Interactions between Documents and People in Britain and Cyprus. *Anthropological Theory* 7(1): 79–98.
Open Society Justice Initiative (2021). *New Kenya High Court Judgement Sets Precedent for Digital ID Protections and Processes*. www.justiceinitiative.org/newsroom/new-kenya-high-court-judgment-sets-important-precedent-for-digital-id-privacy-protections-and-processes [Accessed 12/12/2021]
Oppenheim, B. and B. M. Powell (2015). *Legal Identity in the 2030 Agenda for Sustainable Development: Lessons from Kibera, Kenya*. Open Society Foundation.
Petrozziello, A. J. (2019). (Re) producing Statelessness via Indirect Gender Discrimination: Descendants of Haitian Migrants in the Dominican Republic. *International Migration* 57(1): 213–228.
Privacy International (2020). *A Guide to Litigating Identity Systems*. https://privacyinternational.org/sites/default/files/2020-09/PI_A%20Guide%20to%20Litigating%20Identity%20 [Accessed 13/05/2021]
Recalde-Vela, M. J., S. Jaghai-Bajulaiye and C. Vlieks (2019). The State of Statelessness Research: 5 Years Later. *Tilburg Law Review* 24(2): 139–141.
Reddy, M. (2015). Identity Paper/Work/s and the Unmaking of Legal Status in Mae Sot, Thailand. *Asian Journal of Law and Society* 2(2): 251–266.
Sadiq, K. (2016). Limits of Legal Citizenship: Narratives from South and Southeast Asia, in Lawrance, B. N. and Stevens, J. (eds), *Citizenship in Question: Evidentiary Birthright and Statelessness*. Duke University Press. 165–176.

Salim Ullah Armany (2022). Love in the Rohingya Camps. *Unheard Journalism Project*. https://journal.unheardproject.com/love-in-the-rohingya-camps/ [Accessed 19/01/2022]

Siegelberg, M. L. (2020). *Statelessness: A Modern History*. Harvard University Press.

Tiwari, A. D. and J. Field (2020). Bureaucratic Gaps and Exclusions: The Limits of Documentary 'Protection' for Rohingyas in India. Kaldor Centre, University of New South Wales. www.kaldorcentre.unsw.edu.au/publication/bureaucratic-gaps-and-exclusion-limits-documentary-%E2%80%98protection%E2%80%99-rohingyas-india [Accessed 13/05/2021]

Torpey, J. (2000). *The Invention of the Passport: Surveillance, Citizenship, and the State*. Cambridge University Press.

World Bank Group (2018). *Identification for Development: ID4D Annual Report 2018*. https://id4d.worldbank.org/sites/id4d.worldbank.org/files/2018_ID4D_Annual_Report.pdf [Accessed 20/03/2019]

Index